Models of Teaching

Models of Teaching

NINTH EDITION

Bruce Joyce
Booksend Laboratories

Marsha Weil
ETR Associates

Emily Calhoun
The Phoenix Alliance

PEARSON

Boston   Columbus   Indianapolis   New York   San Francisco   Upper Saddle River
Amsterdam   Cape Town   Dubai   London   Madrid   Milan   Munich   Paris   Montréal   Toronto
Delhi   Mexico City   São Paulo   Sydney   Hong Kong   Seoul   Singapore   Taipei   Tokyo

Vice President, Editor in Chief: Jeffery W. Johnston
Senior Acquisitions Editor: Meredith D. Fossel
Editorial Assistant: Maria Feliberty
Marketing Manager: Darcy Betts
Program Manager: Janet Domingo
Project Coordination and Text Design: Electronic Publishing Services Inc., NYC
Operations Specialist: Linda Sager
Electronic Composition: Jouve
Cover Design: Diane Lorenzo

Library of Congress Cataloging-in-Publication Data

Joyce, Bruce R.
  Models of teaching / Bruce R. Joyce, Marsha Weil, and Emily Calhoun.
    pages cm
  Includes bibliographical references and index.
  ISBN 978-0-13-489258-0   1. Education—Experimental methods.
2. Educational innovations.   3. Teaching.   I. Title.

  LB1027.3.J69 2015
  371.102—dc23

                                                                2013038897

1   17

ISBN 10: 0-13-489258-5
ISBN 13: 978-0-13-489258-0

To those who hold high the candle that brings new light to education
as exemplified by the credo of the Bank Street College of Education,
written about 100 years ago by Lucy Sprague Mitchell . . .

What potential in human beings—children, teachers, and ourselves—
do we want to develop?

- A zest for living that comes from taking the world with all five senses alert.
- Lively intellectual curiosities that turn the world into an exciting laboratory and keep one ever a learner.
- Flexibility when confronted with change and ability to relinquish patterns that no longer fit the present.
- The courage to work, unafraid and efficiently, in a world of new needs, new problems, and new ideas.
- Gentleness combined with justice in passing judgment on other human beings.
- Sensitivity, not only to the formal rights of the other fellow, but to him as another human being seeking a good life through his own standards.
- A striving to live democratically, in and out of schools, as the best way to advance our concept of democracy

We fervently hope that the models of teaching we open in this book
will live up to her manifesto and keep her candle burning.

Contents

This book, *Models of Teaching*, is the central component in the multimedia system that supports the study of the major research-based approaches to teaching. However, two other components are very important.

The website **www.modelsofteaching.org** provides suggestions on ways of using the book and videos in courses, including online offerings and self-instruction. PowerPoints for each model and a variety of other materials are also available. These materials are designed for both instructors and students, providing support in the design of campus and online courses and for personal study.

The second component is our YouTube channel, which offers video demonstrations of many of the models of teaching, as well as several talks on models and how to learn them: **www.youtube.com/user/BooksendLab.** The site provides access to 25 video demonstrations of a variety of models as well as videos providing tips for learning each model.

PART ONE

MODELS OF TEACHING: A WORKING PROFESSIONAL REPERTOIRE

The models are introduced briefly, along with ideas about how to build learning communities in classes and the school as a whole.

CHAPTER ONE

Where Models of Teaching Come From
*Constructing Knowledge and Skill to Help
Our Students Construct Knowledge and Skill*

The product of teacher-researchers comes to us in the form of models of teaching that enable us to construct optimal learning environments for our students. From the time of the academies in Greece and Rome, teachers have generated innovative approaches to learning and teaching. Succeeding generations have given birth to additional ways of helping students learn. As teachers we can draw on these products and use them to help our students become effective and creative learners.

We celebrate learning and the virtues of social support for learning. Classes and student bodies need to be developed into learning communities and provided with the models of learning that enable students to become expert learners. We study how to build these communities, including developing hybrid approaches to teaching/learning, with the resources of ICT integrated with campus teaching. Increasingly, a community of learners will be made up of students from more than one venue, linked by electronic communication.

How can we and our students best acquire information, organize it, and explain it? Here are several models that are directly aligned with the new curriculum standards—frameworks that embrace teaching students with the methods of the disciplines underlying them.

As we remind ourselves continuously, a major outcome of these models is the development of capacity to learn, to collect and approach information confidently, and to help one another become a community of learners. The tools learned by finding and managing information support the social, personal, and behavioral families. Information-processing models provide academic substance to social models, ways of thinking for personal inquiry, and goals for many of the behavioral models.

Human beings are born to build concepts. The infant, crawling around, feeling things and bumping into them, observing people's actions and listening to them, is born to acquire information that is sifted and organized, building the conceptual structures that guide our lives. The inductive model builds on and enhances the inborn capacity of human beings to organize information about their environments and build and test categories—concepts—that make their world more comprehensible and predictable.

This model is placed first in this part because many other models draw on it, and because when it is combined with others, particularly some social models (e.g., group investigation), student learning can be dramatic.

CHAPTER FOUR

Scientific Inquiry
Building Learning around Investigations   **71**

From the time of Aristotle, we have had educators who taught science in the making rather than teaching a few facts and hoping for the best. We introduce you to a model of teaching that is science in the making. Today, students can identify a domain of study or problem, conduct investigations of their own, and connect to studies available on the web. Virtual investigations and simulations can shorten time and bring students into labs and field studies where complex equipment is available and faraway settings can be studied.

CHAPTER FIVE

The Picture Word Inductive Model
Developing Literacy through Inquiry   **91**

Built on the language experience approach, the picture word inductive model enables beginning readers to develop sight vocabularies, learn to inquire into the structure of words and sentences, write sentences and paragraphs, and thus become powerful language learners.

PART THREE

SPECIAL PURPOSE INFORMATION-PROCESSING MODELS   **123**

The models in Part Two can be used for some very broad purposes, including designing lessons, units, courses, and distance offerings. The more specialized models in Part Three, however, are designed specifically to:

- Teach concepts
- Teach students to memorize more effectively, including facts, concepts, and even the core ideas of philosophies

- Teach students to think divergently by learning to use synectics processes to make metaphoric comparisons to break set and learn unfamiliar material better, develop more solutions to problems, and build richer and more productive social relationships
- Design presentations with advance organizers, including lectures, media, and distance offerings
- Teach basic inquiry skills

presentations, readings, distance offerings, and on-campus inquiries that ease the way to long-term retention of key information.

CHAPTER NINE

Using Advance Organizers to Design Presentations
Scaffolding Lectures, ICT, and Distance Offerings   197

Learning from presentations has had almost as bad a name as learning by memorization. David Ausubel developed a system for creating lectures and other presentations that will increase learner activity and, subsequently, learning. A scaffold provides a cognitive map of the material for students to organize their study and assess their progress. This is a particularly useful model for the design of distance learning packages. Students can learn to develop scaffolds as a part of their inquiries.

CHAPTER TEN

The Inquiry Training Model
Training Inquiry Skills Directly   213

Here we have a nicely structured model that begins with puzzling situations and continues with exercises that teach students to ask questions and assay the responses they get.

PART FOUR

THE SOCIAL FAMILY OF MODELS OF TEACHING   229

Working together just might enhance all of us. The social family expands what we can do together and generates the creation of democratic relationships in venues large and small. In addition, the creation of learning communities can enhance the learning of all students dramatically. Interestingly, collaboration among people in different settings is remarkably satisfying, as witnessed in the rise of social media. With respect to collaboration in academic learning, a vast network of systems is fast developing as people interested in particular things find colleagues who share their interests.

CHAPTER ELEVEN

Partners in Learning
Getting Everybody on Board   231

Can two students increase their learning when paired? Yes. Will they develop better social and academic skills if they work together on projects? Yes. Can most students profit from training to collaborate? Yes. Do collaborative classrooms increase productive study and time on task and decrease unproductive and disruptive behavior? Yes. Are cooperative learning models applicable to K–12 and across curriculum areas? Yes. This chapter looks at some of the basic, easy-to-implement forms of cooperative learning.

Can students organized into a democratic learning community learn to apply scientific methods to their learning? You bet they can. Group investigation can be used to redesign schools; increase personal, social, and academic learning among all students; and satisfy both learners and teachers. The project method is a recent variant that organizes students to attack specific social problems. The vast resources of the web are putting new wheels under the complex social models. And, online courses do not have to be presentation only or step-by-step drill. They can be designed with vigorous collaborative models, albeit at a distance.

Values provide the center of our behavior, helping us get direction and understand others. Policy issues involve the understanding of values and the costs and benefits of selecting some solutions rather than others. In these models, values are central. Think for a moment about the issues that face our society right now—research on cells, international peace, including our roles in the Middle East, the battle against AIDS, poverty, and who controls the decisions about pregnancy and abortion, not to mention just getting along together.

The learner always does the learning. His or her personality interacts with the learning environment. How do we give the learner centrality when we are trying to get that same person to grow and respond to tasks we believe will enhance growth? And how can electronic connections be shaped so that they are not just a matter of arguing online, but reflection and growth? Oddly, some kinds of distance counseling can be quite helpful. Virtual counseling will be a developing field.

How do we think about ourselves as learners? As people? How can we organize schooling so that the personalities and emotions of students are taken into account? Let us inquire into the person who is the center of the education process.

Nondirective methods can be supported through distance means. During the school years and later, students can be better connected to their teachers and counselors and supported as they reflect on themselves and take steps to build their self-esteem and ability to relate to others. Much of the support that students need when undertaking investigations involving ICT resources, including online courses and other types of distance courses, can be provided in a nondirective fashion.

If you feel good about yourself, you are likely to become a better learner and have a generally better quality of life. But you begin where you are. Self-concept is a likely avenue. The wonderful work by the SIMs group in Kansas has demonstrated what can be done to help students improve their self-images (and their achievement).

We are what we do. So how do we learn to practice more productive behaviors? This chapter explores some of the possibilities that are variations on themes developed by therapists, particularly Abraham Maslow, Carl Rogers, Erich Fromm, and Karen Horney from the heyday of innovation in psychology.

We enter the world of tasks, performances, and positive and aversive reactions. The study of how behavior is acquired has led to a wide variety of approaches to training. Here we will deal with some of the major behavioral models.

For a long time the teaching of comprehension seemed elusive, although reading without much comprehension is not actually reading at all. Then researchers began to study the skills that expert readers use and develop ways of teaching those skills to all students. The resulting model is generally referred to as *explicit strategy instruction.*

This is the fundamental training model, where new content and skill are introduced, modeled, practiced, and added to the working repertoire. Planning and assessment are the complex parts of the model, but the investment pays off handsomely.

Why beat around the bush when you can just deal with things directly? Let's go for it! However, finesse is required, and that is what this chapter is all about. The basic model here is derived from social learning theory. Many distance models—a good deal are of the online variety—are direct, but several need better designs and students need to learn how to use learning strategies to get the most out of them.

Even young children develop learning styles that interact with their environments, including the kinds of teaching they are exposed to. Major types of learning, like identifying and perfecting new ways of learning, involve some degree of discomfort. Learning new material is a product of the school environment and students need to learn to cope with this discomfort or they will, inevitably, hide from new content. We explain the use of conceptual systems theory to match students to models and scaffold them toward integrating information that advances their growth.

We summarize the growing lines of research and suggest ways that every teacher can add a bit by teaching from an action research perspective, and we discuss and apply Robert Gagné's marvelous framework for applying research to the task of building curricula.

Robert Gagné's framework still guides us as we develop effective curricula. His groundbreaking work combined research on levels and types of learning with the problem of designing instruction that builds on how we think and build knowledge.

By definition, learning requires knowing, thinking, or doing things we couldn't do before the learning took place. Curricula and teaching need to be shaped to take us where we haven't been. The trick is to develop an optimal mismatch so that we are pushed but not overwhelmed. Vygotsky popularized the term *zone of proximal development* to refer to content, conceptual understanding, skills, and processes that are just beyond our current development but not so demanding that we get lost. These concepts are very important because content and process that are well within our comfort zone, while soothing, do not challenge us to grow.

Preface

Models of Teaching connects educators—new and experienced teachers, school and district administrators, school and literacy coaches, providers of professional development, and college educators—to a storehouse of well-developed and studied ways of teaching. These models have strong rationales, use different lines of research, and provide expected student learning examples. All of them are informed by the experience of the hundreds of educators who have used and refined them. Thus, the models represent a base for professional teaching—*professional* meaning "using research to guide practice."

Years ago many educators expected that research on teaching would result in a single model that was superior for all types of educational objectives. However, that was not the case when Bruce Joyce began writing *Models of Teaching*, and it is not the case today. Excellent teaching is made up of a repertoire of models that are very good for particular purposes but need to be assembled to generate a top-drawer learning environment for our students. In other words, teaching is not a one-dimensional operation. Rather, teaching reaches toward different students and across disciplines, responsible for a panoply of standards that require corresponding sets of teaching strategies and ways of reaching students.

Even today some policymakers hope that research will boil down the characteristics of effective teaching into a few principles. Though there are, in fact, some things that we all should do as teachers—and other things we should avoid—the kinds of teaching that will make the most difference to our students and give them the skills for lifelong learning are embodied in teaching strategies or models that provide those skills.

Although the comparison of various professions to medicine is somewhat shopworn, there are important parallels here. In medicine, we don't have one antibiotic, one regimen, one type of test. Furthermore, some medical specialties are directed toward prevention as well as treatment. Complicating the assessment of both preventive measures and treatment is that interactions are probabilistic. Obesity is bad for the heart, but some thin people have heart trouble. In education we have models that help students learn how to think more clearly, to organize information better, to feel more confident—but like medical treatments, educational treatments are probabilistic. Education is not like a game of billiards, where a properly struck ball goes where it is supposed to all the time. In our case, it is *most* of the time.

Over the last 30 years, three important developments have enhanced teaching. One is the continued research on particular models and the development of new ones. Refinements have enhanced their effectiveness. The second is the development of combinations of models into curricula that have great power. Third is the development of electronic technologies that enlarge the library and bring massive amounts of information into the classrooms of even the youngest children. In modern classrooms, hundreds of physical books—fiction and nonfiction—surround the students, and electronic media access to vast resources provides encyclopedias and dictionaries that represent a real advance over print media. The Internet connects modern classrooms to a global network. The study of history is supported by original documents that are easy to access, including graphic material such as the 1,000,000 photos in the Library of Congress collection (www.loc.gov). NASA provides information about space exploration that was available to only a few insiders a dozen years ago. ScienceFriday.com is a delightful site for students and teachers, with simulations available to incorporate into units and courses. Email enables any class to be connected with classes in many of the countries of the world. Young children can follow Jane Goodall's career from her earliest studies to the development of the worldwide organization of children and adults who work together to create a better environment for all living things (including ourselves).

A note on information and communication technology (ICT) promises and worries: Everybody can profit by reading *The Shallows* (Carr, 2010) and *Smarter Than You Think* (Thompson, 2013). Carr lays out the worries that ICT will have seriously negative effects on certain skills and habits. For example, is the use of GPS navigation systems eroding skills in understanding and using maps? Can habitual web-surfing, tweeting, and texting friends generate a goalless, immediate-gratification-oriented state of mind? Or, on balance will the new activities generate new skills and intelligences? This debate will go on for some time.

In our case, we have come from writing manuscript on yellow tablets and typing the result with gallons of corrective fluid on hand. From there, the process evolved to writing and communicating with editors with word processors and graphics files. And at present the print book is also an ebook and is backed up by www.modelsofteaching.org, which brings materials for instructors and students and leads readers to video demonstrations of models, talks providing tips for learning them, PowerPoint tutorials, and more. You don't just write, today, you relearn how to write.

However, as teachers, we need to teach the models of learning that enable our students to understand and exploit the web and use the communication channels to inform themselves and create global connections where interaction with other societies and their cultures becomes the new normal.

The newly developed science frameworks and literacy standards are greatly improved over their predecessors and provide direction for K–12 teaching and learning. Thus, developed models of teaching can become even more effective because support materials, both print and electronic, have become richer.

Yet the field of education is being fiercely criticized at this time in history. Governmental agencies are pressing schools with unprecedented force because current examinations of student learning, particularly the national studies of educational progress, have indicated serious problems. One such problem is that a third or more of our students are not learning to read and write effectively. How can that be, when teaching strategies and learning resources are developing so well?

A major reason is that those powerful models of teaching are unknown to many educators. They need to be known, learned, and used. This book and the resources connected to it can enable new and experienced teachers to broaden their repertoires, develop rich curricula, and enable all students to succeed. All these models work well with students who come to school with limited backgrounds and knowledge of the English language. Our cause is passionate. Education is not only present life; it is also the life of the future. As time passes, all of these models of teaching will be radically changed or replaced by better ones. For now, let us give the students the best that we know.

What students learn today affects their lives in the long term. When we teach our children to read, we are helping them become lifelong readers. When they are learning to work together, they are becoming collaborative citizens of our democracy. When they learn science, they are developing the inquiry skills and habits to educate themselves and solve current and future problems.

Teaching is helping people create themselves. The effects of a teacher's work are still maturing a half-century or more after students' formal education is completed.

NEW TO THIS EDITION

This edition is enhanced by productive changes in the written prose, the addition of pictures depicting the teaching/learning process in action, and multimedia dimensions where video demonstrations are integrated with the print book.

Multimedia additions include:

- Integrated demonstrations of models of teaching. The demonstrations were captured in classrooms where expert teachers used the models of teaching with their students. These can be streamed on demand by both instructors and students.

- The website, www.modelsofteaching.org, which extends additional support to learn the models of teaching with PowerPoint presentations, application guides, and video talks.

Text updates include:

- Newly developed analyses of research and applications of the models. Approximately 30 percent of the prose is new to this edition.
- Applications which demonstrate current policy for school improvement. The models in the book are essential to the implementation of the new Common Core State Standards.
- Updates which shape this book into a core text of Professional Learning and School Improvement Initiatives.
- References to lines of research which constitute the field of education can be found within the text and online at www.modelsofteaching.org. The 9th edition provides an extensive guide for graduate study in education.

ACKNOWLEDGMENTS

Bruce and Emily cannot thank these folks enough.

Lisa Mueller has been a wonderful professional partner. She is a fine provider of professional learning opportunities and demonstrations. We have made videos of her marvelous demonstrations, and they are used in many professional learning programs. Her work has provided inspiration for this edition of *Models of Teaching*.

Brendan Joyce is a great personal companion and has generously given us his technical competence. The site modelsofteaching.org contains manuals, peer-coaching guides, bibliographies, and papers on a number of topics related to this text. The site leads to our storehouse of video demonstrations and links. These and our blog, which enables readers to talk with us, are among Brendan's contributions.

Lori Kindrachuk, Ralph Kindrachuk, Marilyn and Walter Hrycauk, Ed Witchen, Jim Jutras, and Kim Newlove have been wonderful companions in the organization of our recent Canadian excursions in school enhancement through professional learning.

Grant Dougall, Sharon Champ, and Mary Bishop are enjoyable friends and colleagues and worked with us to develop videos and other materials. For a sample of Mary's books, take a look at *Tunnels of Time* (2000).

Maureen Bezanson, Jordan Carlson, Tracy Poirier, and Nicole Simon taught us a lot as they studied several models and the Read to Succeed curriculum. They enriched our understanding as we worked with them to introduce several hundred teachers to those innovations.

From Pearson we have had fine support from editors who were given the responsibility for this edition. Both Linda Bishop and Meredith Fossel took over as editors and worked as if *Models of Teaching* were one of their new acquisitions. Janet Domingo has managed the production with knowledge, skill, and good-humored determination. She has a dynamic interface with the helpful Katie Watterson of Electronic Publishing Services Inc. Heather Gauen Hutches, the copyeditor, has been a content and stylistic editor as well as setting up the copy for the compositors. She is a real editor in all senses.

Bruce Joyce
Emily Calhoun
Saint Simons Island, GA

A Note on Heritage

THE FIRST 2000 YEARS

This is a sketch, really a reminder, that the development of universal public education is a relatively recent event—in fact, one that is not yet complete. Its emergence is built on the work of serious social thinkers and visionaries that shaped the cultural readiness on which equity in the opportunity to learn can be pursued.

The development of formal education depended on the development of language, although long before language developed there was communication—and teaching. Parents, relatives, and tribe members passed down the tools and lore of their culture. Even taboos, such as incest, were enculturated. But with literacy, many aspects of the culture could be written down and passed on more uniformly. Even when most of the citizens were not literate, the written words could be read to them. Scribes wrote down the words of political and religious leaders so that those words became available not only to current citizens but also to subsequent generations.

The development of reading, writing, and some types of formal schooling began long ago, even where only a small portion of society had access to literacy. The Egyptian alphabet dates from about 3500 B.C. Chinese writing included about 2500 characters by around 1200 B.C. Extensive written works in India date from about 800 B.C. Hebrew writing began a few centuries B.C.

The formal literature on Western education dates from the ancient Greek and Roman educators. Some still-useful models have been around for centuries. Plato and Aristotle both developed models of teaching—Socratic dialogue on the one hand and inductive inquiry on the other—that have validity today. Study the literature from their day to the present and you will find a variety of innovative educators who have contributed useful conceptions of teaching and learning. In any given era, there were only a handful of leaders who were able to leave a written heritage, but we have access to them. In their time, their reflections on educational needs in their societies and how to meet them generated discussions that continue to the present day. Consider just these examples:

- John Amos Comenius (1592–1670) was a Czech religious and educational leader who advocated universal education to provide high qualities of living for individuals and collective knowledge for the improvement of society.
- Jean-Jacques Rousseau (1712–1778) was a French philosopher who also advocated an education to enable all citizens to reach their potential and build a strong base for social improvement. His book *Emile* feels remarkably relevant today, as does writing by his contemporary, Voltaire, whose satirical *Candide* (1759) advanced the development of the novel. Both were influential and productive musicians as well.
- John Locke (1632–1704) was one of a number of important British scientists/philosophers/political activists. He was one of the influential spokesmen for using empirical and logical thinking and scientific methods to seek knowledge and verify ideas. His advocacy of education was closely connected to his beliefs that democratic, rather than authoritarian, processes should make up the social contract and that education for all would underpin democratic behavior and institutions.

In the United States, a number of voices addressed education during the period that led up to independence and the agreement on the Constitution. Benjamin Franklin and Thomas Jefferson represent a small but important group whose talks and writings generated discussions that continue to the present day. Both believed that education should be universal. Jefferson developed a very specific framework where progression through the levels of education would be based on merit. Interestingly, all of the persons we have mentioned thus far came from societies where they had access to education and learning from the most highly educated people of their time—and across national borders. Their belief in a truly democratic society was intertwined with their belief that universal education was an essential condition of democracy. They set forth the arguments for their position along with their beliefs that knowledge should be based on reasoned argument and empirical inquiry rather than on superstition, tradition, or rhetoric. These ideas were the basis for the political action to create the educational system of nations and communities. Finally, in fits and starts, universal education came to life—and actually *is still coming to life.*

The development of a formal educational literature, one that could be taught to educators, began in the 1800s. When the common school in the United States began to develop in earnest—1830 is an approximate birth date—much of public education was dominated by a relatively dour view of childhood. A drill-and-practice mode prevailed, backed up by a "spare the rod and spoil the child" belief in harsh discipline. Much of the early formal writing was in reaction to unpleasant and inefficient educational practices. Horace Mann (1796–1859) was a powerful advocate for a more positive view and for methods of teaching that would be more consonant with how knowledge is generated and that would incorporate social processes more aligned with life in a democratic society.

The works of Henry James (1842–1910) and John Dewey (1859–1952) provided the base for modern research and development in education. James was a physician and physiologist; he is regarded as the father of psychology as a discipline. Dewey combined ideas from his own work and that of others to form a different vision of education, specifically educating future citizens by organizing learners into collaborative groups that were taught to use scientific inquiry and disciplined discourse as basic tools for learning. These two men represent the beginning of formal inquiry into education, and their works are influential to the present day.

MODERN EMPIRICAL EDUCATIONAL RESEARCH: BUILDING AND TESTING MODELS OF CURRICULUM AND INSTRUCTION

By the 1920s, there was a community of researchers in education and philosophy who established educational research as a discipline. By the late 1950s, there were a significant number of researchers and inventors who used empirical methods to validate the curricula and models of teaching they were creating, while the social and behavioral sciences contributed methodologies that enabled the inventors of new models to assess them and make them more effective. Much of our current heritage of approaches to teaching and learning are grounded in rationale and empirical work that has occurred in the last 90 years, although they owe a major debt to prior ideas and inquiries.

Our contemporary storehouse of models is grounded from basic and applied research conducted from the mid-1930s to the present—the modern period of research on education. The sets of studies built around movements to create models of teaching derived from the academic disciplines, particularly the sciences and mathematics, and inductive thinking processes constitute a strong line of work that continues to the present. We selected this line of work because so many models draw on it, although each model has its unique set of inquiries that we will discuss in the chapters introducing them.

Because a considerable amount of research on teaching and curriculum has been connected to the academic disciplines, particularly the biological, physical, and social sciences, we can see bursts of innovative activity and research in terms of three phases of the Academic Reform Movements, in which bringing scientific concepts and processes into education were central. The first phase took place from the late 1950s until about 1985. The second phase occurred between 1985 and 2008 and built on the first movement. We are entering the third phase now, as the National Research Council (2012), comprised of members from the National Academy of Sciences, the National Academy of Medicine, and the Institute of Medicine, has published its framework for K–12 science standards (www.nap.edu). The National Academy was initiated in the 1860s to make scientific knowledge available to advise policymakers and provide information to the general public. Influential in the first phase of the Academic Reform Movement in education, its descendants are initiating the third phase.

The First Phase of the Academic Reform Movement

Studies at the Secondary Level

A set of meta-analyses of more than 300 studies on science curriculum and teaching was coordinated at the University of Colorado (Anderson, Kahl, Glass, Smith, & Malone, 1982). Taking into account that the research on science teaching is complex and studies vary considerably in their objectives and conduct, a persistent focus was on the effect of efforts that are characterized within cooperative/inductive inquiry. Particularly, did students acquire information, build and study data sets, form concepts by organizing and analyzing information in those sets, and engage in investigations (formulate questions, devise methods, and study results)? Put another way, did the students learn academic content and processes for solving problems by studying science content with empirical methods and engaging with the inductive processes that cross curriculum areas?

Ronald D. Anderson (1983), a senior researcher at the Laboratory for Research in Science and Mathematics Education at the University of Colorado in Boulder, summarizes concisely the results of the sets of studies: "Pertinent information from four of the meta-analyses is discussed here and, in general, points to a positive vote for inquiry teaching" (p. 500). Anderson, however, was concerned about the extent that inquiry methods are actually implemented in long-term curricular implementations. He points out that in the Shymansky, Kyle, and Alport (1983) meta-analysis of 105 studies (1000 classrooms with, conservatively, 150,000 students), degrees of use of inquiry methods did not generate differences in effects. However, even in the control groups, *all* of the curricula studied were based on science content and processes, and most of the studies were of six months or more, so differences of degree may not be large.

Studies at the Elementary Level

In addition to the set of University of Colorado studies, Bredderman (1983) pulled together the studies of the inquiry-oriented, hands-on science curriculum at the elementary level.

Bredderman drew on research on three "activity-based" programs funded through federal resources and assembled by scholars in education, scholars and district consultants in the sciences, and teachers. The three programs varied considerably in structure, with the Elementary Science Study being the most open ended and *Science: A Process Approach* being the most structured. None were structured around textbooks in elementary science. Students acquired data largely through observation and experimentation. Among the three programs, there were 57 controlled studies reported over a five-year period, involving 900 classrooms and, conservatively, about 13,000 students. Two-thirds of the studies involved 10 or more classrooms. Half of the studies were a year or more long, and most lasted two years or longer.

The mean effect size for learning science processes was 0.52. The effect size for scientific content was 0.16. Attitude toward science and process was 0.28. Smaller subsets examined effects on creativity (0.42) and measures of intelligence (0.48). Computation and mathematical understanding increased modestly. The aggregated mean effect size was 0.30.

> The idea that curriculums should aim at ideas, inductive and other scientific processes, and intellectual capacity and creativity is quite different from the position that the fundamental purpose of education is to imbue students with basic information and skills. One of the often-heard reactions to the activity-based programs has been that they put too much stress on science process at the expense of content learning. However, when activity-based programs are compared with traditional science programs on standardized achievement tests, it appears that those fears have been unwarranted. Content achievement was not affected in a negative way. This was true even if only a subgroup of studies that compared textbook programs with activity programs was considered. (p. 512)

The Second Phase of the Academic Reform Movement

Over the next 20 years, research on inquiry teaching continued, and in 2010 Minner, Levy, and Century presented a synthesis that covered 138 studies from 1984 to 2002. Nearly 2000 classrooms and about 40,000 students were involved.

Like Anderson 27 years before them, Minner, Levy, and Century are able to make a definitive statement about the effectiveness of the inquiry-based science curriculum during what we characterize as the second phase of the Academic Reform Movement.

> Findings . . . indicate a clear, positive trend favoring inquiry-based instructional practices, particularly instruction that emphasizes students' active thinking and drawing conclusions from data. Teaching strategies that actively engage

students in the learning process through scientific investigations are more likely to increase conceptual understanding than are strategies that rely on more passive techniques. (p. 474)

Generally speaking, the results from the Minner, Levy, and Century synthesis are somewhat larger than the results from the studies associated with the Academic Reform Movement. Probably this is a result of the increased refinements in curriculum and instruction—and we can expect more.

The Third Phase of the Academic Reform Movement: Just Beginning

The National Academy of Science's *Framework for K–12 Science Education: Practices, Concepts, and Core Ideas* (National Research Council, 2012) provides the conceptual foundation for the next core curriculum in science and will generate a third phase of the Academic Reform Movement. The inclusion of engineering and technological content should enhance content and process significantly. From the 40 years of studies drawn on previously, we can predict that not only the teaching/learning process will be upgraded, but that student learning will also rise to new levels.

The authors of the framework recommend even more powerful curricula than their predecessors. The development of hybrid curricula that draw on ICT and the increased use of interactive electronic media in and out of school should increase the use of investigation as part of the curriculum. There is now ample evidence that the success of ICT in education will depend on the models of teaching and learning that are implemented.

PART ONE

Models of Teaching: A Working Professional Repertoire

Chapter 1 opens our inquiry. We examine the concept of models of teaching and learning and how the models in this book were selected. We begin to study where models have come from—from gifted teacher-innovators is the short answer—and we prepare to acquire these interesting and effective tools. In Chapter 2, we delve into the social aspects of learning, for effective teaching involves the development of communities of learners and equipping students with ways of learning that will enable them to have high quality lives in school and beyond.

CHAPTER ONE

Where Models of Teaching Come From

Constructing Knowledge and Skill to Help Our Students Construct Knowledge and Skill

Helping new teachers learn to help students learn is more than worthwhile. It's transporting. The satisfaction when the veil lifts and someone realizes that the only barriers to growth are imaginary and self-imposed is almost unbearable. It's like watching the birth of a species.

—*Fritz Perls to Bruce Joyce*

ORGANIZING IDEA

Effective teaching is made up of a toolkit of ways to reach students and help them build their reservoir of knowledge, skills, and enduring values.

SCENARIO

A DAY IN THE LIFE OF SECTION 3A IN SIMONS ELEMENTARY SCHOOL

8:30. Traci Poirier's third-grade students assemble and find their places in the big horseshoe where their desks are arranged. This week they are organized in groups of three. The members of each group discuss something they have done or thought about since leaving class yesterday. Some share books they have read, films or television programs they have seen, places they have gone, or conversations with their family. All are responsible for sharing some current news event.

8:45. Traci asks whether any students wish to share an item that was shared with them. Nancy shares that Billy had received an email from his pen pal at Taipei Market School in Hong Kong (their recently adopted class, which uses them to

3

study life in the United States as they study life in Hong Kong). Billy's pen pal has wondered how many brothers and sisters they have. Everyone writes down his or her number of siblings and passes it to Billy so he can reply. Andy shares that Sharon reported that her sister was getting married on Saturday and wonders whether the class could send her a "best wishes" card. They agree to do so, and Andy volunteers to make a card to send to them.

9:00. The class begins their literacy study. The first inquiry is to get information from a picture of downtown Taipei Market. The class members take turns identifying items in the picture. Traci draws lines from the items to chart paper that surrounds the picture and writes and spells the words, and Andy enters them into the computer. Later they will be printed out on cards for each member of the class. About 30 items are identified and 12 questions generated.

The words are then compared with a set of items they have generated from a picture of the downtown area in their town. To their amazement, about 20 words from each picture are the same. There are more common attributes than different ones. Only six items in the Taipei Market picture are unfamiliar to them. Some of the items are similar, although their representations may be different (a sign in Chinese and English contrasts with a sign only in English). Traci agrees to circle them on the digital picture and email it to the Hong Kong class for identification.

9:30. The class does independent reading. For most students this means reading information from websites that Traci has bookmarked for them and looking through the encyclopedias for information about Hong Kong, taking notes, responding to questions, and developing new questions to explore. Traci tests two students using the Gray Oral Reading Test, looking for fluency and comprehension and searching for clues for her next sessions on comprehension skills for all the students.

10:00. The class works on writing, comparing the two downtown areas using the words they have identified to describe the two pictures. Traci models opening sentences for them, concentrating on how titles and first lines work together to establish topic and theme. She picks up on a prior session where the students classified opening sentences in trade books. Tomorrow they will continue to gather and discuss information as they compare Hong Kong to their own locale, and they will use synectics (see Chapter 7) to explore analogies to structure their writing.

It's only 10:30, but Traci has already designed activities using cooperative learning strategies, the picture word inductive model, group investigation, and the inductive model, and has planned a follow-up lesson using synectics. As the day progresses, she will begin a unit on plants in their vicinity, using the scientific inquiry model (Chapter 4), and continue a unit where the properties of number systems are the focus.

Traci has a good-sized repertoire of models of teaching. She knows that success for the students depends on their mastery of the models of learning that are embedded in each model of teaching.

The classic definition of teaching is *creating environments to facilitate learning.* A model of teaching is a way of building a nurturant and stimulating ecosystem within which the students learn by interacting with its components. Various models pull students into particular types of content (knowledge, values, skills) and increase their competence to grow in the personal, social, and academic domains. We use models in many ways, ranging from planning and using lessons, units, and curricula, to designing instructional materials, including multimedia programs. This concept replaces the "gas station" image of education, where students drop by to be loaded with cognitive fuel. That rather obsolete picture of teaching emphasizes the time-honored picture of a person *imparting* knowledge or skill by talking, exhorting, and drilling students— taking them through their paces in a grinding fashion. Happily, there are models for designing and delivering good lectures, motivating students, and carrying out effective training. There are times when we need to use the traditional delivery or transmission modes, but when we do, we should use the best models available for designing learning experiences and always be aware of the purposes that any approach can and cannot fulfill.

The last few decades have generated an enormous number of ways to enhance learning environments that existed only in dreams when we were writing the first edition of *Models of Teaching.* Even then we were using film, video recording and playback, simulations, transparencies, a dozen or so models of teaching, and a variety of other technologies both in our school and our teacher education programs. Those media are still important, but some are still underused in schools and universities. The best models of teaching in the earlier era are still effective today, along with some new ones, and all are enhanced by information and communications technology (ICT) and the available digital education tools.

OUR PERSONAL AND PROFESSIONAL HERITAGE

We have been fortunate enough to study with many contemporary educators who have developed and tested a variety of approaches to education and have developed the literature from the 1960s to the present. You will meet some of these shortly. We visit schools and classrooms and study current research on teaching and learning. We also study teaching in settings other than K–12 schools, such as therapies and training in industrial, military, and athletic settings.

We have found models of teaching in abundance. Some have broad applications, whereas others are designed for specific purposes. They range from simple, direct procedures that yield immediate results to complex strategies that students acquire gradually from patient and skillful instruction.

For *Models of Teaching*, we selected models that constitute a basic repertoire for schooling. With these models we can accomplish most of the common goals of schools—and at a high standard. In any school, students can achieve many goals that only outstanding students in outstanding schools once aspired to achieve. Using models in combination, we can design schools, curricula, units, and lessons. The selection includes many, but not all, of the major philosophical and psychological orientations toward teaching and learning. All have a solid theoretical basis—that is, their creators provide us with a rationale that explains why we expect them to achieve the goals for which they were designed. The selected models also have histories of extensive practice behind them: They have been refined through experience so that they can be used comfortably and efficiently in classrooms and other educational settings. Furthermore, they are adaptable to the learning styles of students and to the requirements of many curriculum areas. Education comes to the new core curriculum standards with a well-stocked storehouse of effective models that address the most demanding standards.

In addition to being validated by experience, all are backed by formal research and disciplined action research that tests their theories and their abilities to yield positive effects. The amount of related research varies from model to model. Some are backed by a few studies; others have hundreds of items of research. As we discuss each model, we provide key references and links—ones that provide access to the research literature and will include page-long descriptions of some of the more revealing studies. They were designed to have positive effects on student learning, and we try to make the warrants (evidence and reasoned analysis) under their stated effects as transparent as possible.

COMMON CHARACTERISTICS ACROSS ALL MODELS

Before introducing the models and the families into which we have grouped them, we need to discuss some of the characteristics that all of the selected models share. Learning is the reason for all models, but other attributes are common and integral to the teaching stances represented by the models.

Helping Students Learn How to Learn

In their own fashions, each of the selected models includes helping students increase their repertoire of strategies for learning. While using any model, teachers study how the students learn and help them expand their capacity to do so.

• **Helping students take responsibility for learning and supporting their efforts.** Even when being highly directive, which can be the case while introducing students to new ways of learning, we emphasize that they need to build the capacity to take increasing responsibility for their learning. We move from a need to provide extensive coaching to students to a situation where students are coaching themselves.

• **Helping students reach toward new knowledge, skills, and self-understanding.** The essence of learning, in school and out, is acquiring new cognitions, abilities, and even emotions and values. A major part of teaching is helping students learn to go beyond where they are. When a six-year-old says, "I don't like to read!" the underlying emotion is that the child wants to avoid the labor of learning to read and, possibly, the feeling of embarrassment while overcoming difficulties in learning.

A Constructivist Orientation

In their own fashions, all these models seek to help students build knowledge, skills, and values. The instructional aims of several models are almost purely constructivist with respect to academic content (see Vygotsky, 1962). For example, inductive inquiry (Chapter 3) designs the environment so that the student *constructs* categories, tests them, and from them generates inferences and hypotheses, leading to more testing. A very different model, nondirective teaching (Chapter 14), is designed to help students understand themselves better—to *construct* self-knowledge—and set goals in the personal, social, and academic domains.

Scaffolding the Learning Process

Built into their processes, all the selected models provide avenues for teachers to "boost" students over difficulties and into the next levels of learning. Vygotsky described the process as seeking the "zone of proximal development" where learning tasks are at a level slightly above the student's zone of complete comfort, but not so far above that the student cannot manage. Conceptual systems theorists, including the present authors, describe this as providing an "optimal mismatch" designed to enable students to pull themselves into ever-higher levels of capability (see Chapter 20). For example, when teaching new skills with the "training" models (as in Chapter 18), a skill is explained and demonstrated and then the student has to try the skill. At that point, if a student shies away, scaffolding in the form of encouragement may be enough to lift them to try. Possibly more explanation or another demonstration may be in order, but providing motivation may be the difference between success and discouragement. Scaffolding by a teacher on the campus can be a critical support when a student is engaged in distance learning, such as taking part or all of a course online. More than ever, students need to learn to profit from distance offerings. Even those who are highly skilled at downloading and learning to play games may need help when downloading large quantities of information.

Formative Assessment and Adjustments

Closely related to scaffolding is the use of formative assessment to determine whether more or a different kind of support is needed. Sometimes switching to a different model of teaching can help a student find an avenue to learning. ICT is an increasingly important resource for classes as a whole, as well as providing acceleration for students who are sprinting ahead and tutoring for those who need extra help along the way. Helping students become aware of their progress and needs is a critical component of formative assessment. Parents are also brought into the process when they can help, which is frequently.

All models of teaching provide the opportunity for teachers and students to study progress, continue things that are working well, and make adjustments by adding processes and replacing ones that are not working.

21st-Century Skills

A strong movement to improve education has emphasized what have been termed *21st-century skills*—types of expertise that have come to the fore as the global, digital world has emerged. Probably "areas of needed knowledge and competence" is a more accurate and useful term than "skill," but expertise is certainly found in them (see Kay, 2010; Joyce & Calhoun, 2012).

Some 21st-century skills are versions of competence that have been around for a while. Some have been emphasized in the new core state standards, and some are emerging as the digital age ripens. They are *not* just a collection of computer or ICT skills. Though ICT literacy is important, the vital skills are cognitive: learning to inquire, to build and test ideas, to categorize, to summarize. These have been with us a long time, and they continue to be essential as the opportunities to use them expand. However, everyone needs the skills to use software for word processing, graphics, photo and video editing, searching the web, and locating and using distance instructional offerings. For teachers, mastery of interactive whiteboard technology is increasingly important. Let's look at some of the other areas that are emphasized by the 21st-century movement.

Cultural Literacy and Global Awareness

One of the most striking characteristics of the ICT explosion is the rise of a global, cross-national culture and its effects on relations near and far. These effects change the nature of our society, increase interdependence, and generate a considerable need for intercultural understanding. The implications are apparent as nations and their well-being have become more interdependent, economies more unified; and we as individuals are in contact with, well, almost everyone. A provincial perspective today can have devastating consequences.

Collaborative and Cooperative Skills

We need each other. We always have, but the price of failure to work with others near and far has become unsustainable. Schools need to develop a rich culture to teach students to work and play together. In fact, the campus will be a very important place in the future because it is the major social laboratory for the young. As they reach out into cyberspace and information and ideas zip back from global sites, students need each other for perspective. The simpler cooperative learning models must pervade the school, and the most complex models—cooperative/inquiry models and group investigation—should propel major inquiries. Social media have enormous implications and are affecting life all over the world.

We urge teachers to join the International Association for the Study of Cooperation in Education. We greatly enjoy and learn from their newsletter.

Creativity

Convergent thinking enables students to focus on and drive for mastery of knowledge and skills from outside. Divergent thinking plays with information, concepts, pictures, sounds, and objects. Things are moved around, and surprises appear. The process is what the great Bill Gordon called *serious playfulness,* an oxymoron that captures the essence of metaphoric thinking. Ideas that were born on different cognitive planes are placed next to each other, on top of each other, inside each other. Environments populated with analogies lure students into a divergent state. Conception occurs.

The selected models in this book share these characteristics and goals.

THE FAMILIES OF MODELS

We have grouped the models of teaching into four families whose members share orientations toward human beings and how they learn. These are:

- The Information-Processing Family
- The Social Family
- The Personal Family
- The Behavioral Systems Family

We turn now to these four families, what they emphasize, and the models and the people who invented them, studied them, and advocated for them. As you read, keep in mind that, as a teacher, you can begin with a few that have wide applicability and then add others to reach particular goals more readily.

The Information-Processing Family

Information-processing models emphasize ways of enhancing the human being's innate drive to make sense of the world by acquiring and organizing data, sensing problems and generating solutions to them, and developing concepts and language for conveying them. Some models help the learner find information and build concepts and hypotheses to test. Some emphasize teaching concepts directly. Some generate creative thinking. Others teach the processes of the disciplines that underlie the core subjects. All are designed to enhance general intellectual ability.

Eight information-processing models are discussed in Part II and III. Part II is focused on three broadly applicable models and Part III on more narrowly oriented "special purpose" models. Table 1.1 displays their names and the primary developers and redevelopers of each. In some cases, dozens of research-practitioners have contributed to the creation and renewal of particular approaches to teaching.

Inductive Thinking (Chapter Three)

The ability to analyze information and create concepts is generally regarded as the fundamental thinking skill. Although the model has been discussed since ancient times, the contemporary literature was given movement by the work of Hilda Taba (1966) and contemporaries who studied how to teach students to find and organize information and to build and test hypotheses. The model has been used in a wide variety of curriculum areas and with students of all ages—it is not confined to the sciences. Phonetic and structural analysis depend on concept learning, as do rules of grammar. The structure of the field of literature is based on classification. The study of communities, nations, and history requires concept learning. Even if concept learning were not so critical in the development of thought, the organization of information is so fundamental to curriculum areas that inductive thinking would be a very important model for learning and teaching school subjects. The model as presented is based on the recent adaptations by Joyce and Calhoun (1996, 1998), and Joyce, Hrycauk, and Calhoun (2001) in programs designed to accelerate student ability to learn.

This model is listed first because inductive processes are such an important dimension of cognition and cognitive ability, because it inevitably leads to cooperative study and action, and because it combines well with other models.

Scientific Inquiry (Chapter Four)

The National Academy of Sciences has produced a marvelous document that sets forth a forward-looking framework for K–12 science curriculum and teaching. Its comprehensive scope and readable style make it a fine resource for teachers of all grade levels and in all science areas. The inclusion

TABLE 1.1   Information-Processing Models

Model	Developer (Redeveloper)	Purpose
Inductive thinking* (Classification)	Hilda Taba (Bruce Joyce)	Development of classification skills, hypothesis building and testing, and understanding of how to build conceptual understanding of content areas
Scientific inquiry*	Joseph Schwab and many others	Learning the research system of the academic disciplines—how knowledge is produced and organized
Picture word inductive*	Emily Calhoun	Learning to read and write, inquiry into language
Concept attainment*	Jerome Bruner Fred Lighthall (Bruce Joyce)	Learning concepts and studying strategies for attaining and applying them; building and testing hypotheses
Synectics*	William Gordon	Help break set in problem solving and gain new perspectives on topic
Mnemonics*	Michael Pressley Joel Levin (and associated scholars)	Increase ability to acquire information, concepts, conceptual systems, and metacognitive control of information processing capability
Advance organizers*	David Ausubel (and many others)	Increase ability to absorb information and organize it, especially in learning from lectures and readings
Inquiry training*	Richard Suchman (Howard Jones)	Causal reasoning and understanding of how to collect information, build concepts, and build and test hypotheses
Cognitive growth	Jean Piaget Irving Sigel Constance Kamii Edmund Sullivan	Increase general intellectual development and adjust instruction to facilitate intellectual growth

*Indicates a model that has a full chapter or section in this text

of material from engineering and technology make applied science more prominent than in the past and their "cross-cutting concepts" that look across the disciplines are an important contribution to curriculum thought. A good place to begin is the website http://nextgenscience.org.

Social sciences also take a similar approach to curriculum and teaching.

The Picture Word Inductive Model (PWIM) (Chapter Five)

Developed by Emily Calhoun (1999), this model was designed from research on how students acquire print literacy, particularly reading and writing, but also how listening–speaking vocabularies are developed. PWIM incorporates the inductive thinking and concept attainment models as students study words, sentences, and paragraphs. The model is the core of some very effective curricula where kindergarten and primary students learned to read and older beginning readers and writers were engaged in "safety net" programs for upper elementary, middle school, and high school students (see Joyce, Calhoun, Jutras, & Newlove, 2006; and Joyce & Calhoun, 2010, 2012). ICT provides access to enormous reservoirs of pictures that can be used in PWIM and support for investigations initiated with the model.

Concept Attainment (Chapter Six)

Originally built around studies conducted by Bruner, Goodnow, and Austin (1967) and adapted and applied to education by Lighthall, Joyce, and others, concept attainment is a close relative of the inductive model. Whereas the inductive process calls on students to *form* concepts, concept analysis leads the students to *attain* concepts developed by others. The teacher develops a data set containing exemplars of a concept and items where the attributes of the concept are not present. The students then study pairs of contrasting items until they are clear about the concept. The model is an efficient method for presenting organized information from a wide range of topics to students at every stage of development and also enables students to become more effective at concept formation. A short and succinct demonstration is available online at www.modelsofteaching.org.

Synectics (Chapter Seven)

Developed first for use with "creativity groups" in industrial settings, synectics was adapted by William Gordon (1961) for use in elementary and secondary education. Synectics is designed to help people "break set" in problem-solving and writing activities and to gain new perspectives on topics from a wide range of fields. In the classroom it is introduced to students in a series of sessions until they can apply the procedures individually and in cooperative groups. Although designed as a direct stimulus to creative thought, synectics has the side effect of promoting collaborative work and study skills and a feeling of camaraderie among students. Some recent studies and development by Keyes (2006) and Glynn (1994) have pushed the model a welcome new distance.

Mnemonics (Chapter Eight)

Mnemonics are strategies for memorizing and assimilating information. Teachers can use mnemonics to guide their presentations of material (teaching in such a way that students can easily absorb the information), and they can teach devices that students can use to enhance their individual and cooperative study of information and concepts. This model also has been tested over many curriculum areas and with students of many ages and characteristics. We include variations developed by Pressley, Levin, and Delaney (1982); Levin and Levin (1990); and popular applications by Lorayne and Lucas (1974) and Lucas (2001). Because memorization is sometimes confused with repetitious, rote learning of obscure or arcane terms and trivial information, people sometimes assume that mnemonics deal only with the lowest level of information. That is by no means true. Mnemonics can be used to help people master interesting concepts, and in addition, they can be a great deal of fun.

Advance Organizers (Chapter Nine)

During the last 50 years this model, formulated by David Ausubel (1963), has accumulated a good-sized body of research. The model is designed to provide students with a cognitive structure for comprehending material presented through lectures, readings, and other media. It has been employed with almost every conceivable content and with students of every age. It can be easily combined with other models—for example, when presentations are mixed with inductive activity.

Inquiry Training (Chapter Ten)

This model is a direct and fun way to train students to look for causal relationships among variables. See a demonstration with students from India through www.modelsofteaching.org.

The Social Family

When we work together, we generate a collective energy called *synergy*. The social models of teaching are constructed to take advantage of this phenomenon by building learning communities. Essentially, classroom management is a matter of developing cooperative relationships in the classroom. The development of positive school cultures is a process of developing integrative and productive ways of interacting and norms that support vigorous learning activity. Table 1.2 identifies the models and several of the developers of the social models.

Partners in Learning (Chapter Eleven)

There has been a great deal of development work on cooperative learning, and great progress has been made in developing strategies that help students work effectively together. The contributions of three teams—led respectively by Roger and David Johnson, Robert Slavin, and Shlomo Sharan—have been particularly notable, but the entire cooperative learning community has been active in exchanging information and techniques and in conducting and analyzing research (see, for example, Johnson and Johnson, 2009). The result is a

TABLE **1.2**   Social Models

Model	Developer	Purpose
Partners in Learning	David Johnson Roger Johnson Elizabeth Cohen	Development of interdependent strategies of social interaction; understanding of self–other relationships and emotions
Structured social inquiry	Robert Slavin and colleagues	Academic inquiry and social and personal development; cooperative strategies for approaching academic study
Group investigation*	John Dewey Herbert Thelen Shlomo Sharan Rachel Hertz-Lazarowitz	Development of skills for participation in democratic process; simultaneously emphasizes social development, academic skills, and personal understanding
Social inquiry	Byron Massialas Benjamin Cox	Social problem solving through collective academic study and logical reasoning
Laboratory method	National Training Laboratory (many contributors)	Understanding of group dynamics, leadership, understanding of personal styles
Role playing*	Fannie Shaftel George Shaftel	Study of values and their role in social interaction; personal understanding of values and behavior
Jurisprudential inquiry	James Shaver Donald Oliver	Analysis of policy issues through a jurisprudential framework; collection of data, analysis of value questions and positions, study of personal beliefs

*Indicates a model that has a full chapter or section in this text

large number of effective means of organizing students to work together. These range from teaching students to carry out simple learning tasks in pairs to complex models for organizing classes and even organizing whole schools into learning communities.

Cooperative learning procedures can facilitate learning across all curriculum areas, ages, and academic learning goals, as well as improve self-esteem, social skill, and solidarity.

Group Investigation (Chapter Twelve)

John Dewey (1916) was the major spokesperson for the idea—extended and refined by a great many teachers and shaped into a powerful definition by Herbert Thelen (1960)—that education in a democratic society should teach the democratic process directly. A substantial part of students' education should be through cooperative inquiry into important social and academic problems. The model also provides a social organization within which many other models can be used when appropriate. Group investigation has been used in all subject areas, with children of all ages, and even as the core social model for entire schools (Chamberlin & Chamberlin, 1943; Joyce, Calhoun, & Hopkins, 1999). The model is designed to lead students to define problems, explore various perspectives on the problems, and study together to master information, ideas, and skills—simultaneously developing their social competence. The teacher or facilitator organizes the group process and disciplines it, helps the students find and organize information, and ensures that there is a vigorous level of activity and discourse. Sharan and his colleagues (1988) and Joyce and Calhoun (1998) have extended the model and combined it with recent findings on the development of inquiring groups.

Role Playing (Chapter Thirteen)

Role playing is included next because it leads students to understand social behavior, their role in social interactions, and ways of solving problems more effectively. Designed by Fannie and George Shaftel (1982) specifically to help students study their social values and reflect on them, role playing also helps students collect and organize information about social issues, develop empathy with others, and attempt to improve their social skills. In addition, the model asks students to "act out" conflicts, learn to take the roles of others, and observe social behavior. With appropriate adaptation, role playing can be used with students of all ages.

The Personal Family

Ultimately, human reality resides in our individual consciousnesses. We develop unique personalities and see the world from perspectives that are the products of our experiences and positions. Common understandings are a product of the negotiation of individuals who must live and work and create families together.

The personal models of learning begin from the perspective of the selfhood of the individual. They attempt to shape education so that we come to understand ourselves better, take responsibility for our education, and learn to reach beyond our current development to become stronger, more sensitive, and more creative in our search for high-quality lives.

The cluster of personal models pays great attention to the individual perspective and seeks to encourage productive independence, so that people become increasingly self-aware and responsible for their own destinies. Table 1.3 displays some of these models and their developers.

Nondirective Teaching (Chapter Fourteen)

Psychologist and counselor Carl Rogers (1961, 1982) was for three decades the acknowledged spokesperson for models in which the teacher plays the role of counselor. Developed from counseling theory, the model emphasizes a partnership between students and teacher. The teacher endeavors to help the students understand how to play major roles in directing their own educations—for example, by behaving in such a way as to clarify goals and participate in developing avenues for reaching those goals. The teacher provides information about how much progress is being made and helps the students solve problems, but it is the student who has to take initiative—the teacher scaffolds the student's investigation. The nondirective teacher has to actively build the partnerships required and provide the help needed as the students try to work out their problems.

The model is used in several ways. First, at the most general (and least common) level, it is used as the basic model for the operation of entire educational programs (Neill, 1960). Second, it is used in combination with other

TABLE 1.3   Personal Models

Model	Developer	Purpose
Nondirective teaching*	Carl Rogers	Building capacity for personal development, self-understanding, autonomy, and self-esteem
Positive self-concepts*	Abraham Maslow	Development of personal understanding and capacity for development
Awareness training	Fritz Perls	Increasing self-understanding, self-esteem, and capacity for exploration; development of interpersonal sensitivity and empathy
Classroom meeting	William Glasser	Development of self-understanding and responsibility to self and others
Conceptual systems	David Hunt	Increasing personal complexity and flexibility in processing information and interacting with others

*Indicates a model that has a full chapter or section in this text

models to ensure that contact is made with the students. In this role, it moderates the educational environment. Third, it is used when students are planning independent and cooperative study projects. Fourth, it is used periodically when counseling students, finding out what they are thinking and feeling, and helping them understand what they are about. Although designed to promote self-understanding and independence, it has fared well as a contributor to a wide range of academic objectives. Cornelius-White's (2007) review of many years of research on learner-centered teacher–student relationships—119 studies involving more than 300,000 students—examined the impact on cognitive, affective, and behavioral outcomes and reported positive effects and, importantly, that for applications where academic content was included, gains in content were correlated with gains in affect, including self-concepts.

Developing Positive Self-Concepts (Chapter Fifteen)

One of the most difficult tasks in teaching is helping students whose confidence has sunk to a level where they wallow helplessly in failure. They approach the ordinary tasks of the curriculum with dread and avoid those tasks when they can. Here we present a multidimensional approach that attempts to confront grade 4 to 12 students with the very thing they fear—learning to read—and bring those students into the world of success. The influential work of Abraham Maslow has been used to guide programs to build self-esteem and self-actualizing capability for 50 years. We explore the principles that can guide our actions as we work with our students to ensure that their personal image functions as well as possible.

Adaptations to the study of teachers as they expand their repertoire of teaching models have provided a means by which teachers can study their learning styles and processes (Joyce & Showers, 2002). The personal, social, and academic goals of education are compatible with one another. The personal family of teaching models provides the essential part of the teaching repertoire that directly addresses the students' needs for self-esteem and self-understanding and how to build support and respect among students.

The Behavioral Systems Family

A common theoretical base—most commonly called *social learning theory*, but also known as *behavior modification, behavior therapy,* and *cybernetics*—guides the design of the models in this family. The stance taken is that human beings are self-correcting communication systems that modify behavior in response to information about how successfully tasks are navigated. For example, imagine a human being who is climbing (the task) an unfamiliar staircase in the dark. The first few steps are tentative as the foot reaches for the treads. If the stride is too high, feedback is received as the foot encounters air and has to descend to make contact with the surface. If a step is too low, feedback results as the foot hits the riser. Gradually, behavior is adjusted in accordance with the feedback until progress up the stairs is relatively comfortable.

Capitalizing on knowledge about how people respond to tasks and feedback, psychologists (see especially Skinner, 1953) have learned how to organize task and feedback structures to make it easy for human beings' self-correcting capability to function. The result includes programs for reducing phobias, learning to read and compute, developing social and athletic skills, replacing anxiety with relaxation, and learning the complexes of intellectual, social, and physical skills necessary to pilot an airplane or a space shuttle. Because these models concentrate on observable behavior and clearly defined tasks and methods for communicating progress to the student, this family of teaching models has a firm research foundation. Behavioral techniques are appropriate for learners of all ages and for an impressive range of educational goals. Table 1.4 displays the models and their developers.

Explicit Instruction (Chapter Sixteen)

Although reading without comprehension is not really reading, the explicit teaching of comprehension strategies has not been common in U.S. schools. However, research and development, practice, and results have given us a serviceable model. *Every* teacher will find this model useful.

Mastery Learning (Chapter Seventeen)

The most common application of behavioral systems theory for academic goals takes the form of what is called *mastery learning* (Bloom, 1971). First, material to be learned is divided into units ranging from the simple to the complex. The material is presented to the students, generally working as individuals, through appropriate media (readings, tapes, activities). Piece by piece, the students work their way successively through the units of materials, after each of which they take a test designed to help them find out what they have learned. If they have not mastered any given unit, they can repeat it or an equivalent version until they have mastered the material.

Instructional systems based on this model have been used to provide instruction to students of all ages in areas ranging from the basic skills to highly complex material in the academic disciplines. With appropriate adaptation, they have also been used with gifted and talented students, students with emotional problems, and athletes and astronauts.

Direct Instruction (Chapter Eighteen)

From studies of the differences between more and less effective teachers and from social learning theory, a paradigm for instructing directly has been assembled. Direct statements of objectives, sets of activities clearly related to the objectives, careful monitoring of progress, feedback about achievement, and tactics for achieving more effectively are linked with sets of guidelines for

TABLE **1.4**   Behavioral Models

Model	Developer	Purpose
Social learning	Albert Bandura Carl Thoresen Wes Becker	The management of behavior: learning new patterns of behavior, reducing phobic and other dysfunctional patterns, learning self-control
Explicit instruction*	P. David Pearson & Margaret Gallagher Ruth Garner Gerald Duffy Laura Roehler and others	Learning to be a strategic reader
Mastery learning*	Benjamin Bloom James Block	Mastery of academic skills and content of all types
Programmed learning	B. F. Skinner	Mastery of skills, concepts, factual information
Direct instruction*	Thomas Good Jere Brophy Wes Becker Siegfried Englemann Carl Bereiter	Mastery of academic content and skills in a wide range of areas of study
Simulation	Many developers Carl Smith and Mary Foltz Smith provided guidance through 1960s when design had matured	Mastery of complex skills and concepts in a wide range of areas of study
Anxiety reduction	David Rinn Joseph Wolpe John Masters	Control over aversive reactions; applications in treatment and self-treatment of avoidance and dysfunctional patterns of response

*Indicates a model that has a full chapter or section in this text

facilitating learning. Two approaches to training have been developed from the cybernetic group of behavior theorists. One is a theory-to-practice model and the other is simulation. The former mixes information about a skill with demonstrations, practice, feedback, and coaching until the skill is mastered. For example, if an arithmetic skill is the objective, it is explained and demonstrated, practice is given with corrective feedback, and the student is asked to apply it with coaching from peers or the instructor. This variation is commonly used for athletic training.

Simulations are constructed from descriptions of real-life situations. A less-than-real-life environment is created for the instructional situation. Sometimes the renditions are elaborate (for example, flight and spaceflight simulators or simulations of international relations). The student engages in activity to achieve the goal of the simulation (to get the aircraft off the ground, perhaps, or to redevelop an urban area) and has to deal with realistic factors until the goal is mastered.

In Sum

The models briefly introduced here have been selected from many other possibilities. We are sure these can be used in classrooms and in cyberspace; their effectiveness has been substantiated by experience and formal research. As we will see later, achieving mastery over them takes practice. Teams of teachers working together to master a model can share reflections and companionship as one progresses from being a novice to achieving executive control over that model.

CHAPTER TWO

Building the Community of Expert Learners

Taking Advantage of Our Students' Capacity to Learn (and Ours)

A school teaches in three ways: by what it teaches, by how it teaches, and by the kind of place it is.

—Lawrence Downey (1967)

In a perfect world, we would come to adulthood knowing we had full-blown wisdom about how to raise children and how to teach them from infancy to adulthood. At least we'd be aware that those knowledges and attendant skills were latent, lying just below the surface and ready to come to life when we had babies or accepted jobs as teachers. In our imperfect world, we are not so lucky; most of us have to learn a lot about how to parent and how to teach. But we are not without equipment, because what we need *does* lie within us if we will allow it to find its way into our consciousness. Models of teaching and learning are designed to make that awakening a stimulating and positive adventure. Information and communication technologies (ICT) are going to help, particularly by bringing information and ideas closer to us and our children and learners all over the globe.

WHAT PEOPLE BRING TO LIFE: NATURAL LEARNING CAPABILITY, CURIOSITY, AND CREATIVITY

From birth, we are programmed to reach out to living and nonliving things. Think how we loved our pillow, our blanket, or some stuffed toy. We not only loved them, we imbued them with a love that they returned to us. In the most desolate circumstances, a baby will treasure a stick or a stone if that's all there is at hand. Those of us who have pets learn how much they are an opportunity to extend our capacity for love and companionship. The other day Bruce interrupted a telephone conversation to say something to our cat. The woman on the other end said, "Don't worry. I talk to my dog all the time."

Knowing how to love and care for things beyond ourselves is a great tool with which to begin our lives. We *know* that we and other creatures need affection and attention, and we know something about how to provide these to others even as we work our way through the egocentricity we were also born with. But we were not born with meanness or cruelty. Those have to be learned in a perverse environment.

People are also natural scientists. We investigate routinely at birth, looking at and touching things and manipulating them to see what happens. We just can't help it, for we want to know how our world works. We are a handful at that point, and those who care for us have to scoop us up at times just before we are about to connect ourselves to the electrical system or the oven. But we continue studying our world, crawling around and poking things to find out what happens.

Children don't just collect information; they also organize it. We're inborn scholars in the sense that we naturally build concepts and generalizations. We're born with an innate ability to discriminate things and organize all sorts of stuff into categories. As infants, we sorted things as hard or soft, comfortable or uncomfortable, rough or smooth, noisy or quiet. We learned to tell Mom from Dad, the cat from either, the cat from furry toys. We learned words. *There's* a big one—as we listened to the world around us, we sorted words, rapidly gaining control and making choices as we shouted *Da* to access Dad, *Baa* for our bottle, and *Ju* for our juice. We *want* to learn language—to listen and speak fluently. Deaf children are exultant when they discover that sign language exists. And there is no more thrilling moment to watch than when an improvement in hearing aids lets the world of sound into their minds and hearts.

Early language acquisition is easy because we're natural linguists. Once we have about 50 words we begin to make sentences, at first just two or three words long. As our minds seek to make sense of our world, we figure out which words are used for what. Wherever we find ourselves, we listen and learn to speak. In Greece, we learn Greek; in Thailand, we learn Thai; in Argentina, we learn Spanish. In Switzerland, we may learn French, German, and Italian, all at once. By the time we're 4 or so, we know the structure of our language and can understand and speak several thousand words—a basic storehouse that we will hear and process all our lives.

Scholars who study language development are continually amazed as they study young children's language development. Infants progress rapidly from when they utter a first word; by age 2, the average speaking vocabulary is 500 to 600 words. By age 5, the speaking vocabulary averages about 5000 words. By then children are also using the basic structures of language (such as syntax), and phonemic and phonological awareness is established for many.

There is considerable variance—a range of 2500 to 7500 words is common in populations that have been studied (Biemiller, 2010).

We are beginning to understand more about why homes and preschools have large effects. A major factor appears to be the amount of talk in the home and the nursery and preschool (Barnett, 2001; Dickinson, McCabe, & Essex, 2006; Hart & Risley, 1995). If the environment is language dense and rich, the natural linguist takes over and the child learns more words and more about the structure of the language in his or her environment. By surrounding the students with language, expertly taught preschools and kindergartens can level the field considerably. But, by age 5, children from the most linguistically poor families can learn to read if the appropriate models of teaching are used. The early years (K–2) curricula need to increase listening and speaking as well as reading and writing vocabulary. Overall vocabulary measured in grade 2 predicts 30 percent of the variance in reading comprehension in grade 11 (see Cunningham, 2009; Graves, 2006).

Just as learning language is a natural capacity, people are born anthropologists. We learn the norms of our culture rapidly by watching the people around us and imitating them. We'll eat literally anything, if our people do, and we'll stay away from any food our social environment shuns. Most of us mimic, then follow, the customs of our immediate world. If the people around us shake hands on greeting, we shake hands; if they hug, we hug; if they bow, we bow. In China, we'll learn Chinese customs. In England, we'll soon look and talk like miniature English people.

What can we—the parent, relative, neighbor, the teacher candidate, the formal educator, the experienced schoolteacher—do to strengthen, nurture, and channel these wondrous human capabilities? What is our role? Our work? *The first principle is learning to work with nature and avoid working against it.* If we learn to build classroom and school environments that capitalize on the way we are—the way *people* are—the natural learning ability of children will make us great teachers and parents. One of the inherent premises of inductive and other effective models of teaching is that we do not have to feed our knowledge of language, science, social studies, and mathematics to our students. Rather, we help them enhance their ability to learn. If we build learning communities that draw the students into inquiry into subject matter and help those students engage with it conceptually, they will master any subject. And, they will be learning more than our specified curriculum objectives: they will *learn how to learn* ever more powerfully, because they are practicing their thinking, because they have more information, because they are using this information, and because learning and understanding are satisfying. (See the introduction to the new science and English language arts standards for an elaborate affirmation of this position: National Governors Association Center for Best Practices & Council of Chief State School Officers, 2010; National Research Council, 2012.)

Let's turn to the process of building those learning communities—the nurturant and stimulating environments that enable the capacities of our students to flourish as they educate themselves.

CREATING COMMUNITIES OF EXPERT LEARNERS

This book could have been called Models of Learning.

—*Emily Calhoun to Bruce Joyce, maybe a hundred times*

Let's begin by visiting two first-grade and two tenth-grade classrooms at 9:00 on the first day of school. All of the teachers are using teaching/learning models. The first part of each scenario describes the teaching/learning processes on the campus; that is, they each take place in a classroom in a school. Then we add connections to resources on the web and ways of obtaining and managing information, and they each become a *hybrid*—the campus and the web are working together.

SCENARIO

THE FIRST HOUR OF SCHOOL IN GRADE 1

The first-grade children are gathered around a table on which a candle and jar have been placed. The teacher, Jackie Wiseman, lights the candle and, after it has burned brightly for a minute or two, carefully covers it with the jar. The candle grows dim, flickers, and goes out. Then she produces another candle and a larger jar, and the exercise is repeated. The candle goes out, but more slowly. Jackie produces two more candles and jars of different sizes and repeats the process. Again the flames slowly go out.

"Now we're going to develop some ideas about what has just happened," she says. "I want you to ask me questions about those candles and jars and what you just observed." The students begin. She gently helps them rephrase their questions or plan experiments. When one asks, "Would the candles burn longer with an even bigger jar?" Jackie responds, "How might we find out?" Periodically, she will ask them to dictate to her what they know and questions they have and writes what they say on newsprint paper. Their own words will be the content of their first study of reading.

Jackie tells the children that she has planned another demonstration to provide them with more information. Using the interactive whiteboard as the monitor, she takes them to a website called The Naked Scientists (www.thenakedscientists.com) and, within that site, to the Kitchen Science page and then to an item called Losing Air.

She reads students the instructions about the demonstration, beginning with needed materials, which she shows and discusses as she readies the experiment.

The materials are

- A transparent Pyrex dish
- A candle designed to float
- A quart-sized wide-mouthed jar without a top
- Three coasters heavy enough to sink in water

Then Jackie pours water into the dish to a level of about 1½ inches, puts the coasters on the bottom of the dish, places the candle on the water, and lights it. After ensuring that it is burning well, she lowers the jar over it until it is resting on the edges of the coasters. In Figure 2.1 you can see the arrangement as if you were looking at it with your eyes level with the top of the dish.

What happens? First, air bubbles escape from the jar, rising through the water. Then, the candle goes out and the water rises in the jar.

Jackie asks the students to describe the materials, their arrangement, and what happened after the candle was lit. She writes their answers on the whiteboard and takes care that the materials are identified and the events are described in order. They read the descriptions in unison after Jackie reads each one.

Then, she asks them to try to provide explanations of what happened: the onset of the bubbles and then the water rising in the jar.

Jackie is beginning her year with the model of teaching we call *inquiry training* (see Chapter 10) and is transitioning to the model we refer to as *scientific inquiry*.

FIGURE 2.1   Demonstration using candles on water

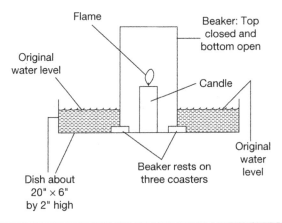

The model begins by having the students encounter what will be, to them, a puzzling situation. Then, by asking questions and conducting other investigations, such as trying larger and smaller jars, they build ideas and test them.

The inquiry leads them to the school library, where the librarian, Cathy Rodelheimer, shows them *Being a Scientist,* by Natalie Lunis and Nancy White. *Being a Scientist* is a big book (approximately 14 × 20 inches), heavily illustrated with photographs, that Jackie can read to students. When she reads the book, she asks her students to describe what they see in the lavish photographs that accompany the text. She also notes on the interactive whiteboard some words they would like to learn to read, including "you," "yes," and "scientist." She spells them as she prints them on the board and asks the children to spell them by repeating after her.

After each page, she also asks the students to dictate a summary or provide an answer to a question posed in the text. She writes these on the board, reading aloud what she writes. For example, one picture discusses the concept of *measuring.* On the next page, the photo shows a girl mixing *ingredients* for a cake and using a beaker to measure flour. The text asks how the young woman can find out how much flour she needs (Lunis & White, 1999).

The inquiry leads to what we call the *great new global library*—the information and ideas indexed on the web. The computer that is connected to the whiteboard contains Encarta (Jackie has an old copy on CD) and Compton and Britannica encyclopedias (see http://kids.britannica.com) that, with her help, the students can consult as the inquiry proceeds. Most important, in this and other projects, Jackie is building a community where the students will work together as they learn to read and write and explore social studies, science, and mathematics.

How does the candle project fit with the spirit of the new core curriculum standards? The science standards suggest that students learn content in such a way that they experience and learn how knowledge is generated. The science core is also unified by continuous hands-on experience. All students, K–12, should conduct investigations in the sciences and participate in projects where the methods and concepts of the sciences are employed. The experiential learning provides the concrete ground for understanding more complex and abstract principles as they are encountered, as well as the application to aspects of life that are within reach. The investigative frame of reference is a lifelong outcome. The Common Core State Standards for English Language Arts & Literacy stress literacy in the sciences—note how Jackie mixes gathering information from books, the web, and hands-on experiences and how this is based on the evidence presented in Chapter 1.

The social studies are similar—learning how to build knowledge and ideas while studying the immediate social environment. (See *Social Education* and *Social Education for the Young Learner,* publications of the National Council for the Social Studies).

In Jackie's classroom, ICT will be present in several ways throughout the school day. An author from Tumblebooks (www.tumblebooks.com/library) will read one of her books to the children, and a clip from "Life in Space" will introduce the international space station (www.discoveryeducation.com).

S CENARIO

INVESTIGATION INTO ELECTROMAGNETS BEGINS THE YEAR NEXT DOOR

Next door, the children are seated in pairs. In front of each pair is a pile of small objects, as well as a large nail, wires, and a battery. Their teacher, Jan Fisher, explains that they are going to study magnetism: "The first thing I want each pair to do is to put your nail next to each of the things I have set in front of you. Then, let's discuss what we learn."

The students take turns exploring the objects with the nail. Each pair reports that nothing happens as the nail passes near or touches the objects. A dozen of those objects are medium-size paper clips. Jan records their statements on the whiteboard.

Then she shows them how to wrap the insulated wire around the nails and attach the uninsulated ends to the batteries through a switch. They connect the ends and turn on the switches. "Now, find out what happens when you bring it close to or touch the things in front of you. Sort the objects according to what happens." The students soon have two piles of objects in front of them: one with items that have been pulled to the nail and one with items that have not. All the paper clips stuck to the nail. One student reports that his nail will hold a string of paper clips. The other students confirm it. The consensus is that the nail will hold a string of about six. Jan records their statements and they read them with her. Like Jackie, Jan also brings up an experiment from The Naked Scientists' collection at www.thenakedscientists.com; hers is "Make Your Own Electromagnet." She explains that the collection shows how to explore various science topics with common materials and also provides explanations and avenues for further inquiry.

Jan has begun with the model we call *inductive thinking* (Chapter 3). That model begins by presenting the students with a data set or having them build one, then helping them study the items in the set and classify those items. As they develop categories—in this case noting how the objects respond to a magnetic field—they will build hypotheses to test. Jan will study how the students think and what they see and don't see to help them learn to attack this and other content areas as a community of inductive thinkers.

Like Jackie, Jan reads *Being a Scientist* to students, and they discuss the content of the text and pictures. That is followed by *Discovering Electricity* by Natalie Lunis, which includes a section on the electromagnet and how it is used. Finally, they make a brief trip to the Internet, where Jackie leads them through the first paragraph of a text that describes the development of the electromagnet some 200 years ago (http://physics.kenyon.edu/EarlyApparatus/Electricity/Electromagnet/Electromagnet.html).

Both teachers have begun to build learning communities and introduce their students to models for learning. Their actions make clear that these communities will be inquiring ones. By writing down the students' statements and questions and reading them with the students, these teachers signal that reading and writing will be emphasized from the beginning.

Each teacher will save the statements and select a number of words that will be printed out so that each student can have a copy of that list with each word on a separate card. Later, we will look in on these classes again and see what is done with the word cards.

Like Jackie's class, Jan's students will be introduced to Tumblebooks (www.tumblebooks.com) and, as the inquiry proceeds, fresh topics will be brought to virtual life through Discovery Education (www.discoveryeducation.com).

SCENARIO

OPENING A HIGH SCHOOL CLASS WITH A CONTEMPORARY SOCIAL ISSUE

About a mile away from the elementary school where Jackie and Jan teach, Marilyn Hrycauk's tenth-grade social studies class begins with a videotape taken in a California courtroom, where litigation is being conducted over whether a mother can prevent a father and their 12-year-old son from having time together. The parents are divorced and have joint custody of their son, who lives with the mother.

The tape presents the opening arguments in the case. Marilyn asks the students to individually generate the issues as they see them and to request further information about the situation. She then urges them to share their ideas and asks each student to list the shared ideas under the headings of "issues" and "questions." They find it necessary to develop another category called "positions and values" for some of these shared ideas.

The inquiry will continue by watching more segments of the tape and analyzing several abstracts of similar cases that Marilyn has collected for them. One such case is their first homework assignment. Gradually, through the week, Marilyn will lead the students to develop sets of policy statements and the values that underlie the various possible policies. As the exercise proceeds, she will be studying how well the students are able to clarify facts, distinguish value positions, and discuss differences between seemingly opposing values and policy positions. She, too, is beginning the development of a learning inquiry and is herself an inquirer into her students and their learning. Inevitably the inquiry will reach to the web, consulting sources like www.courts.ca.gov/selfhelp-custody.htm. They will also examine books like *The Custody Book* by Judge James W. Stewart and *Child Custody* by James C. Black and Donald Cantor.

Marilyn has opened her class with the *jurisprudential model of teaching,* which is designed to lead students to the study of public policy issues and their own values.

SCENARIO

ANOTHER SET OF SOCIAL ISSUES FOR OUR TENTH-GRADE CLASS

Marilyn's class then moves to Shirley Mills's English course, which opens with a scene from the film *The Milagro Beanfield War.* The students share their reactions to the setting, action, and characters. When they want to defend their interpretations or argue against the ideas of others, Shirley announces that, for the time being, she wants to preserve their differences so that they can inquire into them. She then passes out copies of the novel of the same name by the author John Nichols and asks them to begin reading it.

During the week, she will encourage them to explore the social issues presented by the book and film and compare the devices used by the author and filmmakers. She will watch closely what issues and devices students see and don't see as she works with them to build an inquiring community. The search leads the students into investigations into life in the Southwest, beginning with demographic information and from there to websites developed by cities and towns in New Mexico. They begin with www.50states.com/newmexic.htm. They are surprised to find that the average elevation of New Mexico is 5700 feet above sea level, that about a third of the 2,000,000 people have Spanish as their first language, and that the Navajo and Pueblo populations add up to about 300,000.

Shirley has introduced her students to the *group investigation model* (see Chapter 12), a powerful cooperative learning model she has used to design her course. The model begins by having students confront information that will lead to an area of inquiry. They then inquire into their own perceptual worlds, noting similarities and differences in perception as the inquiries proceed.

UNDERSTANDING OUR STUDENTS AND BUILDING COMMUNITIES

Education continuously builds ideas and emotions. The flux of human consciousness gives the process of education its distinctive character and makes teaching and learning such a wondrous, ever-changing process. The children come to school filled with experiences in their heads and hearts and in patterns of behavior that will be built on as they mature. Models of teaching are the product of the teachers who have beaten a path for us and hacked out some clearings where we can start our own inquiries. All teachers create a repertoire of practices as they interact with their students and shape environments intended to educate them. Some of these practices become the objects of formal study—they are researched and polished and become models we can use to develop the professional skills that we bring to the tasks of teaching.

A SCHOOL WHERE EVERYBODY CAN LEARN

Imagine a school where the various models of teaching are not only intended to accomplish a range of curriculum goals (learning to read; compute; understand mathematical systems; comprehend literature, science, and the social world; and engage in the performing arts and athletics) but are also designed to help the students increase their power as learners. As students master information and skills, the result of each learning experience is not only the content they learn, but the increased ability they acquire to approach future learning tasks and to create programs of study for themselves.

In our school the students acquire a range of learning strategies because their teachers use the models of teaching that require them. Our students learn models for memorizing information. They learn how to attain concepts and how to invent them. They practice building hypotheses and theories and using the tools of science to test them. They learn how to extract information and ideas from lectures and presentations, how to study social issues, and how to analyze their own social values.

Our students also know how to profit from training and how to train themselves in athletic, performing arts, mathematical, and social skills. They know how to make their writing and problem solving more lucid and creative. Perhaps most importantly, they know how to take initiative in planning personal study, and they know how to work with others to initiate and carry out cooperative programs of inquiry. These students are both challenging and exhilarating to teach because their expanded learning styles enable us to teach them in the variety of ways that are appropriate for the many goals of education.

When we visited the previous four teaching/learning scenarios, we saw those teachers and students beginning to develop the learning communities they would work in throughout the year. Schools and classes are communities of students, brought together to explore the world and learn how to navigate it productively. We have high hopes for these learning communities. We hope their members will become highly literate, that they will read voraciously and write with skill and delicacy. We hope they will understand their social world, be devoted to its improvement, and develop the dignity, self-esteem, and sense of efficacy to generate personal lives of high quality.

These aspirations are central to the study of teaching and guide the research that has resulted in the rich array of teaching models that give learning tools to our students and stimulate our inquiry. Can we design such schools and classrooms? You bet we can! Can we do it by using the developed teaching strategies as formulas? No, we can't! Do we have to study the kids' responses and continuously adapt the ways we teach? You bet we do! So, let's continue our inquiry. As we prepare to do so, let's again visit some teachers who are beginning to organize their learning communities.

SCENARIO

READ! JUST READ! A TONE IS SET

The first few minutes with a class set a tone.

Evelyn Burnham's fifth-grade class enters the classroom on the first day of school. They find all the computers on. On each screen is the same message: "Please check a book out of the classroom library. Select a desk, which will be yours for the time being, and begin reading the book silently. If you come across a word you can't figure out, write it on a card in your Words to Learn box or look it up in the Talking Dictionary."

The kids are a bit confused, but, looking around the room, they find the bookshelves that are labeled "Classroom Library." They find cards on one of the shelves and sign out their books, locate their desks, and begin to read. Evelyn moves about the room, introducing herself to the students and making name tags for them.

SCENARIO

INVESTIGATING WORDS ON DAY ONE

Bonnie Brigman's second-grade class enters the classroom on the first day of school. They find that their desks have been labeled with their names, and a note on the board asks them to find their desk and begin reading a set of sentences that are on the desks. Bonnie also asks them to write down any words they have trouble pronouncing or understanding.

Like Evelyn, Bonnie moves about the room, introducing herself to the children. She invites parents to stay and asks them to read a description of the Just Read program that she has printed for them.

After about 15 minutes, Bonnie asks the kids to share any words they had difficulty reading. When a child indicates a word, Bonnie asks how many others had difficulty reading the same word. She has her clipboard on her knee with a list of the students' names, and she records the words they have trouble with. The sentences are constructed to include words representing most phonetic combinations, and in each sentence there is a word that she is fairly sure will be new reading vocabulary to them, so that they have to use context clues to comprehend the word.

SCENARIO

BEGINNING WITH GANDHI

Bruce Hall's eighth-grade social studies class enters the room on the first day of school. The students find name tags on the desks and locate their seats. He gives them a minute to get settled, introduces himself, and flips on the DVD player. A scene from the film *Gandhi* appears, and the students watch while Gandhi delivers the famous speech on passive resistance. When the scene is over, Bruce asks the students to write their impressions. "I want us to get started on our study of the world. I also want to get a look at how you write."

"Is this an English class?" asks one of the students.

"Well, it's called social studies, but all classes include literacy. We'll write a lot this year."

GENERAL PRINCIPLES

All three teachers, working with students of different ages, do some similar things. All three let their students know, by the tasks they give them, that they are in a learning environment. They provide instructions and get things moving right away. They do not spend time telling the children how to behave; they assume that their instructions will be followed. And they are right—the kids get right to work. In addition to taking those students into the learning process without delay, they are kind and affirmative. All three teachers are studying their students from the moment they enter the classroom. They are preparing to modulate as they gather information on what the kids can do and how they do it.

All three assume that the students can manage their own activities, checking out books, reading independently, and writing on demand. All three expect independent reading and writing; they begin their Just Read programs (see Joyce, Calhoun, & Hrycauk, 2003) the first day of school. The students record books read each week and set their goals for amount and types of texts they will read. The class tallies the number of books read and sets goals and plans celebrations for when those goals are reached. The program generally quadruples amounts of reading by students with significant effects on the comprehension scores in standardized norm-referenced tests.

All three teachers radiate confidence in themselves and in their students. They let the kids know that they are the adults in the teaching/learning transaction, but do not pretend they are all-knowing gods or goddesses. If the students get stuck, they say, "Well, let's try something else and see if it works." These teachers let the kids see themselves as learners.

FORMATIVE ASSESSMENT

Closely related to scaffolding is the continued use of formative assessment of learning to determine whether more or a different kind of support is needed. Essentially, the teacher watches learning closely and provides support—from simple encouragement to special assignments and possibly tutorial sessions. Sometimes switching to a different model of teaching can help a student find an avenue to learning. We will provide examples as we present each model, but a brief example here may help explain how it works.

SCENARIO

DATA AND DECISIONS

Let's imagine that a fifth-grade teacher (Traci Poirier, from Chapter 1) is studying aspects of her students' knowledge of arithmetic as she plans the year's work. She gives the class a test that includes some examples of multiplication and division. There is quite a difference in the pace with which the students calculate the products and quotients, although the test is not timed and she gives no indication that speed is valued. Further, the slower students made more errors when calculating. She decides to give them a test on knowledge of the multiplication facts and does so by presenting examples on the whiteboard and asking the kids to write down the products privately at their desks. Traci collects their papers and scores them. Ten of her 25 students answer all the examples correctly, eight answer from 60 to 70 correctly, and seven range from 40 to 59, with the majority of their misses in the 6 to 9 times tables.

She decides that for the next two weeks the students will be organized into three groups based on these scores. The group who answered all the examples correctly (she calls them the "ten" group) will engage in inquiries designed to advance their knowledge and test their limits. To begin with, she asks them to explain the "property of 9" phenomenon where the product of 9 and any other number can be divided by 9 with no remainder. They are to develop explanations and present them to the class. In addition, they will be connected to the Everyday

Math group at the University of Chicago and the unit on "Multiplication and Division Numbers Stories" where they can study applying the facts to real-life problems (http://everydaymath.uchicago.edu/parents/4th-grade/em-at-home/unit_5).

The "almost" group is divided into pairs whose task is to help each other master all the facts in any way they choose. However, Traci also leads them to the PBS online package called "A Place for Numbers," which provides a nice review and application to estimation—a very important topic (www.pbslearningmedia.org).

The "worker bees" are also organized into pairs to study the facts they need to learn and they (and their parents) are connected to the PBS site.

Traci takes all the students through exercises with the multiplication facts matrix, having them discover regularities in the products (as in the "threes" table, where products follow a "3, 6, 9" pattern).

After a week she retests their knowledge of the facts and adds problems requiring estimation for the "tens" group. The "almosts" are now "tens" and she adds the everyday number stories unit to their diet. Based on the results, she will continue asking the students to study the multiplication facts and add emphasis on relations to the characteristics of the number system. The class goal is to have all students with mastery of 95 percent or more. For worker bees who have gained just a few facts, she sets up 10-minute peer-tutoring sessions where "tens" students work with the bees on a few facts each day. Her email to the parents of the bees includes a list of the facts each one needs to master and a link to the Everyday Math site (http://everydaymath.uchicago.edu).

The scaffolding orientation involves keeping track of student progress and adjusting instruction to ensure mastery of important basic information and skill. It is important that students are aware of their progress and needs and that parents are brought into the process when they can help.

In SUM

All models of teaching provide the opportunity for teachers and students to study progress, keep doing things that are working well, and adjust by adding processes and replacing ones that are not working. To teach well is to embrace this adventure—learning how the students' knowledge, cognitions, and emotions interact with environments and how both change in the process. To teach well means to be caught up in an inquiry that has no end: we are never finished with this adventure, never satisfied with the arts and sciences of making those inferences, never done with the construction of models of learning and teaching that are built on the guesses we make about what is going on in all those minds. What Ernest Hemingway said about writing we can say about teaching: "We are all apprentices in a craft where no one ever becomes a master."

PART TWO

The Basic Information-Processing Models of Teaching

Conceptual thinking is probably programmed into us during gestation. At birth, we immediately start to learn language by figuring out the concepts that govern the conversations around us and joining them. We study our environment and sort it out. We classify vegetation, objects, and gestures as we try to gain conceptual control of our surroundings. And for centuries—millennia, in fact—scholars have tried to figure out how to improve on what nature provides.

Thus, the information-processing models of teaching and learning have a long history of philosophical advocacy and rationale. As the scientific study of teaching developed during the last 80 years, an accumulation of solid research both tested the theoretical base and created new ways of enhancing student learning by harnessing the inborn capacity to make sense of the environment.

The inductive model and related information-processing models can be the central methods of campus courses. They are often the best available avenue for integrating the riches of information and communication technologies (ICT) into schooling in "hybrid" courses and can also be used to design distance courses, including the online variety.

Joining information and communication technologies to the campus and the classroom is essential. The web is pouring information on us and our students—and modernized courses will increase the flow of information that needs to be managed productively. That is what the information-processing models, particularly when inquiry is cooperative and transparent, are available to accomplish.

The distinctive character of the information-processing models is that, in their particular ways, they all emphasize seeking and operating on information. The development and use of *data sets* is critical in most of these models. Information from particular inquiries is organized into sets—students may collect information or data are presented to them. Working within those sets, analyzing their attributes and comparing and contrasting them, the students organize data, develop categories and look for relationships. They proceed to master that information by developing questions and carrying out investigations to building hypotheses as in the *inductive* and *scientific inquiry* models. Those, plus the *picture word inductive model* are presented in Part II because they have broad applicability to design lessons, courses, curricula, and even schools. Special purpose models will be discussed in Part III.

These models also provide students with powerful tools for managing the enormous quantities of information available on the web. They provide designs for distance courses, including online courses and programs that can bring information, ideas, and processes to the campus. Until the last few years most educational offerings to students were in classrooms supported largely by school libraries, including collections of films and videotapes. Now, we can conceive of education where face-to-face instruction on campus is combined with ICT resources (what we call *hybrid offerings*) and distance programs.

Individual differences can be addressed as never before, with students getting more support and being able to run far ahead of grade-level expectations. Today we see immigrant students who are learning English and simultaneously teaching themselves levels of mathematics previously unavailable until the college years. The creaky old textbook is about to be revolutionized! Scaffolding is built into the instructional environment—students can get help not only from the classroom teachers but from the web as well. For example, a student who is having difficulty learning an arithmetic operation can access an online module in the area of need. Students who are far beyond the usual standards for a given grade will be able to access distance instruction appropriate to their needs.

The heart of education has always been self-education—we teachers have been guides as much as we have been instructors. Now it is clearer than ever that building students' competence as learners is the major legacy of schooling.

CHAPTER THREE

Learning to Learn Inductively

The Really, Really Basic Model of Teaching

The researcher, whether a beginner or an advanced scholar, seeks to populate an inquiry with information. Information changes its character when it is organized. Building categories enriches data and the mind that organizes it.

The long and short of memory. Keeping information present and alive depends on whether it is nested in the categories of the mind.

—Our reflective observer

ORGANIZING IDEA

Building categories that hold information and let us manipulate them is possibly the basic component of what we consider to be intelligence. To look at a scene and see beyond the specific items to how they belong together . . . well, think about what that means to us.

SCENARIO

A PERSONAL INVESTIGATION: WHAT MAKES ELECTRICITY?

Eight-year-old Seamus is apparently playing in the kitchen. In front of him are a number of plates. On one is a potato, cut in quarters. Another contains an apple, similarly cut. The others contain a variety of fruits and vegetables. Seamus pushes into the segments of potato a number of copper and zinc plates that are wired together and to a tiny lightbulb. He nods with satisfaction when the bulb begins to glow. He disconnects the bulb, attaches a voltmeter, examines it briefly, and then reattaches the bulb. He repeats the process with the apple, examining the bulb and voltmeter once again. Then come the raspberries, lemon, carrot, and so on. His father enters the room and Seamus looks up. "I was right about the raspberries," he says, "we can use them as in a battery. But, some of these other things. . . ."

Seamus is, of course, classifying fruits and vegetables in terms of whether they can interact with metals to produce electric current.

SCENARIO

A FIRST GRADE CONDUCTS AN INVESTIGATION

In a first grade in Canada, Lisa Mueller talks to her students about their next project, which is the study of reproductive mechanisms in plants. Using buckets containing seeds, bulbs, and tubers from various plants, she will ask students to classify them according to their characteristics using trays with compartments into which they can sort the seeds, bulbs, and tubers. Then, the students will be asked to raise questions about their categories. Finally, Lisa will give them soil and containers, and the students will plant them under various conditions and watch as they germinate and begin to grow stalks and leaves. Figure 3.1 shows the buckets and trays

FIGURE 3.1   a. Explaining the data and the trays. b. Making categories

Bruce Joyce

a.   b.

Bruce Joyce

FIGURE 3.2 Raising questions

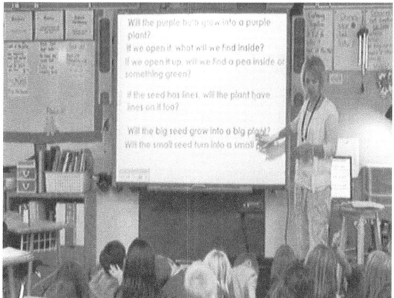

Bruce Joyce

as she explains their use and the students in the act of classifying and reporting their categories to the other students. Then, in Figure 3.2, we see the whiteboard as the teacher records the characteristics focused on by the students and some of the questions they ask, such as "Will the big seed grow into a big plant?" and "Will the purple bulb grow into a purple plant?"

As the students begin to plan their experiments and test their hypothesis, they consider ways they can alter the conditions they provide:

- Will more or less sunlight make a difference?
- Will amounts of water make a difference?
- Will how deeply they are planted affect growth?

Lisa records these questions and provides each student with a manual to record the conditions they will create. The students also begin to label the containers. The assistant principal, who grows plants as a hobby, provides the class with an ultraviolet light so that varying degrees of sunlight can be provided.

Figure 3.3 shows the planting taking place. In Figure 3.4 you can see some of the labeled containers.

FIGURE 3.3   Planting the seeds, bulbs, and tubers

Bruce Joyce

FIGURE 3.4   Planted the seeds, bulbs, and tubers

Bruce Joyce

Bruce Joyce

As the students tend their plantings and observe the results, the teacher can help them connect to sources on the web that provide information about the plants from which the seeds, bulbs, and tubers were selected. For example, see The Better Homes and Gardens Plant Encyclopedia (www.bhg.com/gardening/plant-dictionary) and the United States Department of Agriculture Plants Database (http://plants.usda.gov).

An important reminder: without hands-on experience, consulting the web or print sources can be a superficial exercise—looking for answers developed by others but without the information on which these ideas were grounded can result in misconceptions and shallow understandings. The investigations by the students should provide them with a sense of how knowledge is created. We find ourselves in complete agreement with the recommended standards generated by the Academy of Sciences, where laboratory experience grounds the material that is presented in textbooks and digitally (National Research Council, 2012).

Cooperative/inductive inquiry teaching and learning is similar across grades and curriculum areas. Lisa's first-grade class is working in a fashion we can imagine for upper-grade and secondary students. Classifying poems in a class on English literature is not very different from gathering and classifying plants.

SCENARIO

PLANTING BULBS ON THE FIRST DAY OF SCHOOL

In an investigation in line with Lisa Mueller's inquiry with her first-grade students, Diane Schuetz also provided her first-grade students (on the first day of school!) with sets of tulip bulbs to be classified. The students formed groups according to size, whether two were joined together ("Some have babies on them"), whether they had "coats," or whether they had the beginnings of what looks like roots. Now the students are planting their bulbs, trying to find out whether the variation in attributes they identified will affect how the tulips grow. ("Will the big ones [bulbs] grow bigger?" "Will the babies grow on their own?" and so on.) She has designed the science curriculum around the basic processes of building categories, making predictions, and testing their validity.

We stress that our students are *natural* conceptualizers. Humans organize information all the time, comparing and contrasting objects, events, emotions— everything. To capitalize on this natural tendency, we arrange the learning environment and give tasks to students to increase their effectiveness in forming and using concepts, and we help them consciously develop their skills for doing so. Over the years we have generated guidelines for shaping the environment and tasks that facilitate concept formation. As students become more skilled in inductive learning, we modulate our behavior, helping them create appropriate environments and tasks. Learning how to think inductively is the critical goal and students need to practice it, not just be led through it. We are fortunate to have the benefit of a large body of research as we shape contemporary models for learning and teaching inductively. The result is considerable clarity for remarkably direct ways of teaching a critical and complex process by many investigations experienced throughout the years of schooling. The guidelines for designing those inquiries are straightforward.

One is *focusing the investigation*—helping the students concentrate on a domain (an area of inquiry) they can master, without constricting them so much that they can't use their full abilities to generate ideas. At first we do this by presenting the students with data sets that provide information in the domain that will be the focus of the lesson or unit and by asking them to study the attributes of the items in the set. A simple example is to present kindergarten or first-grade students with cards containing several letters from the alphabet and ask them to examine them closely and describe their attributes. The domain is *the alphabet:* letters and their names. Another example is to present fifth- or sixth-grade students with a data set containing statistical data on the countries from a region of the world—say, Latin America—and ask the students to study the data on each country carefully. The domain is *Latin American countries,* with the subdomain of *statistical data.*

Second is a drive to *conceptual control*—helping the students develop conceptual mastery of the domain. In the case of the alphabet, the goal is to distinguish the letters from one another, and to develop categories by grouping letters that have many, but not all, attributes in common. The students will learn to see the alphabet in terms of similarities and differences. They will also find those letters in words, and when they have made categories of letters with the same shape (as putting a half-dozen Bs together), they will learn the names of those letters. The letters will be placed on charts in the classroom along with words that contain them. In the case of the Latin American countries, the students will classify the countries according to the demographic data provided in the set, moving from single-attribute categories such as population and per capita income to multiple-attribute categories such as determining whether variables like education levels, fertility, and income are related. They will be able to see Latin America in terms of those categories, a step toward the conceptual control that will emerge as they add more data to their set and develop advanced categories, gaining *metacontrol* by developing hierarchies of concepts to gain further mastery of the domain.

The third guideline is converting conceptual understanding to *skill.* In the case of the alphabet, this is exploring letter–sound relationships and how to use them in reading and spelling, where recognition evolves to conscious application in word identification. In the case of the Latin American countries, the skills are in the development of multiple-attribute categories and generating and testing hypotheses (such as studying whether per capita income is related to fertility rates or education levels).

All aspects of the learning environment play important roles, from the development of the learning community, the creation of the data sets, and the learning tasks—classification, reclassification, and development of hypotheses. Also, the teacher observes the students and scaffolds their inquiry by helping them elaborate and extend their concepts. In the alphabet example, tasks like "which letters are most like the 'A' and are most likely to be confused with it?" would be generated. In the Latin American example, tasks like "what other variables might be correlated with levels of literacy?" would be generated.

As the students learn to build and extend categories (concepts), they take on increased responsibility for the process. For example, they learn to build data sets that are relevant to the domains being studied. Our kindergarten/first-grade students use their word charts to develop data sets, at first with explicit guidance ("Here are three words that begin the same. Can you add to my list?") and later by looking at the list and sorting the words independently according to how they begin and end. Our young scholars on Latin America learn to add variables to the data base using statistical sources and expository sources like encyclopedias. As their study of nations proceeds, they will be able to create data sets that enable them to compare and contrast entire regions.

The inductive model leads students to collect information and examine it closely, organize the information into concepts, and manipulate those concepts. Used regularly, this strategy increases students' abilities to form concepts efficiently and increases the range of perspectives from which they can view information.

INTELLECTUAL, SOCIAL, AND PERSONAL GROWTH

Learning to inquire inductively enhances the inborn ability to categorize (Klauer & Phye, 2008). Students construct knowledge (see Vygotsky, 1986) and teachers facilitate (scaffold) their inquiry. As students learn to develop concepts, the learning of information, concepts, and skills are enhanced. Conceptual level—the ability to gather information and integrate it—is enhanced as well (see Hunt & Sullivan, 1974; Joyce, Weil, & Calhoun, 2009).

Aristotle had it right. Humans can learn through disciplined inquiry. When curriculum and instruction capitalize on the inborn ability to study the environment, organize information, and conduct investigations, increased cognitive ability occurs. Other models and other families of models are also effective and reach some of the same goals, and we need those in our repertoire as well.

Students learn to collect data when studying a topic or solving a problem. They learn to organize the data and study its nature—the attributes of the information they are collecting. They further organize the data into categories and develop names for those categories, then build hypotheses and test them, often seeking more data to enrich their inquiry. None of these tasks are complex, but they have to be learned. Superficial classification does not further inquiry and can actually impede it. Even at the K–1 level many worthwhile concepts have multiple attributes, as we can see in Lisa Mueller's first-grade inquiry.

The differences between inductive inquiry in the primary grades and in high school and beyond is more in the complexity of the material being studied and the maturity of the students than in the process. Asking first-grade students to classify nations is not feasible. Classifying vegetation in their environment is well within their capacity, as is their ability to classify words, sentences, and paragraphs. However, we do not want to underestimate our students. First- and second-grade students can enter the world of global information by comparing their neighborhood with a neighborhood in another country using data from the web and later from informants found in those countries. In the previous scenario, in which students classified seeds, bulbs, and tubers, the students connected to a first-grade class in a school in Delhi, India. The students in both settings collected information about life in each other's cultures to make sense of what they learned.

HARNESSING WEB AND PRINT RESOURCES THROUGH INDUCTIVE INQUIRY

Everyone agrees that information and communication technologies (ICT) are providing access to information to an extent that teachers and students have never had in any previous generation. The web represents an evolution of the library (what we call the *great new library*) that enhances self-learning opportunities to a remarkable extent. But there are two caveats. First, unless teachers and students build the tools to organize and use information they retrieve, their minds will be virtually inundated by the sheer mass of material. The possibility of elevating education has never been poised so well, but it will slip away if students do not know how to build concepts and organize their inquiries. Helping students capitalize on new technologies is almost surely going to depend on learning how to scrutinize information and organize it into concepts—basic inductive work. Inductive inquiry allows us to erase this first concern, because building concepts enables us to manage, retain, and use information. There is a high probability that it is the foundation for the 21st-century skills, many higher-order thinking skills, and probably most types of intelligence (see Joyce & Calhoun, 2010, 2012).

The model of inductive teaching and learning is a major key to capitalizing on the marvelous avenues to learning enabled through electronic libraries, the offerings of distance education, and the transformation of campus courses into hybrids as courses capitalizing on both campus interaction and web resources are developed and implemented in schools through the country.

The second caveat about ICTs is that a high level of competence in reading is required to access the riches available in the digital world. Teachers can use the inductive model to teach students to build vocabulary and concepts in order to overcome this obstacle.

However, all the other information-processing models of teaching and learning and those in the other families of models—the social, behavioral, and personal models—share a constructivist view of learning and teaching, in which students are asked to gather and use information and build and apply concepts. Whatever model being used, students still have to build and test ideas in order to gain cognitive control over the content and build their capacity to learn *while* they are learning.

The students do the learning—however, we do the teaching. We design the environment to make it likely that the students will learn. We organize the kids, assemble resources, and provide tasks. We teach the students to work in that organization, use those resources (including ourselves), and respond to those tasks. We draw on various models of teaching to help us design environments, organize students, arrange materials, and decide what kinds of tasks to provide and in what order. We always have objectives in mind: the kinds of learning that we hope will happen.

The inductive model can be used to design extensive and broad units or brief, concentrated lessons or short series of lessons. But some important long-term objectives are always present to guide the process:

• *Thinking inductively.* Every inductive experience should help students learn to work more effectively—collecting and organizing information, forming categories and hypotheses, developing skills, and using the knowledge and skills appropriately. Through these experiences, they learn how to construct and use information while consciously improving their skills in doing so. Thus, the model gives students a powerful tool for learning, one they can use from the time they enter school and that will serve them throughout their lives. As we teach, we want them to get better at learning by thinking. Essentially, we want to help them increase their intelligence.

• *Inquiring collaboratively.* As categories are developed, they are the product of individual minds. We think about data and form categories within our own heads. However, our minds do not exist in a social vacuum. The learning environment needs to operate so that the students learn to build and test ideas with others, helping one another and testing their minds against the ideas of others. Thus, we want to build a learning community in the classroom where individuals learn to share the products of their inquiries and where groups and the whole class plan studies together.

• *Using the ideas in learning resources.* Books and electronic media connect the learner to all manner of sources for information and ideas. Students need to learn to mine those sources for information and to use their contents to test ideas and to find ideas to test. Inquirers are borrowers and the web is an eager lender.

• *Building conceptual control over areas of study.* The inductive process asks students to form concepts by organizing, grouping, and regrouping information so that areas of study become clear and hypotheses and skills can be developed and tested. The goal of mastering the domain needs to be kept in mind—rapid, superficial formation of categories is not a process that pays off.

• *Acquiring and retaining information and skills.* Induction is built on collecting and organizing information and building conceptual structures that provide for long-term retention of information. The process of organizing data, building hypotheses, and converting information into skills is designed to increase the likelihood that what is learned "stays learned." The much-lamented loss of information during the summer is easily explained—what is lost did not find its way into long-term memory. Material in short-term memory decays rapidly.

THE SYNTAX OF THE INDUCTIVE PROCESS

The various models of teaching have distinctive structures or *syntaxes*, composed of the major elements and phases of the model and how they are put together. Some models, such as concept attainment, have relatively fixed structures within which some of the elements or phases need to follow each other for maximum effectiveness. Other models have a rolling or wavelike structure in which phases are recycled. The inductive model has a rolling structure that evolves even in relatively brief inquiries.

The flow of the inductive process is made up of several types of inquiry that overlap considerably:

• *Identifying an area of study—a domain that contains conceptual or actual territory to be explored.* In the scenario that opens this chapter, the domain, *reproductive mechanisms in plants,* was selected by the teacher, who took her time to ensure that it was understood by the students.
• *Collecting and sifting information relevant to that area or domain of inquiry— building data sets.* In the scenario, seeds, bulbs, and tubers constituted the set.

- *Constructing ideas, particularly categories, that provide conceptual control over the topic or topics.* Size, color, number of parts, and texture emerged in this scenario.
- *Generating ideas, sometimes causal hypotheses, to be explored in an effort to understand relationships within that domain or to provide solutions to problems.* The students in this scenario generated ideas such as "Will the little ones grow small plants?" "Will amounts of sunlight influence growth?" and so on.
- *Testing those ideas or hypotheses, including the conversion of knowledge into skills that have practical application.* Some examples from Lisa's class include planting the seeds, bulbs, and tubers and observing the characteristics of their growth.
- *Building concepts and skills, practicing them, and developing "executive control" over them so that they are available for use.* At a minimum, the students should become more capable at the inductive process and the content should affect how they look at plant life—asking things like "Did that big pumpkin grow from that little seed?" The library down the hall and the one in the web wait to extend the inquiry.

In this flow of cognitive operations, we find the definition of induction. In these types of inquiry, the student constructs knowledge and then tests that knowledge through experience and against the knowledge of experts. *Induction,* rooted in the analysis of information, is often contrasted with *deduction,* where one builds knowledge by starting with ideas and proceeding to infer further ideas by logical reasoning.

Although it is convenient to imagine a prototype inquiry that begins with data collection and organization and proceeds to the development of categories, the generation and testing of hypotheses and perhaps then to the development of skills, the inductive process may begin at any of these stages or phases and the inquirer may backtrack, possibly adding data or recategorizing. Let's revisit the phases of the inductive process.

PHASES OF THE INDUCTIVE MODEL

Phase One: Identify the Domain

To begin a given inquiry, we lead the students toward information that is conceptually related. Thus we create—or help them create—territories or arenas for concentrated study. We call these territories *domains for inquiry.* Domains form arbitrary boundaries for study and are quite varied: they can be defined geographically ("Let's study everything in the town center"); they can be selected from domains within the academic disciplines (the economic systems of all nations, the political systems of Asian nations, poems written last year by Chinese women); they can be derived from student work ("We need to learn about organizing ideas more explicitly in our informative pieces"). They can be very broad, such as the mammals living in North America today, or quite narrow, such as specific literary devices like personification and fore-shadowing. Domains can be pragmatic and immediately applicable, as when primary children study the structure of written words, or abstract, as when those same children later study the tenets of the world's religions.

When we think about selecting content and organizing for instruction, we try to select domains that, if studied in-depth, will provide students with greater conceptual control over the world or skills that are needed to navigate it; for example, respectively, understanding how changes in communication technology are affecting the kinds of work we do or developing the ability to write well-organized prose. Essentially, we try to lead students to domains that are significant by some academic standard or that will have practical utility for them.

At this point, the teacher's knowledge of curriculum and what is worthy of sustained study by individuals and the class as a learning community comes strongly into play. Curriculum and resource knowledge are important in other phases of the inductive model as well; however, if the major domains selected for concentrated study are substantive and if worthy materials are selected for analysis, then (as your authors have experienced many times over the years) the teacher can learn along with the students. When it is conducted well, the inductive model of teaching can lead to the clarification of concepts and relationships that have dangled disconnected for years within our minds or the minds of our students.

The academic domains or territories that have developed over the years as part of the curriculum within disciplines (for example, phonetic analysis; the properties of numbers; the study of quality in writing; the relationships among geography, climate, and natural resources; the Romance poets; optics; algebraic equations—just part of an enormous list) provide a rich source for in-depth academic explorations by students across the grades.

Selecting domains for inquiry requires us to think from a curricular point of view. As we organize the year's study in the curriculum areas, we identify the areas or domains that we want to be sure the students study. Other domains will emerge as the year progresses, with smaller domains and lines of inquiry emerging within the major ones, but the long-term planning of the year is the context within which the domains emerge.

Classifying a data set can lead to an inquiry. We can open the study of writing by asking students to classify the first lines of books, looking for styles or strategies employed by the authors and, eventually, asking the students to think about those devices as they write the opening sentences and paragraphs in their own pieces of writing.

Phase Two: Collecting and Enumerating Data

Collecting Data

Moving the inquiry on, we lead the students toward information that forms a domain or is within a given domain or territory. We may begin by presenting information to them or by helping them gather or produce data, because inductive operations involve organizing data, pulling it apart, and reorganizing it in the search for ideas. Thus, collecting data occurs early, and new data may be added or discarded as an inquiry proceeds.

What information will be gathered for analysis, from which disciplines, and in what forms? What material will students burrow into in their inquiry? Will it be a set of words? Poems? Picture storybooks? Opening paragraphs of books or magazine articles? Cartoons? Arithmetic problems? Paintings? Maps? Information about different species of animals?

Within the inductive model of teaching, we call the information presented or gathered *data sets*. These data sets are assemblies of information. This information comes in myriad forms: objects, literature and prose in its many forms, the results of experiments, perceptions, and combinations of various forms. All can be assembled into data sets. Almost any set of related information can become a data set: numbers 1–100, modes of transportation, major cities and their locations, power plants and their locations, accident rates and locations, particular jobs and ethnic prejudice, stars and their locations. In this phase of the model, we bring the learners and the data together.

As learners and data interact, expected and unexpected results transpire. We are born with both the drive and capacity to sort the things we perceive, and we find connections among all kinds of things. The creation of the items we call *constellations* came from the linking of points of light to creatures and legends, which seems an improbable connection from some perspectives but represents a natural function of the human need for understanding. Your students will make many improbable connections; they will often see things in the data that you did not see or make connections that have little utility. For example, in a set of poems students may notice that a number of poems have the word *yellow* in them, that a number of poems mention foreign countries, that a number of them all begin with the word *when*. At other times, students will notice information that you missed, or make useful connections that were not visible to you.

Though we do not want to inhibit our students' spontaneous ability to seek unlikely connections, when we organize them for inquiry we develop boundaries for the search for information. Thus we create, or help them create, sets of data within the domains selected for academic study. For example, if we decide to help upper- or middle-grade students learn to use metaphoric devices in their writing, then they will have to understand categories of metaphors, be able to produce them as they write, and assess the effects of doing so. The data sets thus need to include examples of metaphors as well as other devices so that students can distinguish them from metaphors. To build the set, we draw on samples of writing, possibly sentences, where authors have used metaphors and other devices such as personification or hyperbole.

Similarly, if we want students to be able to generate prepositional phrases, they will need to comprehend the nature of such phrases and practice producing them—our higher-order objective. The data sets will need to include many prepositional phrases and other structures, such as clauses, that need to be distinguished from them.

Let's look at how the two phases we have discussed thus far—the domain identification phase and the data collection phase—might work out in the primary grades, the upper grades, and the middle school.

Primary Grades

In grade 1, we may lead students to the domain of phonetic structures and provide them with a set that contains the subdomain of the sounds represented by the letter *c*. The objective is that they comprehend the rules governing the sounds of *c* and be able to use those rules in reading and spelling. The data set might look like this:

cat	city	cake
catch	canyon	cotton
ice cream	October	nice
Carl	ceiling	cable
Christine	choo-choo	cement
race	accident	act
face	duck	cold
mice	bookcase	luck
chicken	coat	actor

Or we might have the students look through picture storybooks and find words that contain the letter *c*. Or working from devices such as the picture word inductive model (see Chapter 5), we might have them select the words containing *c* from a large word set.

Similarly, we can lead students to the study of plurals by presenting a set of nouns, some of which are plural and some of which are singular. The objective is that they develop categories containing singular and plural words and develop the skill to use those categories when reading and writing. That set might look like this:

book/books	word/words	library/libraries
city/cities	sentence/sentences	window/windows
girl/girls	boy/boys	crayon/crayons

woman/women	church/churches	lady/ladies
story/stories	farmer/farmers	slipper/slippers
cat/cats	teacher/teachers	table/tables
child/children	principal/principals	kitten/kittens
face/faces	man/men	bookcase/bookcases
desk/desks	chair/chairs	blouse/blouses
pan/pans	party/parties	cake/cakes

Again, we might send the students on a hunt for such words or have them sort them from a larger set that includes many types of words. (As an aside, we might do exactly the same thing with older students who have needs in the area of phonetic and structural analysis.)

Upper Elementary Grades and Middle School

To lead students into the domain of Native American Peoples, where we want them to comprehend the types of tribes, their differences, and the consequences to the different tribes as a result of European settlement, we might present a data set containing information about a number of tribes. The data set would include where the tribes lived before European settlement began, their numbers then and now, their type of life (hunting and gathering or agricultural, nomadic or settled, leadership structure), and any pictures and artifacts available. Alternatively, we could present the students with the names of the tribes, plus any good sources they find, and have them locate the information and create the data set.

Enumerating and Labeling Data

The data in the set need to be labeled or numbered so that we can keep track of them. In the upper elementary and middle school sets described previously, the items are numbered so that they can be conveniently referred to. Pictures and objects can be numbered, tagged by color, or provided with meaningful names. For example, if primary students visit a number of local businesses and take notes about them, the data about each business can be labeled with the names of the businesses: bakery, delicatessen, shoe store, and so on. Rocks from the seashore can be tagged with blue labels, rocks from the mountain with yellow labels, rocks from the grasslands with green labels, and so forth. Lines from poems by various poets can be labeled with numbers, along with the poet's names and the titles of the poems.

Enumeration or labeling is extremely important. In a set of any size, we simply cannot manage to communicate with terms like "the one in the middle but slightly left." As we categorize, placing items together in groups, communication is facilitated because we can say, "Items 4, 7, and 17 go together; they have X in common." The listener can refer to those numbers, track down those items, and follow our line of reasoning.

Phase Three: Examine Data

Once a data set is assembled and enumerated, we are ready to have the kids examine the items in the set very carefully, richly teasing out the attributes. The examination of the set needs to be thorough; otherwise the inquiry will be superficial.

Returning to the earlier examples: for the primary grade's data set on the letter *c*, the students need to look carefully at each word, noting the spelling, where the *c*'s are placed, and how the letter, alone and in combination with others, sounds. For the upper elementary grade's data set on Native American tribes, the students need to note each bit of data on each tribe. For the middle school data set on nations, the students need to be sure they are clear about the variables and what they mean and familiarize themselves with the information about each country (its size, population, educational levels, and so on).

We have found that many teachers tend to rush through the examination of data, which is almost always a mistake. Sufficient time must be allowed so that the students have begun to discriminate the items from each other, seeing how their attributes are similar and different.

Phase Four: Form Concepts by Classifying

As we have said before and will reiterate often throughout the book, classification is a natural activity, almost as if it were built into our brains. The inductive model of teaching sets up a learning environment that facilitates and disciplines this natural tendency, making the process formal and conscious.

At this point in the inquiry, data have been collected and organized for examination, the attributes of the items in the set have been studied, and the students are familiar with the material. Their minds have already begun to play over the items, noting similarities and differences. Now, we ask them to reorganize the items into groups according to common characteristics. Using the language of the inductive model, these groups, or *categories*, help students form *concepts* as they put items together that share common characteristics, or *attributes*.

In phase four, we say things like this to students who are just becoming familiar with the inductive process:

To primary school children: "Let's study these words and make groups of them. Group words that have something in common in how they are spelled and how the *c* sounds."

To upper elementary students: "We know something about each tribe. Now, let's put them in groups that have some attributes in common, and see what we can come up with."

To middle school students: "Using what you know about these countries so far, make groups based on common characteristics."

As students become more familiar with the formal inductive process, they will move through the phases with little prompting. They will know what to do before we suggest it, and individuals and groups of students (as well as the class) can carry out the phases while teachers serve as a guide and resource. The students will become more powerful and efficient as they become conscious of the process and gain metacognitive control over it. For now, however, let's continue as if the students have little experience with the process.

Initial Classification
For the classification phase to be most productive, we generally classify data several times. The first passes are important, but we have a tendency to classify on gross characteristics and just use one or two attributes, confining ourselves to one-way classification. For example, when classifying poems, we rely on the more obvious differences in subject matter, mood, and device. Although it is limited, this first pass gets us going at building and sharing categories.

Our primary students might make their first pass by grouping together the words by position of *c,* such as words with *c, cl,* or *cr* at the beginning, regardless of the differences in sound. Thus, *cook, certain, clank,* and *crack* end up in the same category and *back, race,* and *reclaim* in another. That is fine for a beginning.

Our upper elementary and middle school students may make their first pass purely on location, grouping the Eastern, Western, and Plains Indians together. That is also fine for a beginning.

Sharing Categories
Generally, we ask individuals and small groups to share their categories at this point. We ask them to point out the attributes they used and explain why they grouped items together.

Adding Data
Information processing is the essence of inductive inquiry, and without adequate information an inquiry stalls. Fresh information can be needed at any point in the process. For example, when building categories from a set of data, one may find that one has to collect more information because the data set is too thin. Sometimes, after the first exercise in classification, we find we need to add more data to our set. Sometimes, we begin to see things we didn't notice when we were collecting and examining the data. In those cases, we cycle back and collect or examine again, or both.

Further Classification
Digging into the data again, our students reclassify, refine, or collapse categories; split them or make subcategories; and experiment with two- and three-way classification schemes. Categories emerge and are shared. Students gradually gain control of the information.

We ask them to examine the data again and see if they can discover more bases for grouping items. We might even give them some explicit suggestions:

- We might ask our primary students to pay close attention to sounds as they re-examine the data.
- We might ask our upper-grade students to use variables other than location to expand their classifications.
- We might ask our middle school students to develop two-way classifications, prompting them to learn whether size is associated with any other characteristics.

New or Refined Categories Emerge

Our primary students may discover that *cl* generally refers to the same sound regardless of position in a word. They may discover that *c*, *ck*, and *k* can all represent the same sound. They need to learn that *c* followed by *o* or *a* will have the "hard" sound, as in *cone* and *cake*. Gaining full control of how *c* works in the English language provides students an opportunity to learn and apply a number of phonetic generalizations.

Our upper elementary and middle school students may discover relations between methods of gathering food and the region where the tribes lived, or that population was reduced by war or disease among tribes having particular characteristics. They will surely come to have a picture of the overall pattern of change that occurred as a consequence of European settlement.

Reclassification can occur several times, depending on the complexity of the set and the students' experience with the inductive model. Greater experience leads students to develop more refined categories. They will develop a better sense of when to "categorize categories," or collapse them, and when to pull them apart to make more subcategories.

Phase Five: Determine Relationships and Investigate Causal Hypotheses

In this phase of the investigation, students build hypotheses from the data and form generalizations for application and skill use. They continue to analyze information, but the focus is on studying the function and utility of different concepts and how they can be applied.

Of course, just having categories is educative, giving us greater conceptual control over portions of our world. When we classify character sketches drawn from novels and short stories, we discover ways that authors introduce characters; knowing those ways enables us to read with a more refined eye. However, if we keep pushing at the categories, we can form hypotheses about them and convert some of these hypotheses into useful skills. Suppose we discovered that female writers used analogies more frequently than male writers when introducing characters: we might hypothesize that women would use analogies more in all phases of their writing. We can develop a new inquiry to test that hypothesis. If we pursue the subject, test our hypothesis, and find it to be true, we can try to find out why.

To build skills from categories requires students to learn how to produce something that fits the category; to support increasing knowledge and appropriate use, they need to be able to explain their product. Suppose we discover metaphors as a device used by poets. If we want to produce metaphors, we need to practice creating them, and compare our products with the metaphors generated by expert writers.

Generally speaking, we need at least a half-dozen examples to generalize, another half-dozen to consolidate a category, and another half-dozen to convert a category into a skill. Thus, if an initial data set contained a half-dozen metaphors, the students need to find 10 or 15 more items with metaphors as they try to practice making them. Essentially, they need to synthesize their information into operational categories that they can transfer into action, using metaphors powerfully in their own written and oral communication. Thus, they proceed from identifying the characteristics of metaphors into developing a formula (list of attributes and the relationship among the attributes) that tells how to make them.

For example, our primary students need to convert categories into skills for use in reading and writing. We can present more words and ask the students to decode them, using what they have learned (words beginning with *co*, words ending with *ck*, and so forth). We can ask them to look through their books for more examples and place those examples into their categories. We can ask them to spell words that are in their listening–speaking vocabularies, but not in their sight vocabulary, and place them in the correct category. Our goal is for students to be able to use productive categories by recognizing items that belong and creating new items that match the attributes they developed to describe each category.

Our upper elementary and middle school students need to consult authoritative sources that will help them interpret what they have learned. They need to express what they have learned in writing, discussing the similarities and differences among the tribes, formulating hypotheses related to those similarities and differences, and explaining how events evolved into the conditions that exist today.

In this phase, students continue to analyze data, focusing on the similarities and differences among the categories, seeking to understand the reasons and implications of these similarities and differences, and producing items that belong to different categories or relating the hypotheses they have formed to other settings, events, or situations.

Phase Six: Consolidate and Transfer

The concepts and skills produced by the inductive process must be available in the students' minds for use. They need to be consolidated and applied. For this to happen, thinking has to be precise and clear. You can't identify metaphors or use them at an optimum level of expressiveness if your understanding of the definition is vague. Our students, thinking about metaphors, need to call several examples to mind, "see" their attributes, and use them to analyze things they read, identifying metaphors and distinguishing them from other types of imagery. In addition, when writing, the students need to bring those images to bear as they construct metaphors. They need practice in appropriate use, exploring when a metaphor seems to enhance the message and when it doesn't. They need practice, practice, practice.

Let's look at our primary, upper elementary, and middle school students as they make the transfer from "lessons and assignments" to knowledge and skills they own for life.

- Our primary students need to decode and write many words using their letter *c* in all its combinations.
- Our upper elementary and middle school students need to use the concepts they have built about Native American tribes when they think about other groupings of people and when they encounter contemporary discussions about Native Americans. Here, our responsibility as teachers and the students' responsibility as learners is to ensure practice, practice, practice in using what has been learned.

STUDYING STUDENT LEARNING: PRODUCTION, DIAGNOSIS, AND NEXT STEPS

In the context of the inquiry, we study student learning of information, concepts, hypotheses, and skills. During the exploration of each domain, we study how well students are progressing with their mastery of the inductive process itself. We study the students by observing them, examining their products at each stage of the process, and giving them problems to solve that require applications of what they have learned. We will discuss this process again in Chapters 4 and 5. For now, let's see how the study of student learning might look in our primary, upper-grade, and middle school classrooms.

Primary Students

As our primary students classify their words, we note the distinctions they make and the attributes they concentrate on. We find out whether they can "see" both sound and letter. Do they lump the hard and soft *c* sounds together or discriminate between them? We note whether they understand relationships between the sound of the consonant and the vowels that follow it. We note whether they generalize with respect to the position of the *c* in the word. We discover how they handle *ch, cl, cr,* and *ck.* We learn whether they can find, through reading, new words that belong in their categories and whether they can decode them phonetically. We present spoken words to them and learn whether they can spell them. Altogether, we are trying to learn whether they have mastered the domain of *c.*

With respect to the inductive process and transfer of learning, we now provide them with another set and another domain—for example, words defined by the presence of the letter *t*—and we observe whether they are more proficient in the phases of that inquiry than they were with their first. Where they have trouble, we model the process. We might, in fact, choose another domain and demonstrate all the phases to them: gathering the words, enumerating the items, examining them for attributes, classifying, reclassifying, making and testing hypotheses, and sharing examples of how we use the different categories in our own reading (decoding) and writing (encoding).

Upper Elementary Students

We behave similarly with our upper elementary students. We note which attributes they pay attention to as they classify the tribes, and, depending on what we observe, we organize further passes through the items in the data set. We may have to teach them how to classify more than one variable at a time, demonstrating if necessary. ("Here's a category I made to find out whether nomadic or settled tribes lived in particular sections of the country. And here's how I built those categories.") We observe the types of hypotheses they make and what they are curious about: learning, for example, whether they explore how the hunters and gatherers fared when they were confined to reservations. We will provide them with some hypotheses to test and observe the skill with which they explore them.

As we prepare our upper elementary students for their next inquiry, we will use what we have learned to prepare sessions that will add to their knowledge base *and* to their inductive thinking skills. As we present them with a new domain to study, say, the 40 largest population centers in the United States, we will observe whether they are more skillful and, based on these observations, decide what needs to be done next to add to their abilities.

Middle School Students

You can probably now predict what we will look for in our middle school students. As they categorize nations, we will note the variables they concentrate on and how well they can handle categories based on multiple variables.

We will study the hypotheses they develop and the questions they ask ("why is life expectancy so short in Afghanistan, Ethiopia, and Angola?"). And we will give them problems to solve, such as learning how the small, wealthy countries in the world became that way. Depending on what we find, we will demonstrate techniques for handling data and ask them to make new passes through the data using those techniques. And, of course, their next domain of inquiry will be another opportunity for us to observe their developing skills. Table 3.1 summarizes the inductive thinking model.

TABLE   3.1   Inductive Model of Teaching

Syntax

Phase One: Identify the Domain
- Establish the focus and boundaries of the initial inquiry.
- Clarify the long-term objectives.

Phase Two: Collect and Enumerate Data
- Assemble and present the initial data set.
- Enumerate and label the items of data.

Phase Three: Examine Data
- Thoroughly study the items in the data set and identify their attributes.

Phase Four: Form Concepts by Classifying
- Classify the items in the data set and share the results.
- Add data to the set.
- Reclassify, possibly many times.

Phase Five: Generate and Test Hypotheses
- Examine the implications of differences between categories.
- Classify categories, as appropriate.
- Reclassify in two-way matrices, as well as by correlations, as appropriate.

Phase Six: Consolidate and Transfer
- Search for additional items of data in resource material.
- Synthesize by writing about the domain, using the categories.
- Convert categories into skills.

Test and consolidate skills through practice and application.

THE MODEL OF TEACHING

Syntax

The inductive model reaches out to students and invites them to construct knowledge and skill through disciplined inquiry. Long-term retention and the ability to use the knowledge and skills developed during the process are our curriculum goals. The learning that results is not to end with the immediate classroom experience or the end-of-unit assessments, but is to be applied in further schoolwork, out-of-school work, and to life in general. Another goal is the learning of the inductive process itself, so that students have conscious control of a powerful tool for learning.

The best inductive inquiry rolls along naturally, not rigidly, much as does good problem solving in the real world. Thus, it is designed to facilitate, discipline, and extend what the mind does naturally: examine information, develop concepts, generate hypotheses, and take actions whose consequences are assessed.

Therefore, we intentionally design the learning environment—through the classroom organization, the content selected (initially and evolving from individual and collective inquiry), and the tasks we give as instructional moves—so that inductive reasoning occurs and students learn facts, learn concepts, and learn how to learn.

The pace of learning needs to be commensurate with the importance of thorough study. It is important not to let students rush through a shallow exploration; this will not help them consolidate knowledge nor will it lead to transfer and use. Allowing time for thorough study of content and for learning how to think runs counter to normative practice in many classrooms, where rapid but superficial coverage is common. Some teachers allocate as much time to similar topics/content units as those suitable for inductive inquiry, but the content is "covered," not explored for knowledge and use beyond the classroom. Inductive inquiry is an antidote to superficial study.

Social System

The model has high to moderate structure. It is cooperative, but the teacher is very active, continually teaching needed skills and moderating discussions when necessary. When the instructor develops the data set and presents it to the students, a high degree of control is created.

Principles of Reaction

The teacher modulates tasks to take into account conceptual level and whether the students are ready for particular phases to commence, and, importantly, scaffolds the process when needed.

APPLICATIONS

The following scenarios provide examples of this model in action.

BOTANY IN INDIA: A SECONDARY EXAMPLE

At the Motilal Nehru School of Sports in the state of Haryana, India, two groups of tenth-grade students are engaged in the study of a botany unit that focuses on the structure of plant life. One group is studying the textbook with the tutorial help of their instructors, who illustrate the structures with plants found on the grounds of the school. We will call this group the presentation-cum-illustration group. The other group, which we will call the inductive group, is taught by Bharati Baveja, an instructor at Delhi University. This group is presented with a large number of plants that are labeled with their names. Working in pairs, Mrs. Baveja's students build classifications of the plants based on the structural characteristics of their roots, stems, and leaves. Periodically, the pairs share their classifications and generate labels for them.

Occasionally, Mrs. Baveja employs concept attainment (Chapter 6) to introduce a concept designed to expand the students' frame of reference and induce more complex classification. She also supplies the scientific names for the categories the students invent. Eventually Mrs. Baveja presents the students with some new specimens and asks them whether they can predict the structure of one part of the plant from the observation of another part (such as predicting the root structure from the observation of the leaves). Finally, she asks them to collect some more specimens and fit them to the categories they have developed so they can determine how comprehensive their categories have become. They discover that most of the new plants will fit into existing categories, but that new categories have to be invented to hold some of them.

After two weeks of study, the two groups take a test over the content of the unit and are asked to analyze more specimens and name their structural characteristics. The inductive group has gained twice as much on the test of knowledge and can correctly identify the structure of eight times more specimens than the presentation-cum-illustration group.

WORD IDENTIFICATION SKILLS

Jack Wilson is a year 1 teacher in Cambridge, England. He meets daily for reading instruction with a group of children who are progressing quite well. He is studying how his students attack unknown words. He believes that they do well when they

sound out words and recognize them as being in their listening–speaking vocabulary. For example, when they find *war*, they are fine. However, a word like *postwar*
appears to stop them. Deciding that they have trouble with morphological structures when elements like prefixes and suffixes add to the root meanings of words,
Jack plans the following sequence of lessons.

Jack prepares a deck of cards with one word on each card. He selects words
with particular prefixes and suffixes, and he deliberately puts in words that have
the same root words but different prefixes and suffixes. He picks prefixes and suffixes because they are prominent morphological structures—very easy to identify.
(He will later proceed to more subtle features.) Jack plans a series of learning activities over the next several weeks using the deck of cards as a data set. Here are
some of the words:

| set | reset | heat | preheat | plant | replant |
| run | rerun | set | preset | plan | preplan |

When the group of students convenes on Monday morning, Jack gives several
cards to each student. He keeps the remainder, intending to gradually increase the
amount of information. Jack has each student read a word on one of the cards and
describe something about the word. Other students can add to the description. In
this way the structural properties of the word are brought to the students' attention. The discussion surfaces features like initial consonants, begins with an *s*, vowels, pairs of consonants (*pl*), and so on.

After the students have familiarized themselves with the assortment of words,
Jack asks them to put the words into groups. "Put the words that go together in
piles," he instructs. The students begin studying their cards, passing them back
and forth as they sort out the commonalities. At first the students' card groups
reflected only the initial letters or the meanings of the words, such as whether they
referred to motion or warmth. Gradually, they noticed the prefixes and how they
were spelled and looked up their meanings in the dictionary, discovering how the
addition of the prefixes affected the meanings of the root words.

When the students finished sorting the words, Jack asked them to talk
about each category, telling what the cards had in common. Gradually, because
of the way Jack had selected the data, the students could discover the major
prefixes and suffixes and reflect on their meaning. Then he gave them sentences using words not in their deck that had the same prefixes and suffixes
and asked them to figure out the meanings of those words, applying the concepts they had formed to help them unlock word meanings. He found that he
had to teach them directly to identify the root word meaning and then add the
meaning of the prefix or suffix.

By selecting different sets of words, Jack led the students through the categories of consonant and vowel sounds and structures they would need to attack unfamiliar words, providing students with many opportunities to practice inductive learning. Jack studied their progress and adjusted the classification tasks to lead them to a thorough understanding and the ability to use their new knowledge to attack unfamiliar words.

The primary application of the model is to develop thinking capacity. However, in the course of developing thinking capacity, the strategies obviously require students to ingest and process large quantities of information. The model can be used in every curriculum area and from kindergarten through high school. Inducing students to go beyond the given data is a deliberate attempt to increase productive or creative thinking. Inductive processes thus include the creative processing of information, as well as the convergent use of information to solve problems.

The model causes students to collect information and examine it closely, organize it into concepts, and learn to manipulate those concepts. Used regularly, the strategy increases the students' abilities to form concepts efficiently and also the perspectives from which they can view information.

For example, if a group of students regularly engages in inductive activity, the group can be taught more and more sources of data. The students can learn to examine data from many sides and to scrutinize all aspects of objects and events. We can expect that at first their data will be superficial, but their increasingly sophisticated inquiry will turn up more and more attributes that they can use for classifying the data. Also, if a classroom of students works in groups to form concepts and data, then the groups share the categories they develop, they will stimulate each other to look at the information from different perspectives. The students can also learn to categorize categories by building concepts that further cluster those categories.

Another example may serve to pull these ideas together in practical terms. As we have discussed, sometimes we create and organize data sets for our students to classify, and sometimes we help them create and organize sets. In the following example we have organized a set from writing samples produced by the students themselves.

SCENARIO

BUILDING A DATA SET FROM REACTIONS TO A SCENE IN A FILM

The students have watched a scene from the film *Out of Africa* in which three new friends amuse themselves with witty conversation. Then the students were instructed to create a sentence about the scene, beginning each sentence with an adverb. (They are studying the use of adverbs because it was discovered that they are not as comfortable using adverbs as adjectives.)

They opened their sentences in the following ways (the rest of the sentences are omitted to create a focus on the use of adverbs in openings):

1. Profoundly looking into one another's eyes . . .
2. Intently listening to one another's words . . .
3. Wonderingly and as if by magic the love began to flow . . .
4. With relaxed and forthright honesty they shared a part of themselves . . .
5. Anxiously the husband watched as his normally taciturn wife . . .
6. Passionately I gazed at my two companions . . .
7. Playfully at first, but with growing intensity . . .
8. Tentatively, like three spiders caught in the vortex of the same web . . .
9. With heated anticipation, the three formed a web of mystery and emotion.
10. Quietly listening they were engulfed by the tale.
11. With awe and a certain wonderment . . .
12. Tenderly, in the midst of warm candlelight, they . . .
13. Skillfully she met the challenge . . .
14. Boldly they teased one another with their mutual love of language.
15. Effortlessly her practiced mind . . .
16. Awkwardly, like children just learning to walk . . .
17. Softly, slowly, but glowing like the candles about them, they negotiated . . .
18. Boldly she drew them into the fabric of her story.
19. Suspended by the delicate thread of her tale . . .
20. Instinctively she took his cue . . .

Before reading further, read the passages, make notes about the attributes of the writing, and classify the sentences. (If you are alone or in a small group studying the model, classify them independently. If you are in a group of eight or more, classify them with a partner. Then share your classifications, discussing the basis each of you used and the attributes you focused on.)

Now, let's turn to some of the categories developed by our class.

One group classified the sentences by the form of the adverbs, placing single words together (such as *profoundly* from number 1 and *anxiously* from 5), phrases together (such as "with relaxed and forthright honesty" from 4), and the single clause (number 19) by itself. A second group reported that it had classified them according to the mood or tone that was evoked. For example, numbers 12, 17, 19, 11, 3, and 7 were placed together because the group members decided that they all shared the creation of a gentle, loving mood, whereas 5 and 16 emphasized the awkwardness of strangers.

The class then used their categories to experiment with writing, changing single words into phrases and clauses and vice versa, substituting words to change the mood evoked, and so on. For example, one pair experimented with 6, trying "with passion," and "passion flowed as I gazed . . . ." Another changed number 8 to "tentatively and spiderlike" and decided the change altered the mood. One changed *boldly* to *skillfully* in number 18 and judged that it helped the development of the mood.

The episode was followed by a foray into several books of short stories, and the members of the class created a data set of sentences in which authors had made use of adverbs. Classifying them, they proceeded to create categories of adverb use by expert writers and to experiment with them in their own writing.

Thus, the phases of the model built on one another to generate more and more complex mental activity and to increase the likelihood that the study of language would have a yield for their skill in writing. The second inductive activity built on the first as the students added the study of expert writers and tried to learn from them.

The model is adaptable to a wide range of learning styles (see Chapter 20). When the authors and their associates explored inductive processes with both relatively rigid and flexible students, they found that both groups were able to engage in the inductive process but that the more flexible students made the greatest gains initially. More importantly, they found that practice and training increased effectiveness and that all the students could learn to carry on inductive activity independently.

SCENARIO

DEVELOPMENT OF A UNIT

This scenario is built around a series of sets built by Sharon Champ, a literacy trainer in the Saskatoon Public Schools. Sharon decided to build a set where several concepts about syntactic structures of sentences are built in so that they might be discovered as the students build their categories. The objective is to increase the students' study of sentences and how they are structured to convey particular types of meanings. Let's look at the structural characteristics of 21 of the sentences.

1. In the grass, the spider patiently weaves her web.
2. In the trees, birds gather to eat berries.
3. In the forest, a squirrel leaps from tree to tree.
4. In the space station, the astronauts complete their experiment.
5. In the burrow, the rabbit family nestles together to keep warm.
6. In the cockpit, the pilot carefully checks his instrument panel.
7. In the icy water, a penguin dives and splashes.

8. Under the sea, large sharks circle the school of fish.
9. Near the trees, lion cubs scamper in the tall grass.
10. Under the water, the diver silently searches for a dolphin.
11. Under the snow, a hungry mouse burrows deep looking for food.
12. Beside the school, two small boys play catch with a bright red ball.
13. Behind the mountaintops, dark storm clouds are gathering.
14. Between the trees, a small monkey wrestles with its mother.
15. Beside the river, a bear cub scrambles on the rocks.
16. Between the rocks, a snake slithers to search for food.
17. On the surface of the pond, a loon floats peacefully.
18. Hidden under leaves, a spotted frog hides from the sun's brilliant rays.
19. Deep in the forest, a black panther patiently waits to pounce on her prey.
20. High in the sky, the lone eagle glides gracefully.
21. Far below the earth's surface, molten lava rumbles and boils.

From a formal perspective, each of these sentences contains a prepositional phrase that provides information about where the action takes place. Sharon reasons that if the students can build a category that contains those attributes (prepositional phrases and their attributes and the meaningful content *where*), they can use the category as they read, looking for structures that provide particular meanings, and as they write, building a tool for giving their readers information about *where*.

The rest of the set does not contain prepositional phrases that tell us where:

22. Penguins have huge appetites.
23. This bird is a rockhopper penguin.
24. You would not want to fight a grizzly bear!
25. Clouds come in all shapes and sizes.
26. A blue whale is not a fish.
27. This tough bird is an emperor penguin.
28. The small dog yapped impatiently.
29. In the day, bats sleep upside down.
30. At twilight, bats' sharp cries fill the air.
31. At night, the owl hunts silently for mice and rabbits.
32. In the winter, most bears hibernate in caves.
33. Some frogs lay their eggs on land.
34. A duck makes its nest in the reeds.
35. The young penguin stays beside his mother.
36. Many desert animals live underground.
37. Many plants and animals live beside lakes.
38. A woman is standing between her children.

39. The woodpecker searches for insects under the bark of the aspen tree.
40. They build their nests on steep, rocky cliffs and hillsides.
41. Snow leopards live high on snowy mountainsides.
42. Yaks live on some of the tallest mountains in the world.

The sentences numbered 22–42 are mixed with the first 21 as Sharon presents the set to her sixth-grade students. She asks them to look at characteristics of the sentences and the kinds of information that is conveyed. She asks them not to focus on specific bits of information (such as where the yak lives) but on general information conveyed by a particular characteristic of the sentences.

Clearly, this is not the first lesson these students have experienced on sentence structure and purpose, but is a part of a long unit dealing with comprehension in reading and ways of conveying information in writing.

What do you think? What categories do you suppose the students formed in their inquiry?

Tips for Teaching Inductively

Here are a number of tips for teaching inductively that Bruce wrote to a group of teachers a few years ago:

1. Practice, practice, practice. Practice reduces anxiety. Let go and have fun. Build a learning community around the model—designing a weekly lesson won't accomplish that.

2. Study how the kids think—the process of the model gives us a bit of a window into their minds. The better the handle on their minds, the more we can adjust what we do.

3. Keep up front that we are trying to help the kids learn how to learn. A common mistake in teaching is to ask questions without teaching the kids how to answer them—or, even better, to ask the questions themselves and then seek the answers. Teaching comprehension in reading is an example. Many folks ask the kids questions about what they have read to find out whether they have comprehended—or ask them to make predictions. Neither teaches the kids *how* to comprehend or make predictions based on understanding. They need models to follow how we comprehend and make predictions.

4. The inductive process brings kids into the exploration of a domain as a learning community trying to master that content. For example, suppose that initial consonants are the domain for beginning readers. They need to explore a heap of initial consonants, distinguishing the letters and sounds from one another. Giving them a set with the "letter of the week" in it and hoping they will focus on that letter subverts the inquiry. We learn phonics by comparing and contrasting letters and their associated sounds—learning them one at a time without comparison makes life difficult for students.

Remember that the customary ways of teaching reading leave 30 percent of the kids virtually unable to read. They need to inquire actively into phonetic and structural analysis and comprehension skills.

5. Except for very specific concentration on phonetic elements and newly learned vocabulary, words should be introduced in sentences that provide meaningful context for the words.

6. Use the model in the curriculum areas to teach substance, not as a rainy day activity.

7. Make sure the data set has the attributes present, both for concept formation and concept attainment. I probably overuse the example of "food groups." Kids can memorize what food goes in each group and take our word for the meaning of nutrition. They *cannot* use inductive methods to discover the groups. Biochemists can. However, if the data presented are rich enough they can, by the fourth grade, classify the nations of the world by demographic characteristics because no arcane scientific knowledge or process is needed.

8. Be careful how you teach "complete" and "incomplete" sentences. Teach subject and predicate first. A complete sentence is simply an expression that has an explicit or implied subject and predicate.

9. Distinctions between fact and opinion are probably not appropriate for short explorations. Data sets containing each will only work if the kids already know which are facts and opinions—in which case there is no new learning. The distinction requires inference from context or, more often, verification from an authoritative source.

10. In science, try to concentrate on areas where the kids can collect raw data. With respect to rocks, for example, they can study density, hardness, pH, and homogeneity by visual inspection, but they have to consult authoritative sources to find out how the rocks got that way. They can't tell whether a rock was produced from a volcanic process unless they already know or get the information from an authoritative source.

11. Yes, kids can create or attain multiple-attribute categories!

12. When teaching concepts like *adverb, adjective, phrase, clause,* remember that there are many subcategories of all of these. If a data set contains one each of five or six categories of adverbs, it can be tough for the kids. Consider sets where they discover the various subcategories.

13. "Squeeze" the meaning out of complex sets, such as poems. The kids want to approach these with the idea of learning *everything* about them.

14. Studying attributes of subjects such as characters in stories provides interesting problems. Usually, learning what a character is like involves mining the context. You might consider data sets where clues referring to various characteristics are concentrated on, such as physical description and temperament. Again, teach the kids how to answer the question.

15. If students are going to classify characters, they need 20 or so in the set.

16. Figure out the higher-order content objective as you develop a set. A good example is an exercise where the kids classified pictures of clouds and then were given the scientific terms for clouds that have particular appearances. The question was "how do I know when we're done?" That question is not unique to the inductive model—it would apply to a unit taught in any

fashion. The answer is to figure out what they are going to do with their newfound knowledge and design an application task that starts them on their way. For example, have them take a minute at the beginning of several days to look at the sky and write or dictate a description. Or have them look up information about weather or examine a number of weather forecasts and find concepts in them.

INSTRUCTIONAL AND NURTURANT EFFECTS

The inductive model of learning and teaching is designed to instruct students in concept formation and, simultaneously, to teach concepts and the application of concepts/generalizations. It nurtures attention to logic, attention to language and the meaning of words, and attention to the nature of knowledge. Figure 3.5 displays the instructional and nurturant effects of the inductive model.

FIGURE 3.5 Instructional and nurturant effects of the inductive model of teaching

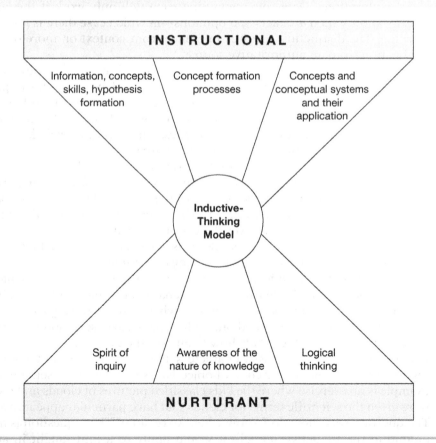

INSTRUCTIONAL

Information, concepts, skills, hypothesis formation

Concept formation processes

Concepts and conceptual systems and their application

Inductive-Thinking Model

Spirit of inquiry

Awareness of the nature of knowledge

Logical thinking

NURTURANT

It is sometimes thought that higher-order thinking is reserved for the mature. Not so. Students of all ages can process information richly. Although the content of primary education needs to be rich with concrete experience, little kids can learn to think well. Similarly, complex, inquiry-oriented models of instruction have turned out to be the best educational medicine for students who start school slowly or who later have the poorest learning histories.

Good thinking combines discipline with flexibility. If we are to help children become more powerful and flexible thinkers, we have to create environments that offer challenge and strong support without smothering the very characteristics we seek to nurture.

CHAPTER FOUR

Scientific Inquiry

Building Learning around Investigations

Modern science is not just the arcane province of a few lucky and gifted people.
It is the way of thinking and learning that brought us out of the Dark Ages.

—*Our reflective observer*

The National Research Council (2012), whose members are drawn from the National Academy of Sciences, the National Academy of Engineering, and the Institute of Medicine, generated a major report on which curriculum reform in science education can be drawn. The report makes clear that the new science standards should apply to *all* students, not just some. When compared with previous curriculum guides and most documents on standards, a major addition to the science curriculum is the inclusion of engineering and technology along with physical sciences, life sciences, earth and space sciences, and the applications of science. All students should have an understanding of the basic concepts of these disciplines and how knowledge is created—the methods of inquiry they employ. All students should learn how these concepts can be applied in their lives and environments and to developments in the global society.

ORGANIZING IDEA

The science curriculum is unified by continuous hands-on experience. All students, K–12, should conduct investigations in the sciences and participate in projects where the methods and concepts of the sciences are employed.

The National Research Council (NRC) states firmly that science education should focus on only a few important concepts from each discipline at any given grade level—and the learning process should be built around in-depth inquiries into topics selected because they contain those concepts. This recommendation is in stark contrast to courses that attempt to touch superficially on a mass of topics—the kilometer-wide but millimeter-deep approach. For example, consider the almost desperately shallow coverage in many of the commercially available textbooks; or, for that matter, the outlines of the "advanced placement" courses.

The framework for K–12 science from the NRC also emphasizes "cross-cutting" concepts—ones that are common to the disciplines and should be learned both to better understand the disciplines and because they have great organizing power. This leads to a more unifying understanding of science as well as helps the learning process as ideas learned in one area are rediscovered in another subject.

The framework is also unified by continuous hands-on experience. All students, K–12, should conduct investigations in the sciences and participate in projects where the methods and concepts of the sciences are employed. Experiential learning provides the concrete ground for understanding more complex and abstract principles as they are encountered, as well as application to other aspects of life. The investigative frame of reference is to be a lifelong outcome.

All students means everyone, not just those who are college-bound or aiming toward careers in scientific or science-related fields. However, knowing the core concepts and methods of inquiry and how to apply them to understand their immediate and distant environment is the foundation for those who will pursue such careers.

The three dimensions of the NRC framework (2012) and the Next Generation Science Standards (NGSS Lead States, 2013) will come to life through models of teaching that include the cooperative/inductive inquiry processes in Chapters 1 and 3 and the investigative methods developed in the formal disciplines. In this chapter, we give extensive attention to the curricular/instructional models developed by the Biological Sciences Study Committee educators over the last 50 years. However, the framework from the NRC cited previously is an excellent guide to content and processes of the major areas of scientific study.

This chapter celebrates science as a teaching strategy. We will deal with the general model and illustrate it with several scenarios and then with a more expansive example from biology. Let's begin in a classroom.

SCENARIO

GINNY'S PRIMARY STUDENTS ASK, "WHAT'S GROWING IN OUR NEIGHBORHOOD?"

Imagine Ginny Townsend's second-grade students as they embark on a study of the vegetation in the neighborhood of their school. The inquiry stemmed from a discussion in which they realized that they had little knowledge of the growing things they pass every day. They had names for only a small proportion of the flora they live with and only superficial knowledge about how the vegetation they see every day gets nourishment, grows, and reproduces. Ginny knows that they begin with very little content knowledge, but they have experienced plant life all their lives and have more information than they realize.

Resources

Ginny's courses are hybrids, where campus and distance experience are intertwined. The campus dimension leads the students to work together and provides them with learning strategies; in this case they will be learning a cooperative/inductive strategy, beginning by collecting data from the living plant life in their neighborhood.

Digital resources provide vastly more information than any human teacher could expect to have. For example, http://knowplants.org is a gateway to dozens of databases that the students can use; quite a few are designed for kids and many were created specifically to support science education. Print sources—books, encyclopedias, and other references—will also be very important. Ginny's class is equipped with a print library of relevant books, computers, email, digital cameras, and camcorders. She has developed a class webpage on which she and they can post ideas and information; it contains a link to http://knowplants.org. As for devices, many of the students are more familiar with tablets and smart phones than with laptops, and most have not used word-processing programs often or made multimedia reports.

So she knows that she will be leading them into relatively unfamiliar content and will have to help them learn to collect and classify information from print and digital sources (and from local experts). They will need to learn to develop and test ideas, and generate attractive and accurate reports about the results of their inquiries, building general computer skills and web skills as the inquiry proceeds.

Initial Process

Ginny begins by leading the students to collect information by observing the vegetation around them the first week in September. Therefore, the inquiry opens with walks around the neighborhood, taking pictures of the specimens as a whole and close-up pictures of their leaves. The pictures are printed and pinned up on a wall so they can be studied. Smaller copies form the beginning of notebooks, with 8" × 10" copies for each student.

Ginny asks the students to look at the leaves and classify them. They use the interactive whiteboard to display and explain their categories, moving the pictures around and talking about them. The photographs are loaded into the folder for this unit so that it is easy for the teacher and students to move them around. Some of the categories are "leaves that look like hands in gloves," "leaves come in sets along the sides of twigs," and "oval leaves." The students agree on those categories and reorganize the pictures to display them.

Next they examine the pictures of the plants, bushes, and trees and classify them, using the general categories and the attributes of the leaves to build more categories, again moving the pictures around on the whiteboard. Gradually they work out a terminology for the categories that most can agree on—tall trees with glove-like leaves, tall trees with oval leaves, and such—and reorganize the pictures to reflect the new categories. Their observation will become more detailed and refined as, for example, they begin to notice the veins in leaves.

Ginny then displays http://knowplants.org on the interactive whiteboard and leads the students to study the lists of databases and select ones that might provide descriptive information about vegetation in their area.

They begin with the Maryland Native Plant Society (www.mdflora.org), a site operated by volunteers. On the featured page "The Year of the Oak," they obtain the names and pictures of oaks that are indigenous to Maryland. They download a picture of a black oak that is bare of most of its leaves. The children look at their pictures, taken when the trees had leaves, but think they have identified a black oak in the group they photographed during their walk. The next task is to see whether they can find a picture of the black oak tree with leaves and, if possible, a close-up picture of its leaves. The Better Homes and Gardens Plant Encyclopedia (www.bhg.com/gardening/plant-dictionary) contains a picture with all the leaves, and it does look like theirs. The United States Department of Agriculture Plants Database (http://plants.usda.gov) provides a picture of the leaves, which also closely matches their picture. The children enlarge the USDA picture and compare it with a leaf they clip off their tree. They conclude that they are 90 percent sure they have a black oak identified and proceed to read about how it reproduces, where it grows, and so on.

The inquiry proceeds, tree by tree, bush by bush, and flower by flower. Teams are organized to search specific bases and particular species. Categories are redeveloped and named, such as "bushes that have flowers." Working in pairs, the students build PowerPoint presentations of categories they have generated, describing the items in the categories. They create a "virtual plant walk" and share it with other classes and their parents.

Some students suggest that they label many of the things they have studied in their neighborhood with their colloquial and scientific names. Ginny leads them to the town council for approval. Their next discussion is over how much information to include on the labels; just the names don't seem enough.

In this scenario, collecting information about the domain (local vegetation) being explored and categorizing members of the category (trees, bushes, and so on) drives the unit. Digital pictures and displays play their part and the web-based data source brings information from specialists to the study. Finally, citizenship found its way into the process.

Reflecting

Building concepts enables us to manage information, retain it, and use it. There is a high probability that it is the foundation for the 21st-century skills—and, generally, for most higher-order thinking skills and most types of intelligence (see Joyce & Calhoun, 2010, 2012).

A complication is that a high level of competence in reading is required to access many of the riches available in the digital world. Ginny's students are able to explore the digital databases because of the scaffolds she provides—and the students support one another also. (See Chapter 6 in Joyce & Calhoun, 2010, and Joyce, Calhoun, Jutras, & Newlove, 2006).

SCENARIO

GENETICS COMES TO FIFTH GRADE

25 June, 2002. John Orr's fifth-grade class has been browsing the Science Times section of the *New York Times* and comes across an extensive report on the genome mapping project in Iceland (Wade, 2002). John's school has a subscription to the electronic edition of the newspaper, and it is well used in his class. He leads the students toward stories that relate to parts of the world they have been studying or items of national and international news he believes they should be conversant with. Working in teams, they also browse sections of the paper, looking for items of interest. Often, as today, John projects an article on the screen, using an LCD monitor on the overhead projector, and reads the article with the class. Information is recorded on newsprint tablets and the major points in the article are summarized by the student "writing leaders of the day."

In this case, he asks the leaders to find a file where information from past forays into genome projects are summarized. He projects those summaries on the whiteboard before turning to the June 25 article. The students have been fascinated with the genome projects. They are amazed to find that 99.9 percent of human genomes are shared by everyone on the planet. The web has been a fine resource, as have been the encyclopedias in the classroom CD-ROM collection, as John has led the class to study the concepts of race and gender. They have begun to realize how many differences are products of socialization.

Today's story interests the students for three reasons:

1. In Iceland, the researchers have genealogical information that goes back for 1,100 years, with a population that has had little immigration over that period of time. Thus, the research strategy differs from the other genomic projects.
2. The project is disease oriented and, in the case of asthma, the researchers have traced current asthmatics who are under treatment to a single common ancestor who was born in 1710.
3. In the 800s A.D. about 10,000 to 15,000 Norsemen founded Iceland. They raided Northern Ireland and England for young women, whom they captured and made into "slave wives." Altogether they enslaved 40,000 to 50,000 young females.

This third fact galvanizes the students. They have trouble coming to grips with it, and they become oriented toward the study of Iceland and Scandinavia. They set out to gather data using encyclopedias and databanks on nations. They also come to realize that the "wife-raids" by the Vikings greatly depleted the female population in Northern Ireland and Northern England and wonder what effect that might have had. Eventually, they will be in touch with a scholar at Oxford who will offer his opinions about the subject.

The students are studying how science is made as well as its findings. John keeps making them aware of the "how" as well as the "what." He keeps reminding them of Carl Sagan's quote that "The method of science, as stodgy and grumpy as it may seem, is far more important than the findings of science."

The subsequent history of the Iceland project has been difficult, largely because of privacy considerations. That history illustrates that science is a socio-cultural activity and does not take place in a vacuum. See Gillham (2011) for a fine analysis in http://www.ftpress.com/article.

You can well imagine that, today, John and his students would be building inquiries from the recent reports of the finding of an ancient skull (Skull 5) in the country of Georgia and generating questions about the implications of these early fossils (Wilford, 2013).

SCENARIO

INVESTIGATING SOUND

In London, Ontario, Mr. Hendricks's fourth-grade students enter their classroom after lunch to find an array of glasses, bottles, bells, wooden boxes of different sizes (with holes in them), tuning forks, xylophones, and small wooden flutes. These objects are spread about the room, and the students spend a few minutes playing with them, creating a most horrendous sound. Mr. Hendricks watches.

After a few minutes the students begin to settle down and one of them asks, "What's going on here, Mr. Hendricks? It looks like you've turned the place into an orchestra."

"Well, in a way," he smiles. "Actually, for the next few weeks this is going to be our sound laboratory." He moves across the room and picks up an instrument made of wood and wires and plucks one of the wires. At the same time he uses a spoon to strike a soft drink bottle on the desk next to him. "Do you notice anything about these sounds?" he asks, and repeats his plucking and striking.

"Hey," says one of the girls, "they sound the same, but different."

"Do it again," suggests one of the students, and Mr. Hendricks obliges. Soon all of the students have noticed that the sound is at the same pitch or level.

"Your problem," explains Mr. Hendricks, "is to find out what makes sound vary and to describe that variation. Given the limitations of the devices we have in this room, I want you to organize yourselves to conduct some investigations and present me with sets of principles that you think describe the variations. When you're finished, I want you to be able to describe to me how you would design an instrument with certain capabilities. I'll tell you what I want the instrument to be able to do, and you can tell me how to make it. Then we'll begin to test your ideas. Now, I think we ought to organize ourselves into groups and decide how we're going to go about this. Does anybody have any ideas?"

"Well," Sally ventures, "I've noticed that the things are made out of five different kinds of materials. Maybe we could get into five groups, and each group would experiment with those for a while. Then we could share what we've learned and trade around and check out the thinking of the other groups. After that we could decide what to do next."

Someone joins in with another suggestion, and the class spends the next half hour planning how the study will begin.

As we discussed in the "A Note on Heritage" section in the Front Matter, during the early 1950s into the 1970s, innovation in U.S. education was propelled mainly by the Academic Reform movement. Scientists sought to modernize the curriculum in an effort to revise the conventional subject areas of the school around conceptions of the major ideas and research methods of the academic disciplines. In the area of mathematics, for example, the curriculum designers attempted to influence the way students would think about both the major ideas and the methods they would use to inquire into mathematics. Similarly, the science curricula reflected both the major ideas of the sciences and the research methods and attitudes of the scientific community. In other words, curricula were built around the information-processing systems of the academic disciplines. Similar curricula continue to be developed, and research and development is active, especially in the sciences and social science education.

Major new curricula were developed in physics, chemistry, biology, and general science courses and the social sciences. Importantly, the National Science Teachers Association has many members who continue to develop lessons, units, and courses and share them on the web. The organization's journal, *Science Teacher*, provides many high-quality, easily accessible ideas and materials. Similarly, the members of the National Council for the Social Studies (NCSS) have been active developers. The NCSS journals *Social Education* and *Social Studies for Young Children* are filled with ideas and guides to instructional materials. If you are a new teacher, we strongly recommend that you join the organizations if possible. The **PBS** collection of videos from the *Nova* and *Nature* programs is also invaluable both to acquaint ourselves with a wide variety of scientific investigations and for our students fourth grade and up. We make these same recommendations for experienced teachers.

Because we cannot deal with all the sciences, engineering, and technology in the scope of this text, we have selected the Biological Sciences Curriculum Study (BSCS) as representative of the curriculum areas (see the concept paper by Schwab, 1965). Incidentally, the **BSCS** organization is still alive and well and continues to generate innovative curricula (see www.bscs.org).

ORIENTATION TO THE MODEL

The essence of the **BSCS** approach is to teach students to process information using techniques similar to those of research biologists—that is, by identifying problems and using a particular method to solve them. BSCS emphasizes content and process. The first emphasis is on human behavior in the ecology of earth:

> The problems created by growing human populations, by depletion of resources, by pollution, by regional development, and the like, all require intelligent government or community action. These are, in part at least, biological-ecological problems, and every citizen should have some awareness of their background. (Schwab, 1965, p. 19)

The second emphasis is on scientific investigation:

> Measured by almost any standard, science has been and continues to be a powerful force in our society. However, although many people may understand some of the products of science, at the same time they may be very ignorant of the nature of science and its methods of inquiry. It is probably a safe generalization to say that the understanding of the products of science cannot be

attained unless the process is also understood. It is apparent that in a free society such as ours, much will depend on the average citizen's evaluation of science. (Schwab, 1965, pp. 26–27)

To help students understand the nature of science, the strategies developed by the BSCS committee introduce students to the methods of biology at the same time that they introduce them to the ideas and facts. The committee put it directly:

If we examine a conventional high school text, we find that it consists mainly or wholly of a series of unqualified, positive statements. "There are so many kinds of mammals." "Organ A is composed of three tissues." "Respiration takes place in the following steps." "The genes are the units of heredity." "The function of A is X."

This kind of exposition (the statement of conclusions) has long been the standard rhetoric of textbooks even at the college level. It has many advantages, not the least of which are simplicity and economy of space. Nevertheless, there are serious objections to it. Both by omission and commission, it gives a false and misleading picture of the nature of science.

By commission a rhetoric of conclusions has two unfortunate effects on the student. First, it gives the impression that science consists of unalterable, fixed truths. Yet, this is not the case. The accelerated pace of knowledge in recent years has made it abundantly clear that scientific knowledge is revisionary. It is a temporary codex, continuously restructured as new data are related to old.

A rhetoric of conclusions also tends to convey the impression that science is complete. Hence, the fact that scientific investigation still goes on, and at an ever-accelerated pace, is left unaccounted for to the student.

The sin of omission by a rhetoric of conclusions can be stated thus: It fails to show that scientific knowledge is more than a simple report of things observed, that it is a body of knowledge forged slowly and tentatively from raw materials. It does not show that these raw materials, data, spring from planned observations and experiments. It does not show that the plans for experiments and observations arise from problems posed, and that these problems, in turn, arise from concepts which summarize our earlier knowledge. Finally, of great importance, is the fact that a rhetoric of conclusions fails to show that scientists, like other men, are capable of error, and that much of inquiry has been concerned with the correction of error.

Above all, a rhetoric of conclusions fails to show that our summarizing concepts are tested by the fruitfulness of the questions that they suggest, and through this testing are continually revised and replaced.

The essence, then, of a teaching of science as inquiry, would be to show some of the conclusions of science in the framework of the way they arise and are tested. This would mean to tell the student about the ideas posed, and the experiments performed, to indicate the data thus found, and to follow the interpretation by which these data were converted into scientific knowledge. (Schwab, 1965, pp. 39–40)

BSCS uses several techniques to teach science as inquiry. First, it uses many statements that express the tentative nature of science, such as, "We do not know," "We have been unable to discover how this happens," and "The evidence about this is contradictory" (Schwab, 1965, p. 40). Current theories, it is pointed out, may be replaced by others as time goes by. Second, in place of a rhetoric of conclusions, BSCS uses what is called a *narrative of inquiry,* in which the history of major ideas in biology is described and the course of inquiry in that area is followed. Third, the laboratory work is arranged to induce students to investigate problems, rather than just to illustrate the text. As they put it, scientists "treat problems for which the text does not provide answers. They create situations in which the students can participate in the inquiry" (Schwab, 1965, p. 40). Fourth, the laboratory programs have been designed in blocks that involve the student in an investigation of a real biological problem. At first students may be presented with materials already familiar to scientists and problems whose solutions are already disclosed, but "as the series of problems progresses, they come nearer and nearer to the frontier of knowledge" (Schwab, 1965, p. 41). Thus, the student simulates the activity of the research scientist. Finally, there is the use of what are called *Invitations to Enquiry.* Like the functioning of the laboratory, the Invitations to Enquiry involve the student in activities that enable him or her to follow and participate in the reasoning related to a front-line item of investigation or to a methodological problem in biology. We present Invitations to Enquiry as the model of teaching drawn from the BSCS materials. Preparing to write this chapter, we obtained contemporary BSCS material and are pleased that it continues the spirit of scientific inquiry that drove the original model of curriculum and instruction. Reading the "Blue" version of the introductory high school course in biology (Greenberg, 2006), we learned a good deal, some updating our knowledge of science and some opening up topics and inquiries that were not in our undergraduate or graduate education programs. The basic text includes about 100 pages of studies for the students to use to conduct their inquiries. The text relentlessly opens up ways of thinking about the collection and organization of information and the generation and testing of explanatory theories.

INVITATIONS TO ENQUIRY

Credited to Schwab, this strategy was designed

> to show students how knowledge arises from the interpretation of data to show students that the interpretation of data—indeed, even the search for data—proceeds on the basis of concepts and assumptions that change as our knowledge grows . . . to show students that as these principles and concepts change, knowledge changes too . . . to show students that though knowledge changes,

it changes for a good reason—because we know better and more than we knew before. The converse of this point also needs stress: The possibility that present knowledge may be revised in the future does *not* mean that present knowledge is false. Present knowledge is science based on the best-tested facts and concepts we presently possess. It is the most reliable, rational knowledge of which man is capable. (Schwab, 1965, p. 46)

Each Invitation to Enquiry (or lesson) is a case study illustrating either a major concept or a method of the discipline. Each invitation "poses example after example of the process itself [and] *engages the participation of the student in the process*" (Schwab, 1965, p. 47).

In each case a real-life scientific study is described. However, omissions, blanks, or curiosities are left uninvestigated, which the student is invited to fill: "This omission may be the plan of an experiment, or a way to control one factor in an experiment. It may be the conclusion to be drawn from given data. It may be an hypothesis to account for data given" (Schwab, 1965, p. 46). In other words, the format of the invitation ensures that the student sees biological inquiry in action and is involved in it, because he or she has to perform the missing experiment or draw the omitted conclusion.

The sets of invitations are sequenced to lead the students to successively more sophisticated concepts. And the nature of investigation is relentless. Even in the first group of Invitations to Enquiry, the focus is topics related to methodology—the role and nature of general knowledge, data, experiment, control, hypothesis, and problems in scientific investigation. The subjects and topics of the invitations in Group 1 appear in Table 4.1.

Take a look at how the content and processes of Invitation 3 in Group 1 lead students to deal with the problem of misinterpretation of data.

Invitation 3
Subject: Seed Germination
Topic: Misinterpretation of Data

It is one thing to take a calculated risk in interpreting data. It is another thing to propose an interpretation for which there is no evidence—whether based on misreading of the available data or indifference to evidence. The material in this Invitation is intended to illustrate one of the most obvious misinterpretations. It also introduces the role of a clearly formulated *problem* in controlling interpretation of the data from experiments to which the problem leads.

To the student: (a) An investigator was interested in the conditions under which seeds would best germinate. He placed several grains of corn on moist blotting paper in each of two glass dishes. He then placed one of these dishes in a room from which light was excluded. The other was placed in a well-lighted room. Both rooms were kept at the same temperature. After four days the investigator examined the grains. He found that all the seeds in both dishes had germinated.

TABLE 4.1   Invitations to Enquiry, Group 1, Simple Inquiry: The Role and Nature of General Knowledge, Data, Experiment, Control, Hypothesis, and Problems in Scientific Investigation

Invitation	Subject	Topic
1	The cell nucleus	Interpretation of simple data
2	The cell nucleus	Interpretation of variable data
3	Seed germination	Misinterpretation of data
4	Plant physiology	Interpretation of complex data
Interim Summary 1, Knowledge and Data		
5	Measurement in general	Systematic and random error
6	Plant nutrition	Planning of experiment
7	Plant nutrition	Control of experiment
8	Predator-prey; natural populations	"Second-best" data
9	Population growth	The problem of sampling
10	Environment and disease	The idea of hypothesis
11	Light and plant growth	Construction of hypotheses
12	Vitamin deficiency	"If . . . , then . . ." analysis
13	Natural selection	Practice in hypothesis
Interim Summary 2, The Role of Hypothesis		
14	Auxins and plant movement	Hypothesis; interpretation of abnormality
15	Neurohormones of the heart	Origin of scientific problems
16	Discovery of penicillin	Accident in inquiry
16A	Discovery of anaphylaxis	Accident in inquiry

Source: Joseph J. Schwab, supervisor, BSCS, *Biology Teachers' Handbook* (New York: John Wiley & Sons, Inc., 1965), p. 52. By permission of the Biological Sciences Curriculum Study.

What interpretation would you make of the data from this experiment? Do not include facts that you may have obtained elsewhere, but restrict your interpretation to those from *this experiment alone.*

Of course the experiment is designed to test the light factor. The Invitation is intended, however, to give the students a chance to say that the experiment suggests that moisture is necessary for the sprouting of grains. Others may say it shows that a warm temperature is necessary. If such suggestions do not arise, introduce one as a possibility. Do so with an attitude that will encourage the expression of unwarranted interpretation, if such exists among the students.

If such an interpretation is forthcoming, you can suggest its weakness by asking the students if the data suggest that corn grains require a glass dish in order to germinate. Probably none of your students will accept this. You should have little difficulty in showing them that the data some of them thought were evidence for the necessity of moisture or warmth are no different from the data available about glass dishes. In neither case are the data evidence for such a conclusion.

To the student: (b) What factor was clearly *different* in the surroundings of the two dishes? In view of your answer, remembering that this was a deliberately planned experiment, state as precisely as you can the specific problem that led to this particular plan of experiment.

If it has not come out long before this, it should be apparent now that the experiment was designed to test the necessity of light as a factor in germination. As to the statement of the problem, the Invitation began with a very general question: "Under what conditions do seeds germinate best?" This is not the most useful way to state a problem for scientific inquiry, because it does not indicate where and how to look for an answer. Only when the "question" is made specific enough to suggest what data are needed to answer it does it become an immediately useful scientific problem. For example, "Will seeds germinate better with or without light?" is a question pointing clearly to what data are required. A comparison of germination in the light with germination in the dark is needed. So we can say that a general "wonderment" is converted into an immediately useful problem when the question is made sufficiently specific to suggest an experiment to be performed or specific data to be sought. We do not mean to suggest that general "wonderments" are bad. On the contrary, they are indispensable. The point is only that they must lead to something else—a solvable problem.

To the student: (c) In view of the problem you have stated, look at the data again. What interpretation are we led to?

It should now be clear that the evidence indicates that light is not necessary for the germination of *some* seeds. You may wish to point out that light is necessary for some other seeds [for example, Grand Rapids Lettuce] and may inhibit the germination of others [for example, some varieties of onion].

Note: This Invitation continues to deal with the ideas of data, evidence, and interpretation. It also touches on the new point dealt with under paragraph (b), the idea of a *problem*. It exemplifies the fact that general curiosity must be converted into a specific problem.

It also indicates that the problem posed in an inquiry has more than one function. First, it leads to the design of the experiment. It converts a wonder into a plan of attack. It also guides us in interpreting data. This is indicated in (c), where it is so much easier to make a sound interpretation than it is in (a), where we are proceeding without a clear idea of what problem led to the particular body of data being dealt with.

If your students have found this Invitation easy or especially stimulating, you may wish to carry the discussion further and anticipate to some extent the topic of Invitation 6 [planning an experiment]. (Schwab, 1965, pp. 57–58)

The format of this investigation exemplifies the BSCS mode. The students are introduced to the problem the biologist is attacking, and they are given some information about the investigations that have been carried out. The students are then led to interpret the data and to deal with the problems of warranted and unwarranted interpretations. Next, the students are led to try to design experiments that would test the factor with less likelihood of data mis-interpretation. This syntax—to pose a problem about a certain kind of investigation, and then to induce students to attempt to generate ways of inquiring that will eliminate the particular difficulty in the area—is used throughout the program.

The course proceeds in the inquiry manner. In one invitation the focus is on how we can infer the function of a given part from its observable characteristics (i.e., what is the evidence of function?). In this model, the question is not posed directly. Rather, the student is guided through an area of investigation, which in this invitation has been framed to embed the methodological concern and the spirit of inquiry. Questions are then posed so that the student himself or herself identifies the difficulty and later speculates on the ways to resolve it.

And the issues surrounding the nature of inferences are surfaced. Schwab notes that during the investigation it is reasonable to conjecture that

> Motion, attachment, and shape taken together suggest that muscles in general move one or all of the other parts of the body to which they may be attached. Such inferences about function are only probable. But so are practically all inferences in science. In later queries, we shall make a point of the doubtful character of functional inference. (Schwab, 1965, pp. 174–176)

The course continues in this vein.

Applications to Other Disciplines

A number of models for teaching the disciplines as processes of inquiry exist, all built around the concepts and methods of the particular disciplines. But the overarching principle is that methods of conducting investigations be central. Necessarily, this means that a curriculum contains fewer areas of inquiry than the textbook-oriented, "rhetoric of conclusions" approach.

A SOCIAL SCIENCE EXAMPLE

Next we discuss a social studies inquiry project shaped in the same spirit of inquiry as the BSCS curricula. The structure and inquiry methods of social psychology are used and the curriculum is built around investigations to be conducted by the students.

The Michigan Social Science Curriculum Project, directed by Ronald Lippitt and Robert Fox, was based on an approach that is potentially very powerful but startling in its simplicity. The strategy is to teach the research techniques of social psychology directly to children using human relations content, including their own behavior. The result presents social psychology as a living discipline whose concepts and method emerge through continuous application to inquiry into human behavior. Another result is a direct demonstration of the relevance of social science to human affairs. This curriculum illustrates how elementary school children can use scientific procedures to examine social behavior.

Both the conception of social psychology held by these curriculum makers and their teaching strategy, which is essentially to lead the children to practice social psychology, are probably best illustrated by looking at their materials and the activities they recommend. They have prepared seven "laboratory units" developed around a resource book or text and a series of project books. The seven units begin with an exploration of the nature of social science, "Learning to Use Social Science," and proceed to a series of units in which the students apply social science procedures and concepts to human behavior: "Discovering Differences," "Friendly and Unfriendly Behavior," "Being and Becoming," and "Influencing Each Other."

The first unit is structured to introduce students to social science methods such as:

1. "What Is a Behavior Specimen?" (How do we obtain samples of behavior?)
2. "Three Ways to Use Observation" (Introduces the children to description, inference, value judgment, and the differences among them.)
3. "Cause and Effect" (Introduces the inference of cause, first in relation to physical phenomena, then in relation to human behavior.)
4. "Multiple Causation" (Teaches how to deal with several factors simultaneously. For example, the children read and analyze a story in which a central character has several motivations for the same action.) (Lippitt, Fox, & Schaible, 1969a, pp. 24–25)

The children compare their analyses of the samples so that they check observations and inferences against one another and come to realize problems of obtaining agreement about observations. They also learn how to analyze interaction through the technique of circular analysis. Finally, a series of activities introduces the children to experiments by social psychologists that have generated interesting theories about friendly and unfriendly behavior and cooperation and competition.

This approach focuses the children's study on human interaction, provides an academic frame of reference and techniques for delineating and carrying out inquiry, and involves the student in the observation of his or her own behavior and that of those around him. The overall intention is that the student will take on some of the characteristics of the social scientist. Thus, the instructional values are in the interpersonal as well as the academic domain.

This model has wide applicability, but unfortunately it is dependent on inquiry-oriented materials (areas of investigation), which are rare in most classrooms, since the didactic text is the standard. However, every subject area has at least one text series that is inquiry oriented or easily adapted to this model. An instructor with a clear understanding of the model will easily discern instructional material that, with a little rearrangement, might provide suitable areas for investigation. Instructors who are quite knowledgeable in their particular disciplines can probably construct their own materials.

THE FUTURE

A number of lines of inquiry are currently in progress that will probably advance thinking about how students can learn to build categories, make inferences, and develop more effective causal reasoning and synthesizing skills. Theories about multiple intelligences may give rise to other ways of thinking about thinking.

Computers are making large databases available to students that will make much more complex types of concept formation easier to research and will permit the development of more intricate and powerful support systems. In the social studies, the journal *Social Education* is a goldmine of topics and resources.

Teaching with real documents has long been on the forefront of innovation in social studies teaching and electronic media is making it more and more interesting. For example, digitized resources from 12 presidential libraries are grist for the mill of studying the U.S. presidency through the 20th century (see Resta, Flowers, & Tothero, 2007). Simulations are burgeoning and opening up areas previously difficult to study inductively (see Bennett & Berson, 2007).

Research continues. A particularly striking example is the work of Philip Adey and his colleagues in the UK (see Adey, Hewitt, Hewitt, & Landau, 2004), who have concentrated on the use of scientific inquiry to increase cognitive development and studied how teachers can acquire the very complex science-based models of teaching. Scholars continue to study the effects of inquiry-based science instruction on students' science knowledge and reasoning skills, for there is much to be learned about supporting teachers and faculties in developing young scientists and scientific thinking. (See, for example, Minner, Levy, & Century, 2009; Wilson, Taylor, Kowalski, & Carlson, 2010.)

THE BIOLOGICAL SCIENCE INQUIRY MODEL OF TEACHING

The essence of the model is to involve students in a genuine problem of inquiry by confronting them with an area of investigation, helping them identify a conceptual or methodological problem within that area of investigation, and inviting them to design ways of overcoming that problem. Thus, they see knowledge in the making and are initiated into the community of scholars. At the same time, they gain a healthy respect for knowledge and will probably learn both the ground of current knowledge and its dependability. Importantly, the resulting skepticism needs to be healthy—students should not come to believe that changes in knowledge mean that grounded knowledge should be dismissed. It is the best we have at *this* time (Schaubel, Klopfer, & Raghavan, 1991).

Syntax (Structure of the Model)

The syntax has phases, but they are not rigidly sequenced. In phase one, an area of investigation is posed to the student, including the methodologies used in that investigation. In phase two, the problem is structured so that the student identifies a difficulty in the investigation. The difficulty may be one of data interpretation, data generation, the control of experiments, or the making of inferences. In phase three, the student is asked to speculate about the problem, so that he or she can identify the difficulty involved in the inquiry. In phase four, the student is then asked to speculate on ways of clearing up the difficulty by redesigning the experiment, organizing data in different ways, generating data, developing constructs, and so on.

Social System

A cooperative, rigorous climate is desired. Because the student is to be welcomed into a community of seekers who use the best techniques of science, the climate includes a certain degree of boldness as well as humility. The students need to hypothesize rigorously, challenge evidence, criticize research designs, and so forth. In addition to accepting the need for rigor, students must also recognize the tentative and emergent nature of their own knowledge as well as that of the discipline, and in doing so develop a certain humility with respect to their approach to the well-developed scientific disciplines.

Principles of Reaction

The teacher's task is to nurture the inquiry by emphasizing the process of inquiry and inducing the students to reflect on it. The teacher needs to be careful that the identification of facts does not become the central issue and should encourage a good level of rigor in the inquiry. He or she should turn the students toward the generation of hypotheses, the interpretation of data, and the development of constructs, which are seen as emergent ways of interpreting reality.

Support System

A flexible instructor skilled in the process of inquiry is a must. The course can be presented at distance, but considerable access to an instructor is important; a hybrid structure with strong teaching on the campus is probably best.

SUMMARY CHART   *Biological Science Inquiry Model*

Syntax

Phase One: Pose Area of Investigation
Phase Two: Students Structure the Problem
Phase Three: Students Identify the Problem in the Investigation
Phase Four: Students Speculate on Ways to Clear Up Difficulties

Social System

The model has moderate structure and a cooperative, rigorously intellectual climate.

Principles of Reaction

Teacher nourishes inquiry, turning students toward inquiry process rather than identification efforts.

Support System

The model requires a flexible instructor skilled in the process of inquiry and a supply of problem areas of investigation.

INSTRUCTIONAL AND NURTURANT EFFECTS OF CONCEPTUAL, INVESTIGATION-ORIENTED CURRICULUM

Scientific inquiry models have been developed for use with students of all ages. In Ginny's second-grade class and in John's fifth-grade class, students learn science content and processes through structured investigations. The biological science inquiry model (Figure 4.1) is designed to teach the content and

FIGURE 4.1   Instructional and nurturant effects of the biological science inquiry model

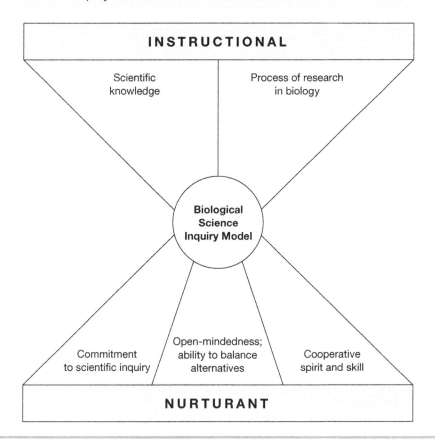

processes of research biology to older students, to affect the ways students process information, and to nurture a commitment to scientific inquiry. It probably also nurtures open-mindedness and an ability to suspend judgment and balance alternatives. Through its emphasis on the community of scholars, it also nurtures a spirit of cooperation and an ability to work with others.

CHAPTER FIVE

The Picture Word Inductive Model

Developing Literacy through Inquiry

It's inquiry, inquiry, *INQUIRY! Do I sound like a broken record?*
Thelen was right! It's inquiry, not activity!

—Emily Calhoun to Bruce Joyce, for the thousandth time

Here are some classroom scenes of the picture word inductive model in action. Figure 5.1 shows Lisa Mueller leading her students as they study a picture of an archeological/anthropological dig and "shake" the labels or words for objects, actions, and ideas out of the picture. In a sense, they are "shaking words out of the picture."

Figure 5.2 shows the wall of the classroom after the students have completed several cycles of the picture word inductive model (PWIM). If you look around the picture of the bucking bronco, you will see words that the students have shaken out of the picture as they have studied it and begun to identify objects, actions, and emotions. Words have been added on cards with subsequent study of the scene. The students study these words, compare and contrast them, and organize them into categories as they have done in all of the PWIM cycles that have begun with the study of a picture.

OVERVIEW OF THE MODEL

The picture word inductive model is an inquiry-oriented, integrated language arts approach to developing literacy. Each cycle of the picture word inductive model (PWIM) uses a large photograph as a common stimulus for the generation of words and sentences. The teacher, working with the whole class or with small groups of students, uses the moves that comprise a PWIM cycle to support the development of students' oral language and vocabulary; their

FIGURE 5.1   An invitation to inquiry

FIGURE 5.2   A wall in Lisa's classroom

phonological awareness and word analysis skills; their reading comprehension and composing at the word, phrase, sentence, paragraph, and extended text levels; and their observation and research skills. The cycles of a PWIM inquiry usually last from two to six weeks.

Each PWIM cycle begins with a picture, usually a photograph that includes many details that students can describe using their developed listening–speaking language (see Figure 5.3). The students study the picture and then *shake out* the words—putting into words the representations and actions they see in the picture. The teacher draws a line from those things to a place outside the picture, reiterates the word, and writes and spells the word or phrase aloud. The students repeat the word and its spelling following a "See, Say, Spell, Say" pattern: the teacher points to the item in the photograph (See); the students pronounce the word (Say); they spell the word together with the teacher (Spell); and they pronounce the word again (Say). This pattern provides a mnemonic chain that helps anchor the pronunciation and spelling of the words. What emerges as students identify items and actions is an illustrated picture-word dictionary.

The next phase begins by providing students with their individual sets of word cards. The students check whether they can recognize words immediately or decode them if necessary, using the picture-word dictionary if they have difficulty. It's easy to assess students' knowledge and skills as the teacher

FIGURE 5.3   Tracy and students start a PWIM chart

Bruce Joyce

moves around among the students. As students begin to read the words, the next phase of the model comes into play: students classify the words in terms of phonetic, structural, or content properties and share their categories and why they put a particular set of words together. The categorization activity occurs regularly during the PWIM cycle.

To expand vocabulary and prior knowledge, teachers collect a set of non-fiction and informational books, including big books if they are available, that relate to the photograph and their purposes for selecting it. Some of these texts are used by the teacher for short content-area read-alouds, and others are used by the students for learning content and practicing literacy skills simultaneously. In the primary grades, teachers often identify and flag websites that have video clips or other types of digital media for extending learning; at the upper elementary level, students are much more involved in identifying and exploring websites. Some of the words from teacher read-alouds and students' reading and exploration are added to the PWIM chart if they are present in the photograph; other words may be added to the Related Words chart; and still others find their way into sentences as students expand their vocabulary and knowledge within each PWIM inquiry.

Frequently, the next phase is generating titles and sentences for the picture. Students are asked to generate factual sentences about the picture, dictating them to the teacher. (The sentences are descriptive. Students do not use the picture to start a fictional story.) New words from the sentences and titles may be added to students' vocabulary banks. After the students can fluently read the sentences, they are asked to classify them into groups by content or common patterns of syntax or structure and provide reasons for their classifications. Beginning writers are starting the study of composing sentences.

As the PWIM cycle continues, the teacher selects one of the sentence categories and models writing a well-organized paragraph, sharing her thinking about how she used the ideas in the sentences and modified the structures, if needed, to form the message about the picture that she wishes to share with her readers. Next, in whatever way is appropriate to the developmental level of the students (e.g., a combination of drawing and writing, dictated pieces), they generate their own paragraphs. The PWIM cycle ends anytime after the paragraph development.

Let's visit a primary grade class for a closer look at PWIM in action.

SCENARIO

PWIM IN A GRADE ONE CLASSROOM

We are in another of Lisa Mueller's first-grade classes. We are looking at a section from Lisa's PWIM planning guide that describes a cycle in which her 23 students were engaged for 22 sessions, each about 50 minutes long, during the second month of school, October 2–30. She continues with more cycles throughout the year and then conducts a set of studies of the students' learning. Figure 5.4 shows a marketplace in Mexico. Lisa says to her students, "You have had a couple of days to look at the picture and identify things in it. Let's take turns putting words to some of the things you have found." As each item is named, Lisa draws a line from the word to a place on the background paper where she prints it, then has the students spell it and say it. The students review the words frequently, spelling them, saying them, and tracing the line from the word to the picture, learning how to use the chart as a picture dictionary. During the first session, 22 words and phrases (such as *umbrellas, woman, palm trees, blue and white striped umbrella*) are shaken out of the picture.

These words are entered into the computer and printed out on cards, a set of which is given to each student. Three activities alternate during the next few days. First is a review of the words as a class: looking at the PWIM chart, selecting a word, tracing it to the element in the picture to which it refers, spelling the word, and so on. ("Look at your cards, one by one. If you can say the word on a card, then look at the picture chart, find the word, trace it to the picture, and make sure you

FIGURE 5.4   A market scene in Mexico

Bruce Joyce

are right.") Second, each student looks at the cards, decides whether he or she recognizes the word correctly, and, if not certain, goes to the PWIM chart to figure it out. Third, each student classifies the words, manipulating his or her cards into groups containing common attributes. ("Look carefully at the words. Then make groups of words that have something in common.") During classification, several categories of words emerged, particularly words with common beginnings (such as beginning consonant blends in *trees, truck, trunk;* "all have two *e's* together and *e* says its name," for the category *trees, wheels, three*); "they have two words and both begin with the letters *t a i l* for *taillights* and *tailgate.*" Plural forms also emerged (such as *umbrellas, trees, wheels*). Lisa prints some of the categories on the interactive whiteboard, and the students discuss what the words have in common and think of other words that might fit into the categories. An additional 12 words appear, some of which Lisa adds to their Word Wall (among them are *standing, walking, leaning,* and *curved*).

At the beginning of the second week of the PWIM cycle, the children are asked to generate titles for the pictures. ("I'm going to show you some other pictures and titles I've made for them. Then I want you to make up a title for our picture. Try to make a title that would help a visitor find our picture from among the other pictures in the room.") Lisa models some titles and asks the students to examine the titles of several books as further models. Each student creates a title.

As the students continue to discuss the picture and what they notice in it, the words *shadow, people,* and *scale* are added to the PWIM Chart; 11 words are added to the Related Words list (e.g., *shopping, market, produce, consumers, farmers, orchards*), and more words are added to the Word Wall (*parked, scale*). Throughout the second week, the children continue to study the words, using the picture-word dictionary and classifying the words on their word cards. Lisa engages them in a number of instructional activities that develop phonemic awareness and the use of analogies. For example, she used the rimes in the words *tail, light,* and *gate* (-ail, -ight, -ate) from two of the compound words, *taillight* and *tailgate,* that students had shaken out of the picture for work on initial consonants, rhyming words, substitutions, and deletions.

Lisa also does many short content area read-alouds to build vocabulary and world knowledge and as a model to encourage her students to explore and learn from the books and texts available. While using the photograph in Figure 5.4 as part of a PWIM cycle, students inquire into books about markets around the world, communities, types and purposes of transportation, and Mexico—to name a few of the text sets available. Some students read these texts; some do picture walks; some collect new words for their PWIM notebooks. From the very first PWIM cycle, Lisa tries to establish a culture of learning from and enjoying texts and gathering information from multiple sources for oral discussions, composing, and research.

At the end of the second week, Lisa and her teaching assistant, Cecile, check the students' knowledge of the words out of the context of the picture, the titles, and the sentences by presenting the words to the students on cards that show only one word. Nine students could correctly read 14 to 22 of the words, and seven could read between 8 and 13. Six students correctly identified only 1 to 7 at the end of the second week.

At the beginning of the third week, Lisa presents sentences she has written about the picture, modeling several sentence structures:

The man is walking into the market.
The scale can be used to weigh the fruits and vegetables.
Umbrellas also provide shade from the sun.

During the week the students dictate their own sentences, using the words they shook out of the picture plus other words that are needed to make sentences. Many of their sentences include high frequency words such as *the, is, are, by,* and *from.* Lisa also has students illustrate at least one sentence in their PWIM notebooks.

The students continue to study the words and read the sentences. At the end of the week, Lisa and Cecile assess the recognition of the words again. During that week there was a considerable gain in words recognized; most students were able to read 20 or more. Only one student did not gain any words. Some students were able to read many of the titles and sentences without assistance.

During the last week of the PWIM cycle, Lisa and the students classified some of the sentences into content categories, such as sentences about the setting, about items in the market, about transportation, all about the truck. Some of the students were curious about the three-wheeled cycle; they did not think that the word *tricycle* would convey to readers what they saw in the picture. So, Lisa used the web to pull up several images, and together they decided the best match and most accurate description was a "cargo tricycle."

Lisa also constructed a paragraph using one of the categories, making some modifications to the sentences the students had generated. The paragraph was printed on a card program, making a booklet the students could take home and read to their parents.

The school participates in the school division's Just Read program (see Joyce & Wolf, 1996; Joyce & Calhoun, 1996). Each week this first-grade class records the number of books that have been read to them, or that, as they learn to read, they read themselves. The goal is for the parents to read at least five books each week to their children. The average by the last three weeks in October was six books, but there was variance; in any given week, two or three parents did not report any books or reported only one. However, the least number during the three-week period was three books—all students were being read to at least occasionally.

There was no gender difference. As the children learn to read, the titles and numbers of the books they read themselves will be recorded, and Lisa and Cecile will make sure that each child selects items at a comfortable level for learning and for at-home reading and sharing.

STUDYING STUDENT LEARNING

During the school year, Lisa conducted several studies, including sight word acquisition and retention, an analysis of the degree to which high-frequency words were included in the body of words, the development of phonetic and structural analysis skills, books read independently, and reading levels attained.

Sight Words

Altogether the students encountered 1029 words during the year, recorded where everyone could read them (picture-word charts, sentences, paragraphs, labeling of objects in the classroom, and words placed on the Word Wall). These were separate from the words encountered and figured out by individuals in their personal reading. Of the 1029, 377 words came from the initial weeks of the PWIM cycles. Cycles began in September and continued at irregular intervals through the year. Retention of those 377 words by individual students was assessed in May—the assessment was in a separate room, and the words were presented individually on flashcards and thus out of the context of the pictures, sentences, and Word Walls. On average, the students read 91 percent of the words correctly. The lowest-performing student read 59 percent correctly.

The following September, as the students were entering the second grade, the students' retention of vocabulary was tested again. On average, the students recognized 91 percent of the words in out-of-context assessments in May and September. The average number read correctly was 90 percent. The lowest-performing student had retained the 59 percent read correctly the previous May. Importantly, Lisa had learned that the students had put many of the words into long-term memory, probably due to their working on them throughout the school year, using them in sentences and paragraphs, and encountering them in books, not only reading them as part of the PWIM inquiries. Lisa also wanted to know how many high-frequency words her students were learning. The words generated in the PWIM cycles are those represented in the pictures; therefore, not all of them are the high-frequency words found in textbook series and the most popular early-level trade books. Lisa tested the students' recognition of the Dolch lists of the 400 highest frequency words that appear in typical texts and basal programs through grade 3. On average, the students recognized 87 percent of the words, with a range of 49 to 100 percent. Fifteen of the 22 students recognized 90 percent or more of the Dolch list words. Thus, although the PWIM cycles do not introduce the sight words systematically according to predetermined lists, these first-grade students appear to be learning them at a good rate.

Skill in Phonics

The PWIM cycles do not introduce phonics skills one by one in a predetermined manner, as is the case in the highly sequenced approaches common in synthetic phonics programs. The students analyze words and develop phonics concepts inductively and through explicit instruction and concept attainment lessons.

Lisa explored the degree to which her students had mastered the basic phonics generalizations. In May she administered the Names Test (Cunningham, 1990, 2005; Duffelmeyer, Kruse, Merkley, & Fyfe, 1994), in which the students try to decode unfamiliar words that, among them, contain all the basic phonics combinations. A perfect score on the test indicates that basic letter–sound relationships have been used correctly when decoding the words. The average score of her students was 81 percent. The lowest was 62 percent. Four students scored 95 percent or better. This picture is considerably better than the typical performance of first-grade classes assessed in this manner.

Books Read Across the School Year

The number ranged from 60 (about two per week) to 300 or more. The average number of books read was about 200 (remember that many of the books in the first months are carried by the pictures). By the end of the year, most of the students were reading grade level and above books. To support her students' learning content while they were also learning to read and learning about how language works, Lisa made sure that students had easy access to a broad range of genres. She made a special effort to ensure that about fifty percent of classroom texts were high quality, nonfiction texts (e.g., concept books, informational/explanatory texts, narrative nonfiction).

End-of-Year Performance on Standardized Tests of Reading Achievement

At the end of the year, 22 students who had been enrolled throughout the year were administered the Alberta Diagnostic Test, which provides estimates of reading achievement in terms of grade levels. Nineteen were at the "end of grade 1" level or above. The distribution was

- Mid-grade 6 level: Two students
- Mid-grade 4 level: Three students
- Beginning of grade 3 level: Six students
- End of grade 2 level: Two students
- End of grade 1/beginning of grade 2 level: Six students
- Mid-grade 1 level: Three students

Individualized, Performance-Based Standardized Tests

Lisa was a member of a team that used the Gray Oral Reading Tests (GORT-4) (Wiederholt & Bryant, 2001), an individualized measure of performance levels used to assess reading across the school district. The team administered the test to 15 students at the end of the year, and the grade level equivalent (GLE) scores are in Table 5.1. The data indicate that many of these end-of-first-grade students are reading and comprehending fluently, well above grade level.

The GORT results are consistent with the provincial achievement tests. A GLE score of 2.0 is the cross-national average for students at the end of grade 1. Importantly, scores of 3.0 or better in grades 1 and 2 indicate that the student is a competent, independent reader who is building a good-sized sight vocabulary and, hopefully, a complement of word-analysis skills.

TABLE **5.1**   Gray Oral Reading Tests (GORT-4) Scores, Students Assessed in June 2010

Grade 1 GLE Scores	
6.0	2.7
2.9	3.7
1.4	5.2
2.7	3.7
3.2	5.7
10.2	5.0
5.0	6.7
4.4	

In sum

Lisa Mueller is a very fine teacher-researcher. She continues to learn new models of teaching and how to use them, as well as study student progress and involve students in studying their own progress as readers and writers. Lisa is the teacher in several of the demonstration videos at http://modelsofteaching.org.

Following the cycle with the first picture of a market, Lisa decides to use another market picture (Figure 5.5), one that students will mine by, again, "shaking out the words," and another cycle will begin.

Rationale of the PWIM model

Whereas many models of teaching have relatively long histories that have been refined through several generations of developers, there are only a handful of powerful new models that we consider for inclusion in *Models of Teaching* as we prepare each edition. The picture-word inductive model is a recent addition and is unusual for the breadth of its grounding and the width of its applications. As the name suggests, inductive learning is built in, drawing on the huge base

FIGURE 5.5   Market street scene

Bruce Joyce

of research on inductive teaching/learning and on cooperative learning research as well.

The grounding is in research in the field of literacy—how students develop literacy in general (particularly how they learn to read and write), inductive teaching and learning, *and* literacy in all curriculum areas. The development of metacognitive control is central—learning how to learn is built into the process. Emily Calhoun developed the model over a 20-year period, and its applications have enabled thousands of students to increase their achievement substantially.

Central is the nature of student learning as students construct knowledge about printed language (phonetic, structural, and contextual analysis) and develop the skills of extracting and organizing information in multiple curriculum areas. In some senses, this is the ultimate constructionist model because general literacy is the base on which curriculum-relevant literacy is developed.

To become an expert reader, people need to read a lot, develop large sight vocabularies, develop skill in phonetic and structural analysis, and learn to comprehend and use extended text. All these are essential as students learn to understand text across the curriculum areas, where the gathering, conceptualization, and application of information is at the core of achievement.

Let's begin with a series of propositions derived from studies of how students become literate.

• **A Natural Social Process.** First, children learn to listen and speak the languages spoken to them in a most natural way. In an Arabic speaking household, they would learn to hear and reproduce Arabic, and they would learn French in a French household. In homes where large vocabularies and complex syntaxes are used, they develop large vocabularies and complex syntaxes. Importantly, the process builds on children's desire to use language as they interact with others and attempts to capitalize on their natural learning capacity.

• **The Concept-Wired Brain.** Second, inductive thinking is built into our brains, as described in Chapters 1, 2, and 3. Children classify from birth, sorting out the world. They are natural conceptualizers.

• **A Need to Understand.** Third, children seek meaning. They want to understand their worlds by organizing what they perceive, and they reach toward language as a source of meaning.

• **The Interactive Environment.** Fourth, interaction with adults and peers is the basic mechanism in socialization. Interaction through reading is an important part of socialization as the young reader encounters information and ideas. The depth of socialization is enormously affected by literacy. Nonreaders have a serious disadvantage in learning the culture and a serious deprivation of the pleasure that accompanies learning through interaction with authors.

All this is not to assert that reading and writing come so naturally that instruction is not necessary, but rather to stress that the natural ways children approach the learning of language can be capitalized on when teaching literacy. A challenge for us is to design curricula that will take advantage of these natural abilities so as to make the learning of reading and writing an extension of what our children are born to do.

The picture-word inductive model was developed to meet the challenge, and its conceptual underpinnings drew on the body of research about how literacy is acquired and on the bodies of research underlying the models of learning we have been describing in the previous chapters.

PWIM AND LITERACY CURRICULUM

Although the model is useful in other curriculum areas, we will concentrate here on its application to the reading/writing curriculum in the early years of schooling. The model (Calhoun, 1999; Joyce & Calhoun, 1998) can be a major component of language arts curricula for primary-level beginning readers and older beginning- or early-stage readers. It resides within the information-processing family because much of the pedagogical focus is on structuring lessons so that students inquire into language and form and use generalizations about how letters, words, phrases, sentences, and longer text work to support communication within the English language arts. The model also contains a number of tools to help teachers study students' progress as they come into literacy. In fact, using the picture word inductive model effectively requires an action research frame of reference, because you don't just adopt or buy into PWIM, you inquire into its theory and rationale, its structure, and its effects on your students. The earlier scenario is an illustration of superior-quality action research at the classroom level. Two recent studies, one in Alberta, Canada, and the other in Saskatchewan, Canada, illustrate the strength of the model in school and district-wide implementations (see Joyce, Hrycauk, Calhoun, & Hrycauk, 2006; and Joyce, Calhoun, Jutras, & Newlove, 2006. See also Chapter 9 in Joyce & Calhoun, 2012, and Chapters 5 and 6 in Joyce & Calhoun, 2010).

The Flow of the Model

We use the model beginning in preschool and kindergarten as well as through the upper elementary grades to support inquiry in the content areas. By the time most children in developed countries are 5 years old, they are able to listen to and speak between 4000 and 6000 words with understanding, and have developed the basic syntactical structure of the language (Chall, 1983; Clark & Clark, 1977). They can listen with understanding to complex sentences and longer communications. They produce sentences that include prepositions and conjunctions and make causal connections like "If we go to the store now, we could watch *Thomas* when we get back." They gobble up words, play with them, and have conversations with stuffed animals and dolls—composing ideas and manipulating words very much like they will later when they write. Children's natural acquisition of language is one of the most exciting inductions into their culture and brings with it a great sense of personal power and satisfaction.

In the first phase of the picture word inductive model, students are presented with enlarged photographs of relatively familiar scenes. They "shake out" the words from the photograph by identifying objects, actions, and qualities they recognize. A line is drawn from the object out to the chart paper, where the word or phrase is written, thus connecting the items they identified to words already in their naturally developed listening–speaking vocabularies. You might take a minute and shake out some of the words in Figure 5.6.

These connections between the items and actions in the picture and the children's language enable them to transition naturally from spoken (and listened to) language to written (and read) language. They see these transformations. They watch the words being spelled and spell them with the teacher. They connect something in the picture with a word and then watch that word appear in print. They can now read that word. Shortly, they learn that we always spell that word the same way. They identify a dog in the picture, see *dog*

FIGURE 5.6 Baby and dog

Bruce Joyce

written, hear it spelled, spell it themselves, and on the way home from school they see a lost dog sign on the street corner and read *dog*.

Thus, a major principle of the model is to build on children's growing storehouse of words and syntactic forms and facilitate the transition to print. Most children want to "make sense" of the language around them, and they will engage with us eagerly in unlocking its mysteries. A corollary principle is that the approach respects the children's language development: their words are used and their ability to make connections is central. Mnemonic principles, especially the development of rich associations to generate long-term retention, are explicitly capitalized on as the vocabulary is developed.

The Process of Learning to Read and Write

Much remains to be learned about the almost magical process whereby children make connections between their naturally developing language and the world of print, surely a cognitive marvel. Our understanding at this time is that several types of learning need to be accomplished as reading and writing develop.

To learn to read and write, children need to build a substantial sight vocabulary—that is, a storehouse of words they can recognize instantly by their spellings. About 400 to 500 words are necessary to bring children to the stage where many easy nonfiction texts and story picture books are available to them. Although, even 100 to 150 words bring very simple books like *Go, Dog, Go* (Eastman, 1961) and *Ten in the Bed* (Dale, 1988) within reach, and when students reach this level, easy informational texts can be used for learning to read and reading to learn, texts such as *My Five Senses* (Aliki, 1989), *About Birds: A Guide for Children* (Sill, 2013), and *Born to be a Butterfly* (2000). Also, once students have about 50 sight words, their study of phonics is greatly facilitated, as are many other aspects of learning, including the development of more vocabulary (Graves, Watts, & Graves, 1994).

The picture word inductive model approaches the development of sight vocabulary directly. First, the students read and spell the words as they are shaken out of the picture. Then, these words are placed on large vocabulary cards that they can look at and the teacher can use for group instruction. Students also get their own set of smaller vocabulary cards. They sort these words and consult the picture dictionary to check their understanding and refresh the meaning of the words. The students keep their word cards in word banks or word boxes, consulting them as they wish and eventually using them to compose sentences.

Children also need to build concepts about the conventions used in language to connect sounds and structures to print forms. With respect to sound/print (*phonetic*) forms (also called *phonics, grapheme/phoneme* or *letter–sound* relationships), they need to learn that nearly all the words that begin with a particular sound begin with particular letters representing those sounds. Periodically, a teacher using PWIM might ask students to pull out all the words they have in their word bank that contain the letter *b,* and they will concentrate on that letter for a while, wherever it is in the word. Another time, all the words with *at* will get attention. After the students have learned to read most of the words on the PWIM chart, the teacher may ask them to pull out all the words in which they can hear a certain sound.

With respect to the structure of words, students need to build an understanding of inflection, the change in form that words undergo to indicate number, gender, person, tense, case, mood, and voice. Students learn to notice the similarities and differences between singular and plural words (as in how *book* and *books* are alike and different).

The picture word inductive model induces students to classify and reclassify their new words, building the concepts that will enable them to unlock words they have not seen before. This active classification and attention to word properties help build sight vocabulary and word recognition skills (Graves, Juel, & Graves, 2001). The English language has about 44 sounds represented in more than 200 forms—some say as many as 250 forms (Morris, 1997)—because some sounds have multiple representations (*shut, nation*). As students work with their words, they will develop many categories: these words all begin like *boy*; these all have two *d*'s in the middle like *ladder.* They will develop phonograms or rhyming families (*bat, cat, hat*) that they will use to read and spell words they have not memorized previously (*mat*). And they will learn that the generalizations they make enable them to unlock about 70 percent of the new words they encounter for they will have learned to read words by sight, by using analogies to words they already know, by using context, by pronouncing common spelling patterns they recognize within the words, and by sounding out and blending graphemes and phonemes into words (decoding). They will have had much practice learning different ways to read words (Ehri, 1999, 2005).

Students will be amused at some of the ways we spell words (*ate, eight*), and, like the rest of us before them, they will sigh occasionally at our insistence that they learn the peculiarities our language has developed. They will be perplexed by *see* and *sea* and will want to know why we made them sound alike. At times, all we can say is what some of our teachers said to us: "You'll just have to memorize them."

In sum, the picture word inductive model capitalizes on children's ability to think inductively. It enables them to build generalizations that form the basis of structural and phonetic analysis. And it respects their ability to think. Thus, a major principle of the model is that students have the capability to make and use those generalizations that reveal to them the conventions of language.

The Reading/Writing Connection

As the students mine a picture for words, those words are spelled correctly by the teacher and written on the picture dictionary, which launches the students into the early stages of formal writing. Later the students will be asked to compose sentences about the picture, and with the help of the teacher, they begin to write longer pieces. Through much repetition, the words in the sentences are added to their storehouse of knowledge, and maybe even physically added to their word banks. Gradually, as they read more and more trade books, the students learn to analyze how other authors write, and they use the devices of these authors to enhance their ability to express themselves. Essentially, they come to use our great literature and prose base (the library of the world) as a model for learning even more about writing to share and communicate ideas. As they read more short informative books and picture storybooks, they will discuss them, and some of these books or sections will serve as mentor texts and models for their own writing. From some texts, they will gather information about the topics and concepts they are studying and consider why the author shared the information in that form and how they, as authors, might share their ideas. Many will come to feel that the reading of a book is not complete until they have said something about it in their own words, completing the communication loop between the writer and the reader in constructing meaning.

As the students study the world through photographs, they will feel the need to understand what they see, to think about its purpose, and to consider what it represents and what it does not represent. For example, when an author includes a photograph like the one in Figure 5.7, students will not only recognize items and actions in the picture, but will think about the purpose, the setting, and the context. They will provide their own caption, mentally or in writing, if one is not present. As students progress through school and use more newspapers and magazines, print or digital, and more web sources, they will think about the author's purpose(s) for including particular images—whether they are photographs, illustrations, graphs, charts—and the nature and source of the evidence presented through the images.

From kindergarten on, students and teachers work together to build words, sentences, paragraphs, and books. As they build paragraphs, they will select and discuss titles. The teacher will lead discussions on why one title is chosen over another, which title is most comprehensive, which title might be most interesting to one audience or another, which sentences would go with one title, which with another. When writing a paragraph or creating a title, the teacher will help students focus on the essence of communication: what do we want to say to our readers, to ourselves? The students will use the reading/writing connection as the teacher has them think about what they want to

FIGURE 5.7   On a photo safari in Africa

Bruce Joyce

share, what they most want the reader to know, how they will help the reader "get" this information, and, finally, to assess whether they shared what they wished. The teacher will continue to work on this link until it becomes explicit and accessible for their use as independent learners.

Thus, the model follows another major principle—that reading and writing are naturally connected and can be learned simultaneously, and later can be used together to advance one's growth in literacy. Relational concepts (see Chapters 3 and 6) are critical. If singular nouns are connected to singular verbs in speech, so should they be connected when writing. If authors write titles that promise readers particular content and approach to content, beginning writers learn to promise readers content and approach as they shape titles.

In the first PWIM scenario, we watched Lisa Mueller teaching grade 1 students. Now, let's watch Lori Kindrachuk as she works with middle school students who are struggling—actually beginning—readers.

S C E N A R I O

LORI'S READ-TO-SUCCEED CLASS

Lori is teaching a Read-to-Succeed class of students from grades 6 and 7. The 90-minute per day class is designed for students who are seriously struggling with reading and writing. At the beginning of this school year, the sixth-grade students' mean grade level equivalent (GLE) score is 3.0, where the overall average for sixth graders would be 6.0.

The picture word inductive model (PWIM) is an important component of the course. On an average day, students will spend about 30 minutes in the PWIM investigations and study, about 20 minutes reading books at their independent and instructional levels, and about 20 minutes writing. And, each day, Lori reads to them and models comprehension and word solving skills, discussing those skills as she reads—and imparting information and ideas from books they are not yet able to read. We will follow Lori and her class through a PWIM cycle.

Phase I: Studying the Photograph and Shaking Out the Words

Lori presents the picture in Figure 5.8 to the students and asks them to study it. The picture is about 24 × 36 inches and is mounted on a large sheet of light yellow paper.

After the students have studied the photograph, Lori asks them to identify objects and actions in the picture and, one by one, to share them. As they do so, Lori draws a line from the object to a space where she writes the word given by the student. She spells the word while the students listen and then spells it with them. Gradually, a picture dictionary is created (see Figure 5.9).

FIGURE 5.8   Two elephants

Bruce Joyce

FIGURE 5.9   Using the PWIM chart to study word properties

Bruce Joyce

Over the next couple of days, the students "shake out" 25 words, which Lori reviews with them—spelling the words and asking students to spell them. She makes a file and prints out copies on card stock, giving a set of word cards to each student. She asks them to study the words by reading them. If they have trouble reading a word, they can refer to the chart, tracing the word to its object or action. Although all the words were within the students' listening–speaking vocabularies, there were several that the students could not read when they looked at the cards out of the context of the picture, necessitating further study. A major objective is to add words to students' sight vocabulary—that is, words that are recognized instantly. Fluent reading requires a sizable sight vocabulary. Lori has also assembled a number of nonfiction books on elephants and on the African savannah, some with small vocabularies; this cycle will add some words that will make it easier for students to read them.

Most of the words the students identify are nouns referring to specific objects or parts of them (e.g., *building, flower,* and *reflection*). Some were two words—an adjective and a noun, such as *stone pillar* and *leathery skin*. About 25 words were in the initial "shake out." More will be added as the students continue to find information in the photograph and explore other resources to answer questions they generate. For example, in their first pass, the unusual structure is referred to only as a "building."

Phase II: Analyzing Word Attributes, Building Categories, and Developing Word Solving Strategies

Analyzing Word Attributes. Lori asks the students to examine the words, thinking about their attributes, and then leads them in a series of exercises where she asks them to look for identifying features in the words. She asks questions to focus their thinking. They locate rimes within the word, such as "-ink" within *pink, drink,* and *wrinkles.* One student noticed the word *leather* in *leathery;* another student noticed that *leathery* had the words *eat* and *her* "inside it." Two other students identified the compound words *grasslands* and *toenails.* This led to a discussion of whether *pine tree* was also a compound word.

Lori has students analyzing word properties and using their phonics and structural analysis skills throughout the word work lessons, asking questions such as, "What did we do to change *water lily* to *water lilies*?" From *trunk,* she asks them what to do to spell *skunk* and *shrunk,* and they explore the "unk" family of words, ending with an assignment to figure out what *debunk* means. She knows that many struggling readers have developed an aversion toward reading, including word analysis, and she wants to lead them to approach their fears and uncertainties directly so that they will have richer sets of attributes with which to associate and remember the words (see the discussion of mnemonics in Chapter 8). And she wants them to develop more word-analysis skills than they currently possess.

Building Categories. Lori now asks the students to sort the words using their word cards, concentrating on what some words have in common. They can build categories based on related content, such as the characteristics of the elephants; or word properties such as how they are spelled, as in *"drinking* and *building* both have the suffix *–ing"; "leaves* and *leathery* both begin with *l-e-a* but the beginnings don't sound the same."*

The students are asked to test their mastery of the words by turning away from the chart and showing themselves each word, card by card, sorting into piles the ones they can read and those where they need to consult the chart. Lori asks them to keep studying the words, aiming for 100 percent recognition. About once a week, she tests the students individually, recording their progress and noting words that a number of the children have trouble reading. She will conduct a quick review of the words each day and give special attention to the "goofy" words, as she calls the more troublesome ones. For some words, spelling patterns, or phonics generalizations that students continue to have difficulty with, Lori may turn to other models such as concept attainment (Chapter 6) and explicit strategy instruction (Duffy, 2009; and Chapter 16 in this text) to ensure mastery.

Phase III: Creating Sentences

Lori announces the next task, which is to create sentences by studying the chart. This provides students opportunities to compose at the sentence level and to use many of the high-frequency words they encounter regularly in text (e.g., *the, of, and, in*). They elaborate their descriptions of what they see, giving them practice using accurate verbs, adverbs, and adjectives and providing Lori with opportunities to expand their syntax and knowledge of the English language and how it works.

In their first PWIM cycle, Lori models making sentences for the students. She begins with a category containing just two items: *building* and *stone pillars*. Lori shares her thinking as she works. "I thought I would just begin with the relationship—what the pillars do for the building. So, I started with 'The building sits on tall stone pillars.' Notice that I focused on one of the unique characteristics of the building. I began my sentence with the word *The*; it is a very useful word. When you are reading silently, notice how many times it is used on a couple of pages in your book. I choose the word *sits* because that seemed to be what the building is doing, perched on the pillars. Actually, I think it's more accurate to say the building is *resting* on the pillars: *sitting* or *perching* sounds as if it might get up and leave. Let's change the sentence to 'The building rests on tall stone pillars.' I added the words *tall* and *stone* to tell the reader both how the pillars looked and something about what they are made of. I started to wonder why the building *is* on pillars. . . ."

Lori models composing another sentence and then asks her students to make some of their own. She says that studying the photograph and/or building on a word category may help get a sentence started because the words often are all about the same topic or action.

The students look at their groups of words and begin to compose their sentences. Over several sessions they generate and share them. Lori writes them on a chart, and they read the list together as sentences are added. She also adds some new words to the original PWIM chart and puts them on word cards that she distributes for students to add to their word banks.

We can easily see the importance of certain useful words as her students compose. *There* is such a word as it appears in nine of the first 26 sentences:

"*There* is a reflection on the water."
"*There* are leaves floating in the water."

Forms of the "to be" verb and several prepositions appear: *in, on, of*. Some compound and complex sentences also appear:

"Two elephants with tusks stand near a waterhole; both are drinking water."

When Lori has the students read the whole list of sentences, the quantity of prose in them exceeds the amount that several of them have ever read in one sitting. Importantly, they are starting to sense progress, even this early in their first PWIM cycle.

Phase IV: Making Titles

Next, Lori gives them the assignment of developing titles for the picture: "I want you to make a title that captures what is there. Imagine that someone had the title and then came in here, where we have lots of big photographs, and could go straight to this photograph. Read through our sentences and see what comes to mind."

In a couple of days, Lori gathers the class into a circle and asks each person to contribute a title. A variety of titles appear, providing students with even more text to read. Here's a sample:

"The Two Elephants"
"A Big Drink of Water"
"The Mystery House on Stilts"
"The Water Hole"
"Elephants at the Water Hole"

Lori then asks her students to identify sentences that could fit under one of those titles.

John offers, "These elephants seem really big."
Mary says, "Their trunks are like giant gray straws."
Sarah muses, "Is that round building on pillars to keep those big elephants out?"

And so we get some more ideas—and sentences to read!

Phase V: Classifying Sentences

Lori's printer hums again and sentence strips appear. "Now, I need you to read the sentences carefully—several times, not just once. And think about their attributes. You can think about their topic, such as what information they contain or about how they are written. Look carefully at them. Then classify them into categories, just as you did the words."

Lori illustrates by putting these two sentences together and sharing her reasoning:

Behind the elephants there are bushes and brown grass.
Elephants live in grasslands in Africa.

"I put these together because one describes where African elephants live in general and the other one describes something about their habitat, the environment where these two actually live. So they have some content in common. Some categories might have how they are written in common." Figure 5.10 displays one of the student categories.

FIGURE 5.10 Students make categories with sentence strips

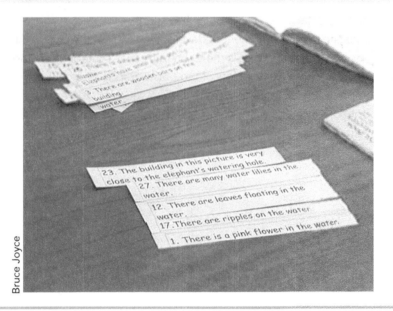

Bruce Joyce

The students work at home and a few minutes each day in class. When she judges that everybody has a couple of categories they can share and explain, Lori gathers them into their work circle.

Josh says, "I put numbers 5, 12, and 17 together because they all say something about the water."

Niento says, "I put numbers 2, 4, 12, and 16 together. Something is happening in all of them."

And the sharing continues. Some categories contain descriptions of the elephants and others deal with the flowers. The students learn that some sentences end up in several categories where different attributes are emphasized. Now, just like categories of words led to the writing of sentences, content categories of sentences lead to the writing of paragraphs.

Note that reading and writing are being learned together. Words are recognized because of how they are spelled, and knowing how to spell them is a fundamental part of writing. Writing sentences provides material to read. Writing paragraphs will provide more passages to read. The print language flows from the already developed listening–speaking vocabularies of the students, building the new form, print, from the previously developed language. New vocabulary and concepts are added as students explore answers to their questions, such as "Where is this? What kind of elephants are these? What are those buildings for? What kind of building is that?" and so on.

Phase VI: Composing—From Sentences to Paragraphs

In the past, Lori's students have barely been able to write legibly, let alone generate a coherent paragraph. By the end of the year, she expects them to be writing short essays and stories, but right now we have arrived at the first formal lesson on composing beyond the sentence level. Figure 5.11 shows Lori during this lesson in which she uses the PWIM chart, the sentences that students generated, one of the sentence categories, and a paragraph she has composed.

"We're going to build paragraphs using our sentences and the photograph. First, I will model how to write a paragraph.

"I have looked through the sentences and put together a category of all the things that happen around this watering hole, that gives me sentences 1, 2, 5, 12, 16, 17, and 27. I had in mind the title, 'The Watering Hole.' Then I took ideas from the sentences, made some of my own, and here is my paragraph." Lori reads it to them.

FIGURE 5.11   The picture word chart, the list of sentences, Lori, and a paragraph

Bruce Joyce

Reflections

The watering hole is a gathering place for African elephants. These enormous creatures set off ripples in the water as they use their trunks to drink. Water lilies grow in clusters along the water's edge. Large floating leaves surround the perfect pink flowers. Reflected in the water, the elephants and the flowers mingle in the ripples.

After she has read her paragraph, Lori does a composing think-aloud (see Figure 5.12) and discusses which sentences she used, how she put them together, and how and why she made modifications or additions.

"Now I want to talk to you about what I was thinking as I wrote the paragraph. I hope it will help you as you think through what you write.

"Let's begin with the title. I put all these sentences in one category because they described things that were occurring at the waterhole, so I thought a good title would be 'The Watering Hole.' And, in my first sentence I wanted to introduce my reader to the place and what was present.

"I changed the word *elephant* in the second sentence to *enormous creatures* to add something more than just repeating *elephant*. In the third sentence, I added

---

FIGURE 5.12   Lori's paragraph for her composing think-aloud

Bruce Joyce

in clusters to our sentence about water lilies growing because it described the groups of flowers near the water's edge and what we learned about how water lilies grow.

"In my fourth sentence, I wanted to provide more detail about the water lilies, so I used information from our sentences 1, 12, and 27. I decided to change 'pretty pink flowers' from one of the sentences to '*perfect* pink flowers' because the lily I can see the best looks so delicate and perfect. Also, I wanted to keep the sound— the alliteration from the consonant sound /p/ at the beginning of each word—of *perfect* and *pink* together.

"One of my favorite things about this picture is the reflection in the water. So in my last sentence I wanted to talk about reflections. I used sentences 2, 5, and 17 and combined the information to make my last sentence. Because I liked the way the reflections mixed or blended in the water, I decided to use the word *mingle* to represent that mixture. I also hoped my reader would think about the contrast of the delicate flowers mixing with the leathery elephants in the reflections.

"My first title was 'The Water Hole,' then I changed it to 'Reflections.' Now, I am thinking about changing it to *Reflections at the Watering Hole* to identify the place and because to me the reflections are a special part of what I noticed when I studied the photograph and thought about what we had said in some of the sentences. That happens sometimes—you get a new idea or clarify one as you write.

"Now, take one of your categories of sentences. Think about what you might say and what title you might use. We will use our writing time each day until you have a whole paragraph. Each day, you'll have a few minutes to share your thinking about what you want your readers to take away and what you are doing as a writer."

In Sum

This PWIM cycle lasts about three weeks. The students study the words and Lori watches their progress. They read and write—just reading their paragraphs will be as much as reading some short books! By the end of the cycle, each student will have acquired about 30 sight words and some new ways of identifying words. Lori is teaching them to print more legibly and has started teaching them cursive writing, which will affect their writing fluency considerably. This year these students will, on average, gain 2.0 GLE—it will be as if they had been in school for two years compared to the national average gain and will be four times the gain any of them made in a previous year.

But we are getting ahead of ourselves.

As their fourth week with Lori begins, she presents students with the photograph in Figure 5.13 and says, "Last month we visited Africa, this month we . . ."

FIGURE 5.13   In the Outback

Bruce Joyce

As they break for recess, the students will notice that, now, a number of books on farms around the world have appeared in the classroom collection. Thus, Phase I of a new cycle begins.

USING THE PICTURE WORD INDUCTIVE MODEL OF TEACHING AND LEARNING

The picture word inductive model is an inquiry-oriented model of teaching whose structure scaffolds the students to ever more complex tasks (see Table 5.2). Hopefully, the scenarios illustrate how a teacher can use the model to structure student inquiry into the English language and how it works.

The model provides a multidimensional curriculum for teaching beginning readers and writers (Calhoun, 1999). Full use of the model includes multiple opportunities for explicit instruction by the teacher and concept formation by the students through structured inductive activities. In the primary grades, and for students learning English as a second language, its focus is on developing skills in reading and writing. However, it is also a useful model for teaching information and concepts in the social sciences when working with older students who are already reading on their own (Joyce & Calhoun, 1998).

The Picture Word Inductive Model   SUMMARY CHART

Syntax and Sequence

1. Select a picture. The teacher does this. The scene may or may not relate to the basic content areas depending on purpose and student needs.
2. Students identify what they see in the picture.
3. Students provide words for what they see. The teacher draws a line from the picture to the word, says the word, spells the word while pointing to each letter, says the word again, then students spell the word with the teacher. A picture-dictionary emerges.
*4. Teacher leads reviews of the picture-word chart, emphasizing characteristics of the words and leading the students to continue to spell and read them. (See/Say/Spell/Say)
*5. Students classify the words and share the categories they develop. (Word cards are printed out and given to each student.)
6. Often, at this point, more words are added to the picture-word chart and to the word banks in the room.
7. Students generate titles for their picture-word chart. The teacher leads students to think about the "evidence" and information in their chart and about what they can say about this information.
*8. The teacher models writing sentences about the picture, using the composing think-aloud processes described in Chapter 16.
*9. The students generate and share sentences directly related to their picture-word chart. The teacher records these, giving students copies from the interactive white board or from the chart paper.
*10. Students classify the shared sentences.
11. The teacher models putting the categories of sentences together into an effective paragraph.
12. The students practice writing or dictating paragraphs. These can be used to build a book to be shared with their parents.

*Indicates moves that occur many times during most PWIM cycles.

Phonics/Grammar/Mechanics/Usage

1. Students hear the words pronounced correctly many times, and they have an immediate reference source to use (the picture-word chart) as they add these words to their sight vocabulary. At the teacher's discretion, almost any sound/symbol relationship can be emphasized (introduced or taken to mastery).
2. Students hear and see the letters identified and formed correctly many times.
3. Students hear the words spelled correctly many times and participate in spelling words correctly.

4. In writing the sentences, the teacher uses standard English usage (transforming student sentences if necessary) and uses correct punctuation and mechanics (commas, capital letters, and so on).

Social System

A cooperative-inquiry environment is developed. The students work together to learn to read and write, listen and discuss, question and investigate.

Principles of Reaction

Knowing how to respond to the students and accelerate their learning depends on a continuous flow of information. The structure of PWIM affords a number of opportunities to study students' learning and application of content and therefore to scaffold moves accordingly. Watching how students identify characteristics of words and how effectively they classify the words provides essential data in regulating review and determining next instructional moves. Examining the sentences students dictate or write has the same function—helping teachers decide how much to model and talk through the composing processes. The model rolls—phases can be repeated and tasks can be modulated to meet the needs of students.

Support System

Enlarged photographs, lots of chart paper, card stock for making word cards, and sentence strips are needed. An interactive whiteboard is excellent for inductive work and composing think-alouds. When the picture is related to a content area unit, many books on the unit concepts need to be available—books at a range of levels. The teacher will use read-alouds, talk-alouds, and think-alouds to help build comprehension and composing skills.

The picture-word chart needs to be posted prominently and provide easy access as a reading/writing resource for students. Encourage students to create their own picture-word charts on plain paper or construction paper.

Most picture word inductive model cycles take five to 15 days. They can take 20 to 30 days depending on the number of words generated, the conceptual richness of photograph(s), and the objectives of the work.

Instructional and Nurturant Effects of the Picture Word Inductive Model

Students build their sight vocabularies, learn how to inquire into word and sentence structures, generate writing (titles, sentences, paragraphs), use the reading/writing connection, develop skill in phonetic and structural analysis, develop interest and capacity to express themselves, increase reading of and learning from informational texts, and develop cooperative skills in working with others. Figure 5.14 highlights some of the instructional and nurturant effects of the picture word inductive model.

FIGURE 5.14   Instructional and nurturant effects of the picture word inductive model

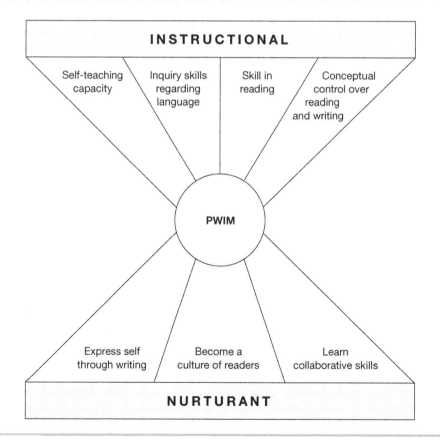

Teachers hold the keys to literacy for many students—keys that provide access and choice. The more words students have in their listening and speaking vocabularies, the more understanding they have of the world around them. The more words they have in their reading and writing vocabularies, the more control and choice they have in life, both in and out of school, along with greater access to knowledge and experience and greater potential for teaching themselves. The more understanding they have of how language works, the more powerful they are and can become as communicators and citizens.

PART THREE

Special Purpose Information-Processing Models

These models emphasize learning to process information and have important places in the advanced repertoire of models of teaching. Some, like advance organizers and mnemonics, boost traditional conceptual and informational outcomes. Others, like concept attainment and synectics, boost specific types of learning—concepts in the former and metaphoric thinking in the latter. Inquiry training is a great deal of fun, builds morale, and is designed to sharpen basic thinking skills.

In the *concept attainment model* students examine data sets to learn categories selected by the teachers. Whereas the students have to organize data and build concepts in the inductive models, here the teachers organize the data sets and lead the students to attain concepts the teachers have selected. With the *synectics model* the students learn to use metaphoric thinking to break set, develop new ideas, and invent novel solutions to problems. Teachers build presentations around *advance organizers*—they increase learning by providing conceptual ladders to scaffold the information and ideas being studied. *Mnemonic devices* help students learn and retain information and ideas, importantly, become tools they can use to become more competent when they need to absorb and maintain information. Finally, *inquiry training* focuses on learning to ask focused questions and thinking carefully about the replies.

As we will remind ourselves continuously, a major outcome of these models is the development of capacity to learn, to collect and approach information confidently, and to help one another to become a community of learners. The tools learned by finding and managing information support the social, personal, and behavioral families. Information-processing models provide academic substance to social models, ways of thinking for personal inquiry, and goals for many of the behavioral models.

CHAPTER SIX

Concept Attainment

The Explicit Teaching of Important Concepts

What that kid did made the point so everybody could hear it. Four times last week he was in concept attainment lessons taught by the student teachers. So he said we owed him one. If we'd get him some second-graders to teach, he'd make a data set and teach the same kind of lesson. And he wanted to be videotaped like the student teachers were. So we got him the kids and he taught the lesson and he did a great job. So now everybody understands that the whole point is to teach the kids the model, and practice will do it.

—Kay Vandergrift, director of the Agnes Russell School, to Bruce Joyce

We will begin with several scenarios. Lori Kindrachuk, coordinator for Literacy for Life in the Saskatoon, Saskatchewan, public schools, designed this series of lessons with the concept attainment model.

ORGANIZING IDEA

We can "form" concepts, as with the inductive, sciencing, and PWIM models. We can also "attain" or learn the concepts developed by others, as in the concept attainment model. In this model students are presented with data sets and led to discover that some items belong to a predetermined category.

LORI'S FIRST LESSON

The first lesson was built for sixth-grade students who are struggling readers and writers (see Joyce and Calhoun, 2010, pp. 104–107). The lesson was part of a series to help the students read more discerningly—many, when reading aloud, read with little inflection, indicating poor comprehension of devices like interjections. This set of lessons was designed to help the students understand these devices as well as add them to their writing repertoire. Let's look at the development of the data sets.

This first lesson was built around the concept of interjections. Lori's notes were to clarify the concept as she built the lesson:

- *Definition:* An interjection is a word added to a sentence to convey emotion. It has no grammatical function in the construction of a sentence. Interjections are usually used when quoting spoken words and should be avoided in business writing.
- *Punctuation:* Either a comma or an exclamation mark can follow an interjection. A comma is used for a mild interjection, whereas an exclamation mark is used for a more abrupt display of surprise, emotion, or deep feeling.

She has developed a set of sentences, some of which contain the attributes of interjections and some of which do not. The students are to arrive at the concept by comparing the positive exemplars and negative exemplars.

1. In this set all the positive exemplars begin with an interjection (a word added to convey emotion).
2. All have a short phrase or sentence following the interjection that quotes spoken words.

The students are presented with the sentences, one by one, after Lori makes an orienting opener to them to help them focus: "All the items in our data set are sentences. The ones I will indicate as positive exemplars (yeses) have two common attributes or characteristics. One of the attributes you are looking for is *something in the way the each statement is written*; the other you will need to think about is the *meaning of the statement* (what it actually says). The negative exemplars do not have those attributes."

> The first six positive sentences are very clear examples of interjection. They start with one colorful word followed by an exclamation mark and a short related phrase, also followed by an exclamation mark. These sentences clearly convey emotion.

Having given the opening orientation and asked for questions of clarification, Lori presents the data set in pairs. The first pair is:

Yippee! We won! (positive)
We won the game. (negative)

The students ponder the differences and make notes.

The next pair is:

Ouch! That hurt! (positive)
It hurt when the needle poked me. (negative)

Again, the students reflect and Lori asks them to compare the differences between the positive and negative exemplars. She mixes the order of positive and negative so that the students can't use order without thinking about the nature of the attributes.

The next pairs are:

Whoa! Hold your horses!
Try to slow down and be patient.

> The first six negative examples state the same information as the positive examples without using an interjection and with less emotion.

Wow! That is a giant pumpkin!
That is a very big pumpkin.

Hey! Put that down!
You shouldn't touch things that don't belong to you.

Yikes! There's a fire in the oven!
The grease is on fire!

Now Lori asks the students whether they have a hypothesis about the attributes that separate the positive and negative exemplars. They do not share their hypotheses orally; if a student states a conclusion, the other students tend to "shut down" their investigation.

Now she presents another series of pairs where the differences are not as dramatic as in the first pairs.

Hurry! The bus is about to leave.
The bus is leaving!

> In the next three examples an exclamation mark follows the interjection in the positive exemplars. The sentence following the interjection does not have an exclamation mark and does not have the same level of surprise emotion or feeling as the first sentence.

Phew! I'm not trying that again.
I'll never do that again!

Oh! You're here.
You're finally here!

Now she asks the students whether they have new hypotheses. Next, she asks them to try to change some positives into negatives: "Please remove the part of the sentence that makes these positives."

> The next three sentences end with an exclamation mark and convey emotion, but they do not start with an interjection.

Ah, now I understand.
Gosh, I'm tired.

Then she has students make some negatives into positives.

> You mean the exam is today!
> That was a real surprise!

If they can do these tasks, then they are probably beginning to attain the concept.

Finally, Lori gives them a short story whose prose contains a good many interjections and asks them to find them. The inquiry will continue. This kind of lesson frequently stretches over several days and, importantly, is part of a long unit where the students are studying reading and writing.

Lori also connects the class to Tumblebooks (www.tumblebooks.com) and they watch and listen as authors read their books. She has selected several books that include interjections and the students can listen to the authors as they inflect those words and phrases.

Several times when an author had read a sentence beginning with an interjection, Lori interrupted the reading, moved the video back to the beginning of the sentence, and had the students read it without the interjection, discussing the effect that adding or removing the interjection had on the meaning and interest of the sentence. If you take a look at Tumblebooks, you will have no difficulty locating books where inflected interjections are employed.

SCENARIO

LORI'S SECOND LESSON

Lori generated this unit after learning that a number of second-grade students were having problems with some structural analysis/phonics concepts. For example, students had overgeneralized the "hard" sound of *g*. They would read or spell *page* as "paggey." This was not their only structural/phonics problem, so Lori wished to draw the students into an inquiry that would help them straighten out the concepts that govern sounds in the context of words.

Her notes indicate how she selected the items in the set. All positive exemplars contain two attributes:

- Successive *ge*
- The *ge* must represent the /j/ sound

Her presentation begins with seven pairs where the differences are relatively unambiguous. She asks the students to compare the positive and negative exemplars and try to develop hypotheses about the attributes that the positives have that are not shared by their partners. The pairs are presented one by one.

Positive Exemplars	Negative Exemplars	
1. age	ace	The first seven words all end with *ge*. These words using the same word family (and vowel) were selected to make it easier for the students to see the pattern. All have one syllable.
2. cage	came	
3. page	plate	
4. rage	rate	
5. wage	wade	
6. sage	sale	
7. stage	grade	

Lori asks the students to reflect on any hypotheses they may have developed, but not to share them with the other students, because each student needs to develop their own—once someone else shares an idea, students tend to stop their independent thinking and try to test the hypothesis that was shared.

Now she presents another set of seven pairs.

Positive Exemplars	Negative Exemplars	
8. bridge	gate	The next seven positive words continue to end in *ge*. They are still one syllable. They now have different vowels and mixed word families.
9. huge	game	
10. range	gave	
11. hedge	gale	
12. urge	grape	
13. large	grade	
14. dodge	great	

In this set the placement of the letters is prominent. The negatives have both *g* and *e* but they are not together in sequence. The idea is for the students to refine their hypotheses as they see that the /j/ sound is generated when the *g* and *e* are together in sequence.

In the next set of positive exemplars placement is changed, showing that the *ge* combination is associated with the /j/ sound whether at the beginning or middle of the word and in multiple-syllable words.

15. germ	The *ge* combination is at the beginning of the first three words. By the fourth word *ge* has moved to the middle of the word. The last four words have two syllables. My students were able to change *agent* to *angry*, *urgent* to *rent*, and *digest* to *dig* to make them into negatives.
16. gel	
17. gem	
18. angel	
19. agent	
20. urgent	
21. digest	

And, finally, Lori presents some negative exemplars where the *ge* combination is in sequence, but the "hard" *g* sound is produced. What is the difference?

> The last seven words all contain a *ge* in succession; however, the *ge* makes the hard sound of /g/. The last four examples are specifically chosen as they are easy to turn into a positive (ragged/rage, anger/angel, forget/forge, singer/singe).

22. getting
23. together
24. forget
25. ragged
26. anger
27. forge
28. singer

Here, we see that bringing the students into inquiry, even in the structure of words and the association of letter combinations with sounds, involves attaining concepts that are not just that simple, but the development of sets can help the students gain control of the concepts and develop the skills to employ them in writing as well as reading. Let's now look at a different application of the same model.

SCENARIO

CITIES IN CATEGORIES

Mrs. Stern's eighth-grade class in Houston, Texas, has been studying the characteristics of the 21 largest cities in the United States. The class members have collected data on size, population, ethnicity, types of industry, location, and proximity to natural resources. The web has helped, including www.infoplease.com and www.quickfacts.census.gov. The information has been summarized on a series of charts now pasted up around the room and available for display on the interactive whiteboard.

One Wednesday in November, Mrs. Stern says, "Today let's try a series of exercises designed to help us understand these cities better. I have identified a number of concepts that help us compare and contrast them. I am going to label our charts either yes or no. If you look at the information we have and think about the populations and the other characteristics, you will identify the ideas that I have in mind. I'm going to start with a city that's a yes and then one that's a no, and so forth. Think about what the yeses have in common. After the second yes, write down the idea that you think connects those two places, and keep testing those ideas as we go along."

"Let's begin with our own city," she says. "Houston is a yes."

The students look at the information about Houston, including its size, industries, location, and ethnic composition. Then she points to Baltimore, Maryland. "Baltimore is a no," she says. Then she points to San Jose, California. "Here is another yes," she comments. The students look for a moment at the information about San Jose. Two or three raise their hands.

"I think I know what it is," one offers.

"Hold on to your idea," she replies. "See if you're right." She then selects another yes—Seattle, Washington; Detroit, Michigan, is a no. Miami, Florida, is a yes. She continues until all students think they know what the concept is, and then they begin to share concepts.

"What do you think it is, Jill?"

"The yeses all have mild climates," says Jill. "That is, it doesn't get very cold in any of them."

"It gets pretty cold in Salt Lake City," objects another.

"Yes, but not as cold as in Chicago, Detroit, or Baltimore," another student counters.

"I think the yeses are all rapidly growing cities. Each one of them increased more than 10 percent during the last 10 years." There is some discussion about this.

"All the yeses have lots of different industries," volunteers another.

"That's true, but almost all of these cities do," replies another student.

Finally the students decide the yeses are all cities that are growing very fast and have relatively mild climates.

"That's right," agrees Mrs. Stern. "That's exactly what I had in mind. Notice that each one shares two attributes, not just one. Now let's do this again. This time I want to begin with Baltimore, Maryland, and now it is a yes."

The exercise is repeated several times. Students learn that Mrs. Stern has grouped the cities on the basis of their relationship to waterways, natural resources, ethnic composition, and several other dimensions.

The students are beginning to see patterns in their data. Finally she says, "Now, each of you try to group the cities in a way that you think is important. Then take turns and lead us through this exercise, helping us see which ones you place in which category. Then we'll discuss the ways we can look at cities and how we can use different categories for different purposes. Finally, we'll use the inductive model and you can see how many relationships you can find."

In this scenario Mrs. Stern is teaching her students how to think about cities. At the same time she is teaching them about the process of categorizing. This is their introduction to the model of teaching we call *concept attainment*.

CATEGORIZING, CONCEPT FORMATION, AND CONCEPT ATTAINMENT

Concept attainment is "the search for and listing of attributes that can be used to distinguish exemplars from nonexemplars of various categories" (Bruner, Goodnow, & Austin, 1967, p. 233). Whereas *concept formation*, which is the basis of the inductive model described in Chapter 3, requires the students to decide the basis on which they will build categories, concept attainment requires a student to figure out the attributes of a category that is already formed in another person's mind by comparing and contrasting examples (called *exemplars*) that contain the characteristics (called *attributes*) of the concept with examples that do not contain those attributes. To create such lessons we need to have our category clearly in mind.

As an example, let us consider the concept *adjective*. Adjectives are words, so we select some words that are adjectives (these become the positive exemplars) and some that are not (these become negative exemplars—the ones that do not have the attributes of the category). We present the words to the students in pairs. Consider the following four pairs:

triumphant	triumph
large	chair
broken	laugh
painful	pain

It is probably best to present the words in sentences to provide more information, because adjectives function in the context of a sentence. For example:

Yes: Our *triumphant* team returned home after winning the state championship.
No: After her *triumph,* Senator Jones gave a gracious speech.
Yes: The *broken* arm healed slowly.
No: His *laugh* filled the room.
Yes: The *large* truck backed slowly into the barn.
No: She sank gratefully into the *chair.*
Yes: The *painful* separation had to be endured.
No: He felt a sharp *pain* in his ankle.

To carry on the model, we need about 20 pairs in all—we would need more if the concept were more complex than our current example.

We begin the process by asking the students to scrutinize the sentences and to pay particular attention to the italicized words. Then we instruct them to compare and contrast the functions of the positive and negative exemplars: "The positive exemplars have something in common in the work they do in the sentence. The negative exemplars do different work."

We ask the students to make notes about what they believe the exemplars have in common. Then we present more sets of exemplars and ask them whether they still have the same idea. If not, we ask what they now think. We continue to present exemplars until most of the students have an idea they think will withstand scrutiny. At that point we ask one of the students to share his or her idea and how he or she arrived at it. One possible response is as follows: "Well, at first I thought that the positive words were longer. Then some of the negatives were longer, so I gave that up. Now I think that the positive ones always come next to some other word and do something to it. I'm not sure just what."

Then other students share their ideas. We provide some more examples. Gradually the students agree that each positive exemplar adds something to the meaning of a word that stands for an object or a person, or qualifies it in some way. We continue by providing some more sentences and asking the students to identify the words that belong to our concept. When they can do that, we provide them with the name of the concept (*adjective*) and ask them to agree on a definition. The final activity is to ask the students to describe their thinking as they arrived at the concept and to share how they used the information given. For homework we ask the students to find adjectives in a short story we assign them to read. We will examine the exemplars they come up with to be sure that they have a clear picture of the concept.

This process ensures that the students learn the attributes that define a concept and can distinguish those from other important attributes that do not form the definition. All the words, for example, are composed of letters. But the presence of letters does not define the parts of speech. Letters are important characteristics of all items in the data set, but are not critical in defining the category we call *adjective*. The students learn that it is the function of the word that is the essence of the concept, not what it denotes. *Pain* and *painful* both refer to trauma, but only one is an adjective.

As we teach the students with this method, we help them become more efficient in attaining concepts. They learn the rules of the model. Let us look at another example, this time language study for beginning readers.

S C E N A R I O

CONCEPTUAL PHONICS

Christine Reynolds presents a class of 6-year-old students with the following list of words labeled *yes* or *no*:

fat	(yes)
fate	(no)
mat	(yes)
mate	(no)
rat	(yes)
rate	(no)

She says, "I have a list of words here. Notice that some have *yes* by them and some have *no* by them." The children observe and comment on the format. "Now, I have an idea in my head, and I want you to try to guess what I'm thinking of. Remember the list I showed you. This will help you guess my idea because each of these is a clue. The clues work this way." The teacher points to the first word and says, "If a word has a yes by it, then it is an example of what I'm thinking. If it has a no by it, then it is not an example."

The teacher continues to work with the students so that they understand the procedures of the lesson and then turns over the task of working out the concept to them.

After a while, the teacher says, "Can you come up with a name for my idea? Do you know what my idea is?" The students decide what they think the teacher's idea is. She continues the lesson: "Let's see if your idea is correct by testing it. I'll give you some examples, and you tell me if they are a yes or a no, based on your idea."

She gives them more examples. This time the students supply the no's and yeses.

kite   (no)
cat   (yes)
hat   (yes)

"Well, you seem to have it. Now think up some words you believe are yeses. The rest of us will tell you whether your example is right. You tell us if we guessed correctly."

The exercise ends with the students generating their own examples and telling how they arrived at the concept.

In this lesson, if the children simply identified the concept as the /at/ vowel–consonant blend and correctly recognized *cat* and *hat* as a yes, they had attained the concept on a simple level. If they verbalized the distinguishing features (essential attributes) of the *at* sound, they attained the concept on a higher level. Bruner outlines these different levels of attainment: correctly distinguishing examples from nonexamples is easier than verbalizing the attributes of the concept. Students will probably be able to distinguish examples correctly before they will be able to explain either the concept name or its essential characteristics.

Concept teaching provides a chance to analyze the students' thinking processes and to help them develop more effective strategies. The approach can involve various degrees of student participation and control and material of varying complexity.

RATIONALE OF THE CONCEPT ATTAINMENT MODEL

We have used terms such as *exemplar* and *attribute* to describe categorizing activity and concept attainment. Derived from Bruner's study of concepts and how people attain them, each term has a special meaning and function in all forms of conceptual learning, especially concept attainment.

Essentially the exemplars are a subset of a collection of data or a data set. The category is the subset or collection of samples that share one or more characteristics that are missing in the others. It is by comparing the positive exemplars and contrasting them with the negative ones that the concept or category is learned.

Attributes

All items of data have features, and we refer to these as *attributes*. Nations, for example, have areas with agreed-on boundaries, people, and governments that can deal with other nations. Cities have boundaries, people, and governments also, but they cannot independently deal with other countries. Distinguishing nations from cities depends on locating the attribute of international relations.

Essential attributes are attributes critical to the domain under consideration. Exemplars of a category have many other attributes that may not be relevant to the category itself. For example, nations also have trees and flowers, but these are not relevant to the definition of nation—although they, too, represent important domains and can be categorized and subcategorized as well. However, with respect to the category "nation," trees and flowers are not essential.

Another important definition is that of *attribute value*. This refers to the degree to which an attribute is present in any particular example. For instance, in any given situation, everyone has some rationality and irrationality mixed together. The question is when is there enough rationality that we can categorize someone as "rational" or enough irrationality that "irrational" is an appropriate description. For some types of concepts, attribute values are not a consideration. For others, they are.

When creating a data set we begin with exemplars where the value of the attribute is high, dealing with the more ambiguous ones after the concept has been well established. Thus, when classifying nations according to wealth, beginning with the very rich and the very poor makes it easier for the students. As we categorize things, we have to deal with the fact that some attributes are present to various degrees. We have to decide whether any presence of an attribute is sufficient to place something in a particular category and what range of density qualifies something to belong to a category. For example, consider the category *poisonous*. We put chlorine in water precisely because chlorine is poison. We judge the amount that will kill certain bacteria and still not harm us, but if we added enough chlorine, it would affect us. So tap water in a city is not an exemplar of poisonous water because although it contains poison, it does not contain enough to harm us. In this case, if the value of the attribute is low enough, its presence does not give the water membership in the category *poisonous to humans*.

Now consider the category *short person*. How short is short enough to be so categorized? People generally agree on a relative value, just as they do for tall. When is something cold? Hot? When is a person friendly? Hostile? These are all useful concepts, yet the categorization issue turns on matters of degree, or what we call *attribute value*.

In other cases, value is *not* a consideration. To be a telephone, an instrument simply must have certain characteristics. Yet there are degrees of quality. A question such as, "When is a sound machine a high-fidelity instrument?" puts us back into the consideration of attribute values.

Once a category is established, we name it so that we can refer to it symbolically. As the students name the categories, they should do so in terms of attributes. Thus, in the scenario at the beginning of the chapter, they will describe the category as words containing "ge" and sounding like /j/. Then, if there is a technical term (such as *adjective* in one of the other previous examples), we supply it. However, the concept attainment process is not one of guessing names. It is to get the attributes of a category clear. Then the name can be created or supplied. Thus, the name is merely the term given to a category. *Fruit, dog, government, ghetto* are all names given to a class of experiences, objects, configurations, or processes. Although the items commonly grouped together in a single category may differ from one another in certain respects (dogs, for example, vary greatly), the common features cause them to be referred to by the same general term.

Often we teach ideas that students already know intuitively without knowing the name itself. For instance, young children often put pictures of fruit together for the reason that they are "all things you can eat." They are using one characteristic to describe the concept instead of the name or label. If students know a concept, however, they can easily learn the name for it, and their verbal expressions will be more articulate. Part of knowing a concept is recognizing positive instances of it and also distinguishing closely related but negative examples. Just knowing terms will not suffice for this. Many people know the terms *metaphor* and *simile* but have never clarified the attributes of each well enough to tell them apart or apply them. One cannot knowingly employ metaphoric language without a clear understanding of its attributes.

Multiple attributes are a critical consideration. Concepts range from cases in which the mere presence of a single attribute is sufficient for membership in a category to those in which the presence of several attributes is necessary.

Membership in the category *red-haired boys* requires the presence of male-ness and red hair. *Intelligent, gregarious, athletic red-haired boys* is a concept that requires the presence of several attributes simultaneously. In literature, social studies, and science we deal with numerous concepts that are defined by the presence of multiple attributes; attribute value is sometimes a consid-eration as well. Consider the theatrical concept *romantic comedy*. A positive example must be a play or film, must have enough humor to qualify as a comedy, and must be romantic as well. Negative exemplars include plays that are neither funny nor romantic, are funny but not romantic, and are roman-tic but not funny.

To teach a concept, we have to be very clear about its defining attributes and about whether attribute values are a consideration. We must also select our negative exemplars so that items with some but not all the attributes can be ruled out.

We call concepts defined by the presence of one or more attributes *con-junctive concepts*. The exemplars are joined by the presence of one or more characteristics. Two other kinds of concepts need to be considered. *Disjunctive concepts* are defined by the presence of some attributes and the absence of oth-ers. Inert gases, for example, have the properties of all other gases but are missing the property of being able to combine with other elements. Bachelors have the characteristics of other men, but are identified by an absence of something—a spouse. Lonely people are defined by an absence of companion-ship. Prime numbers are defined by the absence of a factor other than one and the number itself.

Finally, some concepts require connection between the exemplar and some other entity. Parasites, for example, have hosts, and the relationship between the parasite and its host is crucial to its definition. Many concepts of human relationships are of this type. There are no uncles without nephews and nieces, no husbands without wives, and no executives without organiza-tions to lead.

Strategies for Attaining Concepts

What goes on in the minds of students when they are comparing and con-trasting sets of exemplars? What kinds of hypotheses occur to them in the early stages and how do they modify and test them? To answer these questions, three factors are important to us as we design a lesson or unit. First, we con-struct concept attainment exercises so that we can study how our students think. Second, the students should be able to not only describe how they attain concepts, but also learn to be more efficient by altering their strategies and learning to use new ones. Third, by changing the way we present information and by modifying the model slightly, we affect how students will process information.

The key to understanding the strategies students use to attain concepts is to analyze how they approach the information available in the exemplars. In particular, do they concentrate on just certain aspects of the information (*partistic strategies*), or do they keep all or most of the information in mind (*holistic strategies*)? To illustrate, suppose we are teaching concepts for analyzing literary style by comparing passages from novels and short stories. The first set of positive exemplars includes the following passage:

> A new country seems to follow a pattern. First come the openers, strong and brave and rather childlike. They can take care of themselves in a wilderness, but they are naive and helpless against men, and perhaps that is why they went out in the first place. When the rough edges are worn off the new land, businessmen and lawyers come in to help with the development—to solve problems of ownership, usually by removing the temptations to themselves. And finally comes culture, which is entertainment, relaxation, transport out of the pain of living. And culture can be on any level, and is. (Steinbeck, 1952, p. 249)

The students know that this passage will be grouped with the others to come, on the basis of one or more attributes pertaining to style. Some students will therefore concentrate on just one attribute, say, the use of declarative sentences or the juxtaposition of contrasting ideas about the opening of the frontier. Others will scan the details of the passage, noting the presence or absence of metaphors, the use of evocative language, the author's stance of being an observer of the human scene, and so on.

When comparing this passage with another positive one, a partist (someone who focuses on just one or two aspects of the use of language) will in some sense appear to have an easier task—just looking to see whether the attribute present in the first is also present in the second, and so on. However, if the student's focus does not work out, he or she must return to the earlier examples and scan them for something else on which to concentrate. A holist, on the other hand, has to keep many attributes in mind and eliminate nondefining elements one at a time. But the holistic strategy places the learner in a good position to identify multiple attribute concepts, and the loss of a single attribute is not as disruptive to the overall strategy.

There are two ways that we can obtain information about the way our students attain concepts. After a concept has been attained, we can ask them to recount their thinking as the exercise proceeded—by describing the ideas they came up with at each step, what attributes they were concentrating on, and what modifications they had to make. ("Tell us what you thought at the beginning, why you thought so, and what changes you had to make.") This can lead to a discussion in which the students can discover one another's strategies and how they worked out.

Older students can write down their hypotheses, giving us (and them) a record we can analyze later. For example, in a study of the classification of plants conducted by Baveja, Showers, and Joyce (1985), students worked in pairs to formulate hypotheses as pairs of exemplars (one positive and one negative) were presented to them. They recorded their hypotheses, the changes they made, and the reasons they made them. The holistic students painstakingly generated multiple hypotheses and gradually eliminated the untenable ones. The students who selected one or two hypotheses in the early stages needed to review the exemplars constantly and revise their ideas in order to arrive at the multiple-attribute concept that was the goal. By sharing their strategies and reflecting on them, the students were able to try new ones in subsequent lessons and to observe the effect of the changes.

If we provide students with a large number of labeled exemplars (ones identified as positive and negative) to commence a lesson, they are able to scan the field of data and select a few hypotheses on which to operate. If we provide the exemplars pair by pair, however, the students are drawn toward holistic, multiple-attribute strategies.

Many people, on first encountering the concept attainment model, ask about the function of the negative exemplars. They wonder why we should not simply provide the positive ones. Negative exemplars are important because they help the students identify the boundaries of the concept. For example, consider the concept *impressionism* in painting. Impressionistic styles have much in common with other painting styles. It is important for students to "see" examples that have no traces of impressionism for them to be absolutely certain about the defining attributes. Likewise, to identify a group of words as a prepositional phrase, we need to be able to tell it from a clause. Only by comparing exemplars that contain and do not contain certain attributes can we identify the characteristics of the attributes precisely, and over time. The concept attainment model is designed to produce long-term learning. Having struggled our way to precise definitions of *prime number, element, developing nation, irony,* and so on, we should recognize members of their categories positively and surely when we encounter them in the future.

Tennyson and Cocchiarella (1986) have conducted important research into concept learning and developed a number of models that can be used to improve instructional design. In the course of their explorations, they have dealt with a number of questions that can help us understand the concept attainment model. They have compared treatments where students induce attributes and definitions, finding that the students developed clearer concepts and retained them longer when the examination of the exemplars *preceded* the discussion of attributes and definitions. Tennyson and Cocchiarella also discovered that the first positive exemplars presented should be the *clearest possible prototypes,* especially with multiple-attribute concepts. In other words, the teacher should not try to "fake out" the students with vague exemplars, but should take care to facilitate concept learning by arranging the data sets so that less-clear exemplars are dealt with in the phases where the principles are applied.

Tennyson and Cocchiarella (1986) also concluded that students develop procedural knowledge (how to attain concepts) with practice, and that the more procedural knowledge the students possess, the more effectively they attain and can apply conceptual knowledge. Thus, the analysis of thinking to facilitate concept attainment appears to be very important.

The idea of learning concepts and then clarifying attributes and definitions runs counter to much current teaching practice. We have learned that some teachers, when first using concept attainment, have an urge to provide definitions and lists of attributes. It is important to remember that the appropriate time for clarification is *after* the students have abstracted the concepts.

Data are presented to the students in the form of sets of items called *exemplars*—for instance, a set of poems. These are labeled "positive" if they have characteristics or attributes of the concept to be taught (for example, the sonnet form). The exemplars are labeled "negative" if they do not contain the attributes of the concept (for example, poems that do not have all the attributes of a sonnet).

By comparing the positive and negative exemplars, the students develop hypotheses about the nature of the category. They do not, however, share their hypotheses at this point. When most of the students have developed a hypothesis, some unlabeled exemplars are presented to them and they indicate whether they can successfully identify positive exemplars. They may be asked to produce some of their own (as by scanning a set of poems and picking out some positive and negative ones).

Then they are asked to share their hypotheses and describe the progression of their ideas during the process. When they have agreed on the hypotheses that appear most likely, they generate labels for them. Then the teacher supplies the technical label, if there is one (*sonnet*, for example).

To consolidate and apply the concept, the students then search for more items of the class (poems, in this case) and find which ones most closely match the concept they have learned.

THE MODEL OF TEACHING

The phases of the concept attainment model are outlined in Table 6.1.

Syntax

Phase one involves presenting data to the learner. Each unit of data is a separate example or nonexample of the concept. The units are presented in pairs. The data may be events, people, objects, stories, pictures, or any other discriminable units. The learners are informed that all the positive examples

TABLE **6.1**   Syntax of the Concept Attainment Model

Phase One: Presentation of Data and Identification of Concept
  1. Teacher presents labeled examples.
  2. Students compare attributes in positive and negative examples.
  3. Students generate and test hypotheses.
  4. Students state a definition according to the essential attributes.

Phase Two: Testing Attainment of the Concept
  1. Students identify additional unlabeled examples as yes or no.
  2. Teacher confirms hypotheses, names concept, and restates definitions according to essential attributes.
  3. Students generate examples.

Phase Three: Analysis of Thinking Strategies
  1. Students describe thoughts.
  2. Students discuss role of hypotheses and attributes.
  3. Students discuss type and number of hypotheses.

---

have one idea in common; their task is to develop a hypothesis about the nature of the concept. The instances are presented in a prearranged order and are labeled *yes* or *no*. Learners are asked to compare and justify the attributes of the different examples. (The teacher or students may want to maintain a record of the attributes.) Finally, learners are asked to name their concepts and state the rules or definitions of the concepts according to their essential attributes. (Their hypotheses are not confirmed until the next phase; students may not know the names of some concepts, but the names can be provided when the concepts are confirmed.)

In phase two, the students test their attainment of the concept, first by correctly identifying additional unlabeled examples of the concept and then by generating their own examples. After this, the teacher (and students) confirm or disconfirm their original hypotheses, revising their choice of concepts or attributes as necessary.

In phase three, students begin to analyze the strategies by which they attain concepts. As we have indicated, some learners initially try broad constructs and gradually narrow the field; others begin with more discrete constructs. The learners can describe their patterns—whether they focused on attributes or concepts, whether they did so one at a time or several at once, and what happened when their hypotheses were not confirmed. Did they change strategies? Gradually, they can compare the effectiveness of different strategies.

Social System

Prior to teaching with the concept attainment model, the teacher chooses the concept, selects and organizes the material into positive and negative examples, and sequences the examples. Most instructional materials, especially textbooks, are not designed in a way that corresponds to the nature of concept learning as described by educational psychologists. In most cases, teachers will have to prepare positive and negative examples of the concept, extract ideas and materials from texts and other sources, and design them in such a way that the attributes are clear. When using the concept attainment model, the teacher acts as a recorder, keeping track of the hypotheses (concepts) and attributes as they are mentioned. The teacher also supplies additional examples as needed. The three major functions of the teacher during concept attainment activity are to record, prompt (cue), and present additional data. In the initial stages of concept attainment, it is helpful for the examples to be very structured. However, cooperative learning procedures can also be used successfully.

Principles of Reaction

During the flow of the lesson, the teacher needs to be supportive of the students' hypotheses—emphasizing, however, that they are hypothetical in nature—and to create a dialogue in which students test their hypotheses against each other's. In the later phases of the model, the teacher must turn the students' attention toward analysis of their concepts and their thinking strategies, again being very supportive. The teacher should encourage analysis of the merits of various strategies rather than attempting to seek the one best strategy for all people in all situations.

Support System

Concept attainment lessons require that positive and negative exemplars be presented to the students. It should be stressed that the students' job in concept attainment is not to invent new concepts, but to attain the ones that have previously been selected by the teacher. When students are presented with an example, they describe its characteristics (attributes), looking for shared attributes in the positive ones that are not presented in the negative ones.

Application

The applications in all content areas may emphasize content or process. If the emphasis is on the analysis of thinking, a short sample concept attainment exercise might be developed so that more time can be spent on the analysis of thinking.

The concept attainment model may be used with children of all ages and grade levels. We have seen teachers use the model very successfully with kindergarten children, who love the challenge of the inductive activity. For young children the concept and examples must be relatively simple, and the lesson itself must be short and heavily teacher directed. The typical curriculum for young children is filled with concrete concepts that readily lend themselves to concept attainment methodology. The analysis-of-thinking phase of the strategy (phase 3) should be conducted gently with very young children, but by first grade most can manage it.

When the model is used in early childhood education, concrete materials for examples are often available. Classroom objects, Cuisinaire rods, pictures, and shapes can be found in almost any early childhood classroom. Although helping children work inductively can be an important goal in itself, the teacher should also have more specific goals in mind in using this model.

The concept attainment model is an excellent evaluation tool when teachers want to determine whether important ideas introduced earlier have been mastered. It quickly reveals the depth of students' understanding and reinforces their previous knowledge.

Concept attainment lessons providing important concepts in social studies units—concepts such as *democracy, socialism, capitalism,* and *due process*—can be incorporated periodically into units that otherwise depend on student reading and reporting. Let's look at one more scenario that Lori Kindrachuk created, this time to help her students develop information about settings when they are reading fiction and also to think about how they can generate information about setting when they are writing.

SCENARIO

LORI'S THIRD LESSON

This time we will ask you to look at lists of positive and negative exemplars and draw your own conclusions about the concept.

Here are her notes about the concept.

Definition: A setting is the environment in which the action of a fictional work takes place. It includes information about time and/or place.

Orienting Statement: In this lesson all of the positive exemplars (yeses) have a common attribute. As you read each sentence, focus on its content and the information it provides.

The first seven sentences name specific dates and times, moving from day/month/year to combinations of day, month, or year. The first three sentences name specific holidays. (Halloween and Valentine's Day always fall on the same date.)

Positive Exemplars

1. It was October 31, 1997, and Danny knew he had the best Halloween costume ever.
2. In 2001, Valentine's Day fell on a Friday and Joanne had her cards ready to deliver the night before.
3. Easter Sunday, 1952, fell on April 14, giving Sam five more days to finish decorating the eggs.
4. Mark had just celebrated his twelfth birthday on January 29, 1999, the same day as the Super Bowl game.
5. The spring of 1981 was hot and dry; June 7, graduation day, was no exception.
6. On a Saturday morning, in August of 1862, he left on his first trip.
7. Cold, damp and wet—that was March of 1965.

The next seven sentences begin by naming famous events in history and move towards referring to famous periods in history.

8. The day after Pearl Harbor had been hit, the air was still filled with smoke from the fires.
9. As he read the headline, he realized the *Titanic* had gone down the day before yesterday.
10. The church service this morning marked one year since the events of 9/11.
11. This devastating time in America became known as the Civil War.
12. As Hitler's forces pressed forward, Cal listened to the reports each day, wishing he were old enough to join the fight.
13. After the crash of the stock market, times were tough; they were surviving the years that would become known as the Dirty Thirties.
14. Tom had always wanted to be a pilot—last summer a man had walked on the moon for the first time; who knew what the future would hold?
15. Jake sat down in front of the computer and scanned his email.
16. The crowd roared as the gladiator entered the arena on a chariot trimmed with gold.

The final set of sentences name either modes of transportation or inventions from a certain period, developing the time setting strictly through inference.

17. Mark's new iPod had been stolen out of his locker last week.
18. The covered wagon would be their home during the long trip to the new settlement.
19. With cell phone in one hand and snowboard in the other, Tanis made her way toward the hill.
20. Interplanetary travel was still quite new and they hadn't worked out all of the kinks in the booking system.
21. They had arrived by horse and carriage the night before, as it was the fastest and most comfortable way he could think of to get the entire family home.

Negative Exemplars

1. Sarah was taller than her sister, but they shared the same red hair and freckles.
2. The child in the picture wore a bright blue dress and had ribbons in her hair.
3. June's favorite band was going to play for the dance.
4. He knew that he should help put out the fire, but he couldn't seem to move.
5. She was his second cousin and they had always been good friends.
6. Mrs. Thompson worked in the store and taught piano lessons in her spare time.
7. If they won the game, they would advance to the semifinal.
8. Last month they saw each other three times.
9. She had talked to him yesterday.
10. Two more weeks until the big day!
11. She had only heard the news three days before.
12. In two more hours the celebration would begin.
13. They were still 15 minutes away from the nearest help.
14. During halftime the players would discuss a new strategy.
15. The sale will be three weeks from Saturday.
16. The deal was final at midnight on the 25th.
17. They would attend the lessons the next three Wednesdays in a row.
18. March, April, and May were her favorite months.
19. They always had fish for supper on Friday.
20. Autumn always brought the smells of pumpkin pie and decaying leaves.
21. Next spring they planned to start building their new home.

> The first seven negative exemplars do not mention time in any way. They are related to character/plot development.

> The next seven sentences use time-related vocabulary, without specifically naming times or inferring eras.

> The final seven sentences refer to specific times (e.g., three weeks from Saturday) without revealing a definite period.

INSTRUCTIONAL AND NURTURANT EFFECTS

The concept attainment strategies can accomplish several instructional goals depending on the emphasis of the particular lesson. They are designed for instruction on specific concepts and on the nature of concepts. They also provide practice in inductive reasoning and opportunities for altering and improving students' concept-building strategies. Finally, especially with abstract concepts, the strategies nurture an awareness of alternative perspectives, a sensitivity to logical reasoning in communication, and a tolerance of ambiguity (see Figure 6.1).

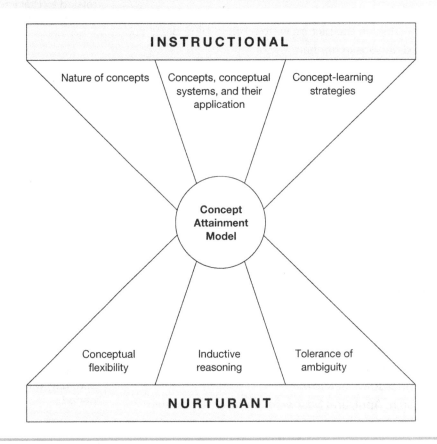

FIGURE 6.1   Instructional and nurturant effects of the concept attainment model

Robert Gagné's 1965 article thoroughly discusses a similar approach to concept attainment. Merrill and Tennyson (1977) describe a similar approach—without, however, an extensive analysis of the thinking processes. McKinney, Warren, Larkins, Ford, and Davis (1983) have reported a series of interesting studies comparing the Merrill and Tennyson approach with Gagné's and a recitation procedure. Their work illustrates the complexity of designing studies to meaningfully compare sets of models built on the same premises but differing in details of execution. However, the differences in approach and the research to build better models are probably of less importance to teachers than the fact that there are models that do a good job of teaching concepts—ones more powerful than the way concepts have traditionally been taught, and therefore represent useful additions to the teaching/learning repertoire. The model we have been discussing is one of them.

The Concept Attainment Model

SUMMARY CHART

Syntax

The syntax proceeds from presentation of the exemplars to testing and naming concepts to application.

Social System

The model has moderate structure. The teacher controls the sequence, but open dialogue occurs in the latter phases. Student interaction is encouraged. The model is relatively structured, with students assuming more initiative for inductive process as they gain more experience (other concept attainment models are lower in structure).

Principles of Reaction

1. Give support but emphasize the hypothetical nature of the discussion.
2. Help students balance one hypothesis against another.
3. Focus attention on specific features of examples.
4. Assist students in discussing and evaluating their thinking strategies.

Support System

Support consists of carefully selected and organized materials and data in the form of discrete units to serve as examples. As students become more sophisticated, they can share in making data units, just as in phase 2 they generate examples.

CHAPTER SEVEN

Synectics

Teaching the Left Brain to Put the Right Side to Work

Of all the models, synectics has got to give the most immediate pleasure when you're leading the exercises. We've been teaching kids (both elementary and secondary) to lead synectics. I have to admit that I always have a little touch of green when I turn it over to the kids, because they're going to have the fun, now.

—*Letter from Bruce Joyce to Bill Gordon*

Here we visit processes for teaching students to think innovatively—to break set and generate new solutions to problems and to use analogies when thinking, writing, and presenting ideas. In the process, the students will learn to decode metaphoric expressions they encounter when reading and listening.

The terms *left-brained* (orderly, logical, rational) and *right-brained* (innovative, unexpected, even *off the wall*) are well publicized today. The jury of neurological scientists is still out on whether the differences are a result of operations within the brain itself, but the concepts are useful. Appropriately, in synectics, we will look at an innovative model that, unexpectedly, uses left-brained means—rational avenues—to generate right-brained styles of reasoning. Students learn to think about their problem-solving processes and gain a measure of metacognitive control over how they solve problems such as figuring out how to begin an essay, approach a conflict, or overcome perplexities. In addition, synectics is delightful and builds empathy, including feelings of warmth in groups in and out of school. Let's begin with a scenario.

A CANADIAN LESSON: TEACHING STUDENTS TO THINK WITH ANALOGIES

Day One

Mary Bishop has conducted two sessions with the students using stretching exercises where they have been introduced to direct, personal, and compressed conflict analogies. Now she begins by asking them to study the picture in Figure 7.1: "We are going to study this picture for the next three days. What are the major things that are going on in it?"

Some of their responses include the following:

"There are people pushing very hard."
"It is on a beach—they are pushing a boat onto the beach."
"It looks very hot." (Mary adds, "The people are dressed for the weather.")
"They are pushing the boat onto the shore."
"There are leaves on the sand."
"It looks like hard work."
"They are leaning really hard."
"There is teamwork."

FIGURE 7.1   Pushing a boat

Emily Calhoun

Now, at the end of this first session, Mary asks the students to "write whatever ideas are most in your mind at this time." Here are some of their products at the end of day one:

"People are pushing."
"The water is on the beach."
"The water is shiny."
"Men are pushing a boat together."

In sum, the students are describing what they see in literal terms.

Day Two

Now Mary opens up the metaphorical dimension—trying to make synectics accessible to the students. "We will begin with direct analogies—I will ask you questions like, 'How is a teacher like a computer?' Then, we will explore personal analogies. I will ask you questions like, 'How do you feel like tennis balls when the day is over and you are put back in the can?' Let's go."

"How is a cracker like toast?"

The students respond with answers such as "crunchy" and "bits of stuff."

"How is a videotape like a book?"

The students respond with: "They have stories in them." "They unwind in your head."

Mary continues to ask the students to create analogies, working within analogies that are relatively easy to generate: "How is a spoon like a shovel?" "How as a rose like a cactus?"

Then she moved to personal analogies: "Now, become a pencil. Pencils, you have to write a laundry list. How do you feel?"

"Scared."
"I have to use my head to write."
"It hurts to write."

She asks, "How is a traffic light like an alarm clock?"

"It gets you going."
"They both tell time."

"How is an earring like a Christmas ornament?" "How is a button like a nail?" "How is riding an elevator like climbing a tree?"

Next, Mary moves to personal analogies. "Be a cellphone—what would you like to control? If you could pick a ring pattern, what would you pick? Who would you want talking on you?"

The students respond with a variety of thoughts as they are being brought into a metaphoric stance.

"I control the world."
"I want to play my own rap."
"I want to talk to my friends, but I'd like to say a few things to the P.M."

Then Mary switches back to direct analogies: "How is tying your shoes like locking the front door?"

"They are both like locking something up."
"How is a map like a skeleton?"
"It looks like one. Like the body of a place."

And then Mary closes the session. "Tomorrow we will take all these words and do something else with them."

Day Three

Mary has prepared a display that shows the words that have been generated during day two. She warms the students up with a few direct and personal analogy stems, and then asks them to try to generate compressed conflicts from the words that have been generated. (In a previous session, she has taught the students the concept of compressed conflicts in concept attainment lessons.)

Mary gives the students a few examples:

Beautiful Nightmare
Silent Sound
Honest Liar

Then she says, "Today we are going to learn to make some of these and use them to guide our writing. First, let's play with analogies a bit. How is a turtle like a helmet?"

"Shells and helmets protect something."
"How is a recipe like a jogging trail?"
"You can use both to get somewhere."
"How is the moon like a mirror?"
"They both shine."

Now Mary asks the students to generate compressed conflicts. "Now, I want you to look at all of the words we came up with yesterday and look for ones that don't quite fit together." The words the students generated yesterday are displayed on a chart. Here are some of the products:

Happy hurt
Tickly hard

Noisily bored
Crazy wind
Crazy control
Crumbly shelter
Crazy energy
Tired energy
Correct mistake
Delicate metal

Then Mary asks, "Now, I want you to think of the ones that have the most tension between them—that don't fit together." After some discussion, "tired energy" is selected and Mary says, "Now, I want you to write about this picture again using tired energy."

Here are some of the products:

"Tired energy fits with the picture because if people push the boat on the shore it looks heavy."
"The men are out of energy because they are working hard."
"First they have energy and then they use all the energy."
"The men are tired because they are pushing so hard."

In Sum

Mary is just beginning to teach the students to think in analogies. However, even in this first training exercise, you can see that the students have moved from fragmentary descriptions of the scene to the development of sentences built around the compressed conflict. An increase in fluency and conceptualization is a typical outcome even of the early experiences with the metaphoric way of thinking. The students generated 2.8 sentences in the second writing, compared with 1.6 in the first descriptive passages.

ORIENTATION TO THE MODEL

In these scenarios, the teachers are introducing metaphoric thinking to their students. Synectics, designed by William J. J. Gordon, is an interesting and delightful approach to the development of innovations. The initial work with synectics procedures was to develop "creativity groups" within industrial organizations—that is, groups of people trained to work together to function as problem solvers or product developers. Gordon has adapted synectics for use with schoolchildren, and materials containing many of the synectics activities are now being published (see Gordon, 1961).

The chief element in synectics is the use of analogies. In synectics exercises, students "play" with analogies until they relax and begin to enjoy making more and more metaphoric comparisons, as did Mary's students. Then they use analogies to attack problems or ideas.

Ordinarily, when we are confronted with a task—say, a problem to be solved or a piece of writing to be produced—we consciously become logical. We prepare to write by making an outline of the points to be made. We analyze the elements of a problem and try to think it through. We use our existing storehouse of words and phrases to set down our ideas; we use our storehouse of learned solutions to face a problem.

For many problems and tasks of expressing ourselves, our logic works well enough. But what do we do when our old solutions or ways of expressing ourselves are not sufficient to do the job? That is when we use synectics. It is designed to lead us into a slightly illogical world—to give us the opportunity to invent new ways of seeing things, expressing ourselves, and approaching problems.

For example, school officials struggle with the problem of how to deal with absenteeism. When a student repeatedly fails to come to school, what do they do? Frequently, they turn to punishment. And what punishment is available? Frequently, suspension. It seems logical to choose a severe punishment to match what is regarded as a severe infraction. The trouble with the solution is that it imposes a penalty on the student that is exactly the same condition that incurred the penalty in the first place. Synectics is used to help us develop fresh ways of thinking about the student, the student's motives, the nature of penalties, our goals, and the nature of the problem. We have to develop empathy for someone who is in conflict with us and recognize that we may have an inadequate definition and may be using a "logical" solution that blinds us to creative alternatives.

When stuck, we have to back away from what appears to be logical thought and then return to see if we can redefine the problem and seek alternative solutions. Through analogies we might conceive of our absentee as an "unhappy lark," as on a "destructive vacation," and the problem as one of ending an "empty feast." Our own needed behaviors may be ones of "seductive strictness," "strong lovingness," and "dangerous peacemaking."

If we can relax the premises that have blocked us, we can begin to generate new solutions. We can consider that we have been taking responsibility for the students in areas where they may need to be responsible for themselves. We can wonder whether the solution lies as much in our administration of the rules as it does in how we teach. We may wonder whether communities of peers might not create the energy and sense of belonging that would attack the problem from a different perspective.

The social and scientific world in which we live abounds with problems for which new solutions are needed. Problems of poverty, international law, crime, just taxation, and war would not exist if our logic did not fail us. Striving for appropriate self-expression—trying to learn how to write and speak lucidly and compellingly—bedevils all of us. Two problems are persistent: grasping the subject clearly and comprehensively and generating appropriate forms of expression.

Let us consider another example from Martin Abramowitz's classroom in Mill Valley, California, this time looking at a current social issue.

SCENARIO

THE FOREST SERVICE DILEMMA

Martin Abramowitz's seventh-grade class is preparing a campaign in opposition to a change in Forest Service regulations that would permit a large grove of redwood trees to be cut down as part of a lumbering operation. They have made posters that they intend to display around their community and send to the members of the state legislature. They have the rough sketches for the posters and their captions, and they are examining them.

"Well, what do you think?" asks Priscilla.

"Well, they're OK," says Tommy. "They sure say where we stand. Actually, though, I think they're a little dull."

"So do I," adds Maryann. "A couple of them are OK, but the others are real preachy and stiff."

"There's nothing really wrong with them," chimes in another, "they're just not very zingy."

"Also, they don't build any bridges with our opponents. They present our side, but I'm not sure they'll reach anybody but people who already agree with us."

After some discussion, it is obvious that nearly everybody feels the same way. They decide that two or three of the posters are well designed and convey their message, but they need some others that would be more poignant.

"Let's try synectics," suggests one of them.

"With pictures and captions?" asks one of the other children. "I thought we could only use synectics with poetry. Can we use synectics with stuff like this?"

"Why, sure we can," says Priscilla. "I don't know why I didn't think of it. We've been doing it with poetry all year long."

"Well, we sure have nothing to lose," adds Tommy. "How would it work?"

"Well," says Priscilla, "we could see these posters we've done as the beginning point and then go through a synectics training exercise and see if it gives us some ideas for pictures and captions. We could think of redwood trees in terms of various personal and direct analogies and compressed conflicts."

"Let's try it," chimes in George.

"Let's start right now," says Sally. "We could go through our exercises and then have lunch time to think about the posters."

"Can I be the leader?" asks Nancy. "I've got some super ideas for some stretching exercises."

"Is that OK?" says Priscilla.

The others agree and Nancy begins.

"How is a redwood tree like a toothpick?" she asks.

"You use the tree to pick the teeth of the gods," laughs George. Everyone joins in the laughter and they are off.

It's clear that Mr. Abramowitz has spent enough time using synectics that the students internalized the process and purpose. They can proceed on their own, drawing on the model when they find it helpful.

The Creative State and the Synectics Process

Gordon (1961) grounds synectics in four ideas that challenge conventional views about creativity. First, creativity is important in everyday activities. Most of us associate the creative process with the development of great works of art or music, or perhaps with a clever new invention. Gordon emphasizes creativity as a part of our daily work and leisure lives. His model is designed to increase problem-solving capacity, creative expression, empathy, and insight into social relations. He also stresses that the meanings of ideas can be enhanced through creative activity by helping us see things more richly.

Second, the creative process is not at all mysterious. It can be described and increased through training. Traditionally, creativity is viewed as a mysterious, innate, and personal capacity that can be destroyed if its processes are probed too deeply. In contrast, Gordon believes that if individuals understand the basis of the creative process, they can use that understanding to increase the creativity with which they live and work, independently and as members of groups. Gordon's view that creativity is enhanced by conscious analysis led him to describe it and create training procedures that can be applied in schools and other settings.

Third, creative invention is similar in all fields—the arts, the sciences, engineering—and is characterized by the same underlying intellectual processes. This idea is contrary to common belief. In fact, to many people, creativity is confined to the arts. In engineering and the sciences, however, it is simply called by another name: *invention*. Gordon maintains that the link between generative thinking in the arts and sciences is quite strong.

Gordon's fourth assumption is that individual and group invention (creative thinking) are very similar. Individuals and groups generate ideas and products in much the same fashion. Again, this is very different from the stance that creativity is an intensely personal experience, not to be shared.

One intriguing idea is that by bringing the creative process to consciousness and developing explicit aids to creativity, we can directly increase the creative capacity of both individuals and groups. Another is that the "emotional component is more important than the intellectual, the irrational more important than the rational" (Gordon, 1961, p. 6). Creativity is the development of new mental patterns. Nonrational interplay leaves room for open-ended thoughts that can lead to a mental state in which new ideas are possible. The basis for decisions, however, is always the rational. The analogistic state is the best mental environment for exploring and expanding ideas, but it is not a decision-making stage. Gordon does not undervalue the linear intellect; he assumes that logic is used in decision making and that technical competence is necessary to the formation of ideas in many areas. But he believes that creativity is essentially an *emotional* process, one that requires elements of irrationality and emotion to enhance intellectual processes. Much of problem solving is rational and intellectual, but by adding the irrational, we increase the likelihood that we will generate fresh ideas.

Also, the "emotional, irrational elements must be understood in order to increase the probability of success in a problem solving situation" (Gordon, 1961, p. 1). In other words, the analysis of certain irrational and emotional processes can help the individual and the group increase their creativity by using irrationality constructively. Aspects of the irrational can be understood and consciously controlled. Achievement of this control, through the deliberate use of metaphor and analogy, is the object of synectics.

Metaphoric Activity

Through the metaphoric activity of the synectics model, creativity becomes a conscious process. Metaphors establish a relationship of likeness, the comparison of one object or idea with another object or idea by using one in place of the other. Through these substitutions the creative process occurs, connecting the familiar with the unfamiliar or creating a new idea from familiar ideas.

Metaphor introduces conceptual distance between the people and the object or subject matter and prompts original thoughts. For example, by asking students to think of their textbook as an old shoe or as a river, we provide a structure, a metaphor, with which the students can think about something familiar in a new way. Conversely, we can ask students to think about a new topic—say, the human body—in an old way by asking them to compare it to the transportation system. Metaphoric activity thus depends on and draws from the students' knowledge, helping them connect ideas from familiar content to those from new content, or view familiar content from a new perspective. Synectics strategies using metaphoric activity are designed, then, to provide a structure through which people can free themselves to develop imagination and insight into everyday activities. Three types of analogies are used as the basis of synectics exercises: personal analogy, direct analogy, and compressed conflict.

Personal Analogies

Making personal analogies requires students to empathize with the ideas or objects to be compared. Students must feel they have become part of the physical elements of the problem. The identification may be with a person, plant, animal, or nonliving thing. For example, students may be instructed, "*Be an automobile engine. What do you feel like? Describe how you feel when you are started in the morning; when your battery goes dead; when you come to a stoplight.*"

The essence of personal analogy is on empathetic involvement. Gordon (1961) gives the example of a problem situation in which the chemist personally identifies with the molecules in action. He might ask, "How would I feel if I were a molecule?" and then feel himself being part of the "stream of dancing molecules."

Personal analogy requires loss of self as one transports oneself into another space or object. The greater the conceptual distance created by loss of self, the more likely it is that the analogy is new and that the students have been creative or innovative. Gordon identifies four levels of involvement in personal analogy:

1. *First-person description of facts.* The person recites a list of well-known facts but presents no new way of viewing the object or animal and shows no empathetic involvement. In terms of the car engine, the person might say, "I feel greasy" or "I feel hot."
2. *First-person identification with emotion.* The person recites common emotions but does not present new insights: "I feel powerful" (as the car engine).
3. *Empathetic identification with a living thing.* The student identifies emotionally and kinesthetically with the subject of the analogy: "When you smile like that, I smile all over."
4. *Empathetic identification with a nonliving object.* This level requires the most commitment. The person sees himself or herself as an inorganic object and tries to explore the problem from a sympathetic point of view: "I feel exploited. I cannot determine when I start and stop. Someone does that for me" (as the car engine).

The purpose of introducing these levels of personal analogy is not to identify forms of metaphoric activity, but to provide guidelines for how well conceptual distance has been established. Gordon believes that the usefulness of analogies is directly proportional to the distance created. The greater the distance, the more likely the student is to come up with new ideas.

Direct Analogies

Direct analogy is the comparison of two objects or concepts. The comparison does not have to be identical in all respects. Its function is simply to transpose the conditions of the real topic or problem situation to another situation in order to present a new view of an idea or problem. This involves identification with a person, plant, animal, or nonliving thing. Gordon cites the experience of the engineer watching a shipworm tunneling into a timber. As the worm ate its way into the timber by constructing a tube for itself and moving forward, the engineer, Sir March Isumbard Brunel, got the notion of using caissons to construct underwater tunnels (Gordon, 1961, pp. 40–41). Another example of direct analogy occurred when a group was attempting to devise a can with a top that could be used to cover the can once it had been opened. In this instance, the analogy of the pea pod gradually emerged, which produced the idea of a seam placed a distance below the top of the can, thus permitting a removable lid.

Compressed Conflicts

The third metaphorical form is compressed conflict, generally a two-word phrase in which the words seem to contradict each other. *Tiredly aggressive* and *friendly foe* are two examples. Gordon's examples are *life-saving destroyer* and *nourishing flame*. He also cites Pasteur's expression, *safe attack*. Compressed conflicts, according to Gordon, provide the broadest insight into a new subject. They reflect the student's ability to incorporate two frames of reference with respect to a single object. The greater the distance between frames of reference, the greater the mental flexibility.

Stretching Exercises: Using Metaphors

These three types of metaphors form the basis of the sequence of activities in this model of teaching. They can also be used separately with groups, as a warm-up to the creative process—that is, to problem solving. We refer to this use as *stretching exercises*.

Stretching exercises provide experience with the three types of metaphoric activity, but they are not related to any particular problem situation, nor do they follow a sequence of phases. They teach students the process of metaphoric thinking before asking them to use it to solve a problem, create a design, or explore a concept. Students are simply asked to respond to ideas such as the following:

Direct Analogies

Direct analogies are elicited with questions that ask for a direct comparison, such as:

An orange is like what living thing?
How is a school like a salad?

How are polar bears like frozen yogurt?
Which is softer—a whisper or a kitten's fur?

Personal Analogies

Personal analogies are elicited by asking people to pretend to be an object, action, idea, or event, such as:

Be a cloud. Where are you? What are you doing?
How do you feel when the sun comes out and dries you up?
Pretend you are your favorite book. Describe yourself.
What are your three wishes?

Compressed Conflicts

Compressed conflict practice is elicited by presenting some conflicts and asking people to manipulate them, such as:

How is a computer shy and aggressive?
What machine is like a smile and a frown?

THE MODEL OF TEACHING: TWO STRATEGIES

Syntax

There are actually two strategies or models of teaching based on synectics procedures. One of these, *creating something new,* is designed to make the familiar strange, to help students see old problems, ideas, or products in a new, more creative light. The other strategy, *making the strange familiar,* is designed to make new, unfamiliar ideas more meaningful. Although both strategies employ the three types of analogy, their objectives, syntax, and principles of reaction are different. We refer to creating something new as strategy one and making the strange familiar as strategy two.

Strategy one helps students see familiar things in unfamiliar ways by using analogies to create conceptual distance. Except for the final step, in which the students return to the original problem, they do not make simple comparisons. The objective of this strategy may be to develop a new understanding; to empathize with a show-off or bully; to design a new doorway or city; to solve social or interpersonal problems, such as a garbage strike or two students fighting with each other; or to solve personal problems, such as how to concentrate better when reading. The synectics process should not be rushed. An important role of the teacher is to guard against premature analyses and closure. The syntax of strategy one appears in Table 7.1.

Strategy two, making the strange familiar, seeks to increase the students' understanding and internalization of substantially new or difficult material.

TABLE **7.1**   Syntax for Strategy One: Creating Something New

Phase One: **Description of Present** **Condition**	Teacher has students describe situation or topic as they see it now.
Phase Two: **Direct Analogy**	Students suggest direct analogies, select one, and explore (describe) it further.
Phase Three: **Personal Analogy**	Students "become" the analogy they selected in phase two.
Phase Four: **Compressed Conflict**	Students take their descriptions from phases two and three, suggest several compressed conflicts, and choose one.
Phase Five: **Direct Analogy**	Students generate and select another direct analogy, based on the compressed conflict.
Phase Six: **Reexamination of the** **Original Task**	Teacher has students move back to original task or problem and use the last analogy and/or the entire synectics experience.

In this strategy, metaphor is used for *analyzing*, not for creating conceptual distance as in strategy one. For instance, the teacher might present the concept of culture to her class. Using familiar analogies (such as a stove or a house), the students begin to define the characteristics that are present and those that are lacking in the concept. The strategy is both analytic and convergent: students constantly alternate between defining the characteristics of the more familiar subject and comparing these to the characteristics of the unfamiliar topic.

In phase one of this strategy, explaining the new topic, the students are provided with information. In phase two, the teacher or students suggest a direct analogy. Phase three involves "being the familiar" (personalizing the direct analogy). In phase four, students identify and explain the points of similarity between the analogy and the substantive material. In phase five, students explain the differences between analogies. As a measure of their acquisition of the new information, students can suggest and analyze their own familiar analogies in phases six and seven. The syntax of strategy two appears in Table 7.2.

TABLE **7.2**   Syntax for Strategy Two: Making the Strange Familiar

Phase One: **Substantive Input**	Teacher provides information on new topic.
Phase Two: **Direct Analogy**	Teacher suggests direct analogy and asks students to describe the analogy.
Phase Three: **Personal Analogy**	Teacher has students "become" the direct analogy.
Phase Four: **Comparing Analogies**	Students identify and explain the points of similarity between the new material and the direct analogy.
Phase Five: **Explaining Differences**	Students explain where the analogy does not fit.
Phase Six: **Exploration**	Students reexplore the original topic on its own terms.
Phase Seven: **Generating Direct Analogies**	Students provide their own direct analogy and explore their understandings of them.

In strategy one, students move through a series of analogies without logical constraints; conceptual distance is increased, and imagination is free to wander. In strategy two, students try to connect two ideas and to identify the connections as they move through the analogies. The strategy the teacher selects depends on whether he or she is trying to help students create something new or to explore the unfamiliar.

Social System: Both Strategies

Both models or strategies are moderately structured, with the teacher initiating the sequence and guiding the use of the operational mechanisms. The teacher also helps the students intellectualize their mental processes. The students, however, have freedom in open-ended discussions as they engage in metaphoric problem solving. Norms of cooperation, "play of fancy," and intellectual and emotional equality are essential to establishing the setting for creative problem solving. The rewards are internal, coming from students' satisfaction and pleasure with the learning activity.

Principles of Reaction: Both Strategies

Instructors note the extent to which individuals seem to be tied to regimented patterns of thinking, and they try to induce psychological states likely to generate a creative response. In addition, the teachers themselves must use the nonrational to encourage reluctant students to indulge in irrelevance, fantasy, symbolism, and other devices necessary to break out of set channels of thinking. Because teachers as models are probably essential to the method, they have to learn to accept the bizarre and the unusual. Instructors must accept all student responses to ensure that students feel no external judgments about their creative expression. The more difficult the problem is, or seems to be, the more necessary it is for teachers to accept farfetched analogies so that individuals develop fresh perspectives.

Teachers should guard against premature analyses. They also clarify and summarize the progress of the learning activity and, hence, the students' problem-solving behavior. They need to remember that, in much of schooling, there is a rush to closure. In all the models we have discussed thus far, careful study and analysis will result in better learning.

Support System: Both Strategies

Most of all the group needs facilitation by a leader competent in synectics procedures. It also needs, in the case of scientific problems, a laboratory in which it can build models and other devices to make problems concrete and to permit practical invention to take place. The class requires a workspace of its own and an environment in which creativity will be prized and utilized. A typical classroom can probably provide these necessities, but a classroom-sized group may be too large for many synectics activities, and smaller groups would need to be created.

APPLICATION

Using Synectics in the Curriculum

Synectics is designed to increase the creativity of both individuals and groups. Sharing the synectics experience can build a feeling of community among students. Students learn about their fellow classmates as they watch them react to an idea or problem. Thoughts are valued for their potential contribution to the group process. Synectics procedures help create a community of equals in which simply having a thought is the sole basis for status. This norm and that of playfulness quickly give support to even the most timid participant.

Synectics procedures may be used with students in all areas of the curriculum. They can be applied to both teacher–student discussions in the classroom and to teacher-made materials for the students. The products or vehicles of synectics activity need not always be written: they can be oral, or they can take the form of role plays, paintings and graphics, or simply changes in behavior. When using synectics to look at social or behavioral problems, you may wish to notice situational behavior before and after synectics activity and observe changes. It is also interesting to select modes of expression that contrast with the original topic, such as having students paint a picture of prejudice or discrimination. The concept is abstract, but the mode of expression is concrete.

Creative Writing

Strategy one of the synectics model can be directly applied to creative writing, not only because it stimulates the uses of analogies, but because it helps "break set" as writers seek to expand the range of devices they can use to approach expressive tasks in expository, persuasive, and narrative genre.

Exploring Social Problems

Strategy one provides an alternative for exploring social issues, especially ones where the students are vested in definitions and solutions. The metaphor creates distance, so the confrontation does not threaten the learner, and discussion and self-examination are possible. The personal analogy phase is critical for developing insight.

Problem Solving

The objective of strategy two is to break set and conceptualize the problem in a new way in order to suggest fresh approaches in personal life as well as in the classroom. Social relations in the classroom, conflict resolution, how to overcome math anxiety, how to feel better about wearing glasses, how to stop making fun of people—the list is endless.

Creating a Design or Product

Synectics can also be used to create a product or design. A product is something tangible, such as a painting, a building, or a bookshelf, whereas a design is a plan, such as an idea for a party or a new means of transportation. Eventually, designs or plans become real, but for the purposes of this model they remain as sketches or outlines.

Broadening Our Perspective of a Concept

Abstract ideas such as culture, prejudice, and economy are difficult to internalize because we cannot see them in the same way we can see a table or building, yet we frequently use them in our language. Synectics is a good way to make a familiar idea "strange" and thereby obtain another perspective on it.

We have found that synectics can be used with all ages, though with very young children it is best to stick to stretching exercises. Beyond this, adjustments are the same as for any other approach to teaching—care to work within their experience, rich use of concrete materials, attentive pacing, and explicit outlining of procedures.

The model often works effectively with students who withdraw from more academic learning activities because they are not willing to risk being wrong. Conversely, high-achieving students who are only comfortable giving a response they are sure is "right" often feel reluctant to participate. We believe that for these reasons alone, synectics is valuable to everyone.

Synectics combines easily with other models. It can stretch concepts being explored with the information-processing family; open up dimensions of social issues explored through role playing, group investigation, or jurisprudential thinking; and expand the richness of problems and feelings opened up by other models in the personal family.

The most effective use of synectics develops over time. It has short-term results in stretching views of concepts and problems, but when students are exposed to it repeatedly, they can learn how to use it with increasing skill—and they learn to enter a metaphoric mode with increasing ease and completeness.

INSTRUCTIONAL AND NURTURANT EFFECTS

As shown in Figure 7.2, the synectics model has both instructional and nurturant value.

Another approach to the stimulation of creativity through metaphoric activity is presented by Judith Sanders and Donald Sanders (1984). Their book is particularly useful for the range of explicit applications it includes. We have noticed that many educators are not automatically aware of the spectrum of useful applications for models designed to induce divergent thinking. For some reason, many people think of "creativity" as an aptitude that defines talent in the arts, especially writing, painting, and sculpture, whereas the creators of these models believe that this aptitude can be improved and that it has applications in nearly every human endeavor and thus in every curriculum area. The Sanderses provide illustrations in the setting of goals, the development of empathy, the study of values, a variety of strategies for problem solving, and the increase of perspectives for viewing topics.

Newby and Ertner (1994) have conducted a nice series of studies where they taught college students to use analogies to approach the learning of advanced physiological concepts. Their results confirm the experience we have had with K–12 students: the analogies both enhanced immediate and long-term learning and increased the pleasure the students had in learning the material.

Baer (1993) reports a set of studies exploring specific and general divergent-thinking skills that confirms that general creativity-inducing strategies probably apply across many domains, but that domain-specific training may be helpful in some areas. Glynn (1994) has reported a study in science teaching

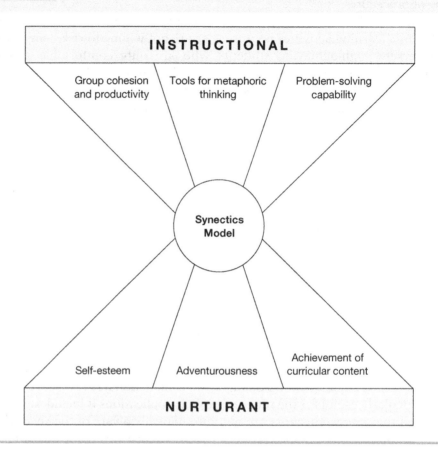

FIGURE 7.2   Instructional and nurturant effects of the synectics model

that suggests that using analogies in textual material enhances both short- and long-term learning. The inquiry continues!

SMALL RICH COUNTRIES—WHY NOT PANAMA?

The following scenario–actually a transcript—illustrates the use of synectics to elaborate on an academic concept. Conducted with students in the country of Panama, it was preceded by two concept attainment lessons, one on the concept of *oxymorons* and the other on the concept of *small, wealthy countries*. Thus, although this was the students' first experience with synectics, they understood the characteristics of oxymorons and were able to construct them in Phase Four of the lesson.

Phase One. Ask students to write a brief characterization of the world's small, wealthy countries. (Students have just finished analyzing a statistical data set on these countries.)

Phase Two. Direct analogies (and examples of student responses).

How is the Panama Canal like a bathtub? [drains]
How is the Panama Canal like a videotape? [long, encased, continuous, viewed]
How is a videotape like a book? [information, pictures]
How is viewing a videotape like dancing? [action, movement]
How is a dream like a skateboard? [falling, adventurous, accelerating]
How is a skateboard like a blender? [spinning, wipe-out]

Phase Three. Personal analogies (and examples of student responses).

Be the Panama Canal. It's midnight and a long string of ships has just begun
    their passage from the Pacific to the Atlantic. How do you feel? [wet, sleepy]
A huge ship, just barely able to clear both sides of the locks, enters the first
    lock. How do you feel? [nervous, stop!]
Pilots are getting on and off of ships. How do you feel about the pilots?
    [friends, protectors]
The tide is coming in with the ships from the Pacific. How do you feel about
    the tides? [smelly, regular, necessary]
Be a raincloud. You're moving into a clear, blue sky. Inside you are hundreds
    of little people with buckets. How do you feel about these little people?
    [(laughter), "go for it"]
You move closer to a town. What are you thinking? [Gotcha]
At a signal from you, all the little people begin emptying their buckets. How
    do you feel? [relieved, light]
You're almost empty. You're starting to break up and you see a little wisp of
    yourself disappearing on the breeze. How do you feel? [nostalgic, sad]

Phase Four. Form oxymorons (actual student responses).

lonely friendship	archaically new
accustomed newness	friendly enemy
apprehensive relief	descending escalation
encased adventure	fictional facts

Phase Five. New direct analogies (and student responses).

What's an example of a "lonely friendship"? [trying to resume a friendship
    after an argument or fight]
What is a "fictional fact"? [a fantasy, like "Alice in Wonderland"]

Phase Six. Reexamination of the original task.

> Think of our small, wealthy nations in terms of "apprehensive relief." [Hong Kong is prosperous but worried about China. Qatar could be swallowed up; they're so small they need a bodyguard; their wealth is based on oil, which could run out or the world market could change with new kinds of fuels; etc. Singapore seems very small.]

> The use of synectics following analysis of data on the world's small, wealthy countries enabled students to elaborate their understanding of these countries. Initial data analysis left the students with an impression that these countries have few problems. The synectics process moved students toward a more differentiated view of the countries that enabled them to hypothesize weaknesses as well as strengths in their relative world positions.

SCENARIO

INDIAN STUDENTS BREAK SET ON A SOCIAL CONCEPT

Another use of synectics is the development of alternative points of view toward social issues, the "breaking of set" when considering solutions. The lesson described here occurred in India with a group of secondary students aged 14 to 17 who were asked to consider the issue of "career women" in their modern culture. Often this topic does not even come up for discussion because the traditional cultural prescriptions for male and female roles are so powerful. Ironically, because access to higher education is based solely on merit, women comprise about half the college and university populations of India, although few women attempt to pursue a career after marriage. Since virtually all Indian women marry, an enormous human resource is being lost to a nation that sorely needs it.

[*Note:* This lesson was conducted in English, a second language for all the students in the session. Their native tongues were either Hindi or Marathi.]

Begin!

Phase One. Write a paragraph about "career women" in India.

Phase Two. Direct analogies (and sample student responses).

> How is a feather like a butterfly? [attractive, soft, flight, pursued]
> How are scissors like a cactus? [sharp, sting]
> How is a snake like a pillow? [slippery, gives you nightmares]
> How is Ping-Pong like getting married? [risk, battle, ups and downs]

Phase Three. Personal analogies (and sample student responses).

> Be a tiger. Good morning, tigers, how do you feel? [grand, kingly, hungry, majestic, untrustworthy]
>
> As you walk through the forest, you come upon a large body of water. You look out over the water and see a whale. What are you thinking, tigers? [greedy, breakfast, threatened, dumbstruck]
>
> Be a feather. Tell me about yourselves, feathers. [no worries, fragile, independent, tramp]

Phase Four. Forming compressed conflicts (oxymorons).

Using words you've generated, construct word pairs that seem to fight each other, word pairs that have a lot of tension or incongruity.

beautiful nightmare	dangerously attractive
carefully threatened	majestically greedy
attractive tramp	grandly majestic

Now select one or two word pairs that have a great deal of incongruity.

beautiful nightmare	dangerously attractive

Phase Five. New direct analogies.

> What is an example of a beautiful nightmare?
> What is dangerously attractive?

Phase Six. Revisiting the original topic.

> Write another paragraph on "career women," using the point of view of one of our oxymorons. You don't have to use the actual words of the compressed conflicts, but try to capture the meaning of the word pairs.

> Here are some of the results, comparing the original (pre) writing with those produced at the end of the exercise:

Pre

If the career woman is married, then the couple gets along with each other only if the husband too pursues an equally good career. Otherwise they tend to split up as the men try to dominate the women, but the women don't like it so they must pursue a career only if it does not interfere with the bringing up of the children.

Post

A career woman can succeed if she is dangerously attractive, especially if she is in the science department. People tend to feast their eyes with her in their sight and leave their stubbornness behind. Then the customer or client realizes later that he has had a beautiful nightmare if the material or the product from the dangerously attractive woman proves to be unworthy of being bought.

Pre

Usually a woman should decide before taking up a career because especially in India if a woman decides to take up a career she's obstructed by her family. I think you can't look after your own family and a career together and usually men do not want their wives to have a career.

Post

A career woman can be equally dangerous and attractive. She can be dangerous to people in the sense that she threatens them and when she [gets] a task accomplished she can be equally sweet or attractive to them.

Pre

What do men feel about career women? They generally think, rather chauvinistically, that women are stupid, inefficient, miserable, subordinate co-workers. So, it is natural for men to feel that, when face to face with career women, they have been brought down to earth. [An] inferiority complex is expressed, giving vent to anger, jealousy, envy, and irritation. But it takes time to realize that career women are generally much more determined and ambitious to make large strides in a severely male-dominated world and once this is realized I think men and women can really work together in one efficient team.

Post

A career woman does give most men beautiful nightmares, some because they have to work in close contact with her and some because they do not want to have a female boss. A career woman has, in my opinion, an inbuilt tendency to be charmingly attractive and complimentary when presented with well done tasks and dangerous when work is performed inefficiently and haphazardly.

THE SYNECTICS MODEL OF TEACHING

Participation in a synectics group invariably creates a unique shared experience that fosters interpersonal understanding and a sense of community. Members learn about one another as each person reacts to the common event in his or her unique way. Individuals become acutely aware of their dependence on the various perceptions of other group members. Each thought, no matter how prosaic, is valued for its potential catalytic effect on one's own thoughts. Simply having a thought is the sole basis for status in this community, and the playfulness of synectics activities encourages even the most timid participant.

Synectics   SUMMARY CHART

Syntax of Strategy One: Creating Something New

- Phase One: Description of the Present Understanding of a Problem or Concept.
- Phase Two: Direct Analogy.
- Phase Three: Personal Analogy.
- Phase Four: Compressed Conflict.
- Phase Five: Direct Analogy from Compressed Conflict.
- Phase Six: Reexamination of the Original Concept, Topic, or Problem

Syntax of Strategy Two: Making the Strange Familiar

- Phase One: Substantive Input.
- Phase Two: Direct Analogy.
- Phase Three: Personal Analogy.
- Phase Four: Comparing Analogies.
- Phase Five: Explaining Differences.
- Phase Six: Exploration.

Social System

The model is moderately structured. Teacher initiates phases, but students' responses are quite open. Norms of creativity and "play of fancy" are encouraged. Rewards are internal.

Principles of Reaction

1. Encourage openness, nonrational, creative expression.
2. Model, if necessary.
3. Accept all student responses.
4. Select analogies that help students stretch their thinking.

Support System

This model requires no special support system.

CHAPTER EIGHT

Memorization

Getting the Facts Straight, Now and for the Long Term

The only way people come to appreciate the real power of the link-word method is to learn to use it themselves to learn new stuff—the more abstract and unfamiliar the better. Folks can't just put it forward as something that is "good for the kids." You have to feel it to be able to teach it well. Come to think of it, maybe that's true of all the models.

—Mike McKibbin to Bruce Joyce

Connections [are] the key. Mnemonics strategies build connections So that items are not just remembered by repetition, but by conceptual connection.

—Bruce Joyce to Bruce Joyce, understanding it at last!

ORGANIZING IDEA

The really, really important process in memorizing is to *pay attention*. No set of effective ways of memorizing will work if you have not been paying attention in the first place.

SCENARIO

ESSENTIAL GLOBAL INFORMATION

The Phoenix High School social studies department has developed a set of mnemonics that are combined with inductive activities to teach students the names and locations of the 191 countries, plus basic demographic knowledge about each of them—population, per capita GNP, type of government, and life expectancy.

The students work in groups using mnemonics like the following one, which is designed to teach the names and locations of the Central American countries.

The exercise begins with the blank map of Central America with the countries numbered (see Map 8.1). The leader describes an imaginary tour they are about to take:

"Imagine that we're about to take a tour of Central America. Our group has learned that there has been a great deal of Spanish influence on the language and the dissemination of a religion based on the Christian Savior—thus, we will see many signs in Spanish and will see mission churches with their distinctive bell towers. We know that the Spanish came for riches and that they expected to find

MAP 8.1

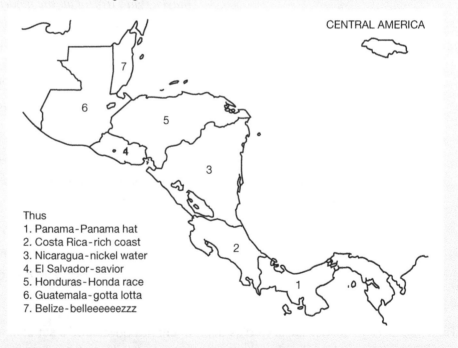

THE TOUR

Imagine that we're about to take a tour of Central America. Our group has learned that there has been a great deal of Spanish influence that has affected the language and the religion based on the Christian savior (we will see mission churches with their distinctive bell towers). We also know that they came for riches. We also know that we have to be careful about the water, except in Panama, and we've got a lot of nickels we will use to buy bottled water. We are going to drive little Hondas and wear Panama hats for identification.

CENTRAL AMERICA

Thus
1. Panama - Panama hat
2. Costa Rica - rich coast
3. Nicaragua - nickel water
4. El Salvador - savior
5. Honduras - Honda race
6. Guatemala - gotta lotta
7. Belize - belleeeeeezzz

Source: Developed by Beverly Showers and Bruce Joyce with the Richmond County, Georgia, Staff Development Cadre. Drawings on this page and on pages 133–135, 141–143, and 147–148 are by Jenna Beard, Eugene, Oregon.

a *rich coast*. We also know we will have to be careful about the water, and we will carry a lot of *nickels* that we will use to buy bottled water. We are going to drive little Hondas, rather than taking a bus, and we will wear Panama hats for identifying our tour group members."

Then the leader points to the first country, Panama, shows the first cartoon, and says, "The link word for Panama is *Panama hat*" (see Cartoon 8.1). The group repeats the link word. The leader then points to the second country and shows the second cartoon, saying "This country stands for the rich coast the Spanish were looking for, which is Costa Rica. The link word for Costa Rica is *rich coast*" (see Cartoon 8.2).

The group repeats the link word and the names of the countries as the leader points to them: "Panama, Panama hat, Costa Rica, rich coast." The exercise continues. The link word for Nicaragua is "nickel water" or "nickel agua" (see Cartoon 8.3), and El Salvador is "Savior" (see Cartoon 8.4). The group repeats the names of the countries and the link words in order as the leader points to the country. The leader proceeds to introduce the link word for Honduras by saying, "We get bored a little and decide to have a 'Honda Race' in our little cars" (see Cartoon 8.5). Guatemala is next and the leader points out that it has the largest population in Central America and that the link word is "gotta lotta" (see Cartoon 8.6). Finally, pointing to the seventh country, the leader reminds them about the bell towers and that the sound from them is "belleeeezzz" (see Cartoon 8.7). The group then names the countries and the link words as the leader points to them in turn.

CARTOON 8.1

CARTOON 8.2

CARTOON 8.3

CARTOON 8.4

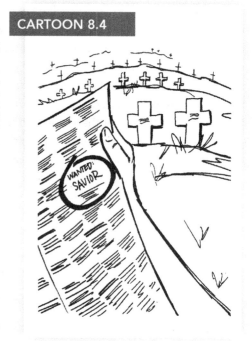

CARTOON 8.5

CARTOON 8.6

CARTOON 8.7

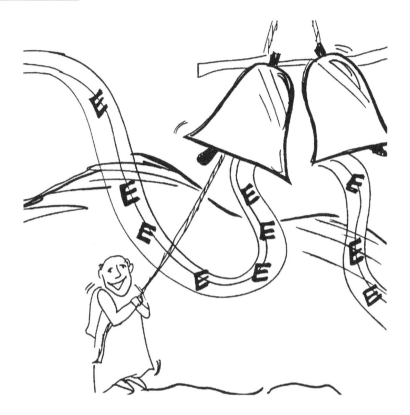

Over the next couple of days the group members study the map, the names of the countries, and the link words until they know them backward and forward. They also consult a database containing information on population, birth and death rates, per capita income, health care, and such, and classify the countries seeking correlations among those variables (e.g., are level of education and life expectancy correlated?).

In this fashion they proceed to examine the regions of the world, comparing and contrasting the countries and learning the names and locations of enough of them that the atlas will seem a familiar place. Eventually, of course, the study goes beyond names, locations, and demographics and proceeds to rich information about a sample of the countries.

FIRST STEPS IN A NEW LANGUAGE

John Pennoyer is the bilingual coordinator of Las Pulgas school district. He works with the teachers to ensure that all the students learn Spanish and English simultaneously. Half the students come to school with English as their primary language; the other half speak Spanish. The students work together to generate link words and pronunciation guides for the two languages.

One of the fifth-grade classes has generated the following list as part of an introduction to Spanish for several students who have newly transferred to their school.

Spanish Words II
por favor (poor fa-BORE)/please [for favor]
gracias (GRA-see-ahs)/thank you [grace to you]
está bién (ess-TA bee-EN)/all right; OK [it's be good]
adiós (ah-dy-OHS)/goodbye
buenos dias (BWE-nos DEE-ahs)/good morning [bonnie day]
buenos tardes (BWE-nos TAR-days)/good afternoon [bonnie late day]
buenos noches (BWEnos NOchays)/good evening [bonnie night]
hasta mañana (AHstah manYAHna)/until tomorrow [no haste, man]

The phonetic pronunciation guides are in parentheses, followed by English equivalents. The link words are in brackets and are designed to provide the flavor of the sounds in English and a sense of the meanings.

The new students study the words, associating the new (to them) Spanish words with the English equivalents and the link words.

GETTING THE PRESIDENTS IN ORDER

Imagine a group of students who are presented with the task of learning the names of the presidents of the United States and the order in which they served. Previously, the students have learned to count from 1 to 40 mnemonically. That is, each number is represented by a rhyming word that has an image attached to it. "One" is "bun," "two" is "shoe," and so on. Also, each set of number decades (1 to 10, 11 to 20) is connected to a location or setting. The decade 1 to 10 is represented by a spring garden scene, 11 to 20 by a summer beach scene, 21 to 30 by a fall football scene, and 31 to 40 by a winter snow scene.

Now, capitalizing on this system of number associations, the name and order of each president are presented to the students in terms of the scene, the mnemonic for the number, and a word—called a *link word*—associated with the president's name. Thus Lincoln (link), number sixteen (sticks), is presented with an illustration of a sand castle on a beach encircled by a set of sticks linked together. Similar illustrations are used for the other presidents. The students study the pictures and the words. They are given a test right after they study and again 60 days later.

How effective was this experience? Did the students learn more than other students who tried to memorize the names and their order using the usual procedures for the same length of time? The answer is yes. In this and other studies, students learn unfamiliar material much more quickly than usual through the application of various mnemonic devices (Pressley, Levin, & Delaney, 1982, p. 83).

Rationale

The humble task of memorizing is with us throughout our lives. From the moment of birth, a world of new artifacts and events is presented to us and has to be sorted out. Moreover, many of the elements of our world have been named by those who have come before us. We have to learn large quantities of words, and we have to learn to connect them to the objects, events, actions, and qualities that they represent. In other words, we have to learn a meaningful language.

In any new area of study, a major task is learning the important words and definitions—the languages, if you will—that pertain to the area. To deal with chemistry, we have to learn the names of the elements and their structural properties. To study a continent, we have to learn the names of its countries, its major geographical features, the important events in its history, and so on. Initial foreign language learning involves developing a vocabulary of words that look and sound unfamiliar.

The study of memory has a long history. Although "the goal of a unified, coherent, and generally satisfying theory of human memory" (Estes, 1976, p. 11) has not yet been achieved, progress has been made. A number of instructional principles are being developed whose goals are both to teach memorization strategies and to help students study more effectively.

For instance, the material on which a particular teacher chooses to focus will affect what information the students retain: "Many items are presented to an individual in a short time, and only those to which attention is directed enter into memory, and only those receiving rehearsal are maintained long enough to secure the processing necessary to establish a basis for long-term recall" (Estes, 1976, p. 7). In other words, if we do not pay attention to something, we are not likely to remember it. Also, we need to attend to it in such a way that we are rehearsing later recall of it. For example, as we wander through a forest, if we do not look carefully at the tree trunks, we are unlikely to remember them, although some visual images may be retained in a haphazard fashion. Even if we notice them, we need to use the information, for example by comparing different trees, to remember it. When we rehearse, we develop *retrieval cues,* which are the basis for sorting through our memories at later times and locating information.

Short-term memories are often associated with *sensory* experiences of various kinds. When we are exposed to the wine called *Chablis,* we may remember it as straw-colored and tasting a certain way. For long-term recall, we may associate things according to *episodic cues*—that is, having to do with the sequences of experience to which we have been exposed. We may remember Andrew Johnson, for instance, as the president who followed Abraham Lincoln. They are connected in time, and their episodes in history are connected to one another. *Categorical cues,* on the other hand, involve conceptualizations of the material. When we compare tree trunks, for example, we form concepts that provide a basis for describing the individual trunks in relation to one another. In other words, we replace specific items with categories, and this categorization provides us with the basis for memory.

Both scholarly and popular sources agree that the ability to remember is fundamental to intellectual effectiveness. Far from being a passive, trivial activity, memorizing and remembering are active pursuits. The capacity to take information, integrate it meaningfully, and later retrieve it at will is the product of successful memory learning. Most important, individuals can improve their capacity to memorize material so that they can recall it later. That is the objective of this model.

ORIENTATION TO THE MODEL

Goals and Assumptions

Our recollection of our early years in school usually includes an image of struggles to master lists of unstructured material such as new words, new sounds, the days of the week, the 50 states, and the nations of the world. Some of us became effective at memorizing. Some did not. As we look back, it is easy to dismiss much of this information as trivial. However, imagine for a moment what our world would be like without the information we acquired in those years of school. We *need* information.

One of the most effective forms of personal power comes from competence based on knowledge; it is essential to success and a sense of well-being.

Throughout our lives, we need to be able to memorize skillfully. To improve this ability increases learning power, saves time, and leads to a better storehouse of information.

The Link-Word Method

Over the last 25 years an important line of research has been conducted on what is termed the *link-word method*. The result is a considerable advance in knowledge about memorization, as well as the development of a system that has practical implications for the design of instructional materials, for classroom teaching and tutoring, and for students.

The method has two components, assuming that the learning task is to master unfamiliar material. The first component provides the students with familiar material to link with the unfamiliar items. The second provides an association to establish the meaning of the new material. For example, when the task involves new foreign language words, one link ties the sounds to those of English words. The second ties the new word to a representation of its meaning. For example, the Spanish word *carta* (postal letter) might be linked to the English word *cart* and a picture showing a letter inside a shopping cart (Pressley, Levin, & Delaney, 1982, p. 62).

An important finding from the research is that people who master material more quickly and retain it longer generally use more elaborate strategies for memorizing material. They use mnemonics—assists to memorization. The less-effective memorizers generally use rote procedures; they "say" what is to be memorized over and over again until they believe it is implanted in their memories.

A second important finding is that devices like the link-word method are even more elaborate than the methods used by the better "natural" memorizers—that is, they require more mental activity than do the rote procedures. When first confronted with the presidential illustrations discussed earlier, many teachers respond, "But why add all the extra stuff? Isn't it hard enough to master the names of the presidents and their order? Why add words like *link* and *stick* and pictures of sand castles on a summer beach?" The answer is that the additional associations provide a richer mental context, and the linking process increases the cognitive activity. The combination of activity and associations provides better "anchors" within our information-processing systems.

Does the link-word method help students who are ordinarily good, poor, and average memorizers? Apparently so (Pressley & Dennis-Rounds, 1980). Further, it appears to help students who are below average in verbal ability, who might have been expected to have greater difficulty with complex learning strategies. In addition, as students use the method, they seem to transfer it to other learning tasks. In other words, mnemonics can be taught so that students can use them independently of the teacher—the students can develop systems for making up their own links.

Finally, even young (kindergarten and first-grade) students can profit from mnemonics (Pressley, Levin, & Miller, 1981a). Obviously, they have greater difficulty generating their own links, but they can benefit when links are provided to them.

The effect sizes from this research are impressive. Even in Atkinson's (1975) early studies, the link-word method was about 50 percent more effective than conventional rote methods. That is, students learned half again more material in the same time period as students not using link words. In some of the later studies, it has been twice as efficient or more (Pressley, 1977; Pressley, Levin, & Miller, 1981a, 1981b). Just as important, retention has been facilitated. That is, more is remembered longer when link words are used. A very long line of research by Mastropieri and Scruggs (1994) has adapted mnemonic devices to the curriculum with particular attention to students having learning disabilities.

As we stated earlier, this research has two obvious uses. The first is to arrange instruction so as to make it as easy as possible for students to make associations and to discourage isolated rote drill. The second is to teach students to make their own links when they are studying new material.

Some of the other models can help us here. Concept attainment provides categories that associate exemplars on the basis of attributes and induce students to make contrasts with the nonexemplars. Inductive teaching causes students to build associations on the basis of common characteristics. Advance organizers provide an "intellectual scaffolding" that ties material together, and comparative organizers link the new with the old. The scientific inquiry methods provide an experiential base for terms and an intellectual structure to "glue" material together.

In an interesting study, Levin and Levin (1990) applied the method to teach what are generally considered higher-order objectives—in this case, a hierarchical system for classifying plants. They compared the effectiveness of using links to familiar concepts with a traditional graphic representation, with the hierarchy presented in a chart featuring boxes connected by lines. The links not only facilitated the learning and remembering of the hierarchical scheme, but also affected problem solving.

For the teacher, the major labor is preparation. Generating the links, and in some cases creating visual materials or working with students to create them, are the chief activities involved. Once the presentations have been prepared, the delivery is straightforward. Let us look at an example accompanied by cartoon figures.

This exercise is similar to the one described in the Central America scenario at the beginning of the chapter and is part of a global literacy program. The link words are phonetic and are created in a sequence following a made-up story of a career woman in the United States. We begin with the map of the Middle East with seven of the countries numbered in the order in which they will be memorized (see Map 8.2).

MAP 8.2

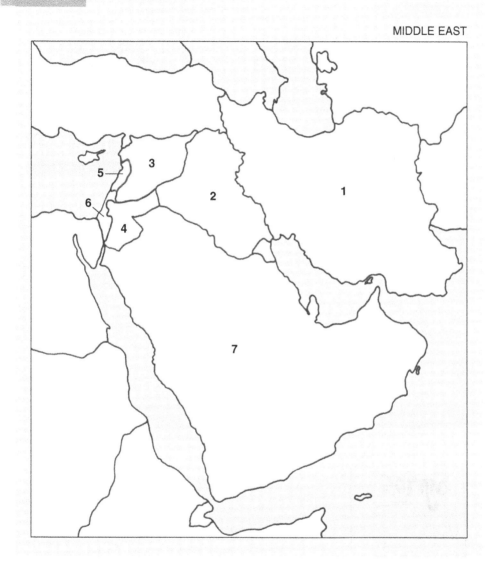

MIDDLE EAST

Our career woman is recounting the beginning of her day. "I got up," she says, and "*I ran* downstairs." *I ran* and its accompanying cartoon are the links to Iran (see Cartoon 8.8). Then she says, "I took the dishes from the *rack*." *Rack,* with its accompanying cartoon, are links to Iraq (see Cartoon 8.9). She continues, "I fixed the children bowls of *Syrios*." *Syrios,* with the accompanying cartoon, are links to Syria (see Cartoon 8.10).

"I fixed myself some English muffins and took out the *jar of jam*." *Jar of jam,* with its cartoon, are the links to Jordan (see Cartoon 8.11). "I also fixed

CARTOON 8.8

CARTOON 8.9

CARTOON 8.10

CARTOON 8.11

myself a cup of tea and sliced a *lemon* for it." *Lemon* is the link, with its cartoon, for Lebanon (see Cartoon 8.12). "Finally, I ran for the *rail*road train." *Rail*road, with its cartoon, is the link for Israel (see Cartoon 8.13). "When I got to my office, I was so hot and thirsty I ran straight to the vending machine and got a *soda* to pick me up." *Soda* (*sody*) is the link for Saudi Arabia (see Cartoons 8.14 and 8.15).

CARTOON 8.12

CARTOON 8.13

CARTOON 8.14

CARTOON 8.15

These are phonetic links, which, with the illustrations, help the students connect the words (new to them) with known words, phrases, and visualizations to help anchor the new material to the familiar. The somewhat humorous and absurd tone helps make the links vivid.

Other Memory-Assist Systems

A number of popular "memory systems" have been developed, none of them backed by the research that Pressley, Levin, and their associates have generated. However, some of these systems use principles congruent with that research. Lorayne and Lucas's *The Memory Book* (1974) and Lucas's *Learning How to Learn* (2001) are two examples, and we have drawn on them for some suggestions of procedures to use with children.

We repeat first the important maxim that before we can remember something we must first attend to it. An effective memory model needs to induce attention to what is to be learned. Because entities we can see, feel, touch, smell, or taste generate powerful associations for remembering, we remember best those ideas that are represented to several of our sensory channels. Each channel contains old material we can associate with the new. If we "see" a flower, for example, as a visual image, something that feels a certain way, has a distinctive smell, and makes a crunchy noise when its stem is cut, we are linked to it through several types of perception. The likelihood of remembering it (or its name) is greater than if we observe it through one sense only. Lorayne and Lucas (1974) quote Aristotle: "It is the image-making part of the mind which makes the work of the higher processes of thought possible. Hence the mind never thinks without a mental picture. The thinking faculty thinks of its form in pictures" (p. 22).

Lorayne and Lucas built their model to increase (1) *attention* to what is to be learned, (2) the *senses* involved in attending, and (3) the *associations* we make between the new material and things that have previously been learned. A sense of how this is done can be seen in the following vignette:

SCENARIO

MAKING A SPEECH

Boris, who is running for student body president of the elementary school, has prepared a speech to deliver before his schoolmates. But he is having difficulty remembering his speech, so he appeals to his teacher for help and support. The teacher encourages him to use the memory strategies they have applied to other seemingly simple learning tasks such as learning new words and the names of African and Latin American countries. Informally, she guides him through the stages of the model much the same way Lorayne and Lucas do with their clients.

First, the teacher has Boris identify (attend to) the main thoughts of his speech. He carefully numbers each main idea. Next she has him identify one word from each main idea that reminds him of the entire thought. One by one, Boris isolates ideas and underlines a *key word* (one that can stand for the point to be made).

Next the teacher has Boris identify familiar words that have vivid meaning for him and connect those words with the key words. He picks his sister Kate for the term *qualifications* and *pear* for peer. To help him remember those two ideas, she asks him to imagine them in any silly way he can. Boris thinks for a minute and then relays the picture of a gigantic pear chasing his sister Kate. He is on his way to remembering! With each pair of key words and substitute words, Boris imagines some outrageous event combining the two.

After he has gone through all of the key thoughts and generated appropriate images, the teacher has Boris repeat words and describe the images several times. Then she asks him to test his memory by giving the whole speech. He is able to go through it comfortably. He has *attended* to his major points, *visualized* the key words and substitutes, and *associated* the key points with vivid sensory images.

If Boris had been learning new vocabulary or important science concepts, the teacher would have asked him to relate the new material to other *related* material he had learned previously, and she would have suggested that he put the new material to use immediately. This active repetition in a natural setting would help Boris retain the material over the long term. However, Boris's speech is a one-time activity requiring only short-term retention, so it is necessary only to review the associations and test his memory by giving the speech several times.

CONCEPTS ABOUT MEMORY

The following concepts are essentially principles and techniques for enhancing our memory of learning material.

Awareness

Before we can remember anything we must give attention to, or concentrate on, the things or idea to be remembered: "Observation is essential to original awareness" (Lorayne & Lucas, 1974, p. 6). According to Lorayne and Lucas, anything of which we are originally aware cannot be forgotten.

Association

Next to *attending,* the important rule is, "You Can Remember Any New Piece of Information If It Is Associated with Something You Already Know or Remember" (Lorayne & Lucas, 1974, p. 7). For example, to help students remember the spelling of *piece,* teachers will give the cue a *piece of pie,* which helps with both spelling and meaning.

Link System

The heart of the association procedure is connecting two ideas, with the second idea triggering yet another one, and so on. Although generally we only expend energy to learn meaningful material, an illustration with material that is not potentially useful helps us see how the method works. Suppose, for example, you want to remember the following five words in order: *house, glove, chair, stove, tree.* You should imagine an unusual picture, first with a house and a glove, then with a glove and a chair. For example, in the first picture you might imagine a glove opening the front door of a house, greeting a family of gloves. The second picture might be a huge glove holding a tiny chair. Taking the time to concentrate on making up these images and then to visualize them will develop associations that link them in order.

Many memory problems deal with the association of two ideas. We often want to associate names and dates or places, names and ideas, words and their meaning, or a fact that establishes a relationship between two ideas.

Ridiculous Association

Even though it is true that association is the basis of memory, the strength of the association is enhanced if the image is vivid and ridiculous, impossible, or illogical. A tree laden with gloves and a family of gloves are examples of ridiculous association.

There are several ways to make an association ridiculous. The first is to apply the rule of substitution. If you have a car and a glove, picture the glove driving the car. Second, you can apply the out-of-proportion rule. You can make small things gigantic or large things miniature—for example, a gigantic baseball glove driving along. The third means is the rule of exaggeration, especially by number. Picture millions of gloves parading down the street. Finally, get action into the association. In the examples discussed earlier, the glove is *ringing* the doorbell and *parading* down the street. Imagining ridiculous associations is not at all difficult for us when we are young children, but making these images gets harder for us as we get older and more logical.

Substitute-Word System

The substitute-word system is a way of making "an intangible tangible and meaningful" (Lorayne & Lucas, 1974, p. 21). It is quite simple. Merely take any word or phrase that seems abstract and "think of something . . . that sounds like, or reminds you of, the abstract material and can be pictured in your mind" (Lorayne & Lucas, 1974, p. 22). As a child you may have said "I'll ask her" to remember the state of Alaska. If you want to remember the name *Darwin* you might visualize a dark wind. The concept of force can be represented by a fork. The pictures you construct represent words, thoughts, or phrases. Cartoons 8.16 and 8.17 illustrate substitute link words and graphics that we use when introducing students to the names of the European countries.

CARTOON 8.16

Key Word

The essence of the key-word system is to select one word to represent a longer thought or several subordinate thoughts. Boris's speech is an example of the use of one word to trigger many verbal statements. Boris chose key-word qualifications to represent a list of his superior qualities. If, as in his case, the key word is abstract, it is necessary to use the substitute-word system before inventing a memorable image.

THE MODEL OF TEACHING

The model of teaching that we have developed from the work of Pressley, Levin, and Delaney (1982) includes four phases: attending to the material, developing connections, expanding sensory images, and practicing recall. These phases are based on the principle of attention and the techniques for enhancing recall (see Table 8.1).

SYNTAX

Phase one calls for activities that require the learner to concentrate on the learning material and organize it in a way that helps that learner remember it. Generally, this includes focusing on what needs to be remembered—the major ideas and examples. Underlining is one way to do this. Listing the ideas separately and rephrasing them in one's own words is another task that forces

TABLE Syntax of Memory Model

Phase One: **Attending to the Material**	Use techniques of underlining, listing, reflecting.
Phase Two: **Developing Connections**	Make material familiar and develop connections using key-word, substitute-word, and link-word system techniques.
Phase Three: **Expanding Sensory Images**	Use techniques of ridiculous association and exaggeration. Revise images.
Phase Four: **Practicing Recall**	Practice recalling the material until it is completely learned.

attention. Finally, reflecting on the material, comparing ideas, and determining the relationship among the ideas is a third attending activity.

Once the material to be learned has been clarified and evaluated, several memory techniques should be used to develop connections with what is to be learned. Phase two includes using techniques such as link words, substitute words (in the case of abstractions), and key words for long or complex passages. The notion is to connect the new material to familiar words, pictures, or ideas, and to link images or words.

Once the initial associations have been identified, the images can be enhanced (phase three) by asking the student to associate them with more than one sense and by generating humorous dramatizations through ridiculous association and exaggeration. At this time the images can be revised for greater recall power. In phase four, the student is asked to practice recall of the material.

Social System

The social system is cooperative: the students and teacher work as a team to shape the new material for commitment to memory.

Principles of Reaction

The teacher's role in this model is to help the student work the material. Working from the student's frame of reference, the teacher helps him or her identify key items, pairs, and images.

Support System

No special support system is required for this model. However, pictures, concrete aids, films, and other audiovisual materials are especially useful for increasing the sensory richness of the associations. We also recommend the "Dr. Memory" series by Lucas Education, which includes books such as *Names and Faces Made Easy* and *Learning How to Learn,* along with audio and video cassettes. Although scholars have documented the considerable effects of the mnemonic techniques, Lucas is the technician of the field and his advice and examples are delightful and effective.

APPLICATION

The other models in the information-processing family all have mnemonic effects. Building and attaining categories create associations. Metaphoric connections *are* connections. The process of science *creates* connections. And connections are the essence of mnemonics. Mastropieri and Scruggs (1991) provide a large number of applications, including developed materials for a number of areas that have been difficult for students, such as geographical and historical places and people.

The memory model is applicable to all curriculum areas where material needs to be memorized. It can be used with groups (a chemistry class mastering the table of elements) or individuals (a student learning a poem, story, speech, or part in a play). Although it has many uses in teacher-led "memory sessions," it has its widest application after students have mastered it and can use it independently. Thus, the model should be taught so that dependence on the teacher is decreased and students can use the procedures whenever they need to memorize. The students are taught the following steps:

1. *Organizing information to be learned.* Essentially, the more information is organized, the easier it is to learn and retain. Information can be organized by categories. The concept attainment, inductive, and advance organizer models facilitate memorization by helping students associate the material in the categories. Consider the following list of words from a popular spelling series, in the order in which the spelling book presents them to the children:

soft	plus	cloth	frost	song
trust	luck	club	sock	pop
cost	lot	son	won	

Suppose we ask the students to classify the words by beginnings, endings, and the presence of vowels. The act of classification requires the students to scrutinize the words and associate words containing similar elements. They can then name the categories in each classification (the "c" group and the "st" group), calling further attention to the common attributes of the group. They can also connect words that fit together ("pop song," "soft cloth," and so on). They can then proceed to rehearse the spellings of one category at a time. The same principle operates over other types of material—say, number facts. Whether categories are provided to students or they create them, the purpose is the same. Also, information can be selected with categories in mind. The previous list is, to outward appearances, almost random. A list that deliberately and systematically provides variations would be easier to organize (it would already have at least implicit categories within it).

2. *Ordering information to be learned.* Information learned in series, especially if there is meaning to the series, is easier to assimilate and retain. For example, if we wish to learn the names of the states of Australia, it is easier if we always start with the same one (say, the largest) and proceed in the same order. Historical events by chronology are more easily learned than events sorted randomly. Order is simply another way of organizing information. We could have the students alphabetize their list of spelling words.

3. *Linking information to familiar material (sounds and meanings are both given consideration).* Suppose we are learning the names of the states. We can connect "Georgia" to "George," "Louisiana" to "Louis," "Maryland" to "Mary," and so on. Categorizing the names of the states or ordering them by size or within region provides more associations.

4. *Linking information to visual representations.* Maryland can be linked to a picture of a marriage, Oregon to a picture of a gun, Maine to a burst water main, and so forth. Letters and numerals can be linked to something that evokes both familiar sounds and images. For example, "one" can be linked to "bun" and a picture of a boy eating a bun, "b" to a bee and a picture of a bee. Those links can be used over and over. "April is the cruelest month, breeding lilacs out of the dead land" is more easily remembered thinking of an ominous metal spring, coiled malevolently over the spring flowers.

5. *Linking information to associated information.* A person's name, linked to information such as a well-known person having the same name, a sound-alike, and some personal information, is easier to remember than the name rehearsed by itself. Louis (Louis Armstrong) "looms" over Jacksonville (his place of birth). Learning the states of Australia while thinking of the points of the compass and the British origins of many of the names (New South Wales) is easier than learning them in order alone.

6. *Use devices that make the information vivid.* Lorayne and Lucas favor "ridiculous association," where information is linked to absurd associations ("The silly two carries his twin two on his back so they are really four"). Others favor the use of dramatization and vivid illustrations (such as counting the basketball players on two teams to illustrate that five and five equal 10).

7. *Practice and give feedback.* Students who have not had past success with tasks requiring memorization will benefit by having relatively short assignments and clear, timely feedback as they have success.

INSTRUCTIONAL AND NURTURANT EFFECTS

The memory model is specifically designed to increase the capacity to store and retrieve information. It should nurture a sense of intellectual power—a growing consciousness of the ability to master unfamiliar material, as well as imagery skills and attention to one's environment (see Figure 8.1).

One of the most important outcomes of the model is the students' recognition that learning is not a mysterious, innate process over which they have no control. As Ian Hunter (1964) points out:

> The mastery of some simple mnemonic system may lead some people to realize, for the first time, that they can control and modify their own mental activities. And this realization may encourage them to undertake that self-critical experimentation with their own learning and remembering procedures which is such an important part of intellectual development. (p. 302)

FIGURE 8.1   Instructional and nurturant effects of the mnemonics model

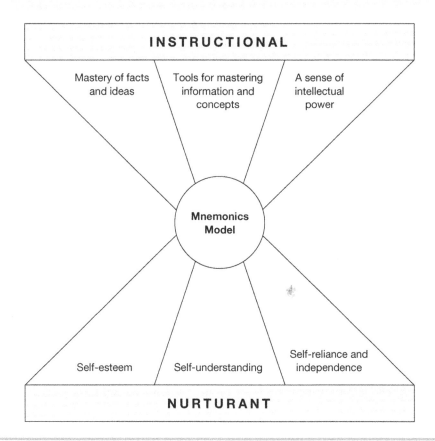

Thus, awareness of how to learn and how to improve learning results in a sense of mastery and control over one's future.

A second outcome is the improvement of imaging capacity and the realization that creative forms of thinking are an essential part of more convergent, information-oriented learning. In training for imagery, creativity is nourished, and ease with playful, creative thought is encouraged. Imaging requires that we observe and attend to the world around us. Consequently, the use of imaging as part of memory work disciplines us to attend to our surroundings automatically.

Finally, of course, our capacity for remembering particular material is strengthened by this model—we become more effective memorizers.

SUMMARY CHART   *The Memory Models Simplified*

Syntax

- Phase One: Attending to the Material.
- Phase Two: Developing Connections.
- Phase Three: Expanding Sensory Images.
- Phase Four: Practicing Recall.

Social System

The social system is cooperative. Teacher and students become a team working with the new material together. The initiative should increasingly become the students' as they obtain control over the strategy and use it to memorize ideas, words, and formulas.

Principles of Reaction

1. Help the student identify key items, pairs, and images.
2. Offer suggestions but work from the students' frames of reference.
3. Familiar elements must be primarily from the students' storehouse of material.

Support System

All of the customary devices of the curriculum areas can be brought into play. Pictures, concrete aids, films, and other audiovisual materials are especially useful for increasing the sensory richness of the associations.

CHAPTER NINE

Using Advance Organizers to Design Presentations

Scaffolding Lectures, ICT, and Distance Offerings

So why not provide the scaffold (of ideas) at the beginning (of the course)? Let the student in on the secret of the structure, including an understanding of how it continually emerges through further inquiry, so that the mind can be active as the course progresses.

—David Ausubel to Bruce Joyce

ORGANIZING IDEA

When developing a presentation, build a scaffold of the important concepts and provide them to the students at the beginning of the talk, written material, video, distance course, or seminar. Help them relate the content to the scaffold. To scaffold yourself, most articles in the Encyclopedia Britannica (www.britannica.com) provide organizing concepts during the presentations.

SCENARIO

A DOCENT AT WORK IN AN ART GALLERY

Beginning a tour of an art museum with a group of high school students, a guide says, "I want to give you an idea that will help you understand the paintings and sculptures we are about to see. The idea is simply that art, although a personal expression, reflects in many ways the culture and time in which it was produced. This may seem obvious to you at first when you look at the differences between Oriental and Western art. However, as each culture changes, so the art will change—and that is why we can speak of *periods* of art. The changes are often reflected in the artists' techniques, subject matter, colors, and style. Major changes are often reflected in the forms of art that are produced." The guide then points out examples of one or two changes in these characteristics. She also asks the students to recall their elementary school days and the differences in their drawings when they were five or six and when they were older. She likens the different periods of growing up to different cultures.

In the tour that follows, the guide points out the differences that result from changing times. "Do you see here," she asks, "that in this painting the body of the person is almost completely covered by his robes, and there is no hint of a human inside his clothes? In medieval times, the church taught that the body was unimportant and that the soul was everything." Later she remarks, "You see in this painting how the muscularity of the man stands out through his clothing and how he stands firmly on the earth. This represents the Renaissance view that man was at the center of the universe and that his body, his mind, and his power were very important indeed."

The docent is using an *advance organizer*—in this case, a powerful concept used by art historians. This organizer contains many subordinate ideas that can be linked to the particular characteristics of the art objects being viewed. In this scenario, the teacher has thus provided students with what David Ausubel calls an "intellectual scaffolding" to structure the ideas and facts they encounter during their lesson.

SCENARIO

THE TABLE OF ELEMENTS

Wendy and Keith open their course on chemistry by using a combination of inductive and mnemonics models to teach their students the table of elements. The students learn the names of the elements and their atomic weights and categorize them in terms of their states at 10 degrees Celsius. They learn the concepts *element*, *atomic weight*, and *chemical bond*.

These concepts and the knowledge of the table itself serve as the conceptual structure of their course. The information to be studied will be linked to this structure, and the concepts themselves will be refined and extended as the course proceeds.

LITERAL AND SUGGESTIVE MEANINGS

Kelly Young is introducing his students to the difference between the literal and figurative meanings of words, or the difference between *denotative* and *connotative language*. He begins by presenting an organizer, which is simply to point out that words represent things, actions, states of beings, and so on, and, while doing so, often *suggest* things. He uses examples. The word *puppy* refers to a young dog, but it also suggests playfulness and cuddliness because we think of puppies as playful and cuddly. *Limousine* refers to a car, but it suggests status, wealth, and perhaps snobbishness and conspicuous consumption.

He then presents students with a set of short stories and asks the students to read them and pick out words that have, in their opinion, only literal or referential meanings and words that also suggest things they do not refer to directly. They develop lists of words and then discuss why some words have only literal and others have literal and figurative meanings. They build categories and then continue their exploration, looking at the works of favorite authors and continuing to develop their lists.

ORIENTATION TO THE MODEL

David Ausubel is an unusual educational theorist. He directly addresses the goal of learning subject matter by advocating the improvement of *presentational* methods of teaching (lectures and readings) at a time when other educational theorists and social critics are challenging the validity of these methods and finding fault with the "passiveness" of expository learning. In contrast to those who advocate discovery methods of teaching, "open education," and experience-based learning—in other words, all the models we have discussed up to now—Ausubel stands unabashedly for the mastery of academic material through presentation.

Ausubel is also one of the few educational psychologists to address learning, teaching, and curriculum simultaneously. His theory of meaningful verbal learning deals with three concerns: (1) how knowledge (curriculum content) is organized, (2) how the mind works to process new information (learning), and (3) how teachers can apply these ideas about curriculum and learning when they present new material to students (instruction).

Goals and Assumptions

Ausubel's primary concern is to help teachers organize and convey large amounts of information as meaningfully and efficiently as possible. He believes that the acquisition of information is an essential goal of schooling and that certain theories can guide teachers in their job of transmitting knowledge to their students. His stance applies to situations in which the teacher plays the role of organizer of subject matter and presents information through lectures, readings, and providing tasks to the learner to integrate what has been learned. In his approach, the teacher is responsible for organizing and presenting what is to be learned. The learner's primary role is to master ideas and information. Whereas inductive approaches lead the students to discover or rediscover concepts, the advance organizers provide concepts and principles to the students directly. Interestingly, Ausubel believes that students have to be active constructors of knowledge, but his route is to teach them the metalevel of the discipline and the metacognitions to respond to instruction productively, rather than beginning with their perceptual world and leading them to induce the structures.

The advance organizer model is designed to strengthen students' *cognitive structures*—their knowledge of a particular subject at any given time and how well organized, clear, and stable that knowledge is (Ausubel, 1963, p. 27). Ausubel maintains that a person's existing cognitive structure is the foremost factor governing whether new material will be meaningful and how well it can be acquired and retained. Before we can present new material effectively, we must increase the stability and clarity of our students' structures. This is done by giving them concepts that govern the information to be presented to them. In the preceding example of the art gallery, the docent presented the idea that art reflects culture and cultural change, which provided the intellectual scaffolding that enabled the students to see the information in the paintings more clearly. Opening the chemistry course as Wendy and Keith did is another example—the students have little knowledge of chemistry, so the organizing concepts provide a conceptual structure on which the course can be built.

Strengthening students' cognitive structure in this way facilitates their acquisition and retention of new information. Ausubel rejects the notion that learning through listening, watching, or reading is necessarily rote, passive, or nonmeaningful. It can be, of course, but it won't be if the students' minds are prepared to receive and process information. If their minds are not prepared, the students must fall back to learning by rote (repeating material over and over), which is arduous and highly subject to forgetting. Any poorly executed teaching methods can lead to rote learning. Expository teaching is no exception. Well done, it promotes the active processing of information. He deals with important questions about what makes meaning and what makes active learning.

What Is Meaningful?

According to Ausubel, whether material is meaningful depends more on the preparation of the learner and the organization of the material than it does on the method of presentation. If the learner begins with the right "set," and if the material is solidly organized, then meaningful learning can occur.

Is Reception Learning Passive?

Ausubel says "No!" provided the proper conditions are set up. During a lecture or other form of expository teaching, the listeners' or watchers' minds can be quite active. But they must be involved in relating material to their own cognitive structure, and advance organizers provide them with a temporary scaffold within that structure. Ausubel speaks about the learners' struggle with the material—looking at it from different angles, reconciling it with similar or perhaps contradictory information, and finally translating it into their own frame of reference and terminology. However, this does not happen automatically.

Organizing Information: The Discipline and Cognitive Structure

According to Ausubel there is a parallel between the way subject matter is organized and the way people organize knowledge in their minds (their cognitive structures). He expresses the view that each of the academic disciplines has a structure of concepts (and/or propositions) that are organized hierarchically (Ausubel, 1963, p. 18). That is, at the top of each discipline are a number of very broad, abstract concepts, with more concrete concepts at lower stages of organization. Figure 9.1 illustrates the hierarchical structure of the discipline of economics, with the more abstract concepts at the top of the pyramid.

Like Jerome Bruner (1961), Ausubel believes that the structural concepts of each discipline can be taught to students, for whom they become an information-processing system—that is, they become an intellectual map that students can use to analyze particular domains and to solve problems within those domains. For example, students can use economic concepts to analyze events from an economic point of view. Suppose we present filmed case studies depicting activities on a farm, in a grocery store, in a suburban household, and in a brokerage house. Each case contains many pieces of information. The students see people engaged in various activities, observe many behaviors, and listen to several conversations. If the students were then to make an economic analysis of these cases, they would catalog the behaviors and activities of the people in terms of such concepts as supply and demand, wants and needs, goods and services, and consumers and producers. These concepts help in several ways. They enable students to make sense of large amounts of data and to compare the four case studies, discovering the underlying commonalities in the apparent differences.

Ausubel describes the mind as an information-processing and information-storing system that can be compared to the conceptual structure of an academic discipline. Like the disciplines, the mind is a hierarchically organized set of ideas that provides anchors for information and ideas and that serves as

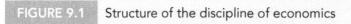

FIGURE 9.1   Structure of the discipline of economics

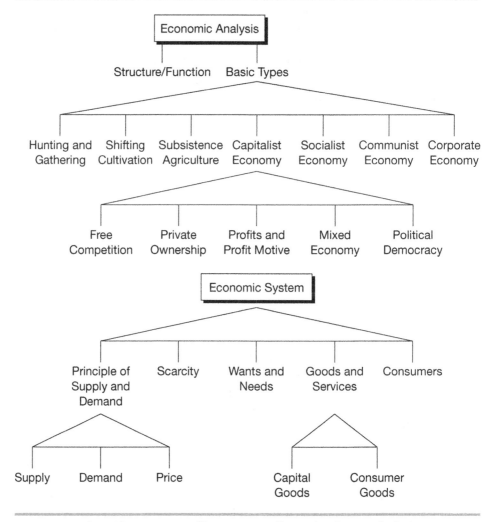

Source: Based on Clinton Boutwell, *Getting It All Together* (San Rafael, CA: Leswing Press, 1972).

a storehouse for them. Figure 9.2 shows the hierarchy of cognitive structure in the discipline of economics. The shaded concepts are the most inclusive. They have been "learned" and exist in a hypothetical learner's cognitive structure. The unshaded concepts are potentially meaningful because they can be *linked* to the existing concepts. The black circles are not yet potentially meaningful concepts because suitable anchors for them are not yet incorporated into the cognitive structure. As this information-processing system acquires new

FIGURE 9.2   An individual's cognitive structure with respect to economics

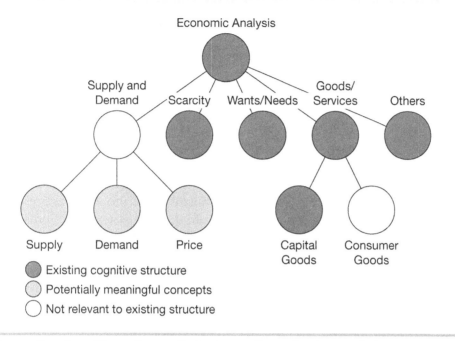

Source: Based on Clinton Boutwell, *Getting It All Together* (San Rafael, CA: Leswing Press, 1972).

information and ideas, it reorganizes itself to accommodate those ideas. Thus, the system is in a continuous state of change.

Ausubel maintains that new ideas can be usefully learned and retained only to the extent that they can be related to already available concepts or propositions that provide ideational anchors. If the new material conflicts too strongly with the existing cognitive structure *or* is so unrelated that no linkage is provided, the information or ideas may not be incorporated or retained. To prevent this from occurring, the teacher must sequence the material to be learned and present it in such a way that the ideational anchors are provided. In addition, the learner must actively reflect on the new material, think through these linkages, reconcile differences or discrepancies, and note similarities with existing information.

Implications for Curriculum

Ausubel's ideas about subject matter and cognitive structure have important and direct implications for the organization of curriculum and instructional procedures. He uses two principles, *progressive differentiation* and *integrative reconciliation,* to guide the organization of content in such a way that the concepts become a stable part of a student's cognitive structure and to describe the student's intellectual role.

Progressive differentiation means that the most general ideas of the discipline are presented first, followed by a gradual increase in detail and specificity. *Integrative reconciliation* simply means that new ideas should be consciously related to previously learned content. In other words, the sequence of the curriculum is organized so that each successive learning is carefully related to what has been presented before. If the entire body of material has been conceptualized and presented according to progressive differentiation, integrative reconciliation follows naturally, though it requires the learner's active cooperation. Gradually, as a result of both principles, the discipline is built into the mind of the learner.

Both the discipline and the sequence of instruction are built from the top down, with the most inclusive concepts, principles, and propositions presented first. Ausubel points out that the organization of most textbooks puts each topic in a separate chapter or subchapter, all at the same level of abstraction and generality. "In most instances," therefore, "students are required to learn the details of new and unfamiliar disciplines before they have acquired an adequate body of relevant subsumers at an appropriate level of inclusiveness" (Ausubel, 1968, p. 153).

At first sight, the approach of providing major ideas gradually followed by subordinate ones seems opposed to the inductive, concept attainment, and scientific inquiry models, but there is great similarity in that the development of concepts is central and the student is to be actively involved in connecting concepts and information. Also, in a curriculum, one might alternate the construction of ideas with the presentation of ideas.

Implications for Teaching

Advance organizers strengthen cognitive structures and enhance retention of new information. Ausubel describes advance organizers as introductory material presented ahead of the learning task and at a higher level of abstraction and inclusiveness than the learning task itself. Their purpose is to explain, integrate, and interrelate the material in the learning task with previously learned material (and also to help the learner discriminate the new material from previously learned material) (Ausubel, 1968, p. 148). The most effective organizers are those that use concepts, terms, and propositions that are already familiar to the learners, as well as appropriate illustrations and analogies.

Suppose, for example, a teacher wants students to acquire information about current energy problems. The teacher provides learning material containing data about possible power sources, general information about U.S. economic growth and technology, and alternative policies on the energy crisis and future planning. The learning material is in the form of newspaper articles, a lecture, and perhaps a film. The learning task for the students is to internalize the information—that is, to remember the central ideas and perhaps the key facts. Before introducing students to the learning material, however, the teacher provides introductory material in the form of an advance organizer to help them relate to the new data.

In this example, the concept of energy might be used as the basis of the organizer, and related concepts such as energy efficiency and energy conservation can provide auxiliary organizers. Other possibilities are the concept of ecology and its various subsystems dealing with the environment, the economy, the political arena, and social structures. This second set of organizers would focus students' attention on the *impact* of old and new energy sources on the subsystems of our ecological system, whereas the first set would encourage them to process the data through a consideration of energy efficiency and energy conservation.

The organizer is important content in itself and needs to be taught. It may be a concept or a statement of relationship. In either case, teachers must take time to explain and develop the organizer, because only when it is fully understood can it serve to organize the subsequent learning material. For example, students must fully understand the concept of *culture* before the teacher can use it effectively to organize factual information about different culture groups. Advance organizers are generally based on the major concepts, propositions, generalizations, principles, and laws of a discipline. For instance, a lesson or text describing the caste system in India might be preceded by an organizer based on the concept of social stratification. Similarly, the generalization, "Technological changes can produce major changes in society and culture" could be the *basis* for an organizer preceding the study of several historical periods and places.

Usually, the organizer is tied closely to the material it precedes. However, the organizer can also be created from an analogy from another field in order to provide a new perspective. For instance, the concept of balance or form, though generic to the arts, may be applied to literature, mathematics, the functioning of the branches of government, or even our daily activities. A study of churches can be viewed under the rubric of many different organizers: those focusing on the economic implications of the church, cultural or sociological perspectives, or architectural perspectives.

EXPOSITORY AND COMPARATIVE ORGANIZERS

There are two types of advance organizers—expository and comparative. *Expository organizers* provide a basic concept and perhaps some lesser concepts at the highest level of abstraction. These represent the intellectual scaffold on which students will "hang" the new information as they encounter it. Expository organizers are especially helpful because they provide ideational scaffolding for unfamiliar material. Thus, the basic concepts of economics would be presented prior to the study of the economic condition of a city.

Comparative organizers, on the other hand, are typically used with relatively familiar material. They are designed to discriminate between the old and new concepts in order to prevent confusion caused by their similarity. For example, when the learner is being introduced to long division, a comparative organizer might be used to point out the similarities and differences between division facts and multiplication facts. Whereas in multiplication, the multiplier and multiplicand can be reversed without changing the product—that is, 3 times 4 can be changed to 4 times 3—the divisor and dividend cannot be reversed in division without affecting the quotient—that is, 6 divided by 2 is not the same as 2 divided by 6. The comparative organizer can help the learner see the relationship between multiplication and division and clarify the differences between the two. The learner can then borrow from knowledge about multiplication when learning division without being confused by the differences.

EVIDENTIAL MATTERS

Ausubel and others have conducted a variety of studies exploring the validity of Ausubel's rationale. The Lawton (1977a,1977b) studies are particularly interesting not only with respect to learning and retention of material but also with respect to the theory's potential for influencing logical operations—that is, to help develop thinking ability.

In general, Lawton's studies seems to support the notion that what is taught will be learned. If we present material to students, some of it will be learned. If it is presented with an organizing structure, somewhat more will be learned. If we use a process that helps students develop certain ways of thinking, some of those ways of thinking will be learned. Thus, if we avoid using those models of teaching that provide certain intellectual structures and employ certain thinking processes, we decrease the chances of those structures and thinking processes being acquired. Generally speaking, the development of an *intellectual structure*—whether through presentational or inductive methods—increases the probability that students will learn those structures and the thinking processes associated with them, and that they will retain material more fully. The effects are strongest with respect to older children. Effects, by the way, can be seen in problem-solving behavior as the students bring the structures to bear on problems they have not previously encountered (Bascones & Novak, 1985; Maloney, 1994).

THE MODEL OF TEACHING

The model of teaching developed here is based on Ausubel's ideas about subject matter, cognitive structure, active reception learning, and advance organizers.

Syntax

The advance organizer model has three phases of activity. Phase one is the presentation of the advance organizer, phase two is the presentation of the learning task or learning material, and phase three is the strengthening of cognitive organization. Phase three tests the relationship of the learning material to existing ideas to bring about an active learning process. A summary of the syntax appears in Table 9.1.

The activities are designed to increase the clarity and stability of the new learning material so that fewer ideas are lost, confused with one another, or left vague. The students should operate on the material as they receive it by relating the new learning material to personal experience and to their existing cognitive structure, as well as by taking a critical stance toward knowledge.

TABLE Syntax of Advance Organizer Model

Phase One: **Presentation of Advance Organizer**	Clarify aims of the lesson. Present organizer: Identify defining attributes. Give examples. Provide context. Prompt awareness of learner's relevant knowledge and experience.
Phase Two: **Presentation of Learning Task or Material**	Present material. Maintain attention. Make organization explicit. Make logical order of learning material explicit.
Phase Three: **Strengthening Cognitive Organization**	Use principles of integrative reconciliation. Promote active reception learning. Elicit critical approach to subject matter. Clarify.

Phase one consists of three activities: clarifying the aims of the lesson, presenting the advance organizer, and prompting awareness of relevant prior knowledge. Clarifying the aim of the lesson is one way to obtain students' attention and orient them to their learning goals, both of which are necessary to facilitate meaningful learning. (Clarifying aims is also useful to the teacher in planning a lesson.)

As mentioned earlier, the organizer is not just a brief, simple statement; it is an idea in itself and, like the learning material, must be explored intellectually. It must also be distinguished from introductory comments, which are useful to the lesson but are not advance organizers. For instance, when we teach, many of us begin our instruction by asking students to recall what we did last week or last year or by telling them what we are going to do tomorrow. In this way, we give them a context or orientation for our presentation. Or we may ask students to recall a personal experience and then acknowledge that what we are about to say resembles that situation or will help students understand a previous experience. We may also tell them the objectives of the session—what we hope they will get out of the presentation or discussion. *None of the just-described techniques is an advance organizer.* However, all are part of a well-organized presentation, and some reflect principles that are central to Ausubel's theory of meaningful verbal learning and are part of the model of teaching.

The actual organizer, however, is built around the major concepts and/or propositions of a discipline or area of study. First, the organizer has to be constructed so that the learner can perceive it for what it is—an idea distinct from and more inclusive than the material in the learning task itself. The chief feature of an organizer is that it is at a higher level of abstraction and generality than the learning material itself. This higher level of abstraction is what distinguishes organizers from introductory overviews, which are written (or spoken) at the same level of abstraction as the learning material because they are, in fact, previews of the learning material.

Second, whether the organizer is expository or comparative, the essential features of the concept or proposition must be pointed out and carefully explained. Thus, the teacher and students must explore the organizer as well as the learning task. To us, this means citing the essential features, explaining them, and providing examples. The presentation of an organizer need not be lengthy, but it must be perceived (the learner must be aware of it), clearly understood, and continually related to the material it is organizing. This means the learner must already be familiar with the language and ideas in the organizer. It is also useful to illustrate the organizer in multiple contexts and to repeat it several times, particularly any new or special terminology. Finally, it is important to prompt awareness of the learner's prior knowledge and experiences that might be relevant to this learning task and organizer.

Following the presentation of the advance organizer in phase one, in phase two the learning material is presented in the form of lectures, discussions, films, experiments, or reading. During the presentation, the organization of the learning material needs to be made explicit to the students so that they have an overall sense of direction and can see the logical order of the material and how the organization relates to the advance organizer.

The purpose of phase three is to anchor the new learning material in the students' existing cognitive structure—that is, to strengthen the students' cognitive organization. In the natural flow of teaching, some of these procedures may be incorporated into phase two; however, we want to emphasize that the reworking of new material is a separate teaching task, with its own set of activities and skills. Ausubel identifies four activities: (1) promoting integrative reconciliation, (2) promoting active reception learning, (3) eliciting a critical approach to the subject matter, and (4) clarification.

There are several ways to facilitate reconciliation of the new material with the existing cognitive structure. The teacher can: (1) remind students of the ideas (the larger picture), (2) ask for a summary of the major attributes of the new learning material, (3) repeat precise definitions, (4) ask for differences between aspects of the material, and (5) ask students to describe how the learning material supports the concept or proposition that is being used as the organizer.

Active learning can be promoted by: (1) asking students to describe how the new material relates to the organizer, (2) asking students for additional examples of the concept or propositions in the learning material, (3) asking students to verbalize the essence of the material, using their own terminology and frame of reference, and (4) asking students to examine the material from alternative points of view.

A critical approach to knowledge is fostered by asking students to recognize assumptions or inferences that may have been made in the learning material, to judge and challenge these assumptions and inferences, and to reconcile contradictions among them.

It is not possible or desirable to use all these techniques in one lesson. Constraints of time, topic, and relevance to the particular learning situation will guide their use. However, it is important to keep in mind the four goals of this phase and specific techniques for effective expository teaching.

Ideally, the initiation of phase three is shared by teachers and students. At first, however, the teacher will have to respond to the students' need for clarification of some area of the topic and for integration of the new material with existing knowledge.

Essentially, Ausubel has provided us with a method for improving not only presentations, but also students' abilities to learn from them. The more we teach students to become active—to *look* for organizing ideas, reconcile information with them, and generate organizers of their own (engaging in inductive activity while reading or watching)—the greater their potential for profiting from presentations becomes.

By the way, can an organizing idea be presented using concept attainment? You bet it can.

Social System

In this model, the teacher retains control of the intellectual structure because it is continually necessary to relate the learning material to the organizers and to help students differentiate new material from previously learned material. In phase three, however, the learning situation is ideally much more interactive, with students initiating many questions and comments. The successful acquisition of the material will depend on the learners' desire to integrate it with prior knowledge, on their critical faculties, and on the teacher's presentation and organization of the material.

Principles of Reaction

The teacher's solicited or unsolicited responses to the learners' reactions will be guided by the purpose of clarifying the meaning of the new learning material, differentiating it from and reconciling it with existing knowledge, making it personally relevant to the students, and helping promote a critical approach to knowledge. Ideally, students will initiate their own questions in response to their own drives for meaning.

Support System

Well-organized material is the critical support requirement of this model. The effectiveness of the advance organizer depends on an integral and appropriate relationship between the conceptual organizer and the content. This model provides guidelines for building (or reorganizing) instructional materials.

APPLICATION

The advance organizer model is especially useful to structure extended curriculum sequences or courses and to instruct students systematically in the key ideas of a field. Step by step, major concepts and propositions are explained and integrated, so that at the end of a period of instruction, the learners should gain perspective on the entire area being studied. We would expect an increase, too, in the learners' grasps of factual information linked to and explained by the key ideas. For instance, the concept of socialization can be drawn on repeatedly in the study of socialization patterns in different cultures and subcultures. This advance organizer thus aids in expanding students' knowledge about cultures.

The model can also be shaped to teach the *skills* of effective reception learning. Critical thinking and cognitive reorganization can be explained to the learners, who receive direct instruction in orderly thinking and in the notion of knowledge hierarchies. Ultimately, they can apply these techniques independently to new learning. In other words, this model can increase effectiveness in reading and watching films and in other "reception" activities.

Other models are also useful for evaluating or applying the material presented by the advance organizer. For example, the advance organizer model, after introducing new material in a deductive, presentational way, can be followed by inductive concept attainment activities that reinforce the material or that informally evaluate students' acquisition of the material.

INSTRUCTIONAL AND NURTURANT EFFECTS

The probable instructional values of this model seem clear—the ideas themselves that are used as the organizer are learned, as well as information presented to the students. The ability to learn from reading, lectures, and other media used for presentations is another effect, as are an interest in inquiry and precise habits of thinking (see Figure 9.3).

FIGURE 9.3   Instructional and nurturant effects of the advance organizer model

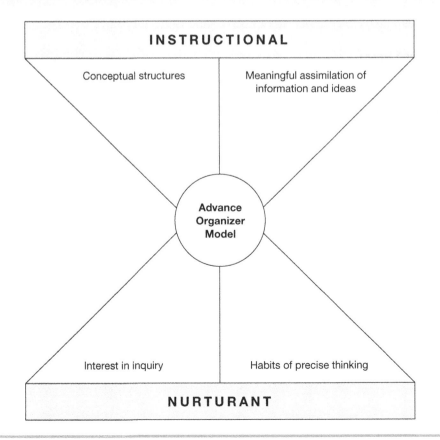

SUMMARY CHART *Advance Organizer Model*

Syntax

- *Phase One: Presentation of Advance Organizer.* Clarify the aims of the lesson. Present organizer. Prompt awareness of learner's relevant knowledge and experience.
- *Phase Two: Presentation of Learning Task or Material.* Present material. Make logical order of learning material explicit. Link material to organizer.
- *Phase Three: Strengthening Cognitive Organization.* Clarify ideas. Apply ideas actively (such as by testing them).

Social System

The social system is highly structured; however, it requires active collaboration between teacher and learner.

Principles of Reaction

1. Negotiation of meaning.
2. Responsively connecting organizer and material.

Support System

The model requires data-rich, well-organized material. (*Caution:* Many textbooks do not feature conceptually organized material. Britannica provides very good models.)

CHAPTER TEN

The Inquiry Training Model

Training Inquiry Skills Directly

Even the most higher-order Twentieth-Century skills require some very specific instruction and practice—the kind usually associated with training in lower-order skills.

—our reflective observer

ORGANIZING IDEA

Reading is *thinking*. Building concepts requires *thinking*. Resolving conflicts requires *thinking*. We can't do much without cognating at least a bit, whether on the left or right side.

So why not teach students how to deal with a puzzling situation by getting the facts straight and looking for causal relationships?

SCENARIO

One morning, as Mrs. Nikki Harrison's fourth-grade students are settling down to their arithmetic workbooks, the lightbulb on Nikki's desk lamp blows out.

"What happened?" asks one student.

"Can't you see?" remarks another. "The lightbulb blew out."

"Yeah," inquires the first, "but what does that mean?"

"What do you mean, 'What does that mean?' "

"Just that we have all seen a lot of lightbulbs blow out, but what does that really mean? What happens?"

Nicki unscrews the lightbulb and holds it up. The children gather around, and she passes it among them. After she gets it back, she says, "Well, why don't you see if you can develop a hypothesis about what happened?"

"What's inside the glass?" asks one of the children.

"I'm afraid I can't answer that," she replies. "Can you put it another way?"

"Is there air inside the glass?" one questions.

"No," Nikki says.

"Is a vacuum inside the glass?"

"A long time ago some of these were made that way, but not now."

"Is there a gas inside?" asks another.

"Yes," says Nikki. The children look at one another in puzzlement.

She prompts, "You might want to learn why they are made without air inside."

"Why not," asks one boy and they all groan. "OK, OK," he responds. "I didn't ask a *yes* or *no* question."

Nikki smiles at him. "Well, can you ask me another question?"

"Lightbulbs get really hot, don't they?"

"Yes."

"Hot enough to burst into flame if air was inside?"

"Yes."

"So some kind of gas is in there that won't be affected by heat?"

"Yep," says Nikki.

"What is that little wire made of?" asks another student.

"I can't answer that," reminds Nikki. "Can you put it another way?"

"Is the little wire made of metal?"

"Yes," she responds.

Asking questions such as these, the children gradually gain information about the bulb and how electricity is involved in generating light.

Then Nikki decides to move the inquiry to information sources. They make a list of questions to ask, categorize them, and assign them to their regular inquiry teams. Then they head to the Internet. She reminds them that information on Wikipedia needs to be checked against Britannica or another encyclopedia but indicates that she will be interested to learn what other kinds of sources they locate. They know that she is reminding them to visit the school library, Nova and other public television sources, and the Library of Congress.

Nikki has prepared her class to carry out a model of teaching/learning that we call *inquiry training*. Normally, the class uses inquiry training to explore preselected areas. That is, either Nikki organizes a unit of instruction and selects puzzling situations to stimulate inquiries, or the students identify puzzlements to explore. In this case, a familiar event got them going—the children used the techniques of inquiry training to formulate theories about an event that was familiar to all of them and yet puzzled them, for none of them had previously developed ideas about what really went on when a lightbulb blew out. Further puzzlements will emerge from their explorations. And, as they learn that only about 10 percent of the electrical energy is converted to light—the rest to heat—they will also find that their inquiry connects to a public policy question as national legislation is making the incandescent lightbulb an artifact of the past. In Australia, legislation was passed in 2009 to replace them. But with what? Another inquiry squirrels its way into their minds.

Inquiry training was developed by Richard Suchman (1981) to teach students a process for investigating and explaining unusual phenomena. Suchman's model takes students through miniature versions of the kinds of procedures that scholars use to organize knowledge and generate principles. Based on an aspect of scientific method, it attempts to teach students some of the skills and language of scholarly inquiry. Suchman developed his model by analyzing methods employed by creative research personnel, especially physical scientists. As he identified the elements of their inquiry processes, he built them into the instructional model called *inquiry training*. He borrowed significantly from the parlor game "20 Questions."

THE EVIDENTIAL DIMENSION

Inquiry training is designed to bring students directly into the scientific process through exercises that compress the scientific process into small periods of time. What are the effects? Schlenker (1976) reported that inquiry training resulted in increased understanding of science, productivity in creative thinking, and skills for obtaining and analyzing information. He reported that it was not more effective than conventional methods of teaching in the acquisition of information, but that it was as efficient as recitation or lectures accompanied by laboratory experiences. Ivany (1969) and Collins (1969) reported that the method works best when the confrontations are strong, arousing genuine puzzlement, and when the materials the students use to explore the topics under consideration are especially instructional. Both elementary and secondary students can profit from the model (Voss, 1982). In an intriguing study, Elefant (1980) successfully carried out the model with deaf children, which suggests that the method can be powerful with students who have severe sensory handicaps.

ORIENTATION TO THE MODEL

Goals and Assumptions

Inquiry training originated in a belief in the development of independent learners; its method requires active investigatory inquiry. Children are curious and eager to grow, and inquiry training capitalizes on their natural energetic explorations, giving them specific directions so that they explore new areas effectively. An important goal is to help students develop the intellectual discipline and skills necessary to raise questions and search out answers. Thus, Suchman is interested in helping students inquire independently, but in a disciplined way. He wants students to question why events happen as they do and to acquire and process data logically, and he wants them to develop general intellectual strategies that they can use to find out why things are as they are.

Inquiry training begins by presenting students with a puzzling event. Suchman believes that individuals faced with such a situation are naturally motivated to solve the puzzle. We can use the opportunity provided by natural inquiry to teach the procedures of disciplined searching.

Congruent with the current core curriculum documents in all areas, students need to embrace the attitude that *all knowledge is tentative*. But tentativeness does not equate with uselessness. Consider that Suchman's formulation, made 50 years ago, has validity today.

Importantly, Suchman believed that students can become increasingly conscious of their process of inquiry and that they can be taught scientific procedures directly. All of us often inquire intuitively; however, Suchman feels we cannot analyze and improve our thinking unless we are conscious of it. Metacognitive awareness is built into the procedure.

The View of Students in the Learning Process

There are four beliefs governing students' role in the learning process:

1. Students inquire naturally when they are puzzled.
2. They can become conscious of and learn to analyze their thinking strategies.
3. New strategies can be taught directly and added to the students' existing ones.
4. Cooperative inquiry enriches thinking and helps students to learn about the tentative, emergent nature of knowledge and to appreciate alternative explanations.

OVERVIEW OF THE TEACHING STRATEGY

Following Suchman's belief that individuals have a natural motivation to inquire, the inquiry training model is built around intellectual confrontations. The student is presented with a puzzling situation and inquires into it. Anything that is mysterious, unexpected, or unknown is grist for a discrepant event. Because the ultimate goal is to have the students experience the creation of new knowledge, the confrontation should be based on discoverable ideas.

In the following example, bending a metallic strip held over a flame begins the inquiry cycle.

> The strip is made of a lamination of unlike strips of metal (usually steel and brass) that have been welded together to form a single blade. With a handle at one end, it has the appearance of a narrow knife or spatula. When this apparatus is heated, the metal in it expands, but the rate of expansion is not the same in the two metals. Consequently, half of the thickness of this laminated strip becomes slightly longer than the other half and since the two halves are attached to each other, the internal stresses force the blade to assume a curve of which the outer circumference is occupied by the metal which has expanded the most. (Suchman, 1981, p 28)

Suchman deliberately selects episodes that have sufficiently surprising outcomes to make it difficult for students to remain indifferent to the encounter. Usually things that are heated do not bend into a big curve. When this metal strip does, the students naturally want to know *why*. The learners cannot dismiss the solution as obvious; they have to work to explain the situation, and the products of that work are new insights, concepts, and theories.

After the presentation of the puzzling situation, the students ask the teacher questions. The questions, however, must be answered by yeses or no's. Students may not ask the teacher to explain the phenomenon to them. They have to focus and structure their probes to solve the problem. In this sense, each question becomes a limited hypothesis. Thus, the student may not ask, "How did the heat affect the metal?" but must ask, "Was the heat greater than the melting point of the metal?" The first question is not a specific statement of what information is wanted; it asks the teacher to do the conceptualizing. The second question requires the student to put several factors together— heat, metal, change, liquid. The student had to ask the teacher to verify the hypothesis that he or she has developed (the heat caused the metal to change into a liquid).

The students continue to ask questions. Whenever they phrase one that cannot be answered by a yes or a no, the teacher reminds them of the rules and waits until they find a way of stating the question in the proper form. Comments such as "Can you restate this question so that I can answer it with a yes or a no?" are common teacher responses when students slip out of the inquiry mode.

Over time, the students are taught that the first stage in inquiry is to verify the facts of the situation—the nature and identity of the objects, the events, and the conditions surrounding the puzzling event. The question "Was the strip made of metal?" helps verify the facts—in this case, a property of the object. As the students become aware of the facts, hypotheses should come to mind and guide further inquiry. Using their knowledge about the behavior of the objects, students can turn their questions to the relationships among the variables in the situation. They can conduct verbal or actual experiments to test these causal relationships, selecting new data or organizing the existing data in new ways to see what will happen if things are done differently. For example, they could ask, "If I turn the flame down, will the bend still occur?" Better yet, they could actually do this! By introducing a new condition or altering an existing one, students isolate variables and learn how they affect one another.

It is important for students and teachers to recognize the difference between questions that attempt to verify "what is" and questions or activities that experiment with the relationships among variables. Each of these is essential to theory development, but fact gathering should precede hypothesis raising. Unless sufficient information about the nature of the problem situation and its elements is verified, students are likely to be overwhelmed by the many possible causal relationships.

> If the child immediately tries to hypothesize complex relationships among all the variables that seem relevant to him, he could go on testing indefinitely without any noticeable progress, but by isolating variables and testing them singly, he can eliminate the irrelevant ones and discover the relationships that exist between each relevant independent variable (such as the temperature of the blade) and the dependent variable (which in this case is the bending of the blade). (Suchman, 1962, pp. 15–16)

Finally, the students try to develop hypotheses that will fully explain what happened. (For instance, "The strip was made of two metals that were fastened together somehow. They expand at different rates, and when they were heated, the one that expanded the most exerted pressure on the other one so that the two bent over together.") Even after lengthy and rich verification and experimentation activities, many explanations may be possible, and the students are encouraged not to be satisfied with the first explanation that appears to fit the facts.

> Inquiry cannot be programmed, and the range of productive inquiry strategies is vast. Thus, students should experiment freely with their own questions, structuring and sequencing [the inquiry session]. Nevertheless, inquiry can be divided into broad phases which, on the whole, should be taken in logical order simply because they build upon one another. Failure to adhere to this order leads either to erroneous assumptions or to low efficiency and duplication of effort. (Suchman, 1962, p. 38)

The emphasis in this model is clearly on becoming aware of and mastering the inquiry process, not on the content of any particular problem situation. Although the model should also be enormously appealing and effective as a mode of acquiring and using information, the teacher cannot be too concerned with subject-matter coverage or "getting the right answer." In fact, this would violate the whole spirit of scientific inquiry, which envisions a community of scholars searching together for more accurate and powerful explanations for everyday phenomena.

THE MODEL OF TEACHING

Syntax

Inquiry training has five phases (see Table 10.1). The first phase is the student's *confrontation* with the puzzling situation. Phases two and three are the *data-gathering* operations of *verification* and *experimentation*. In these two phases, students ask a series of questions to which the teacher replies yes or no, and they conduct a series of experiments on the environment of the problem situation. In the fourth phase, students *organize* the information they obtained during the data gathering and try to *explain* the discrepancy. Finally, in phase five, students *analyze* the problem-solving strategies they used during the inquiry.

TABLE **10.1** Syntax of Inquiry Training Model

Phase One: **Confrontation with the Problem**	Explain inquiry procedures. Present discrepant event.
Phase Two: **Data Gathering—Verification**	Verify the nature of objects and conditions. Verify the occurrence of the problem situation.
Phase Three: **Data Gathering—Experimentation**	Isolate relevant variables. Hypothesize (and test) causal relationships.
Phase Four: **Organizing, Formulating an Explanation**	Formulate rules or explanations.
Phase Five: **Analysis of the Inquiry Process**	Analyze inquiry strategy and develop more effective ones.

Phase one requires that the teacher present the problem situation and explain the inquiry procedures to the students (the objectives and the procedure of the yes/no question). The formulation of a discrepant event such as the bimetallic strip problem requires some thought, although the strategy can be based on relatively simple problems—a puzzle, riddle, or magic trick—that do not require much background knowledge. Of course, the ultimate goal is to have students, especially older students, experience the creation of new knowledge, much as scholars do. However, beginning inquiries can be based on very simple ideas.

The distinguishing feature of the discrepancy is that it involves events that conflict with our notions of reality. In this sense, not every puzzling situation is a discrepant event. It may be puzzling because we do not know the answer, but we do not need new concepts to understand it, and therefore we do not need to conduct an inquiry. We mention this because occasionally teachers do not pick problems that are truly puzzling to the student. In these cases, the learning activity does not progress beyond a "20 Questions" format. Even though the questioning activity has value for its own sake, it should not be confused with the notion of scientific inquiry.

Phase two, verification, is the process whereby students gather information about an event they see or experience. In experimentation, phase three, students introduce new elements into the situation to see if the event happens differently. Although verification and experimentation are described as separate phases of the model, the students' thinking and the types of questions they generate usually alternate between these two aspects of data gathering.

Experiments serve two functions: *exploration* and *direct testing*. Exploration—changing things to see what will happen—is not necessarily guided by a theory or hypothesis, but it may suggest ideas for a theory. Direct testing occurs when students try out a theory or hypothesis. The process of converting a hypothesis into an experiment is not easy and takes practice. Many verification and experimentation questions are required just to investigate one theory. We have found that even sophisticated adults find it easier to say, "I think it has something to do with . . ." than to think of a series of questions that will test the theory. Also, few theories can be discarded on the basis of one experiment. Although it is tempting to "throw away" a variable if the first experiment does not support it, it can be very misleading to do so. One of the teacher's roles is to restrain students whenever they assume that a variable has been disproven when it has not.

A second function of the teacher is to broaden the students' inquiry by expanding the type of information they obtain. During verification they may ask questions about objects, events, conditions, and properties. *Object* questions are intended to determine the nature or identity of objects. (Is the knife made of steel? Is the liquid water?) *Event* questions attempt to verify the occurrence or nature of an action. (Did the knife bend upward the second time?) *Condition* questions relate to the state of objects or systems at a particular time. (Was the blade hotter than room temperature when the teacher held it up and showed that it was bent? Did the color change when the liquid was added?) *Property* questions aim to verify the behavior of objects under certain conditions as a way of gaining new information to help build a theory. (Does copper always bend when it is heated?) Because students tend not to verify all aspects of the problem, teachers can be aware of the type of information needed and work to change the questioning pattern. The web, online encyclopedias, an interactive whiteboard, assisting the sharing of information and categorization, and recategorization also become an integral part of the inquiry.

In phase four, the teacher calls on the students to organize the data and formulate an explanation. Some students have difficulty making the intellectual leap between comprehending the information they have gathered and constructing a clear explanation of it. They may give inadequate explanations, omitting essential details. Sometimes several theories or explanations are possible based on the same data. In such cases, it is often useful to ask students to state their explanations so that the range of possible hypotheses becomes obvious. Together the group can shape the explanation that fully responds to the problem situation. Finally, in phase five, the students are asked to analyze their pattern of inquiry. They may determine the questions that were most effective, the lines of questioning that were productive and those that were not, or the type of information they needed and did not obtain. This phase is essential if we are to make the inquiry process conscious and systematically try to improve it.

Social System

Suchman's intention is that the social system be cooperative and rigorous. The intellectual environment is open to all relevant ideas. Teachers and students participate as equals where ideas are concerned. As the academic year progresses, the students should initiate inquiries more and more.

After a period of practice in teacher-structured inquiry sessions, students can undertake inquiry in more student-controlled settings. A stimulating event can be set up in the room, and students can inquire on their own or in informal groups, alternating between open-ended inquiry sessions and data gathering with the aid of resource materials. In this way, the students can move back and forth between inquiry sessions and independent study. This utilization of the inquiry training model is especially suited to the open-classroom setting, where the teacher's role is that of instructional manager and monitor.

In the initial stages of inquiry, the teacher's role is to select (or construct) the problem situation, referee the inquiry according to inquiry procedures, respond to students' inquiry probes with the necessary information, help beginning inquirers establish a focus in their inquiry, and facilitate discussion of the problem situation among the students.

Principles of Reaction

The most important reactions of the teacher take place during the second and third phases. During the second phase, the teacher's task is to help the students inquire, not to do the inquiry for them. If the teacher is asked questions that cannot be answered by a yes or no, he or she must ask the students to rephrase the questions so as to further their own attempts to collect data and relate them to the problem situation. The teacher can, if necessary, keep the inquiry moving by making new information available to the group and by focusing on particular problem events or by raising questions. During the last phase, the teacher's task is to keep the inquiry directed toward the process of investigation itself.

Support System

The optimal support is a set of confronting materials, a teacher who understands the intellectual processes and strategies of inquiry, and resource materials bearing on the problem.

APPLICATION

Although inquiry training was originally developed for the natural sciences, its procedures are usable in all subject areas; any topic that can be formulated as a puzzling situation is a candidate for inquiry training. In literature, murder mysteries and science fiction stories or plots make excellent puzzling situations. Newspaper articles about bizarre or improbable situations may be used to construct stimulus events. One of the authors was at a Chinese restaurant not too long ago and puzzled over the question, "How is the fortune put into the fortune cookie, since it does not appear burned or cooked in any way?" It occurred to us that this would make an excellent inquiry training topic for young children. The social sciences also offer numerous possibilities for inquiry training.

The construction of puzzling situations is the critical task, because it transforms curriculum content into problems to be explored. When objects and other materials are not available or appropriate to the problem situation, we recommend that teachers make up a *problem statement* for students and a *fact sheet* for themselves. The problem statement describes the discrepant event and provides the information that is shared initially with the students. The fact sheet gives the teacher further information about the problem, and the teacher draws on it to respond to the students' questions. Let's look at an example in social studies.

SCENARIO

THE MYSTERY OF THE MISSING COLONY

For a social studies class, an instructor composed a problem statement and a student fact sheet based on an anthropological issue. The teacher passed the following statement out to his students:

Problem Statement

This map shows an island in the middle of a lake. The island is connected to the shore by a causeway made of stones piled on the bottom of the lake until the pile reached the surface. Then smoothed stones were laid down to make a road. The lake is surrounded by mountains, and the only flat land is near the lake. The island is covered with buildings whose walls are still standing, although the roofs are now gone. It is completely uninhabited.

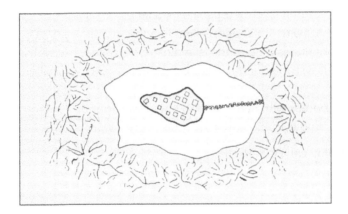

Your task is to discover what happened to the people who lived there. What caused the place to be empty of human beings?

As the students conducted their inquiry, the instructor drew on the following fact sheet:

Instructor Fact Sheet
1. The lake is 500 feet deep, 600 feet across.
2. The lake is 6,500 feet above sea level. The mountains rise to 11,000 feet.
3. The causeway is made of dumped rocks.
4. The houses are close together. Each one is about 20 by 25 feet and has more than one room. They are made of limestone blocks.
5. Some broken tools and pottery have been found in the homes.

6. The edifice in the center is made of marble and has three levels. At the bottom it is six times larger than the houses. At the top level of the edifice, you can sight the planets and stars through a hole slit in a stone. You can sight Venus at its lowest rise, which occurs on December 21.

7. There is evidence that the islanders fished with traps. They also had livestock such as sheep, cows, and chickens.

8. Apparently there was no art, but evidence of graphic writing has been found.

9. Cisterns have been found under limestone streets.

10. There is no habitation within 80 miles.

11. The island has been uninhabited for about 300 years.

12. The area was discovered in 1900.

13. It is located in a subtropical area of South America where there is plenty of drinking water and where every available area was farmed. There is evidence of irrigation but no evidence of crop rotation. In general, the land is marginal for farming.

14. There is a thin layer of topsoil over a limestone shelf.

15. About 1,000 to 1,500 people lived on the island.

16. The mountains around the island can be crossed, but with difficulty.

17. There is a stone quarry in nearby mountains and a burial ground across the lake.

18. Dead bodies with hands folded have been found.

19. There is no evidence of plague, disease, or war.

See what you can do with this.

Age-Level Adaptation

Inquiry training can be used with children of all ages, but each age group requires adaptation. We have seen the method be successful with kindergarten children but encounter difficulty with third graders. As with many other aspects of teaching, each group and each student are unique. However, the model can be simplified in several ways until students are able to engage in all phases.

For very young children, it is best to keep the content of the problem simple—perhaps with more emphasis on discovery than on a principle of causation. Problem situations like "What is in this box?" or "What is this unusual thing?" or "Why does one egg roll differently from the other?" are appropriate. One teacher we know showed her students a picture of a flying squirrel from a magazine for science teachers. Since most of us believe mammals do not fly, this was truly a discrepant event. She asked the students to come up with an explanation for this phenomenon using inquiry procedures.

Bruce and Bruce (1992) provide a large number of discrepant events for use in the social studies that can be used with all grades and over a wide range of common social studies topics. Numerous children's science books are filled with simple science experiments, many of them suitable for primary grades. Mystery stories and riddles work well as stimuli for young children. Another way to adapt inquiry training for young children is to use visual material—props giving clues—which simplifies the stimuli and lessens the requirements for memory. It is useful to aim for only one or two specific objectives in a single inquiry training session. Initially (with students of all ages) it is good to start off with a simple game that requires yes/no questions. This game will give students confidence that they can formulate questions and avoid direct theory questions. Some teachers we know use the mystery bag; others play "I'm thinking of something I'm wearing. Guess what it is." Simple guessing games like this also give the students practice in distinguishing theory questions ("Is it your shirt?") from attribute questions ("Is it made of cotton?"). We recommend that teachers introduce and stress each element of inquiry separately. At first the teachers could pose all yes/no questions. Then they can ask students to convert their theory questions into experiments. One by one the teachers can tighten the constraints of the inquiry as they teach the students each of the elements. Trying to explain and enforce all the elements at once will only frustrate both students and teachers.

At first, older students are better able to handle the inquiry process itself, and their subject matter—especially science—more readily lends itself to inquiry training. Although there are more suitable discrepant events in the upper elementary and secondary curricula, it is usually necessary for the teacher to convert available materials from an expository mode into the inquiry mode—that is, to create a discrepant event.

Discrepant events can be developed through print, film, or audio means. The inquiry can be conducted over a period of several days, and the results of other students' inquiries can be shared. Students should have access to appropriate resources, and they may work together in groups. Students may also develop discrepant events and conduct inquiry sessions for peers.

INSTRUCTIONAL AND NURTURANT EFFECTS

The model promotes strategies of inquiry and the values and attitudes that are essential to an inquiring mind, including:

- Process skills (observing, collecting, and organizing data; identifying and controlling variables; formulating and testing hypotheses and explanations; inferring)
- Active, autonomous learning
- Verbal expressiveness

- Tolerance of ambiguity, persistence
- Logical thinking
- Attitude that all knowledge is tentative

The chief learning outcomes of inquiry training are the processes involved—observing, collecting, and organizing data; identifying and controlling variables; making and testing hypotheses, formulating explanations; and drawing inferences (see Figure 10.1). The model splendidly integrates these process skills into a single, meaningful unit of experience.

The format of the model promotes active, autonomous learning as the students formulate questions and test ideas. It takes courage to ask questions, but it is hoped that this type of risk will become second nature to the students. They will also become more proficient in verbal expression as well as in listening to others and remembering what has been said.

FIGURE 10.1   Instructional and nurturant effects of the inquiry training model

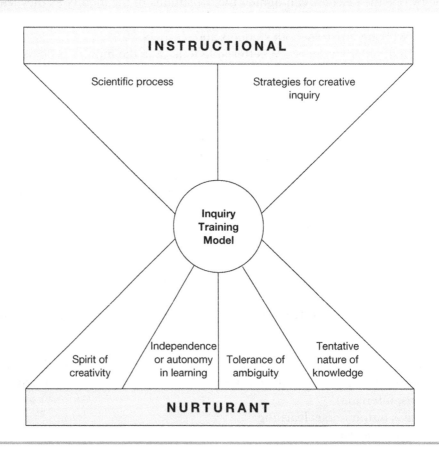

Although its emphasis is on process, inquiry training also results in the learning of content in any curriculum area from which problems are selected. For example, Suchman developed entire curricula in economics and geology. In our opinion, it is adaptable to all elementary and secondary curriculum areas.

Inquiry Training Model   SUMMARY CHART

Syntax

- Phase One: Confrontation with the Problem.
- Phase Two: Data Gathering—Verification.
- Phase Three: Data Gathering—Experimentation.
- Phase Four: Organizing, Formulating an Explanation.
- Phase Five: Analysis of the Inquiry Process.

Social System

The inquiry training model can be highly structured, with the teacher controlling the interaction and prescribing the inquiry procedures. However, the norms of inquiry are those of cooperation, intellectual freedom, and equality. Interaction among students should be encouraged. The intellectual environment is open to all relevant ideas, and teachers and students should participate as equals where ideas are concerned.

Principles of Reaction

1. Ensure that questions are phrased so they can be answered with yeses or no's, and that their substance does not require the teacher to do the inquiry.
2. Ask students to rephrase invalid questions.
3. Point out unvalidated points—for example, "We have not established that this is liquid."
4. Use the language of the inquiry process—for instance, identify student questions as theories and invite testing (experimenting).
5. Try to provide a free intellectual environment by not evaluating student theories.
6. Press students to make clearer statements of theories and provide support for their generalization.
7. Encourage interaction among students.

Support System

The optimal support is a set of confronting materials, a teacher who understands the intellectual processes and strategies of inquiry, and resource materials bearing on the problem.

PART FOUR

The Social Family of Models of Teaching

The models of teaching described in this book rest on beliefs about the nature of human beings and how they learn. Beliefs arise from research, but often the research tests theories that come from intuition about how people learn. In either case the families are distinguished by an orientation toward particular aspects of people and learning. The social models, as the name implies, emphasize our social nature, how we learn social behavior, and how social interaction can enhance academic learning. Nearly all inventors of social models believe that a central role of education is to prepare citizens to generate integrative democratic behavior, both to enhance personal and social life and to ensure a productive democratic social order. They believe that cooperative enterprise inherently enhances our quality of life, bringing joy and a sense of verve and bonhomie and reducing alienation and unproductive social conflict. In addition, cooperative behavior is stimulating not only socially but also intellectually. Thus, tasks requiring social interaction are also designed to enhance academic learning. The development of productive social behavior and academic skills and knowledge are combined.

We are fortunate to be able to draw on the various social models as important parts of our classroom teaching repertoires. Several can be used to design entire school environments as well, for they envision the school as a productive little society, rather than a collection of individuals acquiring education independently. In a cooperative school culture, students can be taught to use the other families of teaching models to acquire the knowledge and skills for which *those* models are developed. Importantly, the social models develop social skills while academic content is being learned. People are inherently cooperative, but the natural tendency can be enhanced and, in multiple-intelligence terms, increase "social intelligence" (see Johnson & Johnson, 2009a, 2009b; Sharan, 1990; Thelen, 1960). The recent review by the Johnsons is particularly helpful and underlines how practice helps generate beliefs, beliefs generate theories, and theories spawn research.

Three active research communities have worked diligently to improve the social models. One is led by David and Roger Johnson at the University of Minnesota. The second is led by Robert Slavin at Johns Hopkins University. The third, in Israel, includes Yael Sharon, Rachel Hertz-Lazarowitz, and several other teacher-researchers. There are differences in the frames of reference of these communities, but they are respectful and cooperative with one another and are appropriately international. Increasingly they are joined by European researchers, and elements of their work are being used and extended by collaborators in Asia, including the current authors. The International Association for the Study of Cooperation in Education's *IASCE Newsletter* (www.iasce.net) describes the ongoing interaction and provides examples of developments and studies as they emerge. We urge all educators to join the organization.

We begin this section with the basic cooperative learning models—ones to use with all students and all subject areas—then proceed to the most complex cooperative learning model, *group investigation,* which has dramatic effects on social and academic learning, and then to models that lead students to study values, resolve conflicts, and consider public policy questions.

CHAPTER ELEVEN

Partners in Learning

Getting Everybody on Board

*If anything is genetically-driven from birth, it's a social instinct.
If it weren't for each other, we wouldn't even know who we are.*

—*Herb Thelen to Bruce Joyce*

ORGANIZING IDEA

Building a respectful, inquiring learning community is fundamental; the developers of social models have concentrated on doing just that. Every other model is enhanced by productive social interaction.

SCENARIO

COOPERATIVE STUDY OF POEMS—CREATING INVESTIGATIONS

Louisa Hilltepper opens the year in her 10th-grade English class by presenting the students with 12 poems she has selected from a set of 100 poems that represent the works of prominent contemporary poets. She organizes the students into pairs, asking them to read the poems and then classify them by structure, style, and themes. As they classify the poems (see Chapter 3 for the structure of the inductive model), they also share their categories with those of the other students. Working together, the class accumulates a list of the ways they have perceived structure, style, and theme. Then, Louisa presents the pairs of students with another dozen poems that they examine, both fitting them into their existing categories and expanding the categories as necessary. This process is repeated until all students are familiar with four dozen poems. She then gives them several other tasks. One is to decide how particular themes are handled by style and structure and vice versa (whether style and structure are correlated with each other and with themes). Another is to build hypotheses about whether some groups of poems were written by particular authors using distinctive combinations of style, structure, and theme.

Only then does she pass out the anthologies and books of critical analysis that are used as the course textbooks, asking students to test their hypotheses about authorship and also to find out if the scholars of poetry employ the same categories they have been developing in their partnerships.

Louisa is organizing her class for partnership-based learning. The cognitive tasks of the classification version of the inductive model of teaching have been used to drive the inquiry. In addition to the substance of this opening unit of study, she is preparing the students to embark cooperatively on their next unit of study—writing poetry or studying the short story. (Which would you use next?) Before long she will introduce them to the more complex activities of group investigation.

SCENARIO

OPENING SCHOOL BY ORGANIZING PAIRS TO STUDY EACH OTHERS' NAMES

As the children enter Kelly Farmer's fifth-grade classroom in Savannah Elementary on the first day of the school year, they find the class roster on each desk. She smiles at them and says, "Let's start by learning all our names and one of the ways we will be working together this year. You'll notice I've arranged the desks in pairs, and the people sitting together will be partners in today's activities. I want each partnership to take our class list and classify the first names by how they sound. Then we will share the groupings or categories each partnership makes. This will help us learn one another's names. It is also to introduce you to one of the ways we will study spelling and several other subjects this year. I know from Mrs. Annis that you have worked inductively last year so you know how to classify, but let me know if you have any problems."

The students *do* know what to do, and within a few minutes they are ready to share their classifications. "We put Nancy and Sally together because they end in 'y.'" "We put George and Jerry together because they sound the same at the beginning even though they're spelled differently." "We put the three Kevins together." A few minutes later the pairs are murmuring together as they help one another learn to spell the list of names.

Kelly has started the year by organizing the students into a "cooperative set," by which we mean an organization for cooperative learning. She will teach them to work in dyads and triads, which can combine into groups of four, five, or six. (Task or work groups larger than that generally have much lower productivity.) The partnerships will change for various activities. The students will learn to accept any members of the class as their partners and will learn that they are to work with each other to try to ensure that everyone achieves the objectives of each activity.

She begins with pairs because that is the simplest social organization. In fact, much of the early training in cooperative activity will be conducted in groups of two and three because the interaction is simpler than it is in larger groups. She also uses fairly straightforward and familiar cognitive tasks for the initial training for the same reason—it is easier for students to learn to work together when they are not mastering complex activities at the same time. For example, she will have them change partners and have the new partnerships quiz and tutor each other on simple knowledge, such as of the states and their capitals. She will change partnerships again and ask them to categorize sets of fractions by size. Each student will learn how to work with any and all of the other students in the class over a variety of tasks. Later she will teach the children to respond to the cognitive tasks of the more complex information-processing models of teaching as well as more complex cooperative sets. By the end of October she expects that they will be skillful enough that she can introduce them to group investigation.

Louise and Kelly have embarked on the task of building learning communities. They will teach the students to work together impersonally but positively, gather and analyze information, build and test hypotheses, and coach one another as they develop skills. The difference in maturity between the classes will affect the degree of sophistication of their inquiry, but the basic processes will be the same.

Each of these teachers possesses a variety of strategies for educating his or her students to work productively together. On their desks are *Cooperative Learning in the Classroom* (Johnson, Johnson, & Holobec, 1994), and *Cooperative Learning Resources for Teachers* (Kagan, 1990). Each is studying the students, learning how effectively they cooperate, and deciding how to design the next activities to teach them to work more effectively together.

Basic assumptions

The assumptions that underlie the development of cooperative learning communities are straightforward:

1. The synergy generated in cooperative settings generates more motivation than do individualistic, competitive environments. Integrative social groups are, in effect, more than the sum of their parts. The feelings of connectedness produce positive energy.

2. The members of cooperative groups learn from one another. Each learner has more helping hands than in a structure that generates isolation.

3. Interacting with one another produces cognitive as well as social complexity, creating more intellectual activity that increases learning when contrasted with solitary study.

4. Cooperation increases positive feelings toward one another, reducing alienation and loneliness, building relationships, and providing affirmative views of other people.

5. Cooperation increases self-esteem not only through increased learning but also through the feeling of being respected and cared for by the others in the environment.

6. Students can respond to experience in tasks requiring cooperation by increasing their capacity to work productively together. In other words, the more children are given the opportunity to work together, the better they get at it, which benefits their general social skills.

7. All students, including primary school children, can learn from training to increase their ability to work together.

THE FOCUS OF RESEARCHERS

Researchers have specifically studied whether cooperative tasks and reward structures affect learning outcomes positively. Also, they have asked whether group cohesion, cooperative behavior, and intergroup relations are improved through cooperative learning procedures. In some of their investigations they have examined the effects of cooperative task and reward structures on "traditional" learning tasks, in which students are presented with material to master.

The community of cooperative learning-oriented educators generate descriptions of productive experiences and informal studies that are available in the IASCE newsletter (www.iasce.net). As we mentioned earlier, we all can glean useful advice from the discussions and reports from our colleagues there. Johnson and Johnson (2009) present a useful typology of cooperative learning applications.

1. Formal cooperative learning: Long-term projects or the way of organizing the learning community.

2. Informal cooperative learning: Kids approach a learning task in ad hoc groups from a few minutes to a class period.

3. Cooperative base groups: Long-term, heterogeneous groups that support one another and may engage in investigations together

4. Cooperative schools: Increase synergy, reduce conflict including bullying.

As you can see, there are several applications of cooperative learning theory that complicate the job of researchers in the area. The more informal types and short-term, formal ones are the most common in school practice.

Do cooperative groups generate the type of energy that results in improved academic learning? The evidence is largely affirmative. In classrooms organized so that students work in pairs and larger groups, tutor each other, and share rewards, there is greater mastery of material than with the common individual-study-cum-recitation pattern. The shared responsibility and interaction also produces more positive feelings toward tasks and others, generates better intergroup relations, and results in better self-images for students with histories of poor achievement. In other words, the results generally affirm the assumptions that underlie the use of cooperative learning methods (see Sharan, 1990).

Some exciting (to us, certainly) studies of the cooperative procedures occur when we combine them with models from other families in an effort to combine the effects of several models. For example, Baveja, Showers, and Joyce (1985) conducted a study in India where concept attainment and inductive procedures were carried out in cooperative groups. The effects fulfilled the promise of the marriage between the information-processing and social models, reflecting gains that were twice those of a comparison group that received intensive individual and group tutoring over the same material. Similarly, Joyce, Murphy, Showers, and Murphy (1989) combined cooperative learning with several other models of teaching to obtain dramatic increases in promotion rates with at-risk students (from 30 to 95 percent) as well as correspondingly large decreases in disruptive activity, an obvious reciprocal of increases in cooperative and integrative behavior.

Those teachers for whom cooperative learning is an innovation find that it is easy to organize students into pairs and triads. And it gets effects immediately. The combination of social support and the increase in cognitive complexity caused by the social interaction have mild but rapid effects on the learning of content and skills. In addition, partnerships in learning provide a pleasant laboratory in which to develop social skills and empathy for others. Off-task and disruptive behavior diminish substantially. Students feel good in cooperative settings, and positive feelings toward self and others are enhanced.

Another nice feature is that students with poorer academic histories benefit so quickly. Partnerships increase involvement, and the concentration on cooperation has the side effect of reducing self-absorption and increasing responsibility for personal learning. Whereas the effect sizes on academic learning are modest but consistent, the effects on social learning and personal esteem can be considerable when comparisons are made with individualistic classroom organization (Joyce, Calhoun, Jutras, & Newlove, 2006; Joyce, Hrycauk, Calhoun, & Hrycauk, 2006). In these studies advances in academic learning are very large.

INCREASING THE EFFICIENCY OF PARTNERSHIPS

Academically Able Students in Cooperative Learning Settings

Curiously, we have found that some parents and teachers believe that students who are the most successful in individualistic environments will not profit from cooperative environments—sometimes expressed as "gifted students prefer to work alone." Though a mass of evidence contradicts that belief (Joyce, 1991; Slavin, 1991), perhaps a misunderstanding about the relationship between individual and cooperative study contributes to its persistence. Developing partnerships does not imply that individual effort is not required. In the scenario in Ms. Hilltepper's classroom, all students read the poems. When classifying poems together, each individual contributed ideas and studied the ideas of others. Individuals are not hindered but are enhanced by partnerships with others. Successful students are not inherently less cooperative. In highly individualistic environments they are sometimes taught disdain for less-successful students, to their detriment as students and people, both in school and in the future.

Training for Cooperation

For reasons not entirely clear to us, the initial reaction of some people to the proposition that students study together is one of concern that they will not know how to work together productively. In fact, partnerships over simple tasks are not very demanding of social skills. Most students are quite capable of cooperating when they are clear about what has been asked of them. However, developing more efficient ways of working together is clearly important, and there are some guidelines for helping students become more practiced and efficient. These guidelines pertain to group size, complexity, and practice.

In the scenarios we have emphasized simple dyadic partnerships used to help students explore both basic and complex content. The pair or dyad is the simplest form of social organization. One way to help students learn to work cooperatively is to provide practice in the simpler settings of twos and threes. Essentially, we regulate complexity through the tasks we give and the sizes of groups we form. If students are unaccustomed to cooperative work, it makes sense to use the smallest groups with simple or familiar tasks to permit them to gain the experience that will enable them to work in groups of larger sizes. Task groups larger than six persons are clumsy and require skilled leadership, which students cannot provide to one another without experience or training. Partnerships of two, three, or four are the most commonly employed. We recommend beginning with groups of two.

Practice results in increased efficiency. If we begin learning with partners and simply provide practice for a few weeks, we will find that the students become increasingly productive.

Training for Efficiency

There are also methods for training the students for more efficient cooperation and "positive interdependence" (see Kagan, 1990; Johnson, Johnson, and Holubec, 1994). Simple hand signals can be used to get the attention of busy groups. One of the common procedures is to teach the students that when the instructor raises his or her hand, anyone who notices is to pay attention to the instructor and raise his or her hand also. Then other students notice and raise their hands, and soon the entire instructional group is attending. This type of procedure is nice because it works while avoiding shouting above the hubbub of the busy partnerships and teaches the students to participate in the management process.

Kagan (1990) has developed several procedures for teaching students to work together for goals and to ensure that all students participate equally in the group tasks. An example is what he calls "numbered heads." Suppose that the students are working in partnerships of three. Each member takes a number from one to three and simple tasks are given ("How many metaphors can you find in this page of prose?"). All members are responsible for mastery of each task. After a suitable interval, the instructor calls out one number—for example, "Number twos." The number two person in each group raises his or her hand. They are responsible for speaking for their groups. The instructor calls on one of them. All group members are responsible for listening and checking the answer of the person who reports. For example, if the response is "seven," the other students are responsible for checking that response against their own. "How many agree? Disagree?" The procedure is designed to ensure that some individuals do not become the "learners" and "spokespersons" for their groups while others are carried along for the ride.

Also, for tasks for which it is appropriate, pretests may be given. An example might be a list of spelling words. After the pretest, a number of tasks might be given to help the students study the words. Then an interval might be provided for the students to tutor one another, followed by a posttest. Each group would then calculate its gain scores (the number correct on the posttest minus the number correct on the pretest), giving all members a stake in everyone's learning. Also, cooperative learning aside, the procedure makes clear that learning expressed as gain is the purpose of the exercise. When posttests only are used, it is not clear whether anyone has actually *learned*—students can receive high marks no better than they would have achieved in a pretest.

Sets of training tasks can help students learn to be more effective in partnerships, to increase their stake in one another, and to work assiduously for learning by all.

Educating for Interdependence

In addition to practice and training for more efficient cooperative behavior, procedures for helping students become truly interdependent are available. The least complex involve reflection on the group process and discussions about ways of working together most effectively. The more complex involve the provision of tasks that require interdependent behavior. For example, there are card games where success depends on giving up valuable cards to another player and communication games where success requires taking the position of another. Familiar games like "Charades" and "Pictionary" are popular because they increase cohesion and the ability to put oneself in the place of another. There are also procedures for rotating tasks so that each person moves from subordinate to superordinate tasks and where members take turns as coordinators.

Johnson and Johnson (2009) have repeatedly demonstrated that sets of these tasks can increase interdependence, empathy, and role-taking ability and that students can become quite expert at analyzing group dynamics and learning to create group climates that foster mutuality and collective responsibility. The role-playing model of teaching, discussed in Chapter 13, is designed to help students analyze their values and to work together to develop interactive frames of reference.

Division of Labor in Groups

A variety of procedures has been developed to help students learn how to help one another by dividing labor. Essentially, tasks are presented in such a way that division of labor increases efficiency. The underlying rationale is that dividing labor increases group cohesion as the team works to learn information or skills while ensuring that all members have both responsibility for learning and an important role in the group. Imagine, for example, that a class studying Africa is organized into groups of four. Four countries are chosen for study. One member of each team might be designated a "country specialist." The country specialists from all teams would gather together and study their assigned nation and become the tutors for their original groups, responsible for summarizing information and presenting it to the other members. Similarly, when tasks requiring memorization are presented to the class, the group will divide responsibility for creating mnemonics for aspects of the data.

A procedure known as *jigsaw* (Aronson, E., Blaney, M., Stephan, C., Sykes, J., & Snapp, M., 1978; Slavin, 1983) has been worked out to develop formal organizations for divisions of labor. It is highly structured and appropriate as an introduction to division-of-labor processes. Whereas individualistic classroom organization allows individuals to exercise their best-developed skills, division of labor procedures require students to rotate roles, developing their skills in all areas. We recommend that *every* student be a recorder in every investigation, because recording increases learning substantially.

Cooperative or Competitive Goal Structures

Some developers organize teams to compete against one another, whereas others emphasize cooperative goals and minimize team competition. Johnson and Johnson (1974, 2009) have analyzed the research and argue that the evidence favors cooperative goal structures, but Slavin (1983) argues that competition between teams benefits learning. The fundamental question is whether students are oriented toward competing with one another or with a goal. Recently several of our colleagues have organized whole classes to work cooperatively toward a goal. For example, the science department of a high school began the year in chemistry by organizing the students to master the essential features of the periodic table of elements. In teams, they built mnemonics that were used by the whole class. Within two weeks, all students knew the table backward and forward, and that information served as the structural organizer (see Chapter 9) for the entire course.

In a group of fifth-grade classes, the exploration of social studies began with memorization of the states, large cities, river and mountain systems, and other basic information about the geography of the United States. Class scores were computed (for example, 50 states times 30 students is 1,500 items). The goal was for the class as a whole to achieve a perfect score. The classes reached scores over 1,450 within a week, leaving individuals with very few items to master to reach a perfect score for the class.

Motivation: From Extrinsic to Intrinsic?

The issue about how much to emphasize cooperative or individualistic goal structures relates to conceptions of motivation. Sharan (1990) has argued that cooperative learning increases learning partly because it causes motivational orientation to move from the external to the internal. In other words, when students cooperate over learning tasks, they become more interested in learning for its own sake rather than for external rewards. Thus, students engage in learning for intrinsic satisfaction and become less dependent on praise from teachers or other authorities. The internal motivation is more powerful than the external, resulting in increased learning rates and retention of information and skills.

The cooperative learning community is a direct challenge to the principles that many schools have relied on to guide their use of tests and rewards for student achievement. Unquestionably, one of the fundamental purposes of general education is to increase internal motivation to learn and to encourage students to generate learning for the sheer satisfaction in growing. If cooperative learning procedures (among others) succeed partly because they contribute to this goal, then the testing and reward structures that prevail in most school environments may actually retard learning. As we turn to group investigation—a powerful model that radically changes the learning environment—consider how different are the tasks, cooperative structures, and principles of motivation we observe in many contemporary schools.

Summary and Effects

Cooperative learning takes many forms (see Figure 11.1). Here is a Summary Chart of a basic strategy that can be used when groups are just learning collaborative procedures.

FIGURE 11.1   Instructional and nurturant effects of simple collaborative activities

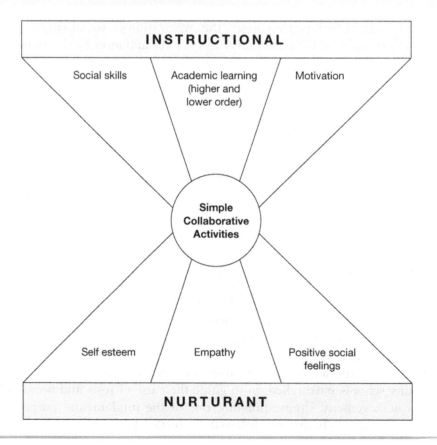

Introductory Procedures

Phase 1. Provide a learning task that is well within the skill-levels of the group. For example, provide a set of illustrated books and suggest that the students classify the covers.

Phase 2. Organize the students in pairs by having them count off by 2's and assigning the adjacent students to be a group.

Phase 3. Ask the pairs to study the covers (or other similar materials) and generate categories.

Phase 4. Ask each pair to share their categories and give reasons for them.

Phase 5. Discuss with the group the similarities and differences in their thinking and whether and what they gained from both common and different perspectives.

Phase 6. Ask each pair to discuss, with each other, whether they approached the task together or divided the labor and why.

Phase 7. Survey the pairs relative to the working-together/division of labor process.

Phase 8. Ask each pair to craft a short paragraph about the categories they formed in their task.

Altogether, this type of exercise gets the cooperative ball rolling—and begins a series of inquiries where cooperative activities are used, improved, and made routine.

CHAPTER TWELVE

Group Investigation

Rigorous Inquiry through Democratic Process

You don't develop democratic investigative processes by just turning things over to the students and hoping for the best. You lead actively, simultaneously teaching the tools of inquiry and ensuring that content is learned. Our species is naturally cooperative, but sophisticated social skills need to be nurtured.

—*Our reflective observer*

ORGANIZING IDEA

Citizenship is learned by practice. From pre-K through 12 we have 14 years to ensure practice in democratic processes that are learned through working together.

SCENARIO

TOM'S STUDENTS INQUIRE INTO THE COUNTRIES OF THE WORLD

The inquiry begins with a series of video clips of families from various cultures. The students begin to ask questions about the variety of human experience: How much behavior is the product of culture? How much is from the makeup of the species?

In Annapolis, Maryland, Tom developed a yearlong course that lays a foundation for global understanding for students from grades 9–12. He designed it as a straightforward cooperative/inductive experience: students collect information on a number of the countries of the world, classify the countries, build and test explanations of similarities and differences, and generate inquiries on specific countries and global issues. In this case the political organization of the world is the topic, and nations are the entities that are focused on. Large databases provide statistics on a range of variables, and encyclopedias, newspapers, and informants provide information as well.

Substantively, the highest order content objective for the course is to build knowledge of regions of the world, their physical and cultural characteristics, and social/political context. The objectives are to develop high-level skill in cooperative/inductive inquiry, to learn to use relevant reference books and ICT systems, to acquaint students with the political globe, to lead them to collect information about the countries of the world, to help them build and test hypotheses or conjectures about causal relationships, and to develop multimedia reports on specific inquiries. Tom knows that increasing the students' capacity to inquire inductively builds not only information and understanding but also long-lasting intellectual power. The specific social science skills they learn will serve them well as social studies students and as world citizens.

Resources

The school provides the students with laptops they can use during class, study periods, and at home. Each student has a Gmail address, and the class has a webpage on which they can post messages and chat. They can use the laptops for personal purposes if they wish. Tom's students have print copies of *The State of the World Atlas* by Dan Smith (2012), which emphasizes information relating to social issues and policy not usually found in other databases, such as measures of equality and inequality. Students can also draw on the online version of the World Factbook (www.cia.gov/library/publications/the-world-factbook), which contains information on nearly all the nations of the world, and Encyclopedia Britannica. Each pair of students has a physical globe, and all have access to virtual globes such as those found on Google Earth. Eventually, they will use a variety of other sources, including authorities on various topics and students and teachers in some of the other countries. Tom's course clearly fits our concept of a *hybrid*. Campus sessions and ICT resources work together. In this case, the campus course generates topics and questions to guide the inquiries and is a forum for sharing and discussing information and hypotheses. ICT sources support and enhance those investigations.

The Students at Entry

With respect to prior knowledge, Tom has ascertained that only about 20 percent of the 40 students who enroll in this course each year can look over a political globe without names and correctly locate as many as 10 countries, and even those students possess very little information about those few nations. In other words, they begin at the beginning with respect to content. They differ quite a bit with respect to the knowledge and skill needed to use digital sources effectively, but only a couple of students have used print or ICT databases dealing with the political globe. Many have constructed PowerPoint presentations, and a few have edited videos for various purposes.

Consequently, Tom knows that in the early stages of the course he needs to introduce the students to inductive learning strategies and information sources and how to use them, as well as ensure that they teach themselves the web and media skills they will need. This year he has started by organizing the students to study 20 countries he has selected (they will study many others by the end of the year). As benchmarks, they begin by looking at a few aspects of the United States, Canada, and Mexico.

He begins by giving the students some tasks designed to get them using the databases and exploring ways of managing and manipulating data, beginning with some demographic variables. He asks them to start with the World Factbook and create a table where the United States, Canada, and Mexico are compared on population size (314, 34, and 114 millions respectively), per capita gross domestic product (47,000; 39,000; and 14,000 respectively), and fertility rate (2.06, 1.58, and 2.29 respectively).

Per capita gross domestic product is new to the students. Tom has them search, discuss, and finally develop a definition that approximates the one in the World Factbook. They are hazy about the meaning of "fertility rate" and have to get it straight. While they are working on those terms, Tom leads them to find out what sources the Factbook developers used to arrive at their estimates—they will need to find the foundations of data whenever they consult secondary sources.

The students were surprised by how much even these three items for three countries interested them—and how much was new, as the number of people in the United States and the population size differences among the three. Only a couple had previously paid attention to fertility rates. The idea that Canada would shrink without immigration was striking. Some had imagined that Mexico's fertility rate would be much larger than it is.

Next, Tom leads them to explore household income and literacy and adds three European countries, where they look at all five variables. He has selected the Netherlands, Luxembourg, and Italy. Again, there were surprises. The students are beginning to generate "why" questions, like "Why does Luxembourg have such a high GDP?" "Why do Italy and the Netherlands have such low fertility rates?" They also express surprise, such as "I didn't know that Italy's population was so much smaller than Mexico's," "We all thought the Netherlands would be tiny, but it has a lot of people in it," "I had no idea that Germany and the Netherlands share a border," and "A few years ago I was amazed when Kim Clijsters won a tennis tournament and gave her 'thank-you' talk in English and French and the announcer said she speaks German as well. Now, I am beginning to understand why she might have three languages."

They look at countries in Africa, South and Middle America, Asia, and the Middle East, all the time recording questions asking for more information, seeking to understand causes, and making conjectures (hypotheses) about differences.

After they have explored a few countries from each region, Tom asks them to build country comparison tables for two variables at a time, such as fertility and literacy rates. That triggers a flurry of conjectures and hypotheses.

Tom leads them to carefully formulate their findings thus far, particularly the confusing picture that has emerged—some large countries have low fertility rates. some small countries have higher ones, and so forth. He pushes them to build a decade-by-decade picture and reclassify the countries in terms of changes in the birth rate, and to develop questions about why changes might have taken place. To track down the likely answer to those questions, students consult encyclopedias, newspaper accounts (a number of the countries have English-language newspapers), and other narrative and visual sources.

Tom mixes this aspect of their inquiries with questions that lead them to add other variables to their study of the 20 countries. As they learn about apparent relationships between variables in the 20 countries, students will expand the base to include other countries in order to test their hypotheses. They will also try to find authorities—specialists in these areas—to see whether they can talk with them. Tom sets them on a search for schools whose students might be willing to exchange information with them.

Tom began by leading his students to study relatively easy-to-understand variables, such as physical size of countries and populations. Then he facilitated their computation of correlations, teaching them how to make cross-breaks; eventually, he will teach them how to test for statistical significance. He led them to develop hypotheses and, using those hypotheses, embark on the further exploration of the databases.

Students have the course outline in their laptops; parents also have a copy. Tom writes notes to the parents about progress and what the students are asked to do on the Infinite Classroom (classroom.infiniteclassroom.com/), a program that makes it easy for teachers and parents to communicate with one another and with the students. A simple use is to post homework so that parents know what is being assigned. Syllabi are also posted in some courses. In this case, the unit is described and progress is posted, including short papers some students have written. Several parents have asked to attend the class, and they are welcomed. In some evening sessions, the students describe their inquiries and findings to the parents. Their written reports are often copied to the parents along with Tom's comments.

As students become more and more knowledgeable about specific regions of the world and/or issues, Tom looks for opportunities for them to present to different groups within and beyond the school, sometimes face to face and sometimes online. He wants students to have the demands of and practice with presenting well-documented information in a variety of formats and practice in responding to a variety of questions from groups and individuals who have perspectives and experiences different from their own. While he's very clear about the inquiry skills and social studies skills his students will develop, Tom is often amazed at some of the issues and questions students delve into as part of their inductive and inquiry work.

Note that Tom's hybrid course is very straightforward. The content is not exotic, but the use of the web takes the students into the study of cultures new to them. Tom considers building on the inquiries by introducing the students to QuadBlogging (http://quadblogging.net), an organization that connects classes with one another all over the world (see Coiro, 2011).

WHERE THE IDEA FOR GROUP INVESTIGATION CAME FROM

John Dewey's ideas have given rise to the broad and powerful model of teaching known as *group investigation*. In it, students are organized into problem-solving groups that attack academic problems and are taught democratic procedures and scientific methods of inquiry as they proceed. The movement to practice democracy in the classroom constituted the first major reform effort in U.S. education and generated a great deal of critical reaction. As schools experimented with democratic-process education, they were subjected to serious criticism during the 1930s and 1940s. The first items of research produced by the reformers were actually developed in defense—in response to questions raised by concerned citizens about whether such a degree of reliance on social purposes would retard the students' academic development. The studies generally indicated that social and academic goals are not at all incompatible. The students from those schools were not disadvantaged; in many respects, in fact, they outperformed students from competitive environments where social education was not emphasized (Chamberlin & Chamberlin, 1943). The reaction continued, however—a seeming anomaly in a democracy whose political and commercial institutions depend so much on integrative organizational behavior.

Educational models derived from a conception of society usually envision what human beings would be like in a very good, even utopian, society.

Their educational methods aim to develop ideal citizens who could live in and enhance that society, who could fulfill themselves in and through it, and who would even be able to help create and revise it. We have had such models from the time of the Greeks. Plato's *Republic* (1945) is a blueprint for an ideal society and the educational program to support it. Aristotle (1912) also dealt with the ideal education and society. Since their time, many other utopians have produced educational models, including St. Augustine (*The City of God*, 1931), Sir Thomas More (*Utopia*, 1965), Comenius (*The Great Didactic*, 1967), and John Locke (*Some Thoughts Concerning Education*, 1927).

It was natural that attempts would be made to use teaching methods to improve society. In the United States, extensive efforts have been made to develop classroom instruction as a model of democratic process; in fact, variations on democratic process are probably more common than any other general teaching method as far as the educational literature is concerned. In terms of instructional models, *democratic process* has referred to organizing classroom groups to do any or all of the following tasks:

1. Develop a social system based on and created by democratic procedures.
2. Conduct scientific inquiry into the nature of social life and processes. In this case, the term *democratic procedures* is synonymous with the scientific method and inquiry.
3. Use inquiry to solve a social or interpersonal problem.
4. Provide an experience-based learning situation.

The implementation of democratic methods of teaching has been exceedingly difficult. They require the teacher to have a high level of interpersonal *and* instructional skills. Also, democratic process is cumbersome and frequently slow; parents, teachers, and school officials often fear that it will not be efficient as a teaching method. In addition, a rich array of instructional resources is necessary, and these have not always been available. Probably the most important hindrance is that the school simply has not been organized to teach the social and intellectual processes of democracy. Instead, it has been directed toward and organized for basic instruction in academic subjects, and school officials and patrons have, for the most part, been unwilling to change that direction or organization. Given the positive effects on student learning in all domains, it is a serious mistake not to make group investigation a staple in the repertoire of all schools.

The perception of alternative frames of reference and courses of action is essential to social negotiations. But one must have great personal development to understand other people's viewpoints. This sharing of perceptions is necessary, however, if a mutual reality is to be constructed (see Berger & Luckmann, 1966).

The essence of a functioning democracy is the negotiation of problem definitions and situations. This ability to negotiate with others also helps each person negotiate his or her own world. Maintaining a sense of meaning and purpose depends on developing a valid and flexible way of dealing with reality. Failure to make life comprehensible or to negotiate reality with others will result in a feeling of chaos. The abilities to continually reconstruct one's value stances and to create compatible value systems are both essential to mature development.

Many approaches to teaching assume that one does something in particular to get a specific outcome from the learner. Models that emphasize the democratic process assume that the outcome of any educational experience is not completely predictable. The democratic model makers reason that if they are successful in persuading students to inquire into the nature of their experiences and develop their own ways of viewing the world, it will be impossible to predict just how they will face any given situation or solve any particular problem. Hence, if the students are taught an academic discipline, it is not so that they will know exactly the discipline known by others, but so that this exposure will help each of them create concepts grounded in, but not smothered by, the discipline.

GOALS AND ASSUMPTIONS

Herbert Thelen is one of the founders of the National Training Laboratory and has drawn on experience and studies in organizational development and academic inquiry to build the group investigation model. He is reaching for an experience-based learning situation, easily transferable to later life situations and characterized by a vigorous level of inquiry.

Thelen (1960, p. 80) begins with a conception of a social being: "a man [or woman] who builds with other men [or women] the rules and agreements that constitute social reality." Any view of how people should develop has to refer to the inescapable fact that life is *social*. A social being cannot act without reference to his or her companions on earth; otherwise in the quest for self-maintenance and autonomy each person may conflict with other people making similar efforts. In establishing social agreements, each individual helps determine both prohibitions and freedom for action. Rules of conduct operate in all fields—religious, political, economic, and scientific—and constitute the culture of a society. For Thelen, this negotiation and renegotiation of the social order are the essence of social process:

> Thus in groups and societies a cyclical process exists: individuals, interdependently seeking to meet their needs, must establish a social order (and in the process they develop groups and societies). . . . as the way of life changes, the

rules must be revised, and new controls and agreements have to be hammered out and incorporated into the social order. (Thelen, 1960, p. 80)

The classroom is analogous to the larger society; it has a social order and a classroom culture, and its students care about the way of life that develops there—that is, the standards and expectations that become established. Teachers should seek to harness the energy naturally generated by the concern for creating the social order. The model of teaching replicates the negotiation pattern needed by society. Through negotiation the students study academic knowledge and engage in social problem solving. According to Thelen, one should not attempt to teach knowledge from any academic area without teaching the social process by which it was negotiated.

> The teacher's task is to lead the development of the social order in the classroom for the purpose of orienting it to inquiry, and the "house rules" to be developed are the methods and attitudes of the knowledge discipline to be taught. (Thelen, 1960, p. 8)
>
> Life in classrooms takes the form of a series of "inquiries." Each inquiry starts with a stimulus situation to which students can react and discover basic conflicts among their attitudes, ideas, and modes of perception. On the basis of this information, they identify the problem to be investigated, analyze the roles required to solve it, organize themselves to take these roles, act, report, and evaluate these results." (Thelen, 1960, p. 82)

The class should become a miniature democracy that attacks problems and, through problem solving, acquires knowledge and becomes more effective as a social group. The group, by the way, has a leader they did not elect—the teacher, who is appointed by the society.

Basic concepts

The concepts of (1) inquiry and (2) knowledge drive Thelen's strategy.

Investigation Begins—the Role of Being Unsure

Inquiry is stimulated by confrontation with a problem, and knowledge results from the inquiry. The social process enhances inquiry and is itself studied and improved. The heart of group investigation lies in its concept of inquiring groups.

The first element of inquiry is an event the individuals in a group can react to and puzzle over—a problem to be solved. Look back to Chapter 10, where puzzling situations are the impetus to inquiry. In the classroom the teacher can select content and cast it in terms of problem situations—for example, "How did our community come to be the way it is?" Simply providing a problem, however, will not generate the puzzlement that is a major energy source for inquiry. The students must add an awareness of self and a desire for personal meaning. In addition, they must assume the dual roles of participant and observer, simultaneously inquiring into the problem and observing themselves as inquirers. Because inquiry is a social as well as individual process, students are aided in the self-observer role by interacting with and observing the reactions of other puzzled people. The conflicting viewpoints that emerge also energize the students' interest in the problem.

Although the teacher can provide a problem situation, it is up to the students as inquirers to identify and formulate the problem and pursue its solution. Inquiry calls for firsthand activity in a real situation and ongoing experience that continually generates new data. The students must thus be conscious of method so that they may collect data, associate and classify ideas recalling past experience, formulate and test hypotheses, study consequences, and modify plans. Finally, they must develop the capacity for reflection, or the ability to synthesize overt participative behavior with symbolic verbal behavior. The students are asked to give conscious attention to the experience—to formulate explicitly the conclusions of the study and to integrate them with existing ideas. In this way thoughts are reorganized into new and more powerful patterns.

THE MODEL OF TEACHING

Syntax

The model begins by confronting (confronting is in the sense of its use in academic inquiry—making clear something to be learned rather *confronting* in the rather nasty move that debaters are taught) the students with a stimulating problem. The confrontation may be presented verbally, or it may be an actual experience; it may arise naturally, or it may be provided by a teacher. If the students react, the teacher draws their attention to the differences in their reactions—what stances they take, what they perceive, how they organize things, and what they feel. As the students become interested in their differences in reaction, the teacher draws them toward formulating and structuring the problem for themselves. Next, students analyze the required roles, organize themselves, act, and report their results. Finally, the group evaluates its solution in terms of its original purposes. The cycle repeats itself, either with another confrontation or with a new problem growing out of the investigation itself (see Table 12.1).

TABLE **12.1**   Syntax of Group Investigation Model

Phase One	Students encounter puzzling situation (planned or unplanned).
Phase Two	Students explore reactions to the situation.
Phase Three	Students formulate study task and organize for study (problem definition, role, assignments, etc.).
Phase Four	Independent and group study.
Phase Five	Students analyze progress and process.
Phase Six	Recycle activity.

Social System

The social system is democratic, governed by decisions developed from, or at least validated by, the experience of the group—within boundaries and in relation to puzzling phenomena identified by the teacher as objects to study. The activities of the group emerge with a minimal amount of external structure provided by the teacher. Students and teacher have equal status except for role differences. The atmosphere is one of reason and negotiation.

Principles of Reaction

The teacher's role in group investigation is one of counselor, consultant, and friendly critic. He or she must guide and reflect the group experience over three levels: the problem-solving or task level (What is the nature of the problem? What are the factors involved?), the group management level (What information do we need now? How can we organize ourselves to get it?), and the level of individual meaning (How do you feel about these conclusions? What would you do differently as a result of knowing about . . .?) (Thelen, 1954, pp. 52–53). This teaching role is difficult and sensitive, because the essence of inquiry is student activity—problems cannot be imposed. At the same time the instructor must: (1) facilitate the group process, (2) intervene in the group to channel its energy into potentially educative activities, and (3) supervise these educative activities so that personal meaning comes from the experience (Thelen, 1960, p. 13). Intervention by the instructor should be minimal unless the group bogs down seriously. Chapters 16 to 18 of *Leadership of Discussion Groups* (1975) by Gertrude K. Pollack provide an excellent advanced discussion of leadership in groups. Although the material was prepared for persons leading therapy groups, it is written at a general level and provides much useful advice for those wishing to build classrooms around group inquiry.

Support System

The support system for group investigation should be extensive and responsive to the needs of the students. The school needs to be equipped with a first-class library with a wide variety of media; it should also be able to provide access to outside resources as well. Children should be encouraged to investigate and to contact resources beyond the school walls. One reason cooperative inquiry of this sort has been relatively rare is that the support systems were not adequate to maintain the level of inquiry.

APPLICATION: A ROLLING MODEL (THAT IS, PHASES GO BACK AND FORTH)

Group investigation requires flexibility from the teacher and the classroom organization. Although we assume that the model fits comfortably with the environment of the "open" classroom, we believe it is equally compatible with more traditional classrooms. We have observed successful group investigation teachers in a context in which other subjects, such as math and reading, are carried out in a more structured, teacher-directed fashion. If students have not had an opportunity to experience the kind of social interaction, decision making, and independent inquiry called for in this model, it may take some time before they function at a high level. On the other hand, students who have participated in classroom meetings and/or self-directed, inquiry-oriented learning will probably have an easier time. In any case, it is probably useful for the teacher to remember that the social aspects of the model may be as unfamiliar to students as the intellectual aspects and may be as demanding in terms of skill acquisition.

Although the examples of the model described here tend to be intellectually and organizationally elaborate, all investigations need not be so complex. With young children or students new to group investigation, fairly small-scale investigations are possible; the initial confrontation can provide a narrow range of topics, issues, information, and alternative activities. For example, providing an evening's entertainment for the school is more focused than resolving the energy crisis. Deciding who will care for the classroom pet and how is even narrower. Of course, the nature of the inquiry depends on the interests and ages of the students. Older students tend to be concerned with more complex issues. However, the skillful teacher can design inquiries appropriate to the students' abilities and to his or her own ability to manage the investigation.

In their study of group investigation, Sharan and Hertz-Lazarowitz (1980a) reported that the more pervasive the cooperative climate, the more positive the students toward both the learning tasks and toward each other. In addition, they found that the greater social complexity increased achievement of more complex learning goals (concepts and theories) as well as the learning of information and basic skills. A nice small study by teachers in an Oregon high school is worth reading both for its insight into the dynamics of the groups and the effects on the students (Huhtala, 1994).

INSTRUCTIONAL AND NURTURANT EFFECTS

This model is highly versatile and comprehensive; it blends the goals of academic inquiry, social integration, and social-process learning. It can be used in all subject areas, with all age levels, when the teacher desires to emphasize the formulation and problem-solving aspects of knowledge rather than the intake of preorganized, predetermined information.

Provided that one accepts Thelen's view of knowledge and its reconstruction, the group investigation model (Figure 12.1) can be considered a direct

FIGURE 12.1   Instructional and nurturant effects of the group investigation model

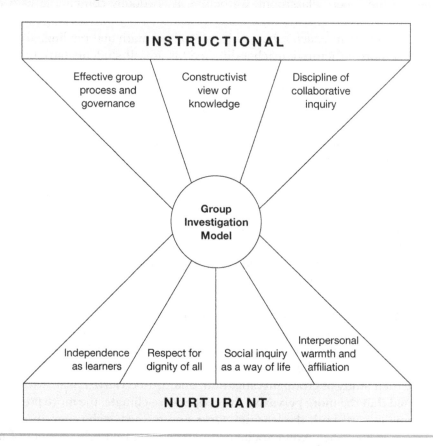

and probably efficient way of teaching academic knowledge as well as social process. It also appears likely to nurture interpersonal warmth and trust, respect for negotiated rules and policies, independence in learning, and respect for the dignity of others.

In deciding whether to use the model, considering the potential nurturant effects may be as important as analyzing the likely direct instructional effects. Another model might be as appropriate for teaching academic inquiry, but a teacher may prefer group investigation for what it might nurture.

Group Investigation Model   `SUMMARY CHART`

Syntax

- Phase One: Encounter Puzzling Situation (Planned or Unplanned)
- Phase Two: Explore Reactions to the Situation
- Phase Three: Formulate Study Task and Organize for Study
- Phase Four: Independent and Group Study
- Phase Five: Analyze Progress and Process
- Phase Six: Recycle Activity

Social System

The system is based on the democratic process and group decisions, with low external structure. Puzzlement must be genuine—it cannot be imposed. Authentic exchanges are essential. Atmosphere is one of reason and negotiation.

Principles of Reaction

Teacher plays a facilitative role directed at group process (helps learners formulate plan, act, manage group) and requirements of inquiry (consciousness of method). He or she functions as an academic counselor. The students react to the puzzling situation and examine the nature of their common and different reactions. They determine what kinds of information they need to approach the problem and proceed to collect relevant data. They generate hypotheses and gather the information needed to test them. They evaluate their products and continue their inquiry or begin a new line of inquiry. The central teaching moves to build the cooperative social environment and teach students the skills of negotiation and conflict resolution necessary for democratic problem solving. In addition, the teacher needs to guide the students in methods of data collection and analysis, help them frame testable hypotheses, and decide what would constitute a reasonable test of a hypothesis. Because groups vary considerably in their need for structure (Hunt, 1971) and their cohesiveness (Thelen, 1981), the teacher cannot behave mechanically but must "read" the students' social and academic behavior and provide the assistance that keeps the inquiry moving without squelching it.

Support System

The environment must be able to respond to a variety of learner demands. Teacher and students must be able to assemble what they need when they need it.

CHAPTER THIRTEEN

Role Playing

Studying Values

The analysis of values is what's important. Playing the roles lets the values become visible if the analysis is right. Understanding that what you do is a living out of your values starts the inquiry.

—*Fannie Shaftel to a group of Palo Alto teachers*

SCENARIO

THE 9/11 TRAGEDY

Laurie's eighth-grade class is reading David Halberstam's marvelous book *Firehouse* (2002), which describes the social system of Engine 40 Ladder 35 (known as 40/35) on the West Side of Manhattan before, during, and after September 11, 2001, a day when 13 of the 40/35 men sped down toward the World Trade Center, only one of them to return alive. Halberstam describes the men, their families, their interaction, and the norms that enabled them, time after time, to go into extremely dangerous situations and work together while risking their lives.

As they reflect on Halberstam's vivid accounts, Laurie's students begin to realize that, all over the United States, there are such little communities of people who know what they are doing and do it with pride and loyalty. She lets the students react randomly for a while until they begin to identify issues. She appoints recorders, and they begin a list of questions and statements that will gradually be organized into needs for information, policy issues, and clarification. The list begins as a jumble of thoughts and observations.

"How many firemen die in fires in New York in a normal year?"

"Why do we pay them less than they could earn doing something else?"

"What must it be like, heading for a dangerous fire at breakneck speed?"

"How can they make themselves go into a fire?"

"How do they stand their grief?"

"Interesting that many are the sons and even grandsons of firemen."

"What would happen if no one would do their job?"

"Why do we build such tall buildings knowing that they are more dangerous than shorter ones?"

"What happens to the families of the ones who are hurt or die?"

They also come up with more local questions:

"What is our fire department like?"

"Are we like New York, just a whole lot smaller?"

Although we are looking at the beginning of a group investigation–style inquiry, Laurie moves to get personal feelings and values into the process prior to the information-processing inquiry that will take place.

Thus, Laurie organizes the students to enact a scene where members of a family confront one of them who is thinking of applying to become a firefighter. The core of the enactment is a confrontation between a brother and sister of the applicant. She selects the students who will play the roles in the first enactment—there will be several—and the other students are organized in various roles as observers and recorders.

To the surprise of the students, the enactment becomes quite heated. The candidate for firefighter becomes more and more determined. The brother and sister role players become more heated. The observers find that the expression of emotion overtakes points where a reasoned position is laid out.

Thus begins an inquiry that will lead down many paths. Eventually the class will have identified a number of values that underlie public policy or are compromised as decisions are made. Then Laurie will open up another area with them. The study of values is the core of their social studies program.

The inquiry will take them to a number of web sources, some providing a good deal of information on the events of the week of 9/11, some with firefighters and other types of *first responders*. A search that begins simply with "firefighters" will lead to heaps of information and commentary.

In this chapter we are going to examine a way of helping our students study values. Role playing begins with problem situations in the lives of the students. It explores how values drive behavior and raises student consciousness about the role of values in their lives and those of others. A direct effect is greater understanding about and empathy with differences in values as people interact. Another direct effect is strategies for resolving conflicts in fashions that respect different points of view without giving up the need for agreed on humane values.

SCENARIO

UNDERSTANDING CONFRONTATION

We are in a seventh-grade classroom in East Los Angeles, California. The students have returned to the classroom from a recess period and are complaining to one another. Mr. Williams, the teacher, asks what the matter is and they all start in at once, discussing a series of difficulties that lasted throughout the recess period. Apparently, two of the students began to squabble about who was to take the sports equipment outside. Then all of the students argued about what game to play. Next, there was a dispute about choosing sides for the games. This included a dispute over whether the girls and boys should play together or separately. The class finally began to play volleyball, but very shortly there was a dispute over a line call, and the game was never completed.

At first, Mr. Williams displays his displeasure toward the class. He is angry, not simply over the incidents, but because these arguments have been going on since the beginning of the year. At last he says, "OK, we really have to face this problem. You must be as tired of it as I am. So we are going to use a method of inquiry that I should have taught you some time ago. This method begins with identifying interpersonal problems. For the next half hour we are going to cool off with a little independent reading. Then we will divide into groups of four and try to identify the types of problems we've been having. Just take today, for example, and outline the situations that got us into this fix."

The students begin with the argument over taking the sports equipment outside, and then identify other arguments. After the separate groups of students have made their lists, Mr. Williams appoints one of the students to lead a discussion in which each group reports the kinds of problem situations that have come up; the groups agree on a half-dozen problems that have consistently bothered the class. Mr. Williams also makes one of *his* objectives clear: "I want you to be able to regulate your behavior as individuals and as a group. I want you to organize yourselves to play games, solve any problems that arise, and, in case you have forgotten, have a good time and get some exercise."

The students begin to categorize the listed problems. One category concerns the division of labor, like taking care of equipment and assigning students to be referees. A second category deals with principles for selecting teams, like choosing sides and dealing with gender. A third category focuses on resolving disputes over the particulars of games, such as whether balls have been hit out of bounds, whether players are out or safe, and so on, including how to deal with the decisions of referees. Mr. Williams then assigns one category of problem to each group and asks the groups to describe situations in which the problems come up. When they have done this, the class votes on which problem to start with. The first problem they select is disputes over rules; the actual problem situation they select is the volleyball game in which the dispute over a line call occurred.

Together, the class talks about how the problem situation develops. It begins when a ball is hit close to the boundary line. One team believes it is in, and the other believes it is out of bounds. The students then argue with one another, and the argument goes on so that the game cannot continue.

Several students are selected to enact the situation. Others gather around and are assigned to observe particular aspects of the role playing that follows. Some students are to look for the particulars of how the argument develops. Some are to study one role player and others another to determine how they handle the situation.

The enactment is spirited. The students select as role players those who have been on opposite sides during the game, and they become as involved in the argument during the role playing as they were during the actual situation. Finally, they are standing in the middle of the room shouting at one another. At this point, Mr. Williams calls, "Time!" and asks the students to describe what has gone on.

Everyone is eager to talk. The discussion gradually focuses on how the attitude of the participants prevented resolving the problem. No one was listening to the other person. And no one was dealing with the problem of how to resolve honest disputes. Finally, Mr. Williams asks the students to suggest other ways that people could behave in this kind of conflict. Some students suggest giving in gracefully. But others object that if someone believes he or she is right, that is not an easy thing to do. Finally, the students identify an important question to focus on: "How can we develop a policy about who should make calls, and how should others feel about those calls?" They decide to reenact the scene by having all the participants assume that the defensive team should make the calls.

The enactment takes place. This time, the players attempt to follow the policy that the defensive team has the right to make the call, but the offensive team has the right to question a call. Once again, the enactment results in a shouting match; however, after it is over, the students who have watched the enactment point out that the role players have not behaved as if there is a resolution to the situation. They recognize that if there are to be games, there has to be agreement about who can make calls as well as a certain amount of trust on both sides. They also begin to discuss values, such as the value of resolving compared to the attitude of "winning the argument."

They decide to try a third enactment, this time with two new role players inserted as dispute referees. The introduction of referees completely changes the third enactment. The referees insist that the other players pay attention to them, which the players do not want to do. In discussing this enactment, the students point out that there has to be a system to ensure reasonable order and the resolution of disputes. The students also agree that as things stand, they probably are unable to resolve disputes without including a referee of some sort, but that no referees will be effective unless the students agree to accept the referees' decisions. They finally decide that in future games, two students will be referees. Those students will be chosen by lot prior to the game; their function will be to arbitrate and to make all calls relevant to the rules of the game, and their decisions will be final. The students agree that they will see how that system works. We can legitimately call Mr. Williams and his class *action researchers*.

The next day Mr. Williams opens up the second set of issues, and the students repeat the process. The exploration of other areas of dispute continues over the next few weeks. At first, many of the notions that are clarified are simply practical ones about how to solve specific problems. Gradually, however, Mr. Williams directs the discussion to a consideration of the basic values governing individual behavior. The students begin to see the problems of communal living, and they develop policies for governing their own behavior, as individuals and as a group. They also begin to develop skills in negotiating. The students who were locked in conflict gradually learn that if they behave in a slightly different way, others may also modify their behavior, and problems become easier to solve.

Esentially, the students need to learn about *circular interactions*, where what any person does may draw a response from someone else and in turn rouse a substantive reaction. When a negative circle ensues in relation to a conflict, bad feelings can be generated and, if the cycle is not interrupted, the conflict can escalate. On the other hand, if the emotional tangent of the cycle is interrupted and integrative behavior pulls the affective level toward neutrality—or, better, reasonability— the conflict can be dealt with on a more rational basis. The students, as anyone else, need to learn how to start an interaction on a calm, integrative basis so that escalation does not occur, as well as how to still the waters and build a peaceful interaction.

Role playing provides us with an opportunity to model the behaviors that begin and maintain interactions on positive notes, as well as how to modify conflictual interactions and build integrative interactions and, thus, relations. The basic social models generate the positive feelings that encourage us to manage conflict politely and seek civil solutions in a civil, democracy-encouraging fashion.

RATIONALE

In role playing, students explore human relations problems by acting out problem situations and then discussing the enactments. Together, students can explore feelings, attitudes, values, and problem-solving strategies. Several teams of researchers have experimented with role playing, and their treatments of the strategy are remarkably similar. The version we explore here was formulated by Fannie and George Shaftel (1967). We have also incorporated ideas from the work of Mark Chesler and Robert Fox (1966).

Role playing as a model of teaching has roots in both the personal and social dimensions of education. It attempts to help individuals find personal meaning within their social worlds and resolve personal dilemmas with the assistance of the social group. In the social dimension, it allows individuals to work together in analyzing social situations, especially interpersonal problems, and in developing decent and democratic ways of coping with these situations. We have placed role playing in the social family of models because the social group plays such an indispensable part in human development and because of the unique opportunity that role playing offers for resolving interpersonal and social dilemmas.

ORIENTATION TO THE MODEL

Goals and Assumptions

On its simplest level, role playing is dealing with problems through action; a problem is delineated, acted out, and discussed. Some students are role players; others observers. A person puts himself or herself in the position of another person and then tries to interact with others who are also playing roles. As empathy, sympathy, anger, and affection are all generated during the interaction, role playing, if done well, becomes a part of life. This emotional content, as well as the words and the actions, becomes part of the later analysis. When the acting out is finished, even the observers are involved enough to want to know why each person reached his or her decision, what the sources of resistance were, and whether there were other ways this situation could have been approached.

The essence of role playing is the involvement of participants and observers in a real problem situation and the desire for resolution and understanding that this involvement engenders. The role-playing process provides a live sample of human behavior that serves as a vehicle for students to: (1) explore their feelings; (2) gain insight into their attitudes, values, and perceptions; (3) develop their problem-solving skills and attitudes; and (4) explore subject matter in varied ways.

These goals reflect several assumptions about the learning process in role playing. First, role playing implicitly advocates an experience-based learning situation in which the "here and now" becomes the content of instruction. The model assumes that it is possible to create authentic analogies to real-life problem situations and that through these re-creations students can "sample" life. Thus, the enactment elicits genuine emotional responses and behaviors from the students.

A related assumption is that role playing can draw out students' feelings, which they can recognize and perhaps release through a legitimate enaction. The Shaftels' version of role playing emphasizes the intellectual content as much as the emotional content; analysis and discussion of the enactment are as important as the role playing itself.

Another assumption, similar to an assumption of the synectics model (Chapter 7), is that emotions and ideas can be brought to consciousness and enhanced by the group. The collective reactions of the peer group can bring out new ideas and provide directions for growth and change. The model deemphasizes the traditional role of the teacher and encourages listening and learning from one's peers.

A final assumption is that covert psychological processes involving one's own attitudes, values, and belief system can be brought to consciousness by combining spontaneous enactment with analysis. Furthermore, individuals can gain some measure of control over their belief systems if they recognize their values and attitudes and test them against the views of others. Such analysis can help them evaluate their attitudes and values and the consequences of their beliefs, so that they can allow themselves to grow.

The Concept of Role

Each individual has a unique manner of relating to people, situations, and objects. One person may feel that most people are dishonest and cannot be trusted; someone else may feel that everyone is interesting and may look forward to meeting new people. People also evaluate and behave in consistent ways toward themselves, seeing themselves as powerful and smart, or perhaps afraid and not very able. These feelings about people and situations and about themselves influence people's behavior and determine how they will respond in various situations. Some people respond with aggressive and hostile behavior, playing the part of a bully. Others withdraw and remain alone, playing the part of a shy or sulking person.

These parts people play are called *roles*. A role is "a patterned sequence of feelings, words, and actions. It is a unique and accustomed manner of relating to others" (Chesler & Fox, 1966, p. 5). Unless people are looking for them, it is sometimes hard to perceive consistencies and patterns in behavior. But they are usually there. Terms such as *friendly, bully, snobby, know-it-all,* and *grouch* are convenient for describing characteristic responses or roles.

The roles individuals play are determined by several factors over many years. The kinds of people someone meets determine his or her general feelings about people. How those people act toward the individual and how the individuals perceive their feelings toward them influence their feelings about themselves. The rules of one's particular culture and institutions help determine which roles a person assumes and how he or she plays them.

Role playing generates feelings that can ruffle feathers. People may not be happy with the roles they have assumed. They may misperceive the attitudes and feelings of others because they do not recognize *their* role and *why* they play it. Two people can share the same feelings but behave in very different ways. They can desire the same goals, but if one person's behavior is misperceived by others, he or she may not attain that goal. However, the untidy melange is an important center of role playing. The emerging situation creates an opportunity to study one's attitudes, beliefs, and values and thus makes them content for personal and social inquiry.

For a clear understanding of oneself and of others, it is extremely important that a person be aware of roles and how they are played. To accomplish this successfully we must be able to put ourselves in another's place, and to experience as much as possible that person's thoughts and feelings. If someone is able to empathize, we, can accurately interpret social events and interactions. Role playing is a vehicle that induces people to take the roles of others.

The concept of role is one of the central theoretical underpinnings of the role-playing model. It is also a major goal. Students need to learn to recognize different roles, and to think of their own and others' behavior in terms of roles. There are many other aspects to this model, and many levels of analysis, which to some extent compete with one another. For example, the content of the problem, the solutions to the problem, the feelings of the role players, and the enactment itself all serve to involve students in the role play.

THE MODEL OF TEACHING

Syntax

The benefits of role playing depend on the quality of the enactment (whether the actors really get into their roles) and, especially, on the analysis that follows. They depend also on the students' perceptions of the role as similar to real-life situations. Children do not necessarily engage effectively in role playing or role analysis the first time they try it. Many have to learn to engage in role playing in a sincere way so that the content generated can be analyzed seriously. Role playing is not likely to be successful if the teacher simply tosses out a problem situation, persuades a few children to act it out, and then conducts a discussion about the enactment. As with successful behaviors in all models, students need to learn how to make this type of inquiry worthwhile.

The Shaftels suggest that the role-playing activity consist of nine steps: (1) warm up the group, (2) select participants, (3) set the stage, (4) prepare observers, (5) enact, (6) discuss and evaluate, (7) reenact, (8) discuss and evaluate, and (9) share experiences and generalize. Each of these steps or phases has a specific purpose that contributes to the richness and focus of the learning activity. Together, these steps ensure that a line of thinking is pursued throughout the complex of activities, that students are prepared in their roles, that goals for the role play are identified, and that the discussion afterward is not simply a collection of diffuse reactions, though these are important too. Table 13.1 summarizes the phases and activities of the model.

Phase one, warming up the group, involves introducing students to a problem so that they recognize it as an area with which everyone needs to learn to deal. The warm-up can begin, for example, by identifying a problem within the group.

> **Teacher:** Do you remember the other day we had a discussion about Jane's lunch money? Because she had put her money in her pocket and had not given it to me when she came into the room, it was lost. We had quite a talk about finding money: whether to keep it or turn it in. Sometimes it's not easy to decide what to do. Do you ever have times when you just don't know what to do? (Shaftel & Shaftel, 1967, p. 67)

The teacher sensitizes the group to a problem and creates a climate of acceptance, so that students feel that all views, feelings, and behaviors can be explored without retribution.

The second part of the warm-up is to express the problem vividly through examples. These may come from student descriptions of imaginary or real situations that express the problem, or from situations selected by the teacher and illustrated by a film, television show, or problem story.

In *Role Playing of Social Values: Decision Making in the Social Studies* (1967), the Shaftels provide a large selection of problem stories to be read to the class. Each story stops when a dilemma has become apparent. The Shaftels feel that problem stories have several advantages. They focus on a particular problem and yet ensure that the children will be able to disassociate themselves from the problem enough to face it. Incidents that students have experienced in their lives or that the group has experienced as a whole, though visually and emotionally involving, can cause considerable stress and therefore be difficult to analyze. Another advantage of problem stories is that they are dramatic and make role playing relatively easy to initiate. The burden of involving the children in the activity is lightened.

The last part of the warm-up is to ask questions that make the children think about and predict the outcome of the story: "How might the story end?" "What is Sam's problem and what can he do about it?" The teacher in the

TABLE **13.1**   Syntax of Role-Playing Model

Phase One: **Warm Up the Group**	Identify or introduce problem. Make problem explicit. Interpret problem story. Explore issues. Explain role playing.
Phase Two: **Select Participants**	Analyze roles. Select role players.
Phase Three: **Set the Stage**	Set line of action. Restate roles. Get inside problem situation.
Phase Four: **Prepare the Observers**	Decide what to look for. Assign observation tasks.
Phase Five: **Enact**	Begin role play. Maintain role play. Break role play.
Phase Six: **Discuss and Evaluate**	Review action of role play (events, positions, realism). Discuss major focus. Develop next enactment.
Phase Seven: **Reenact**	Play revised roles. Suggest next steps or behavioral alternatives.
Phase Eight: **Discuss and Evaluate**	Repeat phase six.
Phase Nine: **Share Experiences and** **Generalize**	Relate problem situation to real experience and current problems. Explore general principles of behavior.

Source: Based on Fannie Shaftel and George Shaftel, *Role Playing of Social Values* (Englewood Cliffs, NJ: Prentice-Hall, Inc., 1967).

preceding illustration handled this step (Original idea here is from the Shaftels' central [1967] book.) as follows:

Teacher: I would like to read you a story this afternoon about a boy who found himself in just such a spot. His parents wanted him to do one thing, but his friends insisted he do something else. Trying to please everybody, he got himself into difficulty. This will be one of those problem stories that stop but are not finished.

Pupil: Like the one we did last week?

Teacher: Yes.

Pupil: Oh! But can't you give us one with an ending?

Teacher: When you get into a jam, does someone always come along and tell you how your problems will end?

Pupil: Oh no! Not very often.

Teacher: In life, we usually have to make our own endings—we have to solve our problems ourselves. That's why I'm reading these problem stories—so that we can practice endings, trying out many different ones to see which works the best for us. As I read this story, you might be thinking of what you would do if you were in Tommy Haines's place.

The story is about a boy caught between his father's views and those of his club. He has committed himself to give money to a club project (a local dating service) his father does not approve of and would not support. Tommy does not have the money and resorts to a somewhat shady means of getting it. He involves himself with a group that is paid for writing term papers and writes one for a community-college student. When the student schedules a time to receive the paper and pay Tommy, he begins to worry seriously and ask himself whether he should go through with the transaction. After reading the story, the teacher focuses the discussion on what might happen next, thus preparing for different enactments of the situation:

Teacher: What do you think Tommy will do?

Pupil: I think he'll take the money.

Teacher: Oh?

Pupil: Because he needs to pay the club.

Pupil: Oh no he won't. He'll get found out, and he knows it.

In phase two, selecting participants, the children and the teacher describe the various characters—what they are like, how they feel, and what they might do. The children are then asked to volunteer to role play; they may even ask to play a particular role. The Shaftels caution us against assigning a role to a child who has been suggested for it, because the person making the suggestion may be stereotyping the child or putting him or her in an awkward situation. A person must want to play a role. Although he or she takes into account the children's preferences, the teacher should exercise some control in the situation.

We can use several criteria for selecting a child for a role. Roles can be assigned to children who appear to be so involved in the problem that they identify with a specific role, those who express an attitude that needs to be explored, or those who should learn to identify with the role or place themselves in another person's position. The Shaftels warn the teacher not to select children who would give "adult-oriented, socially acceptable" interpretations to the role, because such a quick and superficial resolution of the problem dampens discussion and exploration of the basic issues (Shaftel & Shaftel, 1967, p. 67).

In our illustration, the teacher asks a student to be Tommy and then asks the student what roles need to be filled. He answers that he'll need someone to be the club president, someone to be the community college student customer, and other students to be club members. The teacher asks several children to fill these roles.

In phase three, setting the stage, the role players outline the scene but do not prepare any specific dialogue. They simply sketch the setting and perhaps one person's line of action. The teacher may help set the stage by asking the students a few simple questions about where the enactment is taking place, what it is like, and so on. It is necessary only that a simple line of action be identified and a general setting clarified so that participants feel secure enough in the roles to begin to act.

The teacher asks the boy playing Tommy where in the action he wants to begin, and the boy decides to start with the scene where he is delivering the term paper.

In phase four, preparing the observers, it is important that the observers become actively involved so that the entire group experiences the enactment and can later analyze the play. The Shaftels suggest that the teacher involve observers in the role play by assigning them tasks, such as evaluating the realism of the role playing, commenting on the effectiveness and the sequences of the role players' behavior, and defining the feelings and ways of thinking of the persons being portrayed. The observers should determine what the role players are trying to accomplish, what actions the role players took that were helpful or not helpful, and what alternative experiences might have been enacted. Or they can watch one particular role to define the feelings of that person. The observers should understand that there will be more than one enactment in most cases, and if they would have acted out a certain role in a different way, they may have a chance to do so.

In our illustration, the teacher prepares the observers as follows:

> **Teacher:** Now, as you watch, consider whether you think Jerry's way of ending the episode could really happen. How will people feel? You may want to think of what will happen next. Perhaps you'll have different ideas about it, and when Jerry's finished, and we've talked about it, we can try your ideas. (Shaftel & Shaftel, 1967, p. 69)

At phase five, enacting, the players assume the roles and "live" the situation spontaneously, responding realistically to one another. The role playing is not expected to be a smooth dramatization, nor is it expected that each role player will always know how to respond. This uncertainty is part of life, as well as part of feeling the role. A person may have a general idea of what to say or do but not be able to enact it when the time comes. The action now depends on the children and emerges according to what happens in the situation. This is why the preparatory steps are so important.

The Shaftels suggest that enactments be short. The teacher should allow the enactment to run only until the proposed behavior is clear, a character has developed, a behavioral skill has been practiced, an impasse is reached, or the action has expressed its viewpoint or idea. If the follow-up discussion reveals a lack of student understanding about the events or roles, the teacher can then ask for a reenactment of the scene.

The purpose of the first enactment is simply to establish events and roles, which in later enactments can be probed, analyzed, and reworked. In our illustration, the boy playing Tommy can complete the transaction or back off. During the initial enactment, the players of the major role can be changed to demonstrate variety in the role and to generate more data for discussion.

In phase six, discussing and evaluating, if the problem is important and the participants and observers are intellectually and emotionally involved, the discussion will probably begin spontaneously. At first, the discussion may focus on different interpretations of the portrayal and on disagreements over how the roles should have been carried out. More important, however, are the consequences of the action and the motivations of the actors. To prepare for the next step, a teacher should focus the discussion on these aspects.

To help the observer think along with the role players, the teacher can ask questions such as, "How do you suppose John felt when he said that?" The discussion will probably turn to alternatives, both within the roles and within the total pattern of action. When it does, the stage is set for further enactments in which role players change their interpretations, playing the same roles in a different way.

In our illustration, the discussion of the first enactment goes like this:

Teacher: Well, Jerry has given us one solution. What do you think of it?
Pupil: Uh-uh! It won't work!
Jerry: Why not?
Pupil: That man is going to remember how much money he had. He'll phone the druggist about it.
Jerry: So what? He can't prove anything on me. I'll just say he didn't overpay me.
Pupil: You'll lose your job.
Jerry: When they can't prove it?
Pupil: Yes, even if they can't prove it.
Teacher: Why do you think so, John?
Pupil: Because the druggist has to be on the side of his customer. He can fire Tommy and hire another boy. But he doesn't want his customers mad at him.
Pupil: He's going to feel pretty sick inside, if he keeps the money.
Teacher: What do you mean?
Pupil: Well, it bothers you when you know you've done something wrong.
Teacher: Do you have any other way to solve this problem?
Pupil: Yes. Tommy should knock on the door and tell the customer about being overpaid. Maybe the man'll let Tommy keep the money.
Teacher: All right, let's try it your way, Dick. (Shaftel & Shaftel, 1967, p. 71)

In phase seven, reenacting, the reenactment may take place many times. The students and teacher can share new interpretations of roles and decide whether new individuals should play them. The activity alternates between discussion and acting. As much as possible, the new enactments should explore new possibilities for causes and effects. For example, one role may be changed so that everyone can observe how that change causes another role player to behave. Or at the critical point in the enactment, the participants may try to behave in a different way and see what the consequences are. In this way, the role playing becomes a dramatic conceptual activity.

In our illustration, a second enactment produces the solution in which Tommy alerts the man to his overpayment and gets to keep the money for being so honest. In the discussion that follows the second enactment—phase eight, discuss and evaluate—students are willing to accept the solution, but the teacher pushes for a realistic solution by asking whether they think this ending could really happen. One student has had a similar experience but was overpaid only $1.25, which he was allowed to keep. The teacher asks the class whether they think it might be different with $5. She asks for another solution, and it is suggested that Tommy consult his mother. There follows some discussion of Tommy's father, concepts about family, and parental roles. The teacher suggests that this third solution be enacted. Here's what happens in the third enactment:

> **Tommy:** Mom, I'm in an awful jam!
> **Mother:** What's the trouble, Tommy?
> **Tommy:** (Tells his mother the whole story)
> **Mother:** I must say, I can't believe you are in the "ghosting" business. But, I'm sure you can figure a way out of it. The three of us will just have to figure out how.
> **Tommy:** I'm not sure I'm ready for that.
> **Mother:** Well, you have just until this evening to grow up enough to be ready. (Taken from, with alterations, Shaftel & Shaftel, 1967, p. 73)

During the discussion of this enactment, the teacher asks what will happen next, and someone suggests that Tommy will be in the doghouse for a while.

Phase nine, sharing experiences and generalizing, should not be expected to result immediately in generalizations about the human relations aspects of the situation. Such generalizations require much experience. The teacher should, however, attempt to shape the discussion so that the children, perhaps after experience with the role-playing strategy, begin to generalize about approaches to problem situations and the consequences of those approaches. The more adequate the shaping of the discussion, the more general will be the conclusions reached, and the closer the children will come to hypothetical principles of action they can use in their own lives.

The initial goal, however, is to relate the problem situation to the children's experiences in a nonthreatening way. This goal can be accomplished by asking the class members whether they know someone who has had a similar experience. In our illustration with Tommy and the money, the teacher asks whether anyone in the class knows of an instance in which a boy or girl was in a situation like Tommy's. One student describes an experience with his father. The teacher then asks about parental attitudes and the role of fathers with respect to their children's money.

From such discussions emerge principles that all students can articulate and use. These principles may be applied to particular problems, or they can be used by the children as a springboard for exploring other kinds of problems. Ideally, the children will gradually master the strategy so that when a problem comes up, either within their group or from a topic they have studied, they will be able to use role playing to clarify and gain insight into the problem. Students might, for example, systematically use role playing to improve the quality of classroom democracy.

Social System

The social system in this model is moderately structured. Teachers are responsible, at least initially, for starting the phases and guiding students through the activities within each phase; however, the particular content of the discussions and enactments is determined largely by the students.

The teachers' questions and comments should encourage free and honest expression of ideas and feelings. Teachers must establish equality and trust between themselves and their students. They can do this by accepting all suggestions as legitimate and making no value judgments. In this way, they simply reflect the children's feelings or attitudes.

Even though teachers are chiefly reflective and supportive, they assume direction as well. They often select the problem to be explored, lead the discussion, choose the actors, make decisions about when the enactments are to be done, help design the enactments, and most significant, decide what to probe for and what suggestions to explore. In essence, the teachers shape the exploration of behavior by the types of questions they ask and, through questioning, establish the focus.

Principles of Reaction

We have identified five principles of reaction that are important to this model. First, teachers should accept student responses and suggestions, especially their opinions and feelings, in a nonevaluative manner. Second, teachers should respond in a way that helps students explore various sides of the problem situation, recognizing and contrasting alternative points of view. Third, by reflecting, paraphrasing, and summarizing responses, the teacher increases students' awareness of their own views and feelings. Fourth, the teacher should emphasize that there are different ways to play the same role and that different consequences result as they are explored. Fifth, there are alternative ways to resolve a problem; no one way is correct. The teacher helps the students look at the consequences to evaluate a solution and compare it with alternatives.

Support System

The materials for role playing are minimal but important. The major curricular tool is the problem situation. However, it is sometimes helpful to construct briefing sheets for each role. These sheets describe the role or the character's feelings. Occasionally, we also develop forms for the observers that tell them what to look for and give them a place to write it down.

Films, novels, and short stories make excellent sources for problem situations. Problem stories or outlines of problem situations are also useful. Problem stories, as their name implies, are short narratives that describe the setting, circumstances, actions, and dialogue of a situation. One or more of the characters faces a dilemma in which a choice must be made or an action taken. The story ends unresolved.

Real life also provides plenty of dilemmas—some overtly conflictual, some not—that are grist for the mill of role-playing analysis.

APPLICATION

The role-playing model is versatile and can be used to try to achieve several important educational objectives. Through role playing, students can increase their abilities to recognize their own and other people's feelings, acquire new behaviors for handling previously difficult situations, and improve their problem-solving skills.

In addition to its many uses, the role-playing model carries with it an appealing set of activities. Because students enjoy both the action and the acting, it is easy to forget that the role play itself is a vehicle for developing the content of the instruction. The stages of the model are not ends in themselves, but they help expose students' values, feelings, attitudes, and solutions to problems, which then can be explored.

Why use role playing? Two reasons: One is to begin a systematic *program of social education* in which a role-playing situation forms much of the material to be discussed and analyzed; for this purpose, a particular kind of problem story might be selected. The second reason is to counsel a group of children to deal with an *immediate human relations problem;* role playing can open up this problem area to the students' inquiry and help them solve the problem.

Several types of social problems are amenable to exploration with the aid of this model, including:

1. *Interpersonal conflicts.* A major use of role playing is to reveal conflicts between people so that students can discover techniques for overcoming them.
2. *Intergroup relations.* Interpersonal problems arising from ethnic and racial stereotyping or from authoritarian beliefs can also be explored through role playing. These problems involve conflict that may not be apparent. Role-playing situations of this type might be used to uncover stereotypes and prejudices or to encourage acceptance.
3. *Individual dilemmas.* These arise when a person is caught between two contrasting values or between his or her own interests and the interests of others. Such problems are particularly difficult for young children to deal with because their moral judgment is still relatively egocentric. Some of the most delicate and difficult uses of role playing make this dilemma accessible to children and help them understand why it occurs and what to do about it. Individual dilemmas that might be explored are ones in which a person is caught between the demands of the peer group and those of his or her parents, or between the pressures of the group and his or her own preferences.
4. *Historical or contemporary problems.* These include critical situations, past or present, in which policymakers, judges, political leaders, or statespeople have to confront a problem or person and make a decision.

Regardless of the particular type of social problem, students will focus naturally on the aspects of the situation that seem important to them. They may concentrate on the feelings that are being expressed, the attitudes and values of the role players as seen through their words and actions, the problem solution, or the consequences of behavior. It is possible for the teacher to emphasize any or all of these areas in the enactments and discussions. In-depth curriculum sequences can be based on each of the following focuses:

- Exploration of feelings
- Exploration of attitudes, values, and perceptions
- Development of problem-solving attitudes and skills
- Subject-matter exploration

We have found that a single role-playing session is often very rich. Discussion can go in many directions—toward analyzing feelings, consequences, the roles themselves and ways to play them, and alternative solutions. After several years of working with this model, we have come to believe that if any one of these ideas or objectives is to be developed adequately, the teacher must make a concerted effort to explore one particular emphasis. Because all these aspects tend to emerge in the role-playing process, it is easy to consider them only superficially. One difficulty we are faced with, then, is that an in-depth treatment of any one focus requires time. Especially in the beginning, when students are getting accustomed to the model and to exploring their behavior and feelings, we feel it is important to select one major focus, or perhaps two, for any one session. Other aspects, of course, may also need to be considered in the development of ideas, but their place should be secondary. For example, the feelings of the characters may be discussed when the teacher is trying to get the students to concentrate on alternative solutions to the problem, but in this case, the feelings will tie in to a consideration and evaluation of the solutions.

By choosing one or perhaps two emphases for the enactment, carefully questioning and responding to students' ideas, and building on the ideas of the previous phases, the teacher gradually develops each phase so that it supports the particular objectives that have been selected for that session. This is what we mean by developing a focus (see Table 13.2).

The selection of the topic depends on many factors, such as the age of the students, their cultural background, the complexity of the problem situation, the sensitivity of the topic, and the students' experience with role playing. In general, as students gain experience with role playing and develop a high degree of group cohesiveness and acceptance of one another, as well as a close rapport with the teacher, the more sensitive the topic can be. The first few problem situations should be matters of concern to the students but not extremely sensitive issues. Students themselves may develop a list of themes or problems they would like to work on. Then the teacher can locate or develop specific problem situations that fit the themes.

The gender of the students and their ethnic and socioeconomic backgrounds influence their choice of topic and, according to Chesler and Fox (1966), their expectations for the role play. Different cultural groups experience different sets of problems, concerns, and solutions. Most teachers account for these differences in their curricula all the time. Problems that are typical for a particular ethnic or age group, gender, or socioeconomic class can become the basis of problem situations.

Other ideas for problem situations can be derived from: (1) the age and developmental stage of the student, such as personal and social concerns; (2) value (ethical) themes, such as honesty or responsibility; (3) problem behaviors, such as aggression or avoidance; (4) troublesome situations, such as making a complaint at a store or meeting someone new; and (5) social issues, such as racism, sexism, or labor strikes. These various sources of problem situations are summarized in Table 13.3.

Another consideration in choosing a problem situation is its complexity, which may be a result of the number of characters or the abstractness of the issues. There are no definite rules about levels of difficulty in problem

TABLE **13.2**   Possible Focuses of a Role-Playing Session

Feelings

- Exploring one's own feelings
- Exploring others' feelings
- Acting out or releasing feelings
- Experiencing higher-status roles in order to change the perceptions of others and one's own perceptions

---

Attitudes, values, and perceptions

- Identifying values of culture or subculture
- Clarifying and evaluating one's own values and value conflicts

---

Problem-solving attitudes and skills

- Openness to possible solutions
- Ability to identify a problem
- Ability to generate alternative solutions
- Ability to evaluate the consequences to oneself and others of alternative solutions to problems
- Experiencing consequences and making final decisions in light of those consequences
- Analyzing criteria and assumptions behind alternatives
- Acquiring new behaviors

Subject matter

- Feelings of participants
- Historical realities: Crises, dilemmas, and decisions

TABLE **13.3**   Sources of Problem Situations

---

1. Issues arising from developmental stages
2. Issues arising from sexual, ethnic, or socioeconomic class
3. Value (ethical) themes
4. Difficult emotions
5. Scripts or "games people play"
6. Troublesome situations
7. Social issues
8. Community issues

---

situations, but intuitively it seems that the following sequence is a reasonable guide: (1) one main character; (2) two characters and alternative solutions; (3) complex plots and many characters; (4) value themes, social issues, and community issues.

INSTRUCTIONAL AND NURTURANT EFFECTS

Role playing is designed specifically to foster: (1) the analysis of personal values and behavior; (2) the development of strategies for solving interpersonal (and personal) problems; and (3) the development of empathy toward others. Its nurturants are the acquisition of information about social problems and values and comfort in expressing one's opinions (see Figure 13.1).

FIGURE 13.1   Instructional and nurturant effects of the role-playing model

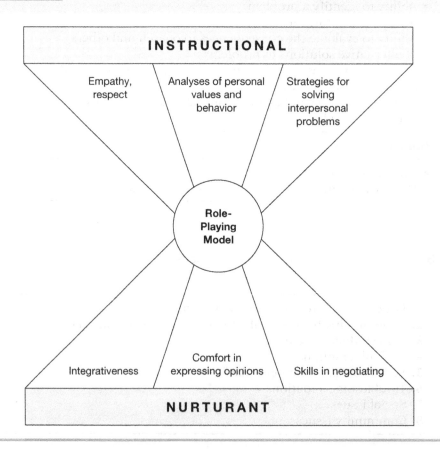

Role-Playing Model

Syntax

- Phase One: Warm Up the Group.
- Phase Two: Select Participants.
- Phase Three: Set the Stage.
- Phase Four: Prepare the Observers.
- Phase Five: Enact.
- Phase Six: Discuss and Evaluate.
- Phase Seven: Reenact.
- Phase Eight: Discuss and Evaluate. Repeat phase six.
- Phase Nine: Share Experience and Generalize.

Social System

The model is moderately structured. The teacher is responsible for initiating the phases and guiding students through the activities within each phase. The particular content of the discussions and enactments is determined largely by the students.

Principles of Reaction

1. Accept all student responses in a nonevaluative manner.
2. Help students explore various sides of the problem situation and compare alternative views.
3. Increase students' awareness of their own views and feelings by reflecting, paraphrasing, and summarizing their responses.
4. Use the concept of role and emphasize that there are different ways to play a role.
5. Emphasize that there are alternative ways to resolve a problem.

Support System

Role playing is an experience-based model and requires minimal support material outside the initial problem situation. The jurisprudential model, which we will visit next, requires more complex materials and information sources.

PART FIVE

The Personal Family of Models

From birth, we are acted on by the world. Our social environment gives us our language, teaches us how to behave, and provides love to us. Even so, our individual selves configure themselves relentlessly and create their own interior environments. Within those worlds each of us creates our identity. Our personalities have remarkable continuity from early in life, yet we have great capacity to change. We can adapt to a wide range of climates and physical environments. We are incomplete without others and can love and receive love, generating perhaps the greatest growth of all when they come together. Paradoxically, we also have the capacity to hold tight to behavior that doesn't work—as if to force the world to yield and make our worst features productive. We are the greatest, and we can be mulish!

Personal models of teaching share two major purposes. The first is to lead us and our students toward greater mental and emotional health by developing self-confidence and a realistic sense of self and through building empathetic reactions to others. The second is to increase the proportion of education that emanates from the needs and aspirations of individuals. As teachers that means partnering with students to determine what they will learn and how they will learn it. A dividend is generating certain kinds of qualitative thinking, such as creativity and personal expression.

Personal models find four types of applications. First, they can be used as general models of teaching. A course or even a school can be designed with a nondirective philosophy as the core approach to education. Advocates have built curricula and schools for hundreds of years (see Rousseau, 1983; Neill, 1960; Chamberlin & Chamberlin, 1943; Calkins, 2000).

Second, they can be used to flavor a learning environment designed around other models. For example, we can "carry around with us" concern for students' self-concepts, and we can think carefully about how to shape everything we do to maximize their positive feelings about self and to minimize the likelihood that our teaching will diminish them as people. In other words, we can use these models to attend to the personal feelings of our students and look for opportunities to make them partners in their learning and to communicate affirmatively with them. We will concentrate on this use of the model.

Third, we can use the unique properties of the personal models to counsel students when we wish to help them learn to reach out to the world more fully and positively.

Fourth, we can build curricula in the academic subjects around the ability and experience of the students themselves. The "experience" methods for teaching reading, for example, use student-dictated stories as the initial reading materials and student-selected literature as the chief materials once initial competence has been established. The PWIM model (see Chapter 5) begins with student-generated words and ideas and continues with student development of categories, titles, sentences, and paragraphs. Combined with other models, the personal models can be used to design independent study courses, including resource-based programs. There are persuasive arguments that a large component of education at all grade levels should be built around self-study.

In addition to the belief that enhancing the learner as a person is a worthwhile educational goal in its own right, a major thesis of this family of models is that better-developed, more affirmative, self-actualizing learners have increased learning capabilities as well. Thus, personal models will increase academic achievement by tending the psyches of the learners. This thesis is supported by a number of studies (Roebuck, Buhler, & Aspy, 1976) that indicate that the students of teachers who incorporate personal models into their repertoires increase their achievement. Sets of studies by Hunt and Joyce and their colleagues (see Joyce, Peck, & Brown, 1981) have indicated how much more effective it is to modulate to the students in the course of using a wide variety of models of teaching.

Personal models are very difficult to research, because by their nature the "treatments" change as the students become more able to take charge of their own development. Therefore, a carefully-designed "X" is not used with the student or client and relentlessly pursued. In our world, conditions change as the student changes. A very interesting review by Cornelius-White (2007) tracks 50 years of study. On the whole, well-implemented personal models positively affect cognitive outcomes (generally substantive learning), affective outcomes (generally feelings of well-being, improved self-concepts), and behavioral outcomes (often the ability for students to take charge of their learning and development). Cornelius-White (2007) provides a thoughtful description of nondirective education and its origins and effects.

From the range of personal models, we have selected several to illustrate the genre. The chapter on Carl Rogers's nondirective teaching model illustrates the philosophy and techniques of the major spokesperson for the family, and the chapter on self-concept and states of growth deals with the organization of communities of learners.

CHAPTER FOURTEEN

Nondirective Teaching

The Learner at the Center

The hard part of figuring out how to teach is learning when to keep your mouth closed, which is most of the time.

—*Carl Rogers, to a seminar at Columbia University*

SCENARIO

WHEN YOUR PARENTS ARE SENT INTO HARM'S WAY

We are in a Department of Defense Dependents School (DODDS) in Germany, in Charley Wilson's fifth-grade class of the children of soldiers. A number of their parents have just been sent to Afghanistan to secure an airfield against attacking forces. Charley has decided that the best course of action is to busy his students in academic study, and he is ready to begin a unit on writing that begins with a set of film clips that the students will write about.

However, as he readies the VCR and turns to the class, he can see unusual stress on the students' faces. He asks, "What's up?" There is no response. He says gently, "You look like you're only half alive."

Silence again. Then one student responds strongly, "We're worried sick." The others nod.

"OK. Now, shall we deal with it? Do you want to talk about it?"

"I don't know what to say. I'm just frozen," says Pamela. More nodding.

"What does frozen feel like?"

"It's like I'm hardly alive. I'm hiding inside a cave."

"That's a good way to put it," says Josh. "It's like I'm somewhere else, trying to freeze out what's happening."

"It's like if you let your fear in—really in—you won't be able to stand it. You have to hide and keep it away," says Nancy.

The students are looking directly at Charley, avoiding each others' eyes. Charley keeps the discussion going, primarily eliciting comments like those above and some heart-rending ones, like "No one cares. They just send the soldiers out to die or get hurt and they sit home and eat popcorn when the news reports the number of casualties on the stupid news shows."

After a while, they take a break for a few minutes. When they reassemble, Charley starts the discussion again.

"You know what? We all fear that something will happen to our friends and mothers and fathers." Everyone nods. "Our fear is a good thing. It's not crazy. There's real danger out there." The students begin to look at each other now, and nod. They are miserable. But they are less alone. Charley keeps on.

"The problem is that we have to support those mothers and fathers and keep ourselves going when we are scared and anxious ourselves." More nods and eye contact with Charley. "So, let's directly face how we are going to do that."

Charley is beginning an inquiry into the very immediate problem of how these children will carry on and help their parents deal with a life-threatening danger.

SCENARIO

THE PSYCHE OF THE STRUGGLING READER

"You expect me to read to myself for twenty minutes every day in this class?"

"Absolutely. You've got to learn to read better and you won't unless you read more."

"Who says so?"

"Well, who is talking to you right now, Tom?"

"I can read all right. Why do I have to be in this class?"

"I'd like you to read something to me, now." Miss Tamron hands Tom an open book. "Begin at the top of the page on the left."

"What's this word?"

"Do you mean the first word, Tom?"

"Yes."

"Is that the heading of the page?"

"Yes, Miss Tamron."

"The word that probably tells us what the page is about?"

"Yes. Come on, what is it?"

"Listen carefully, Tom. That word is *addition.* Kids in first grade have to learn to read that word at sight. You are in the sixth grade. What does that tell you?"

"I don't like to read."

"You may, when you learn how."

In this rather abrupt session, Miss Tamron is trying to get Tom to face himself and what he has to do. For years, Tom has resisted teachers who have tried to teach him to read. The passage illustrates that nondirective doesn't mean "wimpy."

The nondirective teaching model is based on the work of Carl Rogers (1961, 1971) and other advocates of nondirective counseling. Rogers extended to education his view of therapy as a mode of learning. He believed that positive human relationships enable people to grow, and therefore instruction should be based on concepts of human relations in contrast to concepts of subject matter.

As we stated earlier in the introduction to this section of the book, we will concentrate on the use of the model to "flavor" teaching—to keep the students' frames of reference in mind, keep central their growth in self, and help them solve learning problems.

The teacher's role is that of a facilitator who has a counseling relationship with students and guides their growth and development. In this role, the teacher helps students explore new ideas about their lives, their schoolwork, and their relations with others. The model creates an environment where students and teachers are partners in learning, share ideas openly, and communicate honestly with one another.

The nondirective model nurtures students rather than controlling the sequence of learning. The emphases are more on the development of effective long-term learning styles and the development of strong, well-directed individual personalities than they are with short-term instructional or content objectives. The nondirective teacher is patient and does not sacrifice the long view by forcing immediate results.

SCENARIO

LEADING STUDENTS TO TAKE CHARGE OF AN INVESTIGATION

Ann Espinosa, striving to help her tenth-grade students achieve global literacy, introduced them to www.refdesk.com/paper, an online newspapers database, which connects hundreds of newspapers from 80 countries. Ann announced that she was giving students two or three questions and then they were to generate some of their own to focus further inquiries. First, she asked students to find out how many countries, aside from the United States, had an English-language newspaper in the database. They then mapped the countries according to which did and did not have one, seeking to learn whether they were clustered regionally.

Second, because it was World Cup season, she asked the students to find out how many of the countries' newspapers, regardless of language, covered the World Cup soccer games and also reported baseball standings. Much discussion ensued. The students concluded that World Cup soccer matches were being reported virtually everywhere, but baseball was reported in just a few countries. Students speculated on the reasons for the difference.

Third, she asked the students to learn how certain events were described in the English-language newspapers of countries where languages other than English were the most common. Essentially, after opening the topic and source of information, Ann developed the unit by asking questions, reflecting on information acquired—working nondirectively rather than structuring the inquiry for the students.

She was active and challenging, but pulling the students to develop the investigation and collect and analyze information themselves.

SCENARIO

IS SHE A BIT SHY, OR . . .

John Denbro, a 26-year-old high school English teacher in suburban Chicago, is very concerned about Mary Ann Fortnay, one of his students. Mary Ann is a compulsive worker who does an excellent job with literature assignments and writes excellent short stories. She is, however, reluctant to share those stories with other members of the class and declines to participate in any activities in the performing arts.

Denbro recognizes that the issue cannot be forced, but he wants Mary Ann to understand why she is reluctant to allow any public display of her talents. She will make her own decisions about participation that involves sharing her ideas.

One afternoon she asks him to read some of her pieces and give her his opinion.

Mary Ann: Mr. Denbro, could you take a look at these for me?

Denbro: Why sure, Mary Ann. Another short story?

Mary Ann: No, some poems I've been working on. I don't think they're very good, but I'd like you to tell me what you think.

Denbro: When did you write them?

Mary Ann: One Sunday afternoon a couple of weeks ago.

Denbro: Do you remember what started you thinking that you wanted to write a poem?

Mary Ann: I was feeling kind of sad and I remembered last month when we tried to read "The Waste Land," and it seemed to be trying to say a lot of things that we couldn't say in the usual way. I liked the beginning lines, "April is the cruelest month, breeding lilacs out of the dead land."

Denbro: And this is what you wrote down?

Mary Ann: Yes. It's the first time I've ever tried writing anything like this.

Denbro: (Reads for a few minutes and then looks up.) Mary Ann, these are really good.

Mary Ann: What makes a poem good, Mr. Denbro?

Denbro: Well, there are a variety of ways to judge poetry. Some methods are technical and have to do with the quality of expression and the way one uses metaphors and analogies and other literary devices. Others are subjective and involve the quality of expression, the real beauty of the words themselves.

Mary Ann: I felt very good when I was writing them, but when I read them over, they sound a little dumb to me.

Denbro: What do you mean?

Mary Ann: Oh, I don't know. I guess the main thing is that I feel ashamed if anybody else sees them.

Denbro: Ashamed?

Mary Ann: I really don't know. I just know that if these were to be read aloud, say to my class, I would die of mortification.

Denbro: You really feel that the class would laugh at these?

Mary Ann: Oh sure, they wouldn't understand.

Denbro: How about your short stories? How do you feel about them?

Mary Ann: You know I don't want *anybody* to see what I write.

Denbro: You really feel that you want to put them away somewhere so nobody can see them?

Mary Ann: Yes, I really think so. I don't know exactly why, but I'm pretty sure that no one in my class would understand them.

Denbro: Can you think of anybody else that might understand them?

Mary Ann: I don't know. I kind of think there are people out there who might, but nobody around here, probably.

Denbro: How about your parents?

Mary Ann: Oh, they like everything I write.

Denbro: Well, that makes three of us. Can you think of anybody else?

Mary Ann: I guess I think adults would, but I'm not really so sure about other kids.

Denbro: Kids are somehow different from adults in this respect?

Mary Ann: Well, kids just don't seem to be interested in these kinds of things. I feel they put down anybody who tries to write anything.

Denbro: Do you think they feel this way about the authors we read in class?

Mary Ann: Well, sometimes they do, but I guess a lot of the time they really enjoy the stories.

Denbro: Well then, why do you think they wouldn't like what you write?

Mary Ann: I guess I really don't know, Mr. Denbro. I guess I'm really afraid, but I can't put my finger on it.

Denbro: Something holds you back.

Mary Ann: In a lot of ways, I really would like to find out whether anybody would appreciate what I write. I just don't know how to go about it.

Denbro: How would you feel if I were to read one of your short stories but not tell them who wrote it?

Mary Ann: Would you promise?

Denbro: Of course I would. Then we could talk about how everybody reacted. You would know that they didn't know who had written it.

Mary Ann: I don't know, but it sounds interesting.

Denbro: Depending on what happened, we could cook up some kind of strategy about what to do next.

Mary Ann: Well, I guess you've got me right where I don't have anything to lose.

Denbro: I hope we're always where you don't have anything to lose, Mary Ann; but there's always a risk in telling about ourselves.

Mary Ann: What do you mean, telling about ourselves?

Denbro: I think I should go now—but let me pick one of your stories and read it next week, and then let's get together on Wednesday and talk about what happened.

Mary Ann: OK, and you promise not to tell?

Denbro: I promise. I'll see you next Wednesday after school.

Mary Ann: OK. I'll see you then.

ORIENTATION TO THE MODEL

Goals and Assumptions

We will concentrate on the elements that create a nondirective atmosphere for interacting with the students, remembering that counseling, an important component of special education, is designed by the personal models.

The nondirective teaching model focuses on *facilitating* learning. The environment is organized to help students attain greater personal integration, effectiveness, and realistic self-appraisal. Stimulating, examining, and evaluating new perceptions take a central place, because the reexamination of needs and values—their sources and outcomes—is crucial to personal integration. Students do not necessarily need to change, but the teacher's goal is to help them understand their own needs and values so that they can effectively direct their own educational decisions.

The core of the rationale comes from Rogers's stance toward nondirective counseling, in which the client's capacity to deal constructively with his or her own life is respected and nurtured. Thus, in nondirective teaching, the teacher respects the students' ability to identify their own problems and to formulate solutions.

When operating nondirectively, the teacher attempts to see the world as the student sees it, creating an atmosphere of empathetic communication in which the student's self-direction can be nurtured and developed. During interaction, the teacher mirrors students' thoughts and feelings. By using reflective comments, the teacher raises the students' consciousness of their own perceptions and feelings, thus helping them clarify their ideas.

The teacher also serves as a benevolent alter ego, one who accepts feelings and thoughts, even those the students may be afraid of or view as wrong or perhaps even punishable. In being accepting and nonpunitive, the teacher indirectly communicates to the students that all thoughts and feelings are acceptable. In fact, recognition of both positive and negative feelings is essential to emotional development and positive solutions.

The teacher gives up the traditional decision-making role, choosing instead the role of a facilitator who focuses on student feelings. The relationship between student and teacher in a nondirective interview is best described as a partnership. Thus, if the student complains of poor grades and an inability to study, the teacher does not attempt to resolve the problem simply by explaining the art of good study habits. Instead, the teacher encourages the student to express the feelings that may surround his or her inability to concentrate. When these feelings are fully explored and perceptions are clarified, the student tries to identify appropriate changes and bring them about.

The nondirective atmosphere has four qualities. First, the teacher shows warmth and responsiveness, expressing genuine interest in the student and accepting him or her as a person. Second, it is characterized by permissiveness in regard to the expression of feeling; the teacher does not judge or moralize. Because of the importance of emotions, much content is discussed that would normally be guarded against in more customary teacher–student relationships. Third, the student is free to express feelings symbolically but is not free to control the teacher or to carry impulses into action. Fourth, the relationship is free from any type of pressure or coercion. The teacher avoids showing personal bias or reacting in a personally critical manner to the student. Every learning task is viewed as an opportunity to help the student grow as a person.

According to Rogers, responding on a purely intellectual basis to students' problems inhibits the expression of feelings, which are at the root of the problem of growth. For example, if a student is struggling with writing, an intellectual response would be, "Start by making an outline." An empathetic response would be, "When I get stuck I often feel panicky. How do you feel?"

Insight is the short-term goal of the process. By expressing feelings the student becomes better able to look at a problem—in the case of the scenario on pages 286–288, the problem of allowing others to experience one's writing. Indications of insight come from statements by the students that describe behavior in terms of cause and effect or in terms of personal meaning. In the scenario, the student comes to realize that the problem lies in her own fear, rather than the objective possibility of judgments by others. As they begin to understand the reasons for their behaviors, they begin to see other more functional ways of satisfying their needs. Through the release of emotions, the students can perceive options more clearly. New insights enable the students to select delayed goals that are more satisfying than goals that give immediate but only temporary satisfaction.

Ultimately, the test of personal insight is the presence of actions that motivate the students toward new goals. At first, these positive actions may concern minor issues, but they create a sense of confidence and independence in the student. The teacher in the scenario is trying to create a "safe space" for the action of sharing the writing. Gradually, the students' positive actions lead to a new, more comprehensive orientation. This is the integration phase. In the first scenario, Charley is redirecting the students from their misery and fear to the problem of helping themselves and others to create a good life in the midst of a really terrible problem. In the scenario at the end of the chapter, the long-term goal is a mature ability to share writing derived from a better understanding of the social dynamics of sharing. In other words, the student will gradually find that the action of sharing has more good consequences than bad ones and that satisfaction can come from the integrated understanding of the problem of sharing.

The nondirective approach maintains that the most effective means of uncovering the emotions underlying a problem is to follow the pattern of the students' feelings as they are freely expressed. Instead of asking direct questions for the purpose of eliciting feelings, the teacher lets the students direct the flow of thoughts and feelings. If the students express themselves freely, the problems and their underlying emotions will emerge. This process is facilitated by reflecting the students' feelings, thereby bringing them into awareness and sharper focus. This is a difficult skill for most of us because we are more attuned to the objective content of what people are saying than to the affective dimension of the communications.

Taking the Lead

The student and teacher share the responsibility for the discussion. But, frequently, the teacher must make "lead-taking" responses to direct or maintain the conversation (see Table 14.1). These include statements by the teacher that help start the discussion, establish the direction in an open manner, or give the student some indication as to what he or she should discuss, either specifically or generally.

The essential skill is to lead without taking responsibility from the students. Nondirective lead-taking remarks are stated directly in a positive and amiable manner. Some examples are:

- "What do you think of that?"
- "Can you say more about that?"
- "How do you react when that happens?"

Nondirective responses to feelings are attempts to respond either to the feelings the student expresses or to the content of the expressions. In making these comments, the teacher does not interpret, evaluate, or offer advice, but reflects, clarifies, accepts, and demonstrates understanding. The purpose of these comments is to create an atmosphere in which the student is willing to expand the ideas he or she is expressing. Usually, the responses are short statements that are supportive and enable the student to continue the discussion. Some examples are:

- "I think I understand."
- "It's especially hard to be alone."
- "Sort of like it doesn't matter what you do, it will go on the same way."

TABLE **14.1**   Nondirective Responses in Interview

Nondirective Responses to Feelings	Nondirective Lead-Taking Responses
1. Simple acceptance 2. Reflection of feelings 3. Paraphrasing of content	1. Structuring 2. Directive questioning 3. Forcing student to choose and develop a topic 4. Nondirective leads and open questions 5. Minimal encouragements to talk

Interpretation is used sparingly—we want the students to do the interpreting—but it is occasionally useful in moving a discussion forward when a student is unable to offer any explanation for his or her behavior. Interpretative responses are attempts to suggest to the student his or her reasons for being unable to continue the discussion. But interpretation is given only to those feelings that can definitely be accepted by the student. The decision to use interpretation is made cautiously by the teacher and is used only in situations in which the teacher feels confident that interpretation will advance rather than close a dialogue. The whole purpose is to help the student inquire into what have been relatively closed areas:

- "You do this because . . ."
- "Perhaps you feel you won't succeed."
- "It sounds like your reasons for your actions this week are . . ."
- "You are saying to me that the problem is . . ."

Warmth is needed, but reinforcing statements are usually given only when genuine progress has been achieved. It must be used sparingly, or the nondirective relationship is likely to drift rapidly into the traditional teacher–student relationship. But thoughts like the following may help at times:

- "That's a very interesting comment and may well be worth considering again."
- "That last idea was particularly strong. Could you elaborate on it some more?"
- "I think you are really making progress."

Directive counseling moves are also to be used rarely—they imply a relationship in which the teacher attempts to change the ideas of the student or influence his or her attitudes. For example, "Do you think it might be better if . . ." directly suggests a choice to the student. Attempts to support the student directly are usually made to reduce apparent anxiety, but they do not contribute to real problem solving.

THE MODEL OF TEACHING

The nondirective stance presents some interesting problems compared to many of the other models. First, the responsibility is shared. In most models of teaching, the teacher actively shapes events and can picture the pattern of activities that lies ahead, but in most nondirective situations, events emerge and the pattern of activities is more fluid. Second, the nondirective interchanges are "rolling" in nature. A move to help the student initiate a conversation on a difficult (for that student) topic has no completely predictable response. And, sometimes, when progress appears to be happening, the student reverts to a more or less stubborn position, and the teacher needs to backtrack. Thus, to master nondirective teaching, teachers learn general principles, work to increase their sensitivity to others, master the nondirective skills, and then practice making contact with students and responding to them, using skills drawn from a repertoire of nondirective counseling techniques.

Syntax

Despite the fluidity and unpredictability of nondirective teaching, Rogers points out that the nondirective interview has a sequence. We have divided this sequence into five phases of activity, as shown in Table 14.2.

In phase one, the helping situation is defined. This includes structuring remarks that define the student's freedom to express feelings, an agreement on the general focus of the interview, an initial problem statement, some discussion of the relationship if it is to be ongoing, and the establishment of procedures for meeting. Phase one generally occurs during the initial session on a

TABLE **14.2**   Syntax of Nondirective Model

Phase One: **Defining the Helping** **Situation**	Teacher encourages free expression of feelings.
Phase Two: **Exploring the Problem**	Student is encouraged to define problem. Teacher accepts and clarifies feelings.
Phase Three: **Developing Insight**	Student discusses problem. Teacher supports student.
Phase Four: **Planning and Decision** **Making**	Student plans initial decision making. Teacher clarifies possible decisions.
Phase Five: **Integration**	Student gains further insight and develops more positive actions. Teacher is supportive.
Action Outside the Interview	Student initiates positive actions.

problem. However, some structuring or definition by the teacher may be necessary for some time, even if this consists only of occasional summarizing moves that redefine the problem and reflect progress. Naturally, these structuring and definitional comments vary considerably with the specific problem and the student. For example, negotiating academic contracts will likely differ from working with behavioral problem situations.

In phase two, the student is encouraged by the teacher's acceptance and clarification to express negative and positive feelings and to state and explore the problem.

In phase three, the student gradually develops insight: he or she perceives new meaning in personal experiences, sees new relationships of cause and effect, and understands the meaning of his or her previous behavior. In most situations, the student seems to alternate between exploring the problem itself and developing new insight into his or her feelings. Both activities are necessary for progress. Discussion of the problem without exploration of feelings would indicate that the student himself or herself was being avoided.

In phase four, the student moves toward planning and decision making with respect to the problem. The role of the teacher is to clarify the alternatives.

In phase five, the student reports the actions he or she has taken, develops further insight, and plans increasingly more integrated and positive actions.

The syntax presented here could occur in one session or, more likely, over a series. In the latter case, phases one and two could occur in the first few discussions, phases three and four in the next, and phase five in the last interview. Or, if the encounter consists of a voluntary meeting with a student who has an immediate problem, phases one through four could occur in only one meeting, with the student returning briefly to report his or her actions and insights. On the other hand, the sessions involved in negotiating academic contracts are sustained for a period of time, and the context of each meeting generally involves some kind of planning and decision making, although several sessions devoted entirely to exploring a problem might occur. It is very important that the student comes to understand that he or she is ultimately responsible for the outcome rather than being helpless in the hands of outside forces.

Social System

The social system of the nondirective strategy requires the teacher to assume the roles of facilitator and reflector. The norms are open expression of feelings and autonomy of thought and behavior. Rewards, in the usual sense of approval of specific behavior—and particularly punishment—do not apply in this strategy. The rewards in a nondirective interview are more subtle and intrinsic—acceptance, understanding, and empathy from the teacher. The knowledge of oneself and the psychological rewards gained from self-reliance are generated by the student personally.

Principles of Reaction

The principles of reaction are based on bringing the student into inquiry on affect. The teacher reaches out to the students, empathizes with their personalities and problems, and reacts in such a way as to help them define their problems and feelings, take responsibility for their actions, and plan objectives and how to achieve them.

Support System

The support system for this strategy varies with the function of the interview. If a session is to negotiate academic contracts, then the necessary resources for self-directed learning must be made available. If the interview consists of counseling for a behavioral problem, no resources beyond the skills of the teacher are necessary. In both cases, the one-to-one situation requires spatial arrangements that allow for privacy, removal from other classroom forces and activities, and time to explore a problem adequately and in an unhurried fashion. For academic curriculum areas—reading, writing, literature, science, and social science—rich arrays of materials are necessary.

APPLICATION

The nondirective teaching model may be used for several types of problem situations: personal, social, and academic. In the case of personal problems, the individuals explore feelings about self. In social problems, students explore their feelings about relationships with others and investigate how feelings about self may influence these relationships. In academic problems, students explore their feelings about their competence and interests. In each case, however, the interview content is always personal rather than external; it centers on each individual's own feelings, experiences, insights, and solutions.

To use the nondirective teaching model effectively, a teacher must be willing to accept that a student can understand and cope with his or her own life. Belief in the student's capacity to direct himself or herself is communicated through the teacher's attitude and words. The teacher does not attempt to judge the student. Such a stance indicates limited confidence in the student's capabilities. The teacher does not attempt to diagnose problems. Instead, the teacher attempts to perceive the student's world as he or she sees and feels it. And, at the moment of the student's self-perception, the teacher reflects the new understanding to him or her. In this model, the teacher temporarily sets aside personal thoughts and feelings and reflects the student's thoughts and feelings. By doing this, the teacher conveys understanding and acceptance of the feelings.

The nondirective environment raises the emotional elements of the situation more than the intellectual. That is, nondirective counseling strives for reorganization through the realm of feeling rather than through purely intellectual approaches. Often this view leads teachers who are considering adopting the nondirective stance to question the possibility of conflicting roles. How, they reason, can I be a disciplinarian, a referee, an instructor, and a friend—and also be a counselor implementing nondirective principles?

One of the important uses of nondirective teaching occurs when a class becomes "stale" and the teacher finds himself or herself just "pushing" the students through exercises and subject matter. One sixth-grade teacher, exhausted by the failure of more traditional attempts to cope with the discipline problems and the lack of interest on the part of her class, decided to experiment with student-centered teaching. She turned to nondirective approaches to help her students take more responsibility for their learning and to ensure that the subject matter would be related to their needs and learning styles. She has provided an account of that experience, from which excerpts are presented here.

SCENARIO

A TEACHER EXPERIMENTS

March 5: We Begin

A week ago I decided to initiate a new program in my sixth-grade art class, based on student-centered teaching—an unstructured or nondirective approach. I began by telling the class that we were going to try an experiment. I explained that for one day I would let them do anything they wanted to do—they did not have to do anything if they did not want to, as long as it didn't interfere with another student—and they would have to work alone. My usual style is very skill-oriented—my art classes are long on techniques, short on self-direction.

Many started with art projects; some drew or painted for most of the day. Others read or did work in math and other subjects. There was an air of excitement all day. Many were so interested in what they were doing that they did not want to go out at recess or noon!

At the end of the day I asked the class to evaluate the experiment. The comments were most interesting. Some were confused or distressed without the teacher telling them what to do, without specific assignments to complete. The majority of the class thought the day was great, but some expressed concern that a few students just goofed off all day. Most felt that they had accomplished as much work as we usually do, and they enjoyed being able to work at a task until it was completed, without the pressure of a time limit. They liked doing things without being forced to do them and liked deciding what to do. They begged to continue the experiment, so we decided to try it for two more days. We could then reevaluate the plan.

The next morning I implemented the idea of a "work contract." I gave them ditto sheets listing all our subjects with suggestions under each. There was a space provided for their plans in each area and for checking work after completion. Each student was to write his or her contract for the day—choosing the areas in which to work and planning specifically what to do. On completion of any exercise, drill, review, and so on, the student was to check and correct his or her own work using the teacher's manual. The work was to be kept in a folder with the contract.

I met with each person to discuss his or her plans. Some completed theirs in a very short time; we discussed as a group what this might mean and what to do about it. It was suggested that the plan might not be challenging enough, that an adjustment should be made—perhaps going on or adding another idea to the day's plan. Resource materials were provided, suggestions made, and drill materials made available to use when needed.

I found I had much more time, so I worked, talked, and spent the time with individuals and groups. At the end of the third day I evaluated the work folder with each child. To solve the problem of grades, I had each child tell me what he or she had learned.

March 12: Progress Report

Our experiment has, in fact, become our program—with some adjustments. Some children continued to be frustrated and felt insecure without teacher direction. Discipline also continued to be a problem with some, and I began to realize that, although some of the children may need the program more than others, I was expecting too much from them too soon—they were not ready to assume self-direction yet. Perhaps a gradual weaning from the spoon-fed procedures was necessary.

I regrouped the class into two groups. The larger group is nondirected. The smaller is made up of children who wanted to return to the former teacher-directed method and those who, for varied reasons, were unable to function in the self-directed situation. I would have waited longer to see what would happen, but the situation for some disintegrated a little more each day, penalizing the whole class. The disrupting factor kept everyone upset and limited those who wanted to study and work, so it seemed best for the group as a whole as well as the program to modify the plan.

Those who continued the experiment have forged ahead. I showed them how to program their work, using their texts as a basic guide. They have learned that they can teach themselves (and each other), and that I am available when a step is not clear or advice is needed.

At the end of the week they evaluate themselves in each area in terms of work accomplished, accuracy, and so on. We have learned that the number of errors is not a criterion of failure or success. Errors can and should be part of the learning process; we learn through our own mistakes. We have also discussed the fact that consistently perfect scores may mean that the work is not challenging enough and perhaps we should move on. After self-evaluation, each child brings the evaluation sheet and work folder to discuss with me.

Some of the members of the group working with me are most anxious to become "independent" students. We will evaluate together each week their progress toward that goal. Some students (there were two or three) who originally wanted to return to the teacher-directed program are now anticipating going back into the self-directed program. (I sense that it has been difficult for them to readjust to the old program, as it would be for me to do so at this point with that class.)

INSTRUCTIONAL AND NURTURANT EFFECTS

Since the activities are not prescribed but are determined by the learner as he or she interacts with the teacher and other students, the nondirective environment depends largely on its nurturant effects, with the instructional effects dependent on its success in nurturing more effective self-development (Figure 14.1).

FIGURE 14.1   Instructional and nurturant effects of the nondirective teaching model

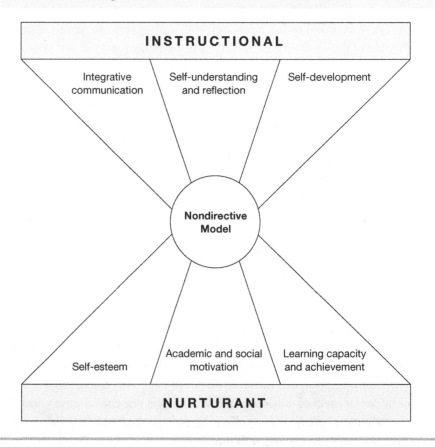

The model thus can be thought of as entirely nurturant in character, dependent for effects on experiencing the nondirective environment rather than carrying content and skills through specifically designed activity.

Nondirective Teaching Model   SUMMARY CHART

Syntax

- Phase One: Defining the Helping Situation.
- Phase Two: Exploring the Problem.
- Phase Three: Developing Insight.
- Phase Four: Planning and Decision Making.
- Phase Five: Integration.

Social System

The structure emerges from the interaction: teacher facilitates; student initiates; and the discussion is problem-centered. Rewards (in the usual sense of approval of specific behavior) and punishment do not apply in this strategy. The rewards are intrinsic and include acceptance, empathy, and understanding from the teacher.

Principles of Reaction

Teacher reaches out to students, empathizes, and reacts to help students define problems and take action to achieve solutions.

Support System

Teacher needs quiet, private place for one-to-one contacts and a resource center for conferences on academic contracts.

CHAPTER FIFTEEN

Developing Positive Self-Concepts

Finding the Inner Person and Learning Self-Actualization

We want to make the school rich, but we also want the kids to know that they can't depend on us forever. They've got to be able to take off on their own.

—*Carlene Murphy to Bruce Joyce*

Although people and their growth are the important substance of this book, this is the first chapter that attempts to deal conceptually with the most important underlying element in general education—the states of growth that result from schooling. Therefore, as we directly approach the subject it is worthwhile to summarize a number of statements about people.

First, the research on the spectrum of models of teaching supports the proposition that all students can learn how to learn and respond to a great variety of teaching/learning environments. Students can accelerate their ability to learn in a number of ways if we provide them with the opportunity.

Second, the more skills students develop and the more they widen their repertoire, the greater their ability to master an even greater range of skills and strategies. (This is true of teachers as well. The better we get, the better we *can* get!)

Third, the learning community developed in the school and the classroom influences how students feel about themselves, how they interact, and how they learn. The social climate, in other words, is part of the substance of schooling. It provides a "curriculum" that affects the results of the academic curriculum.

The important message is that students can learn not only academic content and social skills, but how to become integrated selves that reach out into the world and reciprocally contribute to and profit from their transactions with it.

Now we turn to modeling active states of growth for our students. We will examine a framework for looking at the ways children and adults interact with the world—from states of actively seeking growth to more passive interaction to states of pushing experience away. In many ways, students become what we model for them, and part of our influence on them depends on our own states of growth—our own self-concepts—and how we communicate them to children.

INDIVIDUAL DIFFERENCES

We begin with a frame of reference that will enable us to think about individual differences in growth, particularly readiness to grow. There are a number of ways of thinking about individual differences that we can rely on at the present time. Some of these have been developed to help us think about the learning styles of children (Dunn & Dunn, 1975; McCarthy, 1981) and can be applied to adults as well. Some are developed to distinguish various styles of thinking (Gardner, 1983) and examine how those styles affect problem solving. At least one theory attempts to describe differences between children and adults as learners (Knowles, 1978).

A number of broad conceptualizations of personality can be applied to the behavior of teachers as instructors and as learners (Erikson, 1950; Harvey, Hunt, & Schroeder, 1961; Maslow, 1962). Conceptual systems theory (Hunt, 1971) has been especially heavily studied and has been a useful predictor of teacher–student interaction, the breadth of styles employed by teachers, sensitivity to students and responsiveness to them, and (most pertinent here) aptitude to acquire the competence to use teaching skills and strategies (see Joyce, Peck, & Brown, 1981).

In this chapter we will discuss a framework developed from the study of the professional and personal lives of teachers in the California Staff Development Study (Joyce, Bush, & McKibbin, 1982; Joyce & Showers, 2002). The framework was developed to guide practice in the organization of human resource development programs and school improvement efforts (Joyce, Calhoun, and Hopkins, 1999; Joyce, Hersh, & McKibbin, 1983; McKibbin & Joyce, 1980). A practical orientation, the findings are correlated with the theories of personality growth and take conceptual development, self-concept, and psychological maturity into account. It owes a particular debt to the work of Abraham Maslow (1962).

THE CONCEPT OF STATE OF GROWTH

The objective of the line of inquiry was to build a picture of the opportunities for growth experienced by teachers from their school setting, district, universities, intermediate agencies (county offices of education and professional development centers), and other institutions. In the initial investigation, case studies were made of more than 300 teachers from 21 districts in 7 counties, and more than 2,000 others were surveyed through questionnaires. In addition to information about participation in the formal systems of support (courses, workshops, and the services of administrators and supervisors), interaction with peers was examined, as were those aspects of personal lives that might have implications for professional growth. Thus, data were collected on what came to be termed the *formal*, *peer-generated*, and *personal* domains, depending on the origins of the activities that people engaged in.

The focus was the dynamic of individual interaction with the environment. The thesis was that within any given environment (say, a school in the San Francisco Bay Area), the opportunities for productive interaction leading to growth theoretically would be about equal. That is, formal staff development systems, colleagues, and opportunities to read, attend films and events in the performing arts, engage in athletic activity, and so on, would be available to all personnel in profusion. Thus, differences in activity would be a function of the individual's disposition to interact productively with the environment. If we discovered differences, we could proceed to try to understand their origins and develop ideas for capitalizing on them.

THE FORMAL, PEER-GENERATED, AND PERSONAL DOMAINS

The amount of interaction in all three domains varied greatly. The differences were vast in both urban and rural areas and among elementary and secondary teachers. They are easily illustrated in regions like the Bay Area and the Los Angeles Basin, where literally thousands of courses and workshops are available, most principals and supervisors have been trained to provide active clinical support, many professional development centers in county offices and other agencies involve teachers in the selection of staff development opportunities, and there are active organizations for teachers of writing, science, and other curriculum areas. In addition, the opportunities for personal activity of all sorts abound in these great metropolitan areas, which also are close to mountain ranges, waterways, and oceans. The nature of the differences in each domain is interesting.

The Formal Domain

Participation ranged from persons who experienced only the activities sponsored and required by the district (possibly only one or two workshops or presentations and one or two visits by supervisors or consultants) and who were aware of very few options, to very active, aware persons with definite plans for professional enhancement. A small number effectively exploited the opportunities in universities and the larger teacher centers.

The Peer-Generated Domain

The range here was from persons who had virtually no professional discussions with any other teachers, to persons who had close and frequent interaction, who experienced mentoring relationships (on the giving or receiving end or both), and who gathered with others to instigate the introduction of innovations or initiatives for the improvement of the school.

The Personal Domain

Some teachers were extremely active in their personal lives, with one or two well-developed areas of participation, and some others made virtually no use of the rich environments in which they lived. We found some very active readers and others who barely skim the headlines of the daily paper, some Sierra Club activists and others who had never visited Yosemite, some members of performing arts groups and others who have not seen a film or a live performance in 10 or more years.

STATES OF GROWTH

Somewhat to our surprise, the levels of activity were correlated across domains. That is, those who were more active professionally were also more active personally. Looking for reasons, we concluded that the differences in levels of activity were produced by the individuals' orientations toward their environments, moderated by social influence.

Orientations toward the Environment

The essence of the concept is the degree to which the environment is viewed as an opportunity for satisfying growth. Thus, the more active people view the environment as a set of possibilities for satisfying interaction. They initiate contact and exploit the possibilities. Less active persons are less aware of the possibilities or more indifferent to them. The least active persons expend energy protecting themselves from what they see as a threatening or unpleasant environment, avoiding contact, and fending off the initiatives of others. Also, the persons who are more active and more initiating are also more *proactive*. That is, they *draw* more attention from the environment, bringing more possibilities within their reach. This phenomenon multiplies the opportunities for many people. It was not unusual for us to discover that certain schools that were characterized by a cluster of active people (and generally by an active principal) were regularly approached by central office personnel, teacher centers, and universities to be the "trial" sites for everything from computer technology to community involvement programs. Those people and their schools received more resources and training, whereas schools characterized by a cluster of resistant persons were approached last, and many initiatives passed them by.

Social Influence

Close friends and colleagues, and the social climate of the workplace and the neighborhood, moderate general dispositions toward growth. Affirmative and active friends and colleagues and positive social climates induce persons to engage in greater activity than they would if left to themselves. This finding provides another dimension to the general theme of Chapter 11. The synergistic environment is not only essential for collective action but generates the kind of colleagueship that will be productive for the states of growth of individuals.

Also, as we will emphasize later, a major goal of a human resource development system is to increase the states of growth of the personnel in the system, potentially benefiting the individuals as well as the organization and ensuring that the children are in contact with active, seeking personalities.

Levels of activity

Although the orientations toward growth are best represented on a continuum, people gradually develop patterns that have more clearly discernible edges, and it is not unreasonable to categorize them—provided we recognize that the categories blend into one another. With that caveat, we present the following prototypes, which can be useful in explaining behavior and planning staff development programs and organizing faculties to exploit them vigorously.

A Gourmet Omnivore

Our prototypes here are mature, high-activity people who have learned to canvass the environment and exploit it successfully. In the formal domain they keep aware of the possibilities for growth, identify high-probability events, and work hard at squeezing them for their growth potential.

They constitute the hardcore clientele for teacher centers and district and intermediate-agency offerings for volunteers. They initiate ideas for programs and find ways of influencing the policymakers. However, they are not negative toward system initiatives. They have the complexity to balance their personal interests with the awareness that they belong to an organization.

Our prototype omnivores find kindred souls with whom to interact professionally. They learn from informal interaction with their peers. A group of omnivores may work together and generate initiatives or attend workshops or courses together. When computers appeared on the educational scene, it was often groups of omnivores who learned to use them and developed the computer centers in their schools.

It is in their personal lives that our prototype omnivores become most clearly defined. They are characterized by a general high level of awareness, but their distinguishing feature is one or two areas in which they are enthusiastically involved. These areas vary quite a bit from person to person. One may be an omnivorous reader; another, a theatergoer; a third, an avid backpacker or skier; a fourth, a maker of ceramics. Some run businesses. In close consort with others, they generate activities. The spouses of omnivore tennis players are likely to find themselves with rackets in their hands, and the close friends of moviegoers will be importuned to share films. Because of their proactivity, our mature omnivores have learned to fend off opportunities and protect time for their chosen avocations. What is striking is their habit of both exploiting and enriching whatever environment they find themselves in. In the workplace, they strive to learn all they can about their craft and give and take energy from their peers. In their private lives they find opportunities for development.

They are also distinguished by their persistence. In McKibbin and Joyce's (1980) study, they sought training that would have a high likelihood for transfer and, once back in the workplace, they practiced and created the conditions of peer support that enabled them to implement a remarkably high proportion of the skills to which they were exposed. They are also more likely than others to bring the ideas they gain in their personal lives into the workplace and use them in their teaching. More recent studies (Hopkins, 1990; Joyce & Showers, 2002) have remarkably similar findings.

A Passive Consumer

About 10 percent of the persons we studied fit the profile of our *gourmet omnivores*, and another 10 percent are what we call *active consumers*, also quite engaged with aspects of their environment. By far the largest number, however—about 70 percent—resembled the prototype we term the *passive consumer*.

The distinguishing characteristics of our passive consumers are a more or less amiable conformity to the environment and a high degree of dependence on the immediate social context. In other words, their degree of activity depends greatly on who they are with. In the company of other passive consumers, our prototype is relatively inactive. We studied one school in which all of the personnel in one wing of the building were passive, and their interchange with others was amiable but involved few serious discussions about teaching and learning. They visited one another's classrooms rarely. None attended staff development activities that were not required by the administration. They had no objections to being required to attend those workshops, one day in the fall and one in the spring; they enjoyed them but did nothing with the content.

In another wing of the school, two passive consumers found themselves in the company of two omnivores and an active consumer and were drawn into many of the activities generated by their more enterprising colleagues. They found themselves helping set up computer workstations for the students, cooperating in scheduling and the selection of software, and learning word processing and how to teach their students to use self-instructional programs. They attended workshops on the teaching of writing with the study group instigated by the omnivores and began revamping their writing programs.

In personal life our prototype passive consumer is also dependent on consort. If they have relatively inactive spouses and extended families, they will be relatively inactive. If they are with relatives, friends, and neighbors who initiate activity, their levels of activity will increase.

A Reticent Consumer

Whereas our passive consumer has a relatively amiable, if rather unenterprising, view of the world, about 10 percent of the persons we studied expend energy actually pushing away opportunities for growth. We speak of these persons as "reticent" because they have developed an orientation of reluctance to interact positively with their cultural environment. We can observe this dynamic in both professional and domestic settings.

Our reticent prototype attends only the staff development that is required and is often angry about having to be there, deprecates the content, whatever it is, and tries to avoid follow-up activities. Our reticent treats administrative initiatives and those from peers with equal suspicion and tends to believe that negative attitudes are justified because "the system" is inherently oppressive and unfeeling. Even peers who make initiatives are deprecated because they are "naive" if they believe that they will gain administrative support for their "idealistic" notions. Hence, our reticents tend to view our omnivores as negatively as they do the hated administration. The hardcore reticent even rejects opportunities for involvement in decision making, regarding them as co-opting moves by basically malign forces. In discussions about personal lives, the structure of attitudes was similar. Our reticents tend to emphasize what they see as defects in people, institutions, services, and opportunities in a range of fields. Film, theater, athletic activity, state and national parks, books and newspapers—all are suffering rapid decay. ("Only trash gets published these days." "Movies are full of sex and violence.") In the richness of an urban environment, they tend to emphasize crowding as an obstacle to participation in events ("If I could get tickets . . ." "If you didn't have to wait for a court . . ." "You can never get in to the good movies . . ."). In the rural environments, it is lack of facilities that gets the blame.

Even so, our reticent is not unaffected by the immediate social context. In affirmative school climates they do not "act out" their negative views as much. In the company of omnivores they can be carried along in school improvement efforts. Affirmative spouses who tolerate their jaundiced opinions good-naturedly involve them in a surprising number of activities. In the right circumstances they learn to take advantage of the opportunities in their lives.

CONCEPTUAL SYSTEMS, SELF-CONCEPT, AND STATES OF GROWTH

In an attempt to seek reasons for the differences in states of growth manifested by the teachers we were studying, we turned to a number of developmental theories. Two are of particular interest to us here because their descriptions of development appear to correlate with the states of growth we found (Joyce, McKibbin, & Bush, 1983). One is conceptual systems theory (Harvey, Hunt, & Schroder, 1961; Hunt, 1971), and the other is self-concept theory (Maslow, 1962).

Conceptual Systems

Conceptual systems theory describes people in terms of the structure of concepts they use to organize information about the world. In the lowest developmental stages, people use relatively few concepts for organizing their world, tend to have dichotomous views with few "shades of gray," and much emotion is attached to their views. They tend to reject information that does not fit into their concepts or to distort it to make it fit. Thus people and events are viewed as "right" or "wrong." Existing concepts are preserved.

At higher stages of development, people develop greater ability to integrate new information, are more decentered and can tolerate alternative views better, and their conceptual structure is modified as old concepts become obsolete and new ones are developed. New experiences are tolerated and bring new information and ideas, rather than being rejected or distorted to preserve the existing state.

For an example, let us consider individuals at the lower and higher developmental stages on a first visit to a foreign culture. People characterized by the lower conceptual levels are suspicious of the "different" and tend to find fault with it. ("You can't *believe* what they eat here.") They peer through the windows of the tour buses with increasing gratitude that they will soon be returning to the United States. They speak loudly to the "stupid" hotel personnel who don't speak English. They clutch their wallets to keep them away from the conniving, dishonest natives and their unclean hands.

Their companions at higher conceptual levels are fascinated by the new sights, sounds, and smells. Gingerly they order the local dishes, comparing them with the familiar, finding some new and pleasing tastes, and bargaining for a recipe. They prefer to walk, avoiding the bus unless time forbids. They ask shopkeepers to pronounce the names of things. They brush off the grime to get a better look at the interesting vase in the corner. They speak quietly and wait for the hotel personnel to indicate the local custom.

There is a substantial correlation between conceptual development and the states of growth of the teachers and administrators we studied. The omnivores are in a continual search for more productive ways of organizing information and have more complex conceptual structures as a result. Their openness to new experience requires an affirmative view of the world and the conceptual sophistication to deal with the new ideas they encounter. Our passive consumers have more limited structures and less ability to figure out how to reach for new experience and deal with it. Our reticents are busy protecting their present concepts and act offended by the presence of the unfamiliar. They can be as negative toward children they do not understand as they are toward the facilitators who try to bring new ideas and techniques into their orbit. Conceptual development is correlated with variety and flexibility in teaching styles (Hunt, 1971), ease in learning new approaches to teaching, and ability to understand students and modulate to them (Joyce, Peck, & Brown, 1981).

A change to a more productive orientation involves a structural change—a more complex structure capable of analyzing people and events from multiple points of view and the ability to assimilate new information and accommodate to it.

Self-Concept

More than 50 years ago, Abraham Maslow (1962) and Carl Rogers (1961) developed formulations of personal growth and functioning that have guided attempts since then to understand and deal with individual differences in response to the physical and social environment. Rather than concentrating on intellectual aptitude and development, their theories focused on individuals' views of self or self-concepts. They took the position that our competence to relate to the environment is greatly affected by the stances we take toward ourselves.

Strong self-concepts are accompanied by "self-actualizing" behavior, a reaching out toward the environment with confidence that the interaction will be productive. The self-actualizing person interacts richly with the milieu, finding opportunities for growth and enhancement and, inevitably, contributing to the development of others.

Somewhat less developed persons feel competent to deal with the environment but accept it for what it is and are less likely to develop growth-producing relationships from their own initiatives. They work within the environment and what it brings to them rather than generating opportunities from and with it.

The least developed persons have a more precarious relationship with their surroundings. They are less sure of their ability to cope. Much of their energy is spent in efforts to ensure that they survive in a less-than-generous world.

It is not surprising that we found a relationship between the states of growth of the people we studied and their concepts of self. Our omnivores are self-actualizing. They feel good about themselves and their surroundings. Our passive consumers feel competent but are dependent on the environment for growth-producing opportunities. Our reticents feel that they live in a precarious and threatening world. The faults that they find in their surroundings are products not of being well developed and able to discern problems the rest of us cannot see, but of an attempt to rationalize their need to protect themselves from a world of which they are afraid.

Understanding the Potential for Growth

The theories of conceptual growth and self-concept both help us understand ourselves as growth-oriented programs are planned and carried out. They help us understand why people respond as they do and provide us with a basis for creating environments that are likely to be productive, in terms of both the content of the programs and the people for whom they are intended.

David Hopkins (1990) reported on a study conducted in England in which he studied the implementation by a group of teachers of a new curriculum in the arts for which they had volunteered to be the forerunners. They were to master the curriculum in their classrooms and then become the disseminators to other teachers. Hopkins studied the states of growth and self-concepts of the teachers and the organizational climates of the schools in which they worked. All were influential, but the states of growth alone were predictors of the teachers' uses of the arts curricula. Essentially, the reticent and passive consumers were unable to achieve implementation in any organizational climate, while climate facilitated the work of the active consumers and gourmet omnivores. Not only were the teachers at the lower states of growth unable to profit from the training they received, but their students were deprived of the opportunities to learn presented by the new curriculum!

DEVELOPING RICHER STATES OF GROWTH

We want to grow as people and also to help our students develop richer orientations for growth. These are closely connected, for our primary influence on our students is what we model as people. If we model passivity, we encourage it. If we model activity and reaching out toward the world, we encourage active states. The good news is that we are far more likely to develop an upward progression than a downward one. Also, we develop by practicing reaching out—we simply do it! Thus, the message is that we need to reach out by developing a couple of lines of activity in which we push ourselves for richness and excellence. These areas need to be balanced. Reading or the cinema needs to be balanced by a social or athletic pursuit. We can have confidence that modeling omnivorous reading will not only breed active readers but also will pull students toward different pursuits. The models of teaching described in this book are also strong tools. A cooperative learning community—tooled up with the active models for gathering and interpreting information, examining social issues, and seeking ways of learning more—will have its effect on the students. A rich and active social climate will have its effect.

We are what we eat, not just biologically but socially and emotionally. Rich substance, well organized, in positive circumstances makes us richer, more outreaching, and more productive. And in our professional work, it gives us the tools to develop self-actualizing students.

Self-Actualization in the School Setting

Unquestionably, we want to help our students become self-actualizing—and to develop a high state of growth in their lives. But academic study is the prominent mission of the school and stepping out of it is not easy. Overcoming embarrassment is a major problem in offering counseling for school-age students. Teachers, school administrators, school counselors, and parents also have the built-in problem of being involved in issues that need to be solved. In other words, their attempts to help can be part of a circular problem. Help may come from cyberspace. Browse a little and you will find a wonderful array of websites where you can discuss self-concepts. Actually, you can get a good start in Wikipedia where a nice article opens up the frame of reference and the literature. See wikipedia.org/wiki/self-actualization.

PART SIX

The Behavioral Family of Models

To many people, behavior theory *is* psychology. In part, this conception exists because much early psychological research focused on how behavior is learned through conditioning, making the "behaviorists" the founders of modern psychology and the occupants of the first chapters in most introductory books. Controversy has created the other part of the conception because the science of behavior control, although both illuminating and useful, arouses fears that, should psychological theory become too powerful, malign uses will follow. From *Brave New World* to *Clockwork Orange*, behavior theory has been portrayed as the science of the Dark Side. Also, some find the idea that environmental variables shape behavior to conflict with the idea that we are free to determine ourselves. Educators polarize around programs developed from behavior theory and, at least in academic circles, devotees and critics engage in verbal standoffs.

Our position is that superficial judgment is not wise and that controversy, in this case, is not productive. Behavior theory offers much to teachers and learners, but its models, like the others in this book, are not the treatment of choice in every situation. Let's begin by sorting out some of the assumptions that have led to the research on which we base several models of learning.

BEHAVIOR IS LAWFUL AND SUBJECT TO VARIABLES IN THE ENVIRONMENT

People respond to variables in their environment with a conditioning effect. These external forces stimulate individuals to engage in or avoid certain behaviors. Once a behavior has been learned, the probability that it will occur again can be strengthened or decreased by responses from the environment. Thus, if a two-year-old sees a table in the room (stimulus), points to it, and verbalizes the word *table* (response behavior), he or she is responding to external forces. If, after the child says the word *table*, the child's mother picks him or her up, gives him or her a big hug, and repeats, *"Table, that's right"* (reinforcing stimuli), the child is likely to say the word again (response behavior). On the other hand, suppose the child sees a menacing-looking toy animal curled nearby (stimulus) and experiences a sudden surge of anxiety and fear (response behaviors). If the child runs away (another response behavior) and thereby avoids the toy, the act reduces his or her anxiety (reinforcing stimulus). The reinforcement increases the likelihood that the child will try to avoid that toy. Both examples illustrate the basic behavioral notion that behavior is acquired or enacted through external variables that serve either as the original stimulus or as the reinforcing stimulus. In one case we are learning to do something; in the other case, to avoid something.

Counterconditioning is related, but slightly different in that it always involves relearning. In counterconditioning, a new behavior incompatible with the old behavior is substituted, such as relaxation for anxiety. To cure a phobia toward public places (agoraphobia), the individual substitutes positive feelings for anxiety. One can even prepare oneself to cope with future situations. The Lamaze approach to birthing prepares the woman to trigger relaxation techniques during delivery.

From this stance the task of the psychologist is to discover what kinds of environmental variables affect behavior in which ways. The task of educators is to translate that knowledge—to design instructional materials and interactions that encourage productive learning and to avoid the environmental variables that can discourage it. If we can do that, so can the student learn to do it. Thus, what appears at first to be a technique for controlling others can be used to free people by increasing their capabilities for self-control.

To capitalize on the behaviorist stance, one doesn't need to accept the idea that *all* behavior is shaped by environmental variables. The position that it has partial truth will do. For example, we can use the behaviorist position to build simulations that work—students interacting with them learn something—and simultaneously accept the personalistic position that students can direct their own behavior.

History

Behavioral models of learning and instruction have their origins in the classical conditioning experiments of Pavlov (1927), the work of Thorndike (1911, 1913) on reward learning, and the studies of Watson and Rayner (1921), who applied Pavlovian principles to the psychological disorders of human beings. B. F. Skinner's *Science and Human Behavior* (1953) is in many ways the anchor of the literature in the field and its applications to education. In the late 1950s educators began to employ in school settings some of the behavioral principles, particularly forms of contingency management and programmed learning materials. For some types of learners these have had great success. For example, some youngsters who previously had made no progress in language development and social learning are now trainable and often able to mix with normal individuals. Milder forms of learning problems have responded to behavioral models as well (Becker, 1977; Becker & Carnine, 1980; Becker, Englemann, Carnine, & Rhine, 1981).

During the past 35 years, a great amount of research has demonstrated the effectiveness of behavioral designs for instruction and for help with a wide range of learning problems, including phobias toward subjects such as mathematics, social-skill deficits, behavioral problems, and test anxiety. The research also indicates that these procedures can be used effectively in group settings and by laypeople. We believe that behavior theory presently offers an array of models that are extremely useful to teachers, curriculum planners, and creators of instructional materials.

Terms such as *learning theory, social learning theory, behavior modification,* and *behavior therapy* have been used by various leaders in this field to refer to the models we discuss here (Bandura, 1969; Wolpe, 1969; see also Estes, 1976). Because each term is generally associated with one particular form of the basic theory, we prefer to use the more neutral term *behavior theory* to cover procedures emanating from both operant and counterconditioning principles.

Principles

Behavior as an Observable, Identifiable Phenomenon

Behavior theory concentrates on observable behavior and takes an optimistic view. Given the right conditions and enough time, we can succeed in learning (and unlearning). Essentially, a stimulus evokes a behavior (response), which generates consequences, which, if reinforcing, strengthen the likelihood that a similar stimulus will elicit the behavior that was reinforced. Reciprocally, negative consequences will make it less likely that the behavior will be elicited.

Behavior theorists believe that internal responses (such as fear of failure), which mediate our observable responses (such as avoiding areas that arouse fear of failure), can be changed (Rimm & Masters, 1974). The approach involves continuous inquiry, careful study of the student, the design of the environment, a study of responses, and a continuation or modification of the course of action.

Maladaptive Behaviors Are Acquired, not Programmed

In our society many people have assumed that many children have "blocks to learning" particular kinds of things (such as math) in the form of internal states that cannot be changed. It turns out that many of these blocks are simply learned aversions that the kids can learn to control. If the pattern of avoiding the feared area is left untouched, the aversion becomes more pronounced. The student has greater and greater difficulty as the mathematical content gets more complex. The learning deficit increases. Learning to handle affect in approaching the subject is the key. Some simple techniques can go a long way in mild cases.

Behavioral Goals Should Be Specific and Individualized

Even though behaviorist principles have been used to design instructional materials like simulations that have been used by large numbers of students, the behaviorist frame of reference tends toward the discrete, concrete, and individualized. Two externally similar responses do not necessarily proceed from the same original stimulus (one person may be outwardly friendly because friendliness attracts people, whereas another may behave similarly but to avoid being shunned or ignored). Conversely, no two people will respond to the same stimulus in precisely the same way. Consequently, the procedures for encouraging new behaviors involve setting specific, individualized behavioral goals. This does not mean that group training is not possible. It does mean that the goals for each student may differ and that the training process will need to be individualized in terms of pacing or content. The instructional materials prepared from the behaviorist stance are almost always self-paced (Becker, 1977; Becker & Carnine, 1980; Becker, Englemann, Carnine, & Rhine, 1981). Today, distance and online courses from that stance are usually designed to encourage students to proceed at their own rate of mastery of material.

Behavioral Theory Focuses on the Here and Now

In behavior theory, the role of the past in shaping a person's behavior is deemphasized. Poor instruction may have caused a failure to learn to read, but the focus is on learning to read *now*. The behaviorist concentrates on creating

conditions or helping students create conditions that will enable them to progress and gain satisfaction quickly. The stance regards human behavior with
optimism and does not dwell on the past. The assumption is that past failure
did not result in conditions that cannot be corrected. The more difficult problems just take a little longer to fix.

Behavioral practitioners have often reported that they have been able to
alter maladaptive behaviors in a short time, even in the case of severe phobias
or long-term withdrawal patterns. Many shy people have felt relaxed and
socially effective in a short time, and students who had remained virtually illit-
erate have progressed quickly (Resnick, 1987).

Operant conditioning and counterconditioning

Behaviorists like to arrange instruction so that success is highly probable. Self-
instructional programmed material is sequenced in such small steps as to virtually ensure correct responses, and simulations are designed to generate
successful activity as concepts and skills are being learned. The reinforcement
the learner derives from knowledge of his or her correctness both makes the
achievement enduring and propels the learner toward new tasks. This is one
reason why highly sequenced "programmed" materials often work well with
students who have previously experienced little success. Finally, students are
also reinforced by controlling their environments. Part of the attraction of self-
instructional computer programs is the reinforcement quality of mechanical
manipulation and the ability to control the pace of one's progress.

One should not underestimate the function of social climate to generate
reinforcement. The range of naturally occurring positive reinforcers available
to teachers is broad—for example, a smile, enthusiasm, show of interest, attention, enjoyment, and casual conversation. Perhaps most powerful is a perva-
sively positive atmosphere, where just being in that classroom brings pleasure
and confidence—an environment filled with little positive events just waiting
to attach themselves to appropriate behaviors.

The management mode in some classrooms is based on aversive control;
students are threatened with reprisals if they do not learn or follow rules. Many
years ago the birch rod was used; today the aversive stimuli are less physical
(poor grades, disapproval). According to behavior theorists, punishment has
several drawbacks. First, its effects are temporary; punished behavior is likely
to recur. Second, the aversive stimuli used in punishment may generate
unwanted emotions, such as predispositions to escape or retaliate or disabling
anxieties (Skinner, 1953, p. 183). A negative event can actually reinforce the
very behavior that it is intended to eliminate or reduce. The use of negative
reinforcers can push the student away from the very subject he or she is trying

to learn. Wherever possible, positive rather than negative reinforcement should be used.

Some events are devastating because they violate behavioral principles. Retention in grade ("holding back from promotion") is devastating emotionally and frequently has the effect of destroying interest in school. The embarrassment continues for a long time and generates aversion to the schooling process and even the social interchange in school. It seriously reduces the probability of later successful schoolwork.

Labeling a child as having learning problems can generate aversion as well. No doubt one of the reasons for the general ineffectiveness of special education is that the child, labeled as having a learning disability, feels devastated and approaches learning tasks with poor feelings that become attached to learning itself. In the worst cases, the children so labeled give themselves permission to avoid relevant learning tasks whenever possible.

The effectiveness of reinforcement programs is determined not only by establishing a close temporal relation between reinforcement and behavior and by the type of reinforcement selected, but also by the scheduling or frequency of reinforcement (*reinforcement schedule*). One of the most difficult skills for teachers, or anyone, to master is to be consistent, immediate, and frequent in rewarding the desired responses when they occur. If a response goes unreinforced, it will become less and less frequent until it is extinguished. For example, to teach students to approach writing with confidence and positive feelings, one needs to elicit writing frequently and reinforce production. Eliciting writing too infrequently will diminish positive feelings toward writing tasks and voluntary writing.

Desensitization procedures make use of stimulus control by gradually enlarging the range of stimuli to which individuals can respond without anxiety. Stress reduction models depend on recognizing a range of cues indicating body tension or mental stress and taking action to substitute positive for negative feelings in an increasing variety of situations.

Training models using modeling and practice illustrate the basic behavioral concepts. For example, in an excellent tennis lesson, modeling is followed by practice, verbal reinforcement, and self-reinforcement through observation of results. Only a small number of skills are taught in any one lesson, so that the learner has a high probability of mastering them.

OVERCOMING MATH ANXIETY

Sheila Tobias's (1993) nice book on this subject uses several of the behaviorist principles to help people conquer their negative feelings about themselves as learners of math. Much of her book is about basic arithmetic and mathematical concepts, because one isn't going to get over the anxiety without studying the subject itself. Learning to approach is an essential part of most programs for the treatment of anxiety. Second is the placement of the responsibility squarely on the individual. Third is the use of support groups and the development of positive social climates in mathematics learning centers. Tobias does a particularly nice job of helping people understand the role the anxiety itself plays in inhibiting effective learning.

A CALL FOR INQUIRY

Much has been accomplished; much remains to be done. Considering the field as a whole, carefully designed small-group studies have generated positive effects in a wide variety of areas. Implementation in school districts is more difficult. Probably the most consistent findings are in programs such as Distar, but each teacher, school, and district needs to conduct action research on implementation and effects when a decision is made to implement a curriculum or process based on behavioral theory. On the other hand, that is not so different from the situation with any other model of teaching or family of models of teaching.

TIPS FOR TEACHING FROM THE BEHAVIORAL STANCE

The optimism and positivity of the behavioral stance can perhaps best be summarized in the following tips for teaching that we invite the reader to explore.

Classroom Rules

Which is best, a list of behaviors to avoid combined with negative reinforcers (a one-time violation results in their name on the board, a two-time violation results in . . .), or a list of desirable behaviors and rewards (a certificate proclaiming "You Are the Greatest")?

Tip: The high-probability bet is the positive rules and reinforcers or nurturers.

Off-Task Behavior

If 28 students are on task and two are off task, which teacher behavior has the highest probability of succeeding in bringing the two back on task: reprimanding the off-task students or praising the on-task students?

Tip: Praise the on-task students (positive rather than negative reinforcement). However, placating off-task students is not recommended. The adult is the adult, something not to be forgotten or used as a club. Some students resist challenging tasks and need to learn to take charge of learning on an upward slope.

Instruction or Self-Instruction?

When introducing a new word-processing program to students who can already use another program, one teacher takes the students step by step through the manual. The other gives the students the program and, after a brief orientation, asks them to teach themselves to use it. Which works best?

Tip: Controlling your own learning schedule arouses positive affect. Pacing is under the control of the individual, who can move rapidly or slowly according to individual needs. The ability to learn how to use smartphones, tablets, and computers is a skill these days. A lot of productive self-teaching is going on.

Itchy Students

Certain kids just don't seem to sit still or pay attention for more than a few minutes. Do you give them extra homework when they wander off task, or teach them a relaxation exercise and how to use it when the hyper feeling arises?

Tip: The first solution is a negative reinforcer that also uses academic work as a punishment, which can produce an aversive response. The second provides effective control, makes the students partners in regulating their behavior, and provides the opportunity for positive self-reinforcement as well as external reinforcement.

Motivation

Following a test at the end of a unit in mathematics, one teacher has the students correct their own papers and figure out their gain scores. The other teacher scores the test and provides the students with an analysis of items missed. Which is the best bet for motivating the students?

Tip: Self-scoring, emphasis on progress, and setting of new goals will win almost every time.

Try these, and see whether you agree with the tips.

CHAPTER SIXTEEN

Explicit Instruction

Comprehension When Reading and Composing When Writing

Reading is thinking. Teachers of reading are teachers of thinking. You don't teach children to read or think by leading them by the nose. What you can do is help them develop strategies they can use to learn letters, words and structures and, most important, to tease the meaning from what they read.

—Russell Stauffer, 60 years ago, keynoting the opening of a set of workshops on the inductive, experience-based method of teaching reading

SCENARIO

GRETCHEN MODELS COMPREHENSION STRATEGIES

Every morning Gretchen begins the day in her fifth-grade classroom by reading to the students. Usually she reads from non fiction that will bring new knowledge to them, often about a content unit they are studying. She has several objectives:

Bringing information to her students is one—information from sources above their recreational reading levels.

Modeling fluent and inflected reading is another. Some of her students, when reading aloud, speak in a monotone that does not do justice to the text. And, the students enjoy hearing her read.

A serious objective is to model strategies for comprehending text. She has discovered that many of the students need to build their comprehension skills. Some of them decipher the sounds of words proficiently, but extracting the full meaning is far more difficult for them. So, as she reads, she pauses and discusses her strategies as she uses them. Sometimes she focuses on word meanings, as when she reads directions on making an *electromagnet,* she pauses and pulls the word apart and points out that it refers to a magnet that is activated by *electricity.*

When the text discusses wrapping a large nail with a wire, she points out that the text states that the wire is *insulated* and what that might mean.

Gretchen emphasizes comprehension skills that research has found are used by expert readers but much less often by poorer readers.

Frequently, after she reads and has emphasized a particular skill, Gretchen provides the students with a paragraph where that skill can be applied to understand the content.

Gretchen has been using what is called *Explicit Teaching of Comprehension* where comprehension strategies are modeled, explained, and applied through practice. Much of the research on which it is based compares the skills used by really good readers and struggling readers of all ages. Top readers in grade two use some techniques used by expert adult readers. A strong motive for the research has been the search for ways of helping poor readers. The good news is these skills can be taught, and that is what this chapter is about.

Curricula for struggling readers focus on a critical national need in reading, writing, and literacy at the primary, middle, and secondary school levels (see our description of the Second Chance curriculum in Joyce & Calhoun, 2012, pp. 106–108). Despite efforts to provide for individual needs within the regular curriculum, about 30 percent of students struggle in the essential literacy areas, necessitating the implementation of more intensive instruction—called Tier 2 interventions in the Response to Intervention (RTI) phases for helping students. Teaching reading begins with the curriculum in Kg–1. As students struggle, the classroom teacher provides individual assistance (Tier 1). Then, for students needing more help, Tier 2 is developed—more intensive and tailored to the problems the student has. If success is not forthcoming, Tier 3—specialized learning disability treatments—are invoked. (Readers who are not familiar with this terminology might want to take a few minutes here and consult the web. The Wikipedia article on the subject is a fairly good place to begin.)

It is vital that Tier 2 interventions be successful, and not just for a minor percentage of those students. At the primary level, the pattern of failure needs to be interrupted. The students need to improve not only their level of learning but their capacity to learn at a high level through school and beyond. For struggling readers and writers, the Tier 2 program is a second chance to learn to become competent in literacy—a chance that virtually *has* to be rewarding if they are to succeed in secondary education and beyond.

Built around research on inductive curricula, the explicit teaching of reading comprehension, and the effects of regular and wide reading and writing, the Second Chance Program also includes an extensively researched professional development design. That design enables nearly all teachers to implement complex curricula and models of teaching skillfully in the first year. Thus, the program can be successfully implemented on a scale large enough to reach all the struggling readers in a district and considerably improve their performance in the language arts. The result essentially changes not only their future prospects, but the climate of the classroom and school as a greater proportion of students become capable learners.

THE DEVELOPMENT OF EXPLICIT INSTRUCTION IN THE READING COMPREHENSION AREA

About 25 years after Russell Stauffer's comments, researchers began a serious effort to conduct research on the processes readers use to comprehend extended text—a particularly fertile time was between the mid-1970s and the 1980s, although research continues to the present. Although understanding how students derive meaning was the focus, these researchers also had action in mind. They designed and tested explicit instructional models aimed at teaching better comprehension strategies and teaching them more effectively. These models were developed and modified as research provided more information about how students went about constructing meaning from extended text and the differences between more and less effective readers.

The backstory and rationale for the effort in reading comprehension has several facets. First, studies of student learning indicated that many students had difficulty finding and putting together the meanings in stories and expository text. A certain number of those students possessed relevant sight vocabularies and could sound out words new to them as long as the new words were not too numerous, but much of the content was not processed. In other words, they were not actually reading; they were emitting sounds that they could not really understand. That jarring picture continues to the present day—about one-third of students have a comprehension problem and some have other problems as well (see National Center for Educational Statistics, 2010).

Second, there were a good many studies of classrooms during the 1970s and 1980s that focused on how teachers taught reading, including providing the students with instruction on how to build understanding as they approached texts. These studies concluded that the majority of teachers did not offer much instruction. Many *did* ask students questions about the content—characters, plots, and settings in the case of fiction and topics and main ideas in the case of nonfiction—thus assessing some aspects of comprehension, but they did not have a repertoire of ways to help the uncomprehending. In other words, the picture of student achievement in the comprehension area matched the picture of instruction. By the way, the problem was true of some quite different curricula—some heavily phonics-oriented and general basal-materials programs had the same problem. We hasten to say that there are some models of teaching and curriculum that do a good job in all aspects of learning to read—but they are less used than they should be (see, for example, Duffy, Roehler, & Herrmann, 1988; Garner, 1987; Pressley, 2006).

Another facet is that studies of good readers indicated that many of them used similar basic strategies to dig the meaning out of text. For example, they monitored their comprehension while reading and persisted in trying to achieve a full understanding of the text, displaying a variety of skills as they did so. Poorer readers often plowed ahead without focusing on the extent to which they were acquiring information. Thus, many of the community of researchers decided that it might be worthwhile to teach all the students the strategies used by expert readers (see, for example, Scardamalia & Bereiter, 1984; Pearson & Dole, 1987).

Parallel lines of research suggested that the learning of skills was greatly enhanced by a high degree of consciousness as students used those strategies while reading. Termed *metacognition*, the essence is that when we are learning new practices, understanding the rationale and studying our application as we learn it facilitates the attainment of mastery (see Pressley & Brainerd, 1985).

(A note here on language: Some of the scholars in this field prefer the term *skills* to refer to both simple and complex actions and thoughts, whereas others use the term *skills* to refer to actions that have become relatively automatic and *strategies* to refer to ones that require the reader to pause and consciously decide what to do. We will use the terms interchangeably but will describe the degree of complexity of any skill or strategy we identify.)

Other lines of research emphasized the importance of modeling in the instructional process. In other words, teaching that includes demonstration is more effective than teaching that merely tells the student what to do. This is as true of cognitive skills as it is of motor skills. The tennis pro who demonstrates the half-volley several times will be more effective than the one who shows it once and than asks the student to practice. The algebra teacher who demonstrates setting up equations several times, discussing the rationale in the process, will be more effective than one who demonstrates a particular process once or twice and then asks the students to practice.

Putting these facets together, the community of researchers proceeded to approach the problem of improving the teaching of comprehension by:

- Identifying the strategies used by high-comprehension readers
- Organizing instruction to model those strategies for students
- Asking the students to practice them consciously as they read

- Studying their use of the strategies, identifying areas that need further modeling and practice and, as in the case of most effective models of teaching, lending help (scaffolding)
- Helping the students assess their comprehension of passages and the extent to which they are progressing in the ability to obtain meaning—in other words, learning to judge their own growing capacity

Essentially, the teacher brings the students into an action research partnership, leading strongly but then gradually giving the control to the students. Brown and Palincsar (1984), in the approach they called reciprocal teaching, gave special emphasis to the process that begins with modeling, proceeds to guided practice, and then to students' independent exercise of the skills.

Let's look at some of the strategies used by expert readers to comprehend passages. The material can be only written prose but all manner of illustrations and animations can be included and need to be understood as well.

RECENT REVIEWS OF EVIDENCE

Gersten, Fuchs, Williams, and Baker, 2001; and Duke, Pearson, Strachan, and Billman, 2011, bring together the literature, including studies that easily meet the criteria enunciated in the regulations accompanying the Elementary and Secondary Education Act (www.ed.gov/esea) legislation and many others that have contributed to the development of a supportable set of strategies to help Tier 2 students.

The Nature of Comprehension Strategies

The approach to teaching that resulted from the series of investigations is most often called *explicit instruction of comprehension strategies*, frequently shortened to just *explicit instruction*. The term is often confused with direct instruction, but there is a very important difference: Most practitioners of direct instruction, when they attempt to teach a skill or body of knowledge, will break the skill into subskills or the knowledge into segments and teach them sequentially. Thus, the eventual larger skill will be acquired step by step.

Comprehension skills, however, resist segmentation—just as they are employed to develop understanding of a passage of text as a whole, they operate as a whole. Thus, the explicit instruction modality demonstrates skills as wholes, and the learner acquires them by degrees rather than assembling them from subskills. Several of them work together as an integrated approach to the development of meaning. Thus, the student comes to see them as a coordinated overall approach to understanding (see Pearson & Gallagher, 1983; Pressley, 2006).

An advantageous benefit of the holistic nature of comprehension skills is that a relatively small number may have considerable benefit, thus focusing instruction, rather than generating a long list that diffuses teaching and learning, as the segmentation in direct instruction often does. In one sad example, the investigators attempted to teach a strategy each week for 20 weeks, virtually assuring that none of those skills would be mastered.

Let's take a look at some of the skills that have been given emphasis as intervention studies have been developed.

Continuously Monitoring Comprehension

As this is written, there is virtually complete agreement that this practice is used by expert readers and less by average readers and almost not at all by poor readers. Importantly, it appears that the practice can be taught to beginning readers so that kindergarten and first-grade students can be started off with high payoff skills. Thus, it can be a significant dimension of the curriculum for all, and an important early scaffolding assist in Tier 1 for students who have difficulty mastering it. It is essential for Tier 2. Essentially, the best readers have a metacognitive mind that operates as they read and, like a heart rate monitor, generates a comprehension-emergent awareness chart ready to be consulted.

Summarizing is an important complex skill and one component of continuous monitoring, although the essential component of monitoring is the *awareness* of whether they are understanding the story or message and taking action when they do not. Nearly all top-level readers summarize at intervals and judge what they are learning. Students who learn to summarize effectively usually both learn and retain more of the content they are reading, both fiction and nonfiction.

Strategic Backtracking

Picking up from the studies of Bird (1980), Scardamalia and Bereiter (1984) emphasized that good readers, as they monitored their comprehension, would look back in the text to reinforce or clarify content and try to answer questions that had occurred as they read ("Just how little is the little girl?") and fill in understandings large and small.

Setting Up "Watchers"

Another strategy from Bird's studies is, while reading, thinking of items where more information might be useful to understanding or might be clarified. For example, an author introduces a town, but does not initially provide information about size or history, which *might* be interesting or useful to understanding. The readers' antennae are activated, looking for contextual information that might be useful. Setting up watchers is a sophisticated skill, but quite powerful as the reader not only follows the narrative but is looking for related information.

Prediction

Prediction originated in the old basal readers, when teachers were urged to regularly ask the students "What do you think will happen next?" As a component of comprehending, prediction is much more multidimensional than that. A student who is aware that an author is using a *comparison/contrast* strategy to present information may predict what element of comparison will proceed next or, as clarified, what changes or amplifications will occur, or whether an analogy will be repeated.

We can consider several other skills (strategies), but these are enough for us to step back and see how these few might operate to assist comprehension. Imagine a reader who does not monitor comprehension, doesn't summarize even when tackling long passages, doesn't backtrack to clarify, doesn't think ahead and identify things to watch for and amplify, and doesn't predict, compared to a reader who does all those things. Among other differences, the poorer reader not only lacks the metacognitive train of thought but is probably a passive recipient of parts of the text that are readily understood and lets the others remain as gaps. This kind of analysis on our part helps us understand why a capable person who has poor comprehension skills is likely to find reading unsatisfying and possibly finds the act of trying to read an aversive experience.

IN SUM

As inquiry has continued, there have been additions to the repertoire for teaching comprehension (see Figure 16.1). An important innovation is "thinking aloud," where the instructors read and simultaneously discuss their processes of comprehension, modeling by letting students inside their working minds. Discussions ensue and, eventually, the students learn to discuss *their* thinking while reading. Thus a partnership evolves as teacher and student think together about comprehension and how to strengthen their own modes of thinking about text (see Kucan & Beck, 1997).

Syntax

The instruction occurs when the teacher is reading to the student and pauses periodically to describe a strategy he/she uses to comprehend a passage or even an unfamiliar word, thus *modeling and explaining* the technique. After reading, a passage is provided to the students that enables them to *practice* the illustrated skill. Then they are asked to identify passages in their assigned or independent reading where the technique was or might have been useful.

Social System

The teaching/learning episodes are teacher-directed, but practice involves students in using and finding opportunities to use the content being emphasized.

Principles of Reaction

Particularly during sessions where the students practice a strategy, the teacher observes how well they are able to use the strategy and decides whether to model it soon again. Several sessions of modeling any of the comprehension skills are almost always necessary.

FIGURE 16.1 Instructional and nurturant effects of explicit teaching of comprehension

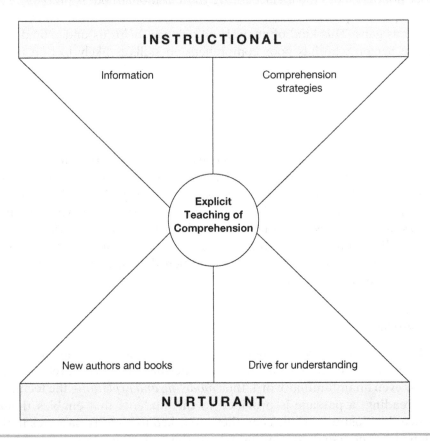

Support System

Books, books, and more books. And, when the class is being led through a search on the web, there are many opportunities to practice all the skills. The interactive whiteboard is a very useful tool.

INSTRUCTIONAL AND NURTURANT EFFECTS

The focus is on the comprehension strategies, but building a community of readers who learn to share their efforts to build understanding is nurtured continually.

Explicit Teaching of Comprehension   SUMMARY CHART

Syntax

While reading the instructor models and explains comprehension strategies. Practice opportunities follow.

Social System

Teacher directed, but warm.

Principles of Reaction

Student acquisition of the strategies is followed by decisions about providing further instruction and practice on the comprehension skills.

Support System

A good supply of books in the classroom is very important. Ways of demonstrating while doing web searches are important—hence projection devices and the interactive whiteboards are very useful.

CHAPTER SEVENTEEN

Mastery Learning

Bit by Bit, Block by Block, We Climb Our Way to Mastery

*If we can allow them time to learn one thing at a time, and then
another, and another, until they can get their feet under them,
we can break the cycle of failure.*

—Berj Harootunian to Bruce Joyce

Mastery learning is a framework for planning instructional sequences formulated by John B. Carroll (1963, 1977) and Benjamin Bloom (1971). Mastery learning provides a compact and interesting way of increasing the likelihood that more students will attain a satisfactory level of performance in school subjects. Recent work has sharpened the idea, and contemporary instructional technology has made it even more feasible.

A CONCEPT OF APTITUDE

The core theoretical idea in mastery learning is based on John Carroll's interesting perspective on the meaning of aptitude. Traditionally, aptitude has been thought of as a characteristic that correlates with a student's achievement—the more aptitude one has, the more he or she is likely to learn. Carroll, however, views aptitude as the *amount of time* it takes someone to learn any given material, rather than his or her capacity to master it. In Carroll's view, students with very low aptitude with respect to a particular kind of learning simply take a much longer time to reach mastery than students with a higher aptitude.

This view is optimistic in the sense that it suggests that it is possible for nearly all students to master any given set of objectives, if sufficient time (the opportunity to learn) is provided along with appropriate materials and instruction. Thus viewed, aptitude becomes primarily a guide to how much time a learner will need. Aptitude also suggests *how* to instruct, because learners of different aptitudes will learn more efficiently if the style of instruction is suited to their configurations. (In *our* terms, some aptitudes are model-relevant—they help us choose and adapt models.) For any given objective, according to Carroll, the degree of learning achieved by any given student will be a function of time allowed, the perseverance of the student, the quality of instruction, the student's ability to understand instruction, and his or her aptitude. The problem in managing instruction is deciding how to organize the curriculum and the classroom so that students will have optimal time, benefit from good instruction, be induced to persevere, and receive assistance in understanding the learning tasks.

Bloom transformed Carroll's stance into a system with the following characteristics:

1. Mastery of any subject is defined in terms of sets of major objectives that represent the purposes of the course or unit.
2. The body of material in the unit is then divided into sets of relatively small learning units, each one accompanied by its own objectives, which are parts of the larger objectives or thought essential to their mastery.
3. Learning materials are then identified and the instructional strategy (model of teaching) selected.
4. Each unit is accompanied by brief diagnostic tests that measure the student's developing progress (the formative evaluation) and identify the particular problems each student is having. Knowledge of progress is fed back to the students to act as a reinforcement. (Praise and encouragement can, if contiguous with correct performance, serve as reinforcement also.)
5. The data obtained from administering the tests are used to provide supplementary instruction to the student to help overcome problems. (Bloom, 1971, pp. 47–63)

If instruction is managed in this way, Bloom believes, time to learn can be adjusted to fit aptitude. Students of lesser aptitude can be given more time and more feedback while the progress of all is monitored with the assistance of the tests.

Bloom, Block, and the other advocates of mastery learning believe that it can be implemented by teachers through modifying traditional group instructional procedures to ensure that some students have more time and that they receive appropriate individual instruction according to the results of the formative evaluation (Carroll, 1963, 1971, pp. 37–41).

However, modern instructional technology, especially the development of self-administering multimedia units and the application of programmed learning procedures, has encouraged curriculum developers to invent comprehensive curricular systems and to reorganize schools to provide for a much greater degree of individualized instruction than is generally possible under conventional school organizations.

An early and important example of an application of systems planning to elementary and secondary school instruction is the Individually Prescribed Instruction (IPI) program, developed by the Learning Research and Development Center of the University of Pittsburgh in collaboration with the Baldwin-Whitehall School District. In IPI, students usually work independently on the materials prescribed for them daily (or every few days), depending on their demonstrated level of competence, learning style, and particular learning needs.

IPI illustrates a modular curriculum developed by applying systems analysis procedures to curriculum materials development. It is a particularly useful case study because it readily demonstrates the steps the IPI planners took in creating the system. As we examine these steps, we stop briefly to show how each reflects the inner workings of the performance model.

The system is designed to:

1. Enable each pupil to work at his or her own rate through units of study in a learning sequence
2. Develop in each pupil a demonstrable degree of mastery
3. Develop self-initiation and self-direction of learning
4. Foster the development of problem solving through processes
5. Encourage self-evaluation and motivation for learning (Lindvall & Bolvin, 1966)

The assumptions regarding the learning process and the related learning environment are as follows. First, students take different amounts of time to practice and become skillful with instructions and objectives. Second, students must be provided with methods to work at their own pace to ensure they get necessary practice. Third, when working in a self-learning, tutorial-heavy environment, elementary age students can learn with minimum teacher instruction. In order for this to be effective, schools must have necessary and proper study supplies and materials. Fourth, in order to begin a new unit of study, a student must meet the prerequisites of the previous unit of study. Fifth, students should be evaluated frequently to map learning progression. These evaluations aid teachers in developing methods to assist students in individual learning. Sixth, teachers are more effective when working with one student or when working with small groups as compared to completing class management tasks like grading and organizing records. Because of this, teacher aids can be a great asset to schools and programs. Seventh, students take a more hands-on responsibility to their learning than is possible in other learning environments. Lastly, students can enhance learning when tutoring or being tutored by a fellow student (Lindvall & Bolvin, 1966, pp. 3–4). Development is crucial. For any curriculum unit, the overall performance model—the objective—is generated.

Then, the performance model is divided into a set of sequentially organized behavioral objectives. IPI planners believe that such a listing is fundamental to other aspects of the program and must have the following characteristics:

a. Each objective should tell exactly what a pupil should be able to do to exhibit his mastery of the given content and skill. This should typically be something the average student can master in such a relatively short period as one class period. Objectives should involve such action verbs as *solve, state, explain, list, describe*, etc., rather than general terms such as *understand, appreciate, know,* and *comprehend.*

b. Objectives should be grouped in meaningful streams of content. For example, in arithmetic the objectives will be grouped (typically) into such areas as numeration, place value, addition, subtraction, etc. Such grouping aids in the meaningful development of instructional materials and in the diagnosis of pupil achievement. At the same time, this grouping does not preclude the possibility of having objectives that cut across areas.

c. Within each stream or area, the objectives should, to the extent possible, be sequenced in such an order that each will build on those that precede it, and, in turn, be a prerequisite to those that follow. The goal here is to let the objectives constitute a "scale" of abilities.

d. Within the sequence of objectives in each area, the objectives should be grouped into meaningful subsequences or units. Such units can be designated as representing different levels of progress and can provide break points so that when a student finishes a unit in that area, he or she may either go on to the next unit in that area or may switch to a unit in another area. (For example, on completing Level B addition, the pupil may either go on to Level C addition or move on to Level B subtraction.) (Lindvall & Bolvin, 1966, p. 3)

SCENARIO

THE YOUNG LADY FROM IRAN

In a *New York Times* article published in 2010, Eric A. Taub, the author, begins with an anecdote about meeting an Iranian woman who recently immigrated to the United States and spoke English. When asked how she perfected her English, she stated she used Rosetta Stone (Taub, 2010).

LANGUAGE LABORATORY

Another prominent example of an instructional system, one in which the machine components paved the way for an entirely different learning environment, is the *language laboratory.* Its development represents vivid application of the combined properties of systems analysis, task analysis, and cybernetic principles in the educational setting. Before the language laboratory became commonplace, the classroom teacher served as the model for foreign speech in a classroom of 25 to 35 students who were trying to reproduce speech sounds. The individual in such a situation might have a maximum of one minute of speech practice per classroom session, hardly enough to produce fluency or accuracy.

Today, in the typical classroom laboratory, learners use electrical equipment to hear, record, and play back spoken materials. The general physical equipment includes student stations and an instructor's central panel. Through this panel, the teacher can broadcast a variety of content materials, new and remedial programs, and instruction to individuals, selected groups, or the entire class. He or she can also monitor the students' performance. The students' stations are often a series of individual, acoustically treated carrels, usually equipped with headphones, a microphone, and a tape recorder. Each student listens through the headphones to live or recorded directions from the instructor to repeat, answer questions, or make other appropriate responses to the lesson. The instructor may also choose to use the chalkboard, textbook, or other visual stimuli to supplement audio inputs. Modern technology has made it possible for almost instantaneous situations in which students might:

1. Hear their own voices more clearly through headphones than they could otherwise
2. Directly compare their speech with that of a model
3. Provide themselves with immediate feedback
4. Isolate items for study
5. Permit pacing for specific drill
6. Permit more finely sequenced instructional content

Learning a foreign language requires that the student hear vocabulary and speech patterns repeatedly. The exercises are carefully sequenced and followed by new combinations of varying complexity. The ultimate goal is to have the student readily comprehend what he or she hears and make immediate and appropriate responses. From the student's viewpoint, the language laboratory serves as a base for extensive practicing of finely sequenced behavior, matching aural models, and developing speech fluency. From the instructor's viewpoint, it provides the facilities (hardware and software) for a more effective language-learning situation.

In systems analysis terminology, the language laboratory represents the development of a human-machine system based on the performance objectives and requirements of foreign language proficiency. Prior to the development of the language laboratory, it was possible to provide reasonably sequenced visual materials. But the critical elements of language training—individualized audial practice and dynamic feedback—far outran the human management capacities and support facilities of the self-contained classroom teacher with 25 students. With electronic hardware and software support subsystems, instructors can now divide their time more effectively between monitoring (management), diagnosis, and instruction. Students are given immediate, direct sensory feedback so that they can compare their performance with the desired performance and make the necessary self-corrective adjustments.

Many programs now available for personal computers create miniature language laboratories that function in self-instructional mode. For computers without sound cards, phonetic spelling is used to assist with pronunciation. For computers with sound cards, the computer "speaks" words and phrases. Combined with the use of the picture-word inductive model (Chapter 5), "talking" dictionaries helped kindergarten students in French immersion to reach levels equal to those of most second- and third-grade English-speaking students in French immersion classes.

Very few United States schools currently have language labs, but if you consult the web, you will find virtual labs, such as Rosetta Stone, that are about as effective as many campus labs and courses. See also the MIMI demonstration on BooksendLab's YouTube channel (www.youtube.com/user/BooksendLab), where PWIM is the basis for French immersion in primary grades.

Mastery learning has been investigated extensively. Slavin's (1990) reanalysis of the literature generally agrees with Kulik, Kulik, and Bangert-Drowns's (1990) analysis that it usually increases learning modestly but consistently on curriculum-relevant tests. (The average student places at about the 65th percentile when compared with students in control groups studying the same material without the careful sequencing of objectives and modules of instruction.)

A NOTE ON PROGRAMMED INSTRUCTION

Many mastery learning programs use programmed instruction, a system for designing self-instructional materials. It is one of the most direct applications of Skinner's writings. It provides for highly systematic stimulus control and immediate reinforcement. Although Skinner's initial programmed instruction format has undergone many transformations, most adaptations retain three essential features: (1) an ordered sequence of items, either questions or statements to which the student is asked to respond; (2) the student's response, which may be in the form of filling in a blank, recalling the answer to a question, selecting from among a series of answers, or solving a problem; and (3) provision for immediate response confirmation, sometimes within the program frame itself but usually in a different location, as on the next page in a programmed textbook or in a separate window in the teaching machine.

Programmed instruction has been successfully employed for a variety of subject matter, including English, math, statistics, geography, and science. It has been used at every school level from preschool through college. Programmed instructional techniques have been applied to a great variety of behaviors, such as concept formation, rote learning, creativity, and problem solving. Some programs have even led students to discover concepts, using a format reminiscent of inductive thinking.

How is programmed instruction different from traditional workbooks that classroom teachers have used for years with no startling effects? With workbooks the emphasis is on practice (response maintenance) rather than on behavioral acquisition through carefully sequenced material. Workbooks provide endless "frames" of review material. Obviously, review is of little value unless the behavior has first been successfully established; the traditional workbook is not designed to do this. Also, the reinforcing effect of continuous review is bound to suffer diminishing returns as the learner only goes over material already mastered. Finally, most workbooks make no provision for immediate feedback, supplying the answer only in the teacher's copy!

In sum

Mastery learning is straightforward, optimistic, and clear. To create a mastery learning system takes careful development, but in a positive social climate, this system directly approaches many of the learning problems that have vexed teacher-driven instruction. It also places the teacher in an encouraging, assisting role that has a positive effect on the self-esteem of the students.

Although individual teachers can teach from a mastery-learning point of view, most applications are developed by teams and published for use in the classroom.

However, it is an important model for developers of online courses, where the highly sequenced tasks with quick feedback and clear objectives are very useful.

Syntax

The syntax is straightforward—objectives are stated clearly at the beginning and then a sequence of tasks is provided along with information about how successfully the tasks were completed. A summary assessment is provided at the end of each unit of study. Incidentally, units can be relatively short or quite long. Often the longer units are divided into sections.

Social System

The tendency is for students to work as individuals. However, it is important that students understand that individuals may vary in the time they need and the atmosphere should be positive toward all.

Principles of Reaction

Instructors need to keep track of student progress and provide encouragement when students labor to complete tasks or find success to be laborious. Instructors need to try to ensure that the units in an instructional system are at an appropriate level for the students.

Applications

Nearly all curriculum area includes content that can be approached from a mastery perspective. Foreign language learning systems frequently use a mastery framework and initial instruction in music, computer science, and graphics abound with systems.

INSTRUCTIONAL AND NURTURANT EFFECTS

The model has a good track record with highly motivated students and, with careful support by instructors, can pull struggling learners into a higher state of progress and elevate their academic self-concepts (see Figure 17.1). Even when a mastery-learning unit is well-matched to the students' prior knowledge, those students will vary considerably in their need for support by instructors.

FIGURE 17.1   Instructional and nurturant effects of the mastery learning model

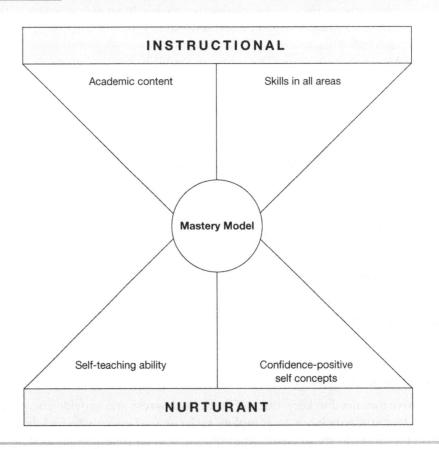

CHAPTER EIGHTEEN

Direct Instruction

Applied Psychology Goes to Work

The idea that you teach kids how to ask and answer questions, rather than just asking them questions, came as a revelation to me.

—*A teacher of 20 years, to Bruce Joyce*

Although based on the studies of effective teachers, direct instruction has its theoretical origins in the behavioral family, particularly in the thinking of training and behavioral psychologists. Training psychologists have focused on training people to perform complex behaviors that involve a high degree of precision and often coordination with others—for example, being a crew member on a submarine. Their main contributions to learning situations are task definition and task analysis. The instructional design principles they propose focus on conceptualizing learner performance into goals and tasks, breaking these tasks into smaller component tasks, developing training activities that ensure mastery of each subcomponent, and, finally, arranging the entire learning situation into sequences that ensure adequate transfer from one component to another and achievement of prerequisite learning before more advanced learning.

Whereas training psychologists have emphasized the design and planning of instruction, behavioral psychologists address the interaction between teachers and students. They speak of modeling, reinforcement, feedback, and successive approximation. Behaviorists sometimes refer to their approach as "modeling with reinforced guided performance."

GOALS AND ASSUMPTIONS

Direct instruction plays a limited but important role in a comprehensive educational program. Critics of direct instruction caution that the approach should not be used all the time, for all educational objectives, or for all students—cautions we agree with. Despite the cautions and the caveats, direct instruction has a relatively solid empirical track record, getting consistent if modest effects. A materials-based curriculum, DISTAR (Direct Instruction System for Teaching Arithmetic and Reading), based on social learning theory (see Becker, 1977) was developed about 40 years ago and continues as a commercial program to the present, published by SRA/McGraw-Hill. While DISTAR is not the only such program, it is a very useful example here because it combines grounded theory with careful development. Some dimensions of *Success for All* (see Slavin and Madden, 2001) use similar principles.

THE LEARNING ENVIRONMENT FOR DIRECT INSTRUCTION

The most prominent features of the learning environment are an academic focus, a high degree of teacher direction and control, high expectations for pupil progress, a system for managing time, and an atmosphere of relatively neutral affect. Academic focus means one places highest priority on the assignment and completion of academic tasks. During instruction, academic activity is emphasized; the use of nonacademic materials—for example, toys, games, and puzzles—is deemphasized or even discouraged, as is nonacademically oriented student–teacher interaction, such as questions about self or discussions of personal concern. Several studies have shown that a strong academic focus produces greater student engagement and, subsequently, achievement (Fisher et al., 1980; Madaus, Airasian, & Kellaghan, 1980; Rosenshine, 1985).

Teacher direction and control occur when the teacher selects and directs the learning tasks, maintains a central role during instruction, and minimizes the amount of nonacademic pupil talk. Teachers who have high expectations for their students and concern for academic progress demand academic excellence and behavior conducive to academic progress. They expect more of their students in terms of quantity and quality of work.

Two major goals of direct instruction are the maximization of student learning time and the development of independence in seeking educational goals. Many teacher behaviors found to be associated with student achievement are in fact associated with student time on task and student rate of success, which in turn are associated with student achievement. Thus, the behaviors incorporated into direct instruction are designed to create a structured, academically oriented learning environment in which students are actively engaged (on task) during instruction and are experiencing a high rate of success (80 percent mastery or better) in the tasks they are given. Time spent by pupils in both these conditions is referred to as *academic learning time* (ALT), which is to be maximized.

Finally, there is substantial evidence that negative affect inhibits student achievement (Rosenshine, 1985; Soar, Soar, & Ragosta, 1971). Teachers should create an academic focus and avoid such negative practices as criticism of student behavior. Research is less clear on the role of positive affect on student outcomes: some students may benefit more from large amounts of praise than others; some types of praise are more effective than others (Brophy, 1981).

The direct instruction environment is one in which there is a predominant focus on learning and in which students are engaged in academic tasks a large percentage of time and achieve at a high rate of success. The social climate is positive and free of negative affect.

ORIENTATION TO THE MODEL

The term *direct instruction* has been used by researchers to refer to a pattern of teaching that consists of the teacher's explaining a new concept or skill to students, having them test their understanding by practicing under teacher direction (that is, controlled practice), and encouraging them to continue to practice under teacher guidance (guided practice).

Before presenting and explaining new material, it is helpful to establish a framework for the lesson and orient the students to the new material. Structuring comments made at the beginning of a lesson are designed to clarify the purposes, procedures, and actual content of the subsequent learning experience. Such comments are associated with improved student engagement during the learning activity and with overall achievement (1980; Fisher, C., Berliner, D., Filby, N., Marliave, R., Ghen, L., & Dishaw, M., 1980; Medley, 1977; Medley, Soar, & Coker, 1984). These orienting comments can take various forms, including: (1) introductory activities that elicit students' relevant existing knowledge structures (Anderson, Evertson, & Brophy, 1979), such as reviewing the previous day's work (Rosenshine, 1985); (2) discussing the objective of the lesson; (3) providing clear, explicit directions about work to be done; (4) telling the students about the materials they will use and the activities they will be engaged in during the lesson; and (5) providing an overview of the lesson.

Once the context for learning has been established, instruction can begin with the presentation of the new concept or skill. Students' success in learning the new material has much to do with the thoroughness and quality of the teacher's initial explanation. Effective teachers spend more time explaining and demonstrating new material than less effective teachers (Rosenshine, 1985). Presentation practices that appear to facilitate learning include: (1) presenting material in small steps so that one point can be mastered at a time; (2) providing many, varied examples of the new skills or concepts; (3) modeling, or giving narrated demonstrations of the learning task; (4) avoiding digressions, staying on topic; and (5) reexplaining difficult points (Rosenshine, 1985). From research on concept learning we also know that when teaching a new concept it is important to clearly identify the characteristics (attributes) of the concept and to provide a rule or definition (or sequence of steps in skill learning). Finally, providing a visual representation of the concept or skill along with the verbal explanation assists students in following the explanation. Later, at other points in the learning process, the visual representation serves as a cue or prompt.

Following the explanation comes the discussion, in which the teacher checks for students' understanding of the new concept or skill. A common error is simply to ask students if they understand or have any questions and then to assume that if no one or only a few students respond, everyone understands well enough to move on to seatwork. Effective teachers ask more questions that check for student understanding than less effective teachers (Rosenshine, 1985). Such questions call for specific answers or ask for explanations of how answers were found. According to Rosenshine (1985), effective teachers not only asked more questions, but they also spent more time on teacher-led practice and on repeating the new material they were teaching. Other aspects of effective questioning behavior for direct instruction approaches are:

1. Asking convergent, as opposed to divergent, questions (Rosenshine, 1971, 1985).
2. Ensuring that all students get a chance to respond, not just those who raise their hands or call out the loudest. This can be accomplished by calling on students in a patterned order; for example, by calling the students' names in reading groups before asking them questions or calling for a choral response (Gage & Berliner, 1983; Rosenshine, 1985).
3. Asking questions within students' "reach" a high percentage of the time (75 to 90 percent) (Rosenshine, 1985).
4. Avoiding nonacademic questions during direct instruction (Rosenshine, 1985; Soar, Soar, & Ragosta, 1971).

Once the teacher has initiated a question and a student has responded, the teacher needs to give the student feedback on his or her response. Research indicates that effective teachers do a better job of providing feedback than noneffective ones (Rosenshine, 1971). They do not let errors go uncorrected, nor do they simply give the answers to students who have responded incorrectly. They use techniques for correcting responses or they reteach the material.

In addition, effective teachers maintain a brisk pace during this recitation activity. When they provide corrective feedback or reteach, they do it efficiently so that many practice opportunities are provided and many students have the opportunity to respond. For example, when a correct answer has been given, the teacher simply asks a new question. In the early stages of learning, when answers may be correct but somewhat tentative, the teacher provides knowledge of results and quick-process feedback. ("Very good. You remembered that 'i' goes before 'e' when it comes after 'c.'") If the student has carelessly provided an incorrect answer, the teacher provides corrective feedback and moves on. If the incorrect response indicated lack of understanding, the teacher should provide hints or clues, such as referring back to the visual representation. It is important to probe for clarification and improved answers. Effective feedback is academically oriented, not behaviorally oriented (Fisher et al., 1980). It is also substantive in that it tells students *what* they have done correctly. Feedback may be combined with praise; however, it is important that praise be deserved based on the quality of the response (Gage & Berliner, 1983). Students differ in the amount of praise they need; some students, particularly low-achieving students, need a lot, whereas others do not need as much. Even if a student's need for praise is great, he or she should not be praised for an incorrect response (Brophy, 1981).

The major point is that the kind of feedback students receive during structured practice has much to do with their later success. Feedback helps students find out how well they understand the new material and what their errors are. To be effective, feedback must be academic, corrective, respectful, and deserved.

The need for students to be given thorough explanations and structured practice with feedback before they begin their practice seems obvious. However, it is clear both from the research and from the authors' own experiences that students are often asked to work from their texts or workbooks with almost no explanation and/or practice. Students need to have a high degree of success when they are engaged in reading or practicing skills. In order for this to occur, they should move from structured practice to open practice only when they have achieved about 90 percent accuracy on the structured-practice examples.

In the average classroom, students spend between 50 and 75 percent of their time working alone on tasks (Rosenshine, 1985). If this large amount of time is to be productively directed toward learning, students need to remain engaged in the learning task. What is most conducive to engagement is being well prepared by the teacher's presentation and by teacher-led practice. Practice that is directly related to the presentation and that occurs right after teacher-led practice facilitates student engagement. It is also helpful for the teacher to circulate while students are working, monitoring individual students with relatively short contacts (Rosenshine, 1985).

Practice

As its name implies, the "heart" of this teaching strategy is its practice activities; three phases of the model deal with practice under varying conditions of assistance. The three levels of practice function in the following manner: When the students are first introduced to a new skill or concept, the teacher leads the group through each step in working out the problem. The idea is to ensure that few errors are produced in the initial learning stages, when memory is most vulnerable to remembering incorrect practice and when errors reinforce incorrect information. After the highly structured practice, the students practice on their own while the teacher monitors. During this time the teacher provides corrective feedback for any errors produced as well as reinforcement for correct practice. When students are able to practice with accuracy, they are ready for independent practice—that is, for practice under conditions when assistance is not as available. Homework is an example of independent practice. This last step in the practice progression is the mastery level; students are performing the skill independently with minimal error.

The second principle has to do with the length of each practice session. Research indicates that, on the whole, the more a person practices a skill, the longer it takes him or her to forget it. The general principle guiding the length of time recommended for practice is: *Short, intense, highly motivated practice periods produce more learning than fewer but longer practice periods.* For example, with younger students, short, 5- to 10-minute practice sessions interspersed over the day or a series of days will be more effective than long, 30- to 40-minute sessions. Older students are able to handle longer practice sessions, but, many short sessions with clear feedback about progress pay off for them also.

The third principle is the need to *monitor the initial stage of practice,* because incorrect performance at this stage will interfere with learning. Students need corrective feedback to prevent incorrect procedures from becoming embedded in their memories. Immediate corrective feedback (that is, information on how to perform correctly) will reverse misconceptions early in the instructional process. It also reduces performance anxiety because students practice with the assurance of immediate feedback. In addition to catching incorrect performance in the early stages, it is also important to reinforce correct performance. This gives students the knowledge of results that stabilizes the new learning more quickly.

Having students achieve an 85 to 90 percent *level of accuracy* at the current practice level before going to the next level is the fourth practice principle. Paying attention to accuracy rates ensures that students experience success and do not practice errors.

The next guideline is to *distribute practice,* using multiple practice sessions spread out over a period of time. Without practice, as much as 80 percent of new information is forgotten within 24 hours. With periodic reviews spread out over an extended period of time, such as four or five months, nearly all new information can be retained. A common mistake in instruction is to deal with a topic, end the topic, and never review the information or skills again until a final examination. The important material needs to be reviewed regularly.

And, finally, the general guideline is that practice periods should be close together at the beginning of learning; once learning is at an independent level, the practice sessions can be spaced farther and farther apart. Thus, guided practice sessions should occur immediately after new learning has been introduced and should continue frequently until independence is achieved. When this has occurred, independent practice sessions can be distributed farther apart—that is, for example, 1, 2, 6, and then 15 days apart.

THE MODEL OF TEACHING

Syntax

The direct instruction model consists of five phases of activity: orientation, presentation, structured practice, guided practice, and independent practice. However, the use of this model should be preceded by effective diagnosis of students' knowledge or skills to be sure that they have the prerequisite knowledge or skills to achieve high levels of accuracy in the different practice conditions.

Phase one is orientation, in which a framework for the lesson is established. During this phase the teacher's expectations are communicated, the learning task is clarified, and student accountability is established. Three steps are particularly important in carrying out the intent of this phase: (1) the teacher provides the objective of the lesson and the level of performance; (2) the teacher describes the content of the lesson and its relationship to prior knowledge and/or experience; and (3) the teacher discusses the procedures of the lesson—that is, the different parts of the lesson and students' responsibilities during those activities.

Phase two is the presentation—explaining the new concept or skill and providing demonstrations and examples. If the material is a new concept, it is important that the teacher discuss the characteristics (or *attributes*) of the concept, the rule or definition, and several examples. If the material is a new skill, it is important to identify the steps of the skill with examples of each step. (Another common mistake is to provide too few demonstrations.) In either case, it is helpful to convey this information both orally and visually so that students will have the visual representation as a reference in the early stages of learning. Another task is to check to see that students have understood the new information before they apply it in the practice phases. Can they recall the attributes of the concept that the teacher has explained? Can they recall the number and list of steps in the skill they have just been shown? Checking for understanding requires that students recall or recognize the information that they have just heard. In structured practice, they will apply it.

Phase three, structured practice, comes next. The teacher leads students through practice examples, working through each step. Usually the students practice as a group, offering to write answers. A good way to accomplish the lockstep technique is to use an overhead projector, doing practice examples on a transparency so that all students can see the generation of each step. The teacher's role in this phase is to give feedback on the students' responses, to reinforce accurate responses, and to correct errors and point out the objective. By referring to it while working the practice examples, the teacher is ensuring that students understand it so that they can use it as a resource during their semi-independent practice phase.

Phase four, guided practice, gives students the opportunity to practice on their own with support. Guided practice enables the teacher to make an assessment of the students' abilities to perform the learning task by assessing the amount and types of errors the students are making. The teacher's role in this phase is to monitor students' work, providing corrective feedback when necessary.

In phase five, we reach independent practice. It begins when students have achieved an accuracy level of 85 to 90 percent in guided practice. The purpose of independent practice is to reinforce the new learning to ensure retention as well as to develop fluency. In independent practice, students practice on their own without assistance and with delayed feedback. The independent practice work is reviewed soon after completion to assess whether the students' accuracy level has remained stable and to provide corrective feedback for those who need it. An independent-practice activity can be short in length of time and number of practice items; however, it should not be a one-time venture. As discussed earlier, five or six practice sessions distributed over a month or more will sustain retention.

Social System

The social system is highly structured. Nonetheless, pains need to be taken to ensure that students know what is to be learned and how. The concentrated effort of the students generates the learning.

Principles of Reaction

The principles of reaction are governed by the need to provide knowledge of results, help students pace themselves, and offer reinforcement. The support system includes sequenced learning tasks, sometimes as elaborate as the sets developed by the individually prescribed instruction team.

APPLICATION

The most common applications are in the study of basic information and skills in the core curriculum areas. A number of large-scale programs built around direct instruction have been directed at economically poor, low-achieving children. In the evaluation of Project Follow Through, a federal program that extended Head Start into the elementary grades, the University of Oregon's direct instruction model produced significant differences on both cognitive and affective measures (Becker, 1977). Overall, the students in this program went from being well below the 25th percentile nationally in reading, math, and spelling before starting the program to being in the 50th percentile or above by the third grade. The program emphasizes "small-group, face to face instruction by a teacher using carefully sequenced, daily lessons in reading, arithmetic, and language" (Becker, Engelmann, Carnine, & Rhine, 1981). "A positive self-concept was viewed as a by-product of good teaching rather than as a goal to be achieved in the abstract" (Becker, 1977, pp. 921–922).

INSTRUCTIONAL AND NURTURANT EFFECTS

The model is, as the name implies, "direct." It approaches academic content systematically. Its design is shaped to generate and sustain motivation through pacing and reinforcement. Through success and positive feedback, it tries to enhance self-esteem (see Figure 18.1).

FIGURE 18.1 Instructional and nurturant effects of the direct instruction model

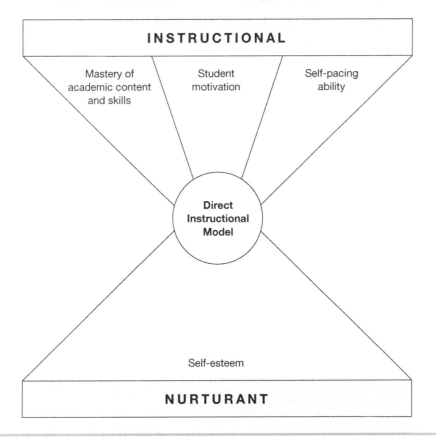

Direct Instruction Model

Syntax

- *Phase One: Orientation.* Teacher establishes content of the lesson, reviews previous learning, establishes lesson objectives, and establishes the procedures for the lesson.
- *Phase Two: Presentation.* Teacher explains/demonstrates new concepts or skill, provides visual representation of the task, and checks for understanding.
- *Phase Three: Structured Practice.* Teacher leads group through practice examples in lockstep. Students respond to questions. Teacher provides corrective feedback for errors and reinforces correct practice.
- *Phase Four: Guided Practice.* Students practice semi-independently. Teacher circulates, monitoring student practice, and provides feedback.
- *Phase Five: Independent Practice.* Students practice independently at home or in class. Feedback is delayed. Independent practices occur several times over an extended period.

Social System

The social system should be positive but realistic, with students and instructor sharing knowledge about accomplishments and the need for review and second tries at success.

Principles of Reaction

In this model reaction is closely tuned to progress. Continual encouragement is needed, but, again, with a realistic appraisal of gain.

PART SEVEN

The Conditions of Learning, Learning Styles, and Conceptual Levels

Here we pull together knowledge on models of teaching and apply them to some serious problems in education and our society. We take another look at the development of knowledge about teaching and learning. We also look at the yield of studies of personality, particularly integrative complexity, and how we profit from the discomfort that inevitably nips at us when we are learning new things, for a really good education takes us into new information, understanding, skills, and commitment to the betterment of our society—both our current social environment and the community, national, and world environments that invite us to participate in the quest for ever-better qualities of life for everyone.

CHAPTER NINETEEN

Creating Curricula

The Conditions of Learning

*Lessons, courses, and curriculums need to be opened with
the identification of the concepts, skills, and information
that are to literally become part of the learner, carried
on to the future, to be used and reused again and again.*

—*Our reflective observer*

Planning curricula, courses, units, and lessons is a sine qua non of good teaching. In this chapter, we study planning with a master and then try to apply his framework to the problem of planning instruction.

One of the most important books on learning and teaching is Robert N. Gagné's *The Conditions of Learning* (1965). Gagné gives us a careful analysis of the important variables in learning and how to organize instruction to take these variables into account. His picture of the "varieties of chance called learning" enables us to classify and specify learning objectives and the relationships *between* various kinds of performances. Gagné identifies six varieties of performances that can be the result of learning:

1. Specific responding
2. Chaining
3. Multiple discrimination
4. Classifying
5. Rule using
6. Problem solving

Varieties of performance

Specific responding is making a specific response to a particular stimulus. An example occurs when a first-grade teacher holds up a card (the stimulus) on which the word *dog* is printed and the children say "dog" (the response). Specific responding is an extremely important type of learning and is the basis for much of the information we possess. In order for the student to learn to make correct, specific responses, we must assume he or she has the ability to make connections between things. In the previous example, the printed word *dog* is associated, or connected, with the verbal statement "dog." Note that we are describing evidence of *learning* here—the student, able to respond, has learned at that level. How the learning was accomplished is a different matter. In other words, whether flashcards are or are not used is immaterial, as is whether any particular model of teaching was or was not used.

Chaining is making a series of responses that are linked together. Gagné uses the example of unlocking a door with a key and of translating from one language to another. Unlocking a door requires us to use a number of specific responses (selecting a key, inserting it, turning it) in an order that will get the job done. When one takes the English words "How are you?" and puts them together into a meaningful phrase, chaining is occurring. Similarly, translating them to "¿Cómo está usted?" in Spanish is chaining by taking a series of specific responses and linking them into phrases in both languages.

Multiple discrimination is involved in learning a variety of specific responses and chains and in learning how to sort them out appropriately. Discrimination applies to learned responses; one learns to associate colors with their names under similar conditions, such as learning to identify the colors of various objects in a particular room in one's home or in a school. Then one has to sort out the colors and apply them to varieties of objects under different conditions, such as in a shopping center (blue, first learned in relation to a blanket, is applied to a sweater in a store). More complex is sorting out and combining chains. Similarly, when learning a language, one develops a storehouse of words and phrases (chains). When spoken to, one has to sort out the reply, adjusting for gender, number, tense, and so forth. Multiple discrimination, then, involves learning to handle previously learned chains of various sorts.

Classifying is assigning objects to classes denoting like functions. Learning to distinguish plants from animals or automobiles from bicycles involves classifying. The result of this process is *concepts*, ideas that compare and contrast things and events or describe causal relations among them. When learning languages, one builds concepts that pertain to the structure of the language, such as *subject, predicate, phrase, clause,* and *parts of speech.* The young language learner, by the age of four or five, has learned many of these concepts without having names for them, including relational concepts, such as modifying nouns with adjectives.

Rule using is the ability to act on a concept that implies action. For instance, in spelling we learn varieties of concepts that describe how words are spelled. Then we apply those concepts in rule form in the act of spelling itself. As an example, one learns that in consonant-vowel words ending in "t," such as *sit*, the consonant is doubled when *-ing* is added. This becomes a rule (double the "t") that one usually follows in spelling such words.

Finally, *problem solving* is the application of several rules to a problem not encountered before by the learner. Problem solving involves selecting the correct rules and applying them in combination. For example, a child learns several rules about balancing on a seesaw and then applies them when moving a heavy object with a lever.

FACILITATING THE CLASSES OF LEARNING

Gagné believes that these six classes of learning form an ascending hierarchy; thus, before one can chain, one has to learn specific responses. Multiple discrimination requires prior learning of several chains. Classifying builds on multiple discrimination. Rules for action are forms of concepts learned through classification and the establishment of causal relations. Problem solving requires previously learned rules. Each level of learning requires certain conditions. The task of the instructor is to provide these conditions by using the appropriate model of teaching.

To facilitate specific responding, a stimulus is presented to the student under conditions that will bring about his or her attention and induce a response closely related in time to the presentation of the stimulus. The response is then reinforced. Thus the teacher may hold up the word *dog*, say "dog," ask the children to say "dog," and then smile and say "good" to the students. A teacher who does this repeatedly increases the probability that the students will learn to recognize words and be able to emit the sounds associated with the symbols. The memory and training models (see Chapters 8 and 10) are approaches that facilitate specific responding.

To facilitate the acquisition of chaining, a sequence of cues is offered and appropriate responses are induced. A language teacher may say, "How are you? ¿Cómo está usted?" and invite the students to repeat the phrases, providing sufficient repetition that the students will acquire the chain and achieve fluency. The memory model, advance organizer, and inductive thinking models are appropriate to helping build chains.

To facilitate multiple discrimination, practice with correct and incorrect stimuli is needed so that the students can learn to discriminate. For example, suppose the students are learning the Spanish expressions for "How are you?" and "Good morning"; they must learn to discriminate which one to use in a given situation. The instructor provides sets of correct and incorrect stimuli until the students learn the appropriate discrimination. Advance organizers and inductive reasoning are useful in this process.

Classification is taught by presenting varieties of exemplars and concepts so that the students can gradually learn bases for distinguishing them. Concept attainment and inductive thinking are appropriate, among other models.

Rule using is facilitated by inducing the students to recall a concept and then apply it to a variety of specific applications. In the earlier spelling example, students recall the rule about doubling the final consonant when adding -*ing* and are presented with examples they can practice. Inquiry training can help students move from concepts to rules, as can the application phases of concept attainment and inductive thinking.

Problem solving is largely done by the students themselves, because problem situations are unique. It can be facilitated by providing sets of problems that the students can attempt to attack, especially when the instructor knows that the students have acquired the rules needed to solve the problem. Inquiry training, group investigation, synectics, simulation, and nondirective teaching can be used for problem-solving activities.

Functions of the Instructor

Gagné emphasizes that it is the learner's activity that results in the learning. The function of the instructor is to provide conditions that will increase the probability that the student will acquire the particular performance. Practice is extremely important so that the learner makes the necessary connections, but it is the learner who makes the connections even when they are pointed out to him or her. The instructor cannot substitute his or her own activity for that of the student. We agree completely with Gagné on this point.

Instructors (or perhaps instructional systems) operate through the following instructional functions:

1. Informing the learner of the objectives
2. Presenting stimuli
3. Increasing learners' attention
4. Helping the learner recall what he or she has previously learned
5. Providing conditions that will evoke performance
6. Determining sequences of learning
7. Prompting and guiding the learning

Also, the instructor encourages the student to generalize what he or she is learning so that the new skills and knowledge will be transferred to other situations.

Informing the learner of the performance expected is critical for providing him or her with a definite goal. For example, the teacher might say, "Today we're going to try to learn about three presidents of the United States. We'll learn their names, when they lived, and what they are most known for." The teacher then presents the pictures of Washington, Lincoln, and Theodore Roosevelt. Their names are printed under the pictures. Pointing to the pictures and names and saying the names will draw the students' attention.

To recall previous learning, the teacher may say, "Do you remember that we discussed how the country has grown and changed in various ways? Can you tell me what some of these changes were?" The students can reach into their memories for material that will later be connected to the presidents.

To induce performance, a teacher may ask the students to name the three presidents and then read printed material describing the life of each. Then the teacher can ask them to tell him or her what they have learned.

A variety of sequences can be used, depending on the type of learning and the subject matter in question. Generally, however, presenting a stimulus, evoking attention, helping the learner understand the objectives, inducing performance, and then helping the learner to generalize are the major instructional tasks, which follow one another naturally.

Gagné's paradigm reminds us of a variety of important general principles of teaching: informing the learner of the levels of objectives being sought, encouraging generalization, and pushing for application of what is learned. He emphasizes that we cannot control learning but can only increase the probability that certain kinds of behavior will occur. We can present stimuli in close connection with others and ask the student to perform, but it is the *learner* who makes the connection between the printed and spoken word:

> Essentially, however carefully one controls the aspects of external learning conditions described previously, instruction nevertheless can only make the occurrence of the crucial internal, idiosyncratic event of learning more probable. The careful design of instruction can surely increase its probability, and, by so doing, make the entire process of learning more sure, more predictable and more efficient. But the individual nervous system must still make its own individual contribution. The nature of that contribution is, of course, what defines the need for the study of individual differences. (Gagné, 1965, pp. 291–313)

From this point of view, a model of teaching brings structures to the student that change the probability that he or she will learn certain things. The syntax presents tasks to the student, the reactions of the teacher pull the student toward certain responses, and the social system generates a need for particular kinds of interaction with others. The net effect is to make it more likely that various kinds of learning will take place.

Gagné's hierarchy is useful in helping us select models appropriate for varieties of educational objectives. It also reminds us of the multiple types of learning promoted by individual models and the attention that must be given to the varieties of performance as the students engage in the study of any important topic. For example, students using inductive thinking to explore a problem in international relations, such as the balance of imports and exports, will gather data (specific responding and chaining), organize it (multiple discrimination and classifying), and develop principles (rule using) to explore solutions to problems (problem solving).

PLANNING A COURSE IN GLOBAL EDUCATION

Let's see what happens when we put Gagné's hierarchy to work. Let's design a global education curriculum that we can use from the primary grades through high school. Such a complex curriculum will give us the opportunity to consider quite a range of models, and we will almost certainly want to use several of them to design the instructional aspects of such a curriculum.

We'll begin with a somewhat arbitrary statement of our overall objectives. Note that we begin with objectives at the problem-solving level because those will guide our selection of objectives at the other levels of Gagné's hierarchy. A common mistake to be avoided in planning is to begin at the response level and then try to "squeeze" the more complex types of learning from responses. Rather, one should begin at the most complex level (problem solving) and then determine what needs to be learned to make problem solving possible.

Overall Objectives

Our social studies curriculum seeks to ensure that the students have a working knowledge of human geography, can think about some of the critical issues facing the peoples of the world, and are prepared to interact productively with people from cultures other than theirs. Our rationale is that the global perspective is essential for personal understanding, for the guidance of our nation, for the betterment of the world, and for economic competence. At one level, we want our students to graduate with the learning that will enable them to spin a globe, put a finger down on a land mass, and know considerable information about the nation it lights on. At another level, we want them to have considerable knowledge of several representative cultures and to be able to think of the world and our nation in terms of cultural history and cultural comparison. At yet another level, we want them to have experience thinking about and generating solutions to important global problems.

A secondary overall objective is to use the study of the globe to further the reading/writing curriculum, especially the reading and writing of expository prose. (This objective appears across all curriculum areas!)

Building Operational Objectives

Several models of teaching can help us clarify our objectives and transform them into goals for which we can plan.

Integrative Complexity, Cognitive Development, and Concept of Self

Let's begin with the models that highlight individual differences. Understanding the globe and its multiple cultures will require a high level of integrative complexity as the students try to develop a perspective on complex problems, how to understand the concept of culture, and how to reconcile one's own cultural perspective with that of another.

The framework for studying cognitive development helps us think about the kinds of objectives that can be reasonably aimed for at different ages. The littlest kids can certainly absorb information about one or two other cultures, but thinking abstractly about the cultural spectrum would be a bit much. Upper elementary students can learn to manipulate demographic data about the nations of the world and can search for correlations among variables; they can learn to ask, for example, whether the wealth of nations is correlated with educational levels, fertility, and so on. They can compare cultures with respect to the more visible and concrete variables—housing, family styles, occupations, and so forth. Secondary students can handle complex multicultural problems, compare and contrast cultures with respect to more abstract variables, such as norms, and make inferences about how various nations would respond to particular types of problems, such as population growth, threats of war, and the global ecology.

Studies of self-concept help us in several ways. First, the general orientation reminds us that the entire curriculum should be conducted in a manner to increase the students' sense of ability to learn and master complex material. Second, it reminds us that self-understanding is vital. Thinking about world cultures is practically ready-made for aspects of self-understanding; it should help the students think about their own culture in relation to others and understand how cultural values affect thinking and behavior.

Let us also think from the perspective of the families of models of teaching.

Cooperative Action and Mutual Understanding

The social family offers the perspective of building a cooperative community of learners (not a bad objective in itself) and helping that community explore the world together and surface the important value questions. Role playing offers us a tool for helping the students study their own values as the inquiry progresses. Jurisprudential inquiry (see Chapter 13) invites us to approach issues by clarifying them and the value positions underlying various alternatives.

Learning Concepts, Hypothesis Building, and Testing

The information-processing family places at our disposal a set of relevant tools. The development of concepts will be necessary to manage the mass of information, and thinking about relationships will give our students many hypotheses to test. Synectics can help students break set and generate alternative solutions to global problems and international relations. The link-word method is there to help the students master unfamiliar terms—and there will be many of them.

Self-Actualization and Self-Direction

If the makers of the personal models have their way, we will provide much opportunity for self-directed inquiry and urge our students not just to follow immediate interests or work at their current level of development, but to stretch themselves into new areas and toward "personal bests" in learning. We will make their feelings a part of the subject matter and will recognize always that knowledge is a personal construction.

LITERACY AND THE PICTURE WORD INDUCTIVE MODEL

Now, let us turn to the picture-word inductive model and plan a sequence of lessons using Gagné's framework. Consider the following scenario.

SCENARIO

Judith's 5-year-olds at Hempshill Hall Primary School are working on building their reading vocabularies. They are also beginning their study of phonics by analyzing the structures (spelling) of words that are in their listening, speaking, and reading vocabularies.

The children are seated on the floor, facing a poster that features a teddy bear in the countryside (Figure 19.1). The poster is mounted in the middle of a large blank sheet of paper. Judith says, "We're going to get some of the words for this week's reading vocabulary by shaking words out of this picture. I want you to study the picture carefully and then, when I call on you, come up and point to something in the picture and say what it is. Then I'll write the word and draw a line from the thing in the picture to the word. We'll start learning to read the words as we go along."

The children study the picture. After a while, Judith asks them if they have found something they'd like to share. All the hands go up and Judith calls on Jessica.

FIGURE 19.1   The teddy bear

Emily Calhoun

Jessica reaches up, points, and says, "That's a ladder." Judith draws a line from the ladder and writes the word, saying the letters as she does so. She then spells "ladder" again, while the children watch and listen.

"Now, I'll spell it again, and you say each letter after me." She does, and then asks another child for a word.

"Sit," says Brian, and points to the teddy bear. "The bear's sitting."

Specific Responding

Judith draws a letter from the bear and writes, "The bear's sitting." She spells each word as she writes it and then takes the children to each word in turn, saying them, spelling them, and asking the children to spell them after her. She then points to the first word. "What is this word?"

"Ladder," they chorus.

"And if you saw the word and couldn't remember it, what could you do?"

"Go down the line to the ladder in the picture," they say.

"Right. And what's this word?" She points to the word *the*.

"The," they chorus again. She repeats the process with *bear's* and *sitting* and then asks for the whole sentence, but calls on Nancy.

"The bear's sitting," says Nancy.

"Who thinks she's right?" asks Judith. The children's hands go up. Judith continues to elicit words from the children, continuing the pattern as before, examining each word and regularly reviewing all of them.

Chaining

By the end of the session, the following list has been accumulated, and the children can say each one as she points to it. Judith finishes by asking them to see if they notice any of the words in the books they are taking home for the evening to share with their parents. As they break, an older child who has been recording the words on a computer saves the file.

ladder	apple	leaf	bear
teddy bear	sitting bear	half-eaten	trunk
tree	apple tree	apples	trees
ate	basket	basketgrass	tree trunk
little trees	ladder	apple core	teddy
core	half-eaten apple	sit leaves	

The following day, as the children enter the classroom, some of them go up to the picture and look at the words, saying them to each other and following words they don't remember down the lines to the objects those words are connected to. Again, the children sit next to the poster and Judith has them read the words, using the picture to help them locate the referents for the words.

Multiple Discrimination

Judith has taken the file of words that were shaken out of the picture, put them into a large font, and printed them out, making a set of word cards for each child. Now she asks the children to read their sets and, if they can't remember a word, to go to the poster, find the word, and trace it down to the part of the picture it represents.

Much activity ensues. The children peer at the words, saying them, usually aloud, to themselves. Occasionally, they ask Judith if they are right, and she sends them to the picture to find out for themselves. Soon children are getting up and down, holding a word card and locating the word on the chart.

Elaborate Multiple Discrimination

Judith then asks them for sentences that describe the picture as a whole, and gets sentences like, "The teddy bear is sitting in the countryside" and "There are apples all over the place." One child asks a question. Pointing to an apple core, she wonders, "Who do you suppose ate that apple? Can teddy bears eat apples?" Judith records the sentences, and they read them together before closing the session.

Classification

The following morning she again reviews the poster chart with the children. Then she asks them to take out their word cards and put words together according to how they are spelled.

Here are some of the categories they came up with.

Jessica says, " 'Tree' and 'trees' and 'ladder' have two letters the same in them."

"Super! Can you point to the letters?" Jessica does so. "Did anyone else put words together for the same reason? Nancy?"

"I put 'apple' and 'teddy' together because one has two p's together and the other has two d's together."

Brian adds, "I put 'teddy' and 'ladder' together because they have two d's in the middle."

Judith says, "Let's look at 'apple' and 'apples.' How are they the same and how are they different?" Several children volunteer and she calls on Dylan.

"They're spelled the same except for the s's. And 'apple' is just one apple and 'apples' is two apples."

Rule Using

Judith asks why "tree" and "trunk" might be put together.

The children are puzzled for a minute, and then hands begin to go up. Judith waits until nearly all the kids have an idea and then calls on Brendan. "Probably because 'tree' and 'trunk' sound the same at the beginning." They discuss Brendan's answer and then Judith writes "sound the same."

Finally, the children read the set of words on the chart once more and end for the day, requested to hunt for the words in their evening's reading.

Problem Solving

Judith has been using a strategy called the *picture-word inductive model* (as in Chapter 5). This is a model for eliciting words from the children's listening and speaking vocabulary so that those words can be studied and mastered and, through classification, be a basis for the early exploration of phonics. Ultimately, solving the problems of word identification and developing sight vocabularies are the students' problems. But we can help by using the models of teaching that foster these skills.

CHAPTER TWENTY

Expanding Our Horizons

Making Discomfort Productive

If we get too comfortable, we stop growing. Students can put pressure on us to work within their comfort zone. Let's be kind about that. Kind enough to help them learn to be uncomfortable.

—*Herb Thelen to Bruce Joyce*

SCENARIO

MATCH AND MISMATCH

First Student: That guy keeps insisting on more ideas. He's driving me crazy. I have to write everything over a dozen times.

Second Student: I'm happy in there. The other one gives me the heebie jeebies. He uses his heavy blue pencil and wants me to get rid of metaphors and allegories.

First Student: It's like we have to change personalities on the way down the hall.

Second Student: For sure, THEY are not going to change.

That scenario depicts an all-too-common sad story. In this chapter, we deal explicitly with the relationship between styles of learning, styles of teaching, and models of teaching. We present a general stance toward individual differences and how to teach students to learn productively from a variety of models. Conceptual systems theory (see Harvey, Hunt, & Schroeder, 1966; Hunt, 1971) is an incredibly important foundation of our thinking.

Individual differences are to be prized because they are the expression of the uniqueness of personalities. Learning styles are important because they are the education-relevant expressions of this uniqueness. Individually, our configurations give us our personal identities; together, they also exemplify the richness of our culture.

We hope to provide our children with a common education that enhances their individuality and encourages their personalities and simultaneously passes along our culture and its tools. We need to use our teaching repertoires in such a way that we capitalize on the characteristics of our students to help them achieve increasing control over their own growth.

With respect to models of teaching, we can begin by avoiding two mistakes. The first is to assume that a model of teaching is a fixed, inflexible formula, which should be employed rigidly for best results. The second is to assume that each learner has a fixed style of learning that is unlikely to change or grow. Both mistakes lead us into an impossible dilemma, for if unyielding teaching methods are mismatched with rigid learners, a destructive collision is inevitable. Fortunately, teaching methods have great flexibility, and students have great learning capacities—and, thus, adaptability.

Consider the nature of the models of teaching we have been discussing. By its very nature, the personal family begins with the uniqueness of the learner, and each personal model tries to help the students take charge of their own growth. The social models depend on the synergy caused by the interaction of heterogeneous minds and personalities. The group investigation model explicitly generates the energy for learning from different perceptions of academic and social problems. The behavioral models build into instructional sequences the ability to adjust pace and complexity of tasks to the ability and prior achievement of the student. The information-processing models provide ways of adjusting instruction to cognitive development and style and will increase both learning ability and the ability to adapt productively. Importantly, you don't have to give up your important center in order to learn in multiple ways.

Then—perhaps most important to this discussion—we not only employ a model to teach information, concepts, skills, the analysis of values, and other content objectives, but we also teach the students to use the strategies of each model to educate themselves. In the previous chapters we have cast each model as a way of teaching students to learn particular ways of thinking. From that perspective, each model of teaching can be seen as a model of learning—a way of helping students expand their styles of approaching problems now and in their futures.

Yet, as we expose students to content and learning styles that are new to them, we will inevitably cause varying degrees of discomfort. Real growth often requires us to make our learners uncomfortable, and we have to help them deal with the unfamiliar situations that we must create for them as well as manage their discomfort productively.

Discomfort and learning

I (Bruce Joyce) would like to begin on a personal note that explains why discomfort is so prominent in this discussion of learning styles and educational environments. At the University of Chicago, I ended a conversation with Herbert Thelen by borrowing a copy of his *Education and the Human Quest* (1960); I spent much of the night reading the book. The next day we had a chance to talk again. Among the powerful ideas Thelen had generated, one left me most stimulated and uncomfortable: significant learning is frequently accompanied or impelled by discomfort.

Sometimes he put it pungently: "The learner does not learn unless he does not know how to respond" (Thelen, 1960, p. 61). Wow! So many educators were seeking ways that students could learn easily and comfortably—stress free—and Thelen was stating the obvious dilemma that the very concept of learning means that learners need to come to understand ideas or be able to perform skills that were not in their repertoires before the teaching/learning episode occurred. Let's say this again: if you already know something or possess a skill, you can call on that knowledge or skill when it is needed. Otherwise, you are faced with a situation in which "you do not *know* what to think or do." So, if you *learn*, you have changed. Learning means changing, if only in a small way at times.

Sometimes Thelen put this in terms of the dynamics of the inquiry process, as in the approach to teaching he called *group investigation*. Group investigation begins with a "stimulus situation to which students . . . can react and discover basic conflicts among their attitudes, ideas, and modes of perception" (p. 8). In other words, they need to learn (change) to be able to handle the type of situation that puzzles them at present.

In several earlier chapters we dealt with this frame of reference as we examined some other models. Think about Chapter 10, where inquiry training begins with a puzzlement—a situation in which our present knowledge does not solve the puzzle. Or think about synectics, where we learn to use analogies to think about a task or resolve a dilemma in which our present knowledge is not up to the demands of the situation. Or consider how the picture-word inductive model leads students to read and write previously unknown words, generate sentences they could not produce before, and follow the pictures into content they did not know existed before the inquiry developed. However, going where we have not been before can make us uncomfortable unless we accept that growing means to go "where we haven't been able to respond before" and relax into the adventure of learning rather than pushing change away.

Thelen also believed that education was seriously hampered by beliefs that schooling should be smooth and comfortable—that learning tasks should not stress the learners but move them along by easy stages. Thus he challenges the effects of the "norms of comfort and accommodation" (p. 80) that exist in so many classrooms and that mitigate the argumentation and difficult, uncomfortable tasks that characterize effective learning environments.

My first reaction was confusion. Thelen's ideas appeared to conflict with what I had been taught regarding learners as fragile egos that had to be protected by a supportive environment, so that they would in fact feel *comfortable* enough to stretch out into the world. How can the learner be made comfortable and uncomfortable at the same time? I asked Thelen that question, and he only smiled and replied, "That is a puzzling situation you will have to think about."

Psychologists from otherwise different orientations have dealt with the concept of discomfort for some time, albeit not always using the term as such. Personalistic psychologists are an example. Interpreters of Carl Rogers frequently concentrate on his argument for providing a safe place for learners to explore themselves and their environments. However, Rogers (1982) also emphasizes that our natural tendency as learners is to confine ourselves to domains in which we already feel safe. A major task of counselors and teachers is to help the learner reach into those domains that are shrouded in fear. To grow, learners have to acknowledge discomfort and set tasks to help break the barriers of fear. The educator's task is not simply to unloose the environmental bonds that constrict the learners but to help them become active seekers after new development.

Self-actualization, as described by Maslow (1962), is a state that not only enables people to venture and take risks, but also to endure the inevitable discomfort felt when attempting to use unfamiliar skills. Maslow's constructs apply to adults as well as children. In a four-year study of teachers exposed to a wide variety of staff development activities, it appeared that the teachers' self-concepts were important predictors of their abilities to use new skills and knowledge in their classroom situations (McKibbin & Joyce, 1980). We have also learned that a major part of successful staff development is helping people deal productively with the discomfort attendant to working their way to new levels of competence.

The role of discomfort and the ability to manage it productively appears in a different guise when we consider developmental stage theories (see Erikson, 1950; Harvey, Hunt, & Schroeder, 1961; Piaget, 1952). Most developmental stage theories emphasize not only the naturalness of growth through the stages, but the possibility of arrestation, and the accommodation that is necessary if higher levels of development are to be reached. Consider Piaget: Interpreters of Piaget are often most impressed by the naturalness of growth described from his stance—the position that the assimilation of new information will inevitably force the accommodations that lead to the successive stages of development. However, not everyone makes it upward through the Piagetian stages. Arrestation is possible. Accommodation sufficient to bring about the reconfiguration necessary to a new stage requires a "letting go" of the confines of one level so that the essentials of the next level can be reached. If the comfort of any given level of development is not challenged, the learner may happily forgo the important leaps in cognitive structure.

In conceptual systems theory, Hunt (see, especially, his 1971 essay) stresses the relationship of the environment to development. He describes stages of development and the characteristics of environments that permit people to function effectively at each stage while progression to the next stage is facilitated.

If the environment is perfectly matched to the developmental level of the learners, they may become satisfied at that level and become stuck there. The very language that Hunt and his colleagues use is provocative. If the environment is too comfortable or "reliable," the learners may be satisfied at the stage of concrete thinking, where the ability to integrate new information and form new conceptual systems is limited indeed. To impel learners to diverge from the familiar sets of concepts that enable them to view the world in "black and white," the environment must be dissatisfying in some ways. Although he approaches development from a very different perspective from Thelen, Hunt (1971) states explicitly that discomfort is a precursor to growth. To stimulate development, we *deliberately* mismatch student and environment so that the student cannot easily maintain the familiar patterns but must move on toward greater complexity. (But not too much—we seek an optimal mismatch where the learner's conceptual systems are challenged but not overwhelmed.)

Research on teacher training has repeatedly uncovered a "discomfort factor" as teachers acquire new repertoires, which helps us understand adults as they acquire new skills. Between 1968 and the present, a series of investigations inquired into teachers as they acquired larger repertoires of teaching strategies (Joyce, Peck, & Brown, 1981; Joyce & Showers, 2002; and Joyce & Calhoun, 2010). Teachers could acquire skill by studying the theories of various models of teaching or skills, seeing them demonstrated a number of times (15 or 20, the researchers came to believe), and practicing them about a dozen times with carefully articulated feedback. However, some teachers experienced considerable discomfort as they attempted to use approaches new to them. Only a small percentage (about 5 or 10 percent) of the teachers who had learned teaching strategies new to their repertoires were able to handle the discomfort without assistance. Most teachers never tried an unfamiliar strategy at all unless support personnel were available to them. Even then, during the first half-dozen trials, most teachers found the use of the new teaching strategies, whatever they were, to be extremely uncomfortable. The explanation was that the discomfort resulted in part because the teachers needed to adapt other, well-ingrained skills in order to use the new strategies; in part because students exposed to the new strategies needed to learn complementary skills so they could relate to them; and in part because the teachers felt less confident with any new strategy than they felt with their older repertoires.

The result was that many teachers would have withdrawn from the use of strategies new to them, even after their training had enabled them to produce these strategies with relative ease. However, after a number of trials with the new strategies, they became more comfortable with and developed power in their use. A major function of peer study groups is to provide the support necessary to work through the period of discomfort.

Conceptual level (CL) is a predictor of the ability to acquire new repertoires. The higher-CL teachers mastered sets of new models more fully and also tended to use them more (Joyce, Weil, & Wald, 1981). The relationship between conceptual level and the ability to learn new teaching strategies is partly related to how one manages feelings of discomfort attendant to learning the new repertoire. The more conceptually flexible teachers managed the process of discomfort more effectively. They incorporated the new information from their students, accommodated the discomfort of their students, and— most important—learned how to live through their periods of learning until the new teaching strategies worked in their classrooms.

It also became apparent that a critical part of a teacher's task in learning to use a new teaching strategy has to do with helping the learners acquire the skills necessary to relate to the new approach to teaching. Hunt and his associates initiated a series of studies to investigate the process by which learners respond to unfamiliar teaching strategies (Harvey, Hunt, & Schroder, 1961). These researchers identified students of varying conceptual levels and exposed them to teaching strategies that were matched and mismatched to their levels of development. Nearly all learners were able to respond to a wide variety of teaching strategies, but there were considerable individual differences in their responses. Students with a high need for structure (low CL) were more uncomfortable with teaching strategies that provided low degrees of structure, whereas learners who preferred independent direction were more uncomfortable with teaching strategies that provided higher structure.

Moreover, the students "pulled" the behavior of the teachers toward their preferred styles. Those who required the higher degrees of structure "asked" for that structure, and the teachers responded by adapting the strategies to conform to the personalities of the students. Curiously, the more a given model of teaching was mismatched with the natural learning style of the student, the more it presented a challenge to the student to take an affirmative stance so as to pass through the period of discomfort and develop skills that would permit a productive relationship with the learning environment.

For example, gregarious students are initially the most comfortable with social models and can profit from them quickly. However, the less gregarious students are in the greatest need of the models least comfortable for them. Hence, the challenge is not to select the most comfortable models but to enable the students to develop the skills to relate to a wider variety of models, many of which appear, at least superficially, to be mismatched with their learning styles.

The formulation gradually developed that significant growth requires discomfort. If the environment and the student are too much in harmony, the student is permitted to operate at a level of comfort that does not require the challenge of growth. To help students grow, we need to generate what we currently term a *dynamic disequilibrium*. Rather than matching teaching approaches to students in such a way as to minimize discomfort, our task is to expose the students to new teaching modalities that will, for some time, be uncomfortable to them.

LEARNERS LIVING ON THE MARGINS

Most of the literature on learners and educational environments emphasizes explicit matching, the adjustment of environments to the optimal "comfort level" of the students. The comfort-level matching concept appears frequently in most discussions of learning styles (hemispheric dominance, sensory modalities, multiple intelligences, and such). To consider the productive possibilities of discomfort, let us now discuss the *marginal learners*—students who experience great discomfort in the environments in which they find themselves. Currently many educators are concerned with these learners and are seeking ways to make the school environment more productive for them. (This is often discussed under the concept of *diversity*, where students who do not fit into an idea of an ideal mainstream are regarded as difficult to reach.) If we consider the concept of marginality, we can join the issues of discomfort and growth directly. When learners relate only marginally to educational environments, we tend to change the environments and reestablish the "norms of comfort." In fact, the discomfort they feel may be a clue to how we should behave to help them reach new plateaus of growth.

Marginality is a condition that exists when a learner has difficulty relating to an educational environment and profiting from it. Learners may relate marginally to some environments but not others. The theoretically possible range of marginality is from *none* (when learners relate productively to all the environments to which they are exposed) to *all* (when learners experience virtually no environments that are productive for them). Educators create environments, but they clearly cannot do the learning—which is why the condition of the learner accounts for so much of the variance when we consider the productivity of any given environment. If the learner is marginal with respect to a particular environment, educational productivity for that learner is likely to be depressed; worse, if the marginality is acute, serious side effects are likely to occur. The learner becomes frustrated and, very likely, "learns" that he or she cannot be productive in that environment. If the learner generalizes from enough frustrating experiences, a likely derivative lesson may be that the process of education is hopeless (from the perspective of that particular person).

Assumptions about Learners

How do we think about our students? We think about them from a variety of perspectives, each of which gives us assumptions about what they are like.

Enculturation

Assumption: our learner has been enculturated to a certain degree, having been exposed to the behavior patterns, artifacts, and cognitions that make up U.S. culture. The learner may (or may not) have a smaller vocabulary than the average person but does possess a vocabulary, has internalized the basic linguistic properties of our language, has been a participant in the cultural process, and has been an observer of adults as they behave in our society. In other words, our learner is not culturally different from the rest of us, although, within the cultural boundaries, the learner may be relatively unsophisticated. This may seem like an obvious point, but much language about marginal learners connotes, if it does not actually denote, that the people who relate marginally to the common educational environments are essentially members of a subculture so different from the mainstream that they have to be treated as foreigners. That is rare indeed. Human beings are born with the capacity to learn a culture, and it is the rare person who develops cultural patterns that do not in some way match the major configurations of his or her society.

Intellectual Capacity

The position about intellectual differences articulated by Carroll (1977) and Bloom (1971) has considerable validity. Specifically, this position is that differences in intellectual ability as we currently measure them translate substantially into temporal differences with respect to the mastery of particular learning objectives. This second assumption relates to the first; one way of restating Carroll and Bloom's position is that the "less intelligent" learner is not culturally different with respect to what can be learned, but may require more time, perhaps *considerably* more time, to acquire a particular cognition. In other words, the learner is one of us. Some of us are slower than others to acquire some of the elements of the culture in given educational situations. We can make the optimistic assumption that our marginal learner is capable of learning but may require more time than some people do, given the situation.

Stigmatization

A third assumption is that the inability to relate to a given educational environment productively has social stigma attached to it. The learner who does not fit in will be socially stigmatized by other people and, probably more damaging, will internalize the norms of the culture; failing to fit in with these norms, the learner will stigmatize himself or herself. Education, as manifested in formal institutions, is largely a public activity, and the full power of the society comes down on the learner when a marginal condition exists—hence, the latent side effects. The marginal learner is punished twice, first by being frustrated and second by being stigmatized by others (or by self-stigmatization).

Flexibility

An important assumption about learners is that people are flexible. They are not fixed. They are growing entities and have considerable adaptive capabilities. Nearly all learners have the potential to relate to a wide variety of learning environments, provided they are not made *too* uncomfortable and that they are assisted in relating productively to any given environment.

Assumptions about Learning Environments

Learning environments, viewed from a cultural perspective, are variations on a basic cultural theme that has its origins in Western societies. Put another way, all our models of teaching represent variety within the culture, but they are not culturally different. They have originated with scholars and teachers who belong not only to the same genus and species but to the same normative configuration. Thus, both teaching models and learners have the same cultural roots. That said, every learning environment produces a range of responses by students. No learning environment will produce exactly the same effects on all students.

Learning environments can be adaptive if we design them to respond to differences in learners. A model of teaching should not simply bore into the learner in an unyielding and unforgiving fashion. Properly constructed, a learning environment fits soft rather than hard metaphors. It curls around the students, conforming to their characteristics just as, properly treated, learners also curl around the features of the learning environment.

Alternative Environments and Educational Outcomes

Certain approaches to teaching increase the probability that certain kinds of learning outcomes will eventuate and decrease the probability that others will happen. For example, contrast the role-playing model with the inquiry training model. The Shaftels' model of role playing (Shaftel & Shaftel, 1967) is designed to enable students to examine their values. Suchman's (1981) model of inquiry training is designed to increase the probability that students will build capability to make causal inferences. As such, all things being equal, if the Shaftels' model is used to design a learning environment, it will increase the probability that students' social values will be made available to them. Suchman's model will increase the probability that the students will become more able to reason causally. We are not dealing with an orthogonal world, however. The examination of values *can* improve causal reasoning, and, vigorously conducted, *ought* to do so. Similarly, there is no law that dictates that Suchman's model cannot be used to increase the ability to reason causally about values. At any given moment it is conceivable that the Shaftels' model might be more effective in teaching causal reasoning than Suchman's or that Suchman's might be more effective as an approach to social values. Over the long term, however, each model is more likely to pay off in the direction for which it was designed. Thus, it is wise for educators to have in their repertoires the models of choice for given categories of learning objectives.

Solutions for Correcting Marginality

Returning now to marginal learners, our problem is to consider what to do when a learner has a marginal reaction to any given learning environment. To keep the discussion within boundaries, let us imagine two learners who are exposed to the previous two models. Each learner responds positively to one environment and not to the other. What do we do?

In this example, each learner is marginal in one environment but not in the other. We can predict that one will engage in the study of values in a relatively comfortable way and that the other will increase the capability to engage in causal reasoning. If we do nothing, the differences between the two learners will probably increase. One will get better and better at the study of values and the other better and better in reasoning ability. For the time being, let us put aside the question of explanation—that is, let us not begin by sorting out the reasons *why* each learner responds to one environment and not to the other; instead, let us concentrate on what we can do.

First, we reject a "do-nothing" approach. We do not want to leave either of our learners in an unproductive, frustrating, and perhaps phobia-producing situation. We also reject removing the learner from the offending environment, thus eliminating the frustration. For each learner we eliminate the models of discomfort and identify the ones of greatest comfort. On the positive side, enough models of teaching exist that we can be relatively sure that almost any learner can relate productively to some of them. In our example we already have an initial diagnosis.

The Industrial Solution

In what Hunt (1971) calls the *industrial solution,* we search for the approaches to teaching in which our learners are least marginal, and then we employ them. This approach makes a certain amount of pragmatic sense. Its obvious difficulty is that for certain learners, it eliminates the instructional models of choice for the achievement of various kinds of objectives. Consider the case of our two learners. Because the Shaftels' model is elegantly constructed to promote the study of values, eliminating it for the learner who is marginal in it means that we are going to have to use a model less elegantly appropriate for the study of values. For any given learner that might be only a moderate loss of efficiency, but if we consider large numbers of learners over a long period of time, the industrial solution has a built-in deficit.

However, this is certainly a more efficient solution than ignoring the problem. It also reduces the likelihood that the most damaging side effects of mismatching will occur. The success of the industrial model depends on the assumption that we can find enough industrial models that accommodate both our students and our objectives.

Adaptation of the Models of Choice

Another solution is to adapt the models to conform to the characteristics of the learners. We identify the reasons why a given learner has trouble relating to a particular learning environment and then modulate the features of that environment to make it easier for the learner to fit in. For example, suppose that we are using inquiry training in elementary science. It is possible that our learner who is not comfortable with the model may be reacting to the ambiguity of inductive reasoning. Our learner may like a direct route to the correct answer and may be uncomfortable asking questions that may be wrong and that do not provide quick resolution. We could moderate the task complexity of the inquiry training exercises by providing puzzles for which there are plainly only two or three possible avenues of inquiry and to which the learner can bring considerable knowledge.

Our learner who has trouble relating to role playing may be somewhat embarrassed during the enactments of the puzzling situations, may have difficulty taking the role of the "other," or may find the discussion of values to be uncomfortable. To compensate, we can guide the enactments to make them relatively simple and straightforward, or we can provide practice in the skills necessary to analyze values.

Hunt (1971) has pointed out that if we "drill a model through" the learner we exacerbate our problem. If we take the trouble to find out what is bothering the learner, we have many options for modifying the environment. We can increase the structure of unstructured models, decrease the structure of highly structured ones, modulate the degree of learner control, manipulate task complexity, and in other ways make the learning environment safe for the person who would otherwise be marginal in it.

The merits of this solution are that it permits us to continue to use the "models of choice" for given objectives—that is, the models likely to produce certain kinds of learning—and that it reduces the likelihood that the student will be acutely uncomfortable. It depends on the assumption that the natural mismatch between the learner and the model is not too great to overcome. Because learners are members of the same culture from which the models of teaching came, we can have some confidence that they will bring some developed tools to the environment. Relatively few learners lack the capacity to function within a fairly wide range of models.

Much research is needed in this area. We need to study how to adapt a wide spectrum of models to learners who, on first contact with the models, display varying degrees of marginality. Without such knowledge, we are left with uncertainty about how far we can go. One of the major findings of the match–mismatch studies mentioned earlier was the extent to which the students exerted modifying influences on the environment. Students who needed more structure asked more questions about procedures and literally forced instructors to provide them with more explicit information about what they were doing, even in the open-ended models. They required teachers to interrupt themselves periodically and to reexplain what was going on. They made teachers break up the model into bite-sized chunks that better fit their intellectual mouths. Other learners vied for control of the procedures, lowering the degree of imposed structure and actually increasing the amount of ambiguity in task complexity. I was the teacher in some of these studies, and I came away from that work with the feeling that many learners will help us out if we let them. They would like to have a productive learning environment and will work with us to adapt the environment if we will give them the opportunity.

Learner Flexibility Training

A third solution for correcting marginality is to attempt to teach the learners to relate to a wide spectrum of learning environments. Maintaining our earlier example, we teach one learner the skills necessary to relate to inquiry training. Again, Hunt's (1971) experiments with direct model-relevant skills training have contributed significantly to our knowledge in this area. To provide skill training requires diagnosing what it is about the learner that makes for a marginal relationship to the instructional model. This training is provided to help that learner become more powerful in that kind of environment. Some of the recent studies in teacher training are instructive on this point. The more a model is different from a teacher's developed and customary style, the more uncomfortable they are when beginning to use it. Practice with the model combined with model-relevant skill training appears to make a difference. As we coach teachers who are trying to learn a new model, they identify the particular areas where they are having difficulty and we provide direct training adapted to their particular learning problems (Showers, 1982a).

We need to learn much about helping learners develop environment-relevant skills. It is interesting to observe students in schools that have distinctive approaches to learning and that pay attention to helping their learners become effective in the environments they are creating. Schools that emphasize self-directed activity need to teach students how to engage in self-direction. Learning laboratories with highly sequenced activities need to help students learn to receive diagnoses and prescriptions and relate to those highly sequenced activities. Again, some of my own clinical experience is relevant. When I was the director of the laboratory at Teachers College, Columbia University, we built a set of learning centers that operated on very different models, and the students contracted for activities within those centers. We became convinced that nearly all of our learners were increasing their capabilities to learn in a variety of ways and that they adapted their learning styles to the requirements of the different centers to which they were exposed (Joyce & Clift, 1983).

If we take the skill-training approach seriously, then we devote substantial energy to teaching students to relate to an appropriate variety of learning environments. We help them master the skills of learning that will enable them to master facts, concepts, and skills, and to solve problems collectively. We include the skills of learning as basic skills in the curriculum, and we measure our success as teachers partly by our abilities to help students become more effective as learners.

From this perspective, we see individual differences in relating to learning environments in a fresh light. When a learner is uncomfortable with a particular learning environment, we know we have identified an objective—to help the learner become competent in relating to that environment. Rather than giving up, we proceed to give that learner protected practice and the special help necessary for a productive relationship to develop between learner and environment. Thus, our learner who has trouble relating to role playing is not viewed as being immutably unable to study values using that technique, but as someone who, through practice, can develop competence.

We also modify pace, using Carroll's (1971) and Bloom's (1971) formulations as a heuristic. We assume that all learners can become able to profit from a variety of environments but that some need more time than others to become productive in specific environments. One reason learners become marginal is because they are asked to work at a faster pace than will permit them mastery of the environment. Even though most of the applications of mastery learning have been within the basic skill areas of the elementary school, we suggest that the principles would apply to the ability to master all manner of learning objectives. Hence, some learners will be slower profiting from a Rogerian environment. Others will be slower working their way through the models that are appropriate to divergent thinking. Others will be slower attaining concepts with the models appropriate to concept learning.

There are no special models for marginal learners. All learners are part of this culture and practically all can learn to relate to a considerable array of environments, provided that the environments are adapted to the learners' characteristics and that we pay attention to teaching them how to learn more effectively.

Experience with persons with severe sensory handicaps provides us with a case in point. From a models of teaching point of view, there are no special models for the blind or the deaf. They can learn to relate to a great variety of environments and, more important, profit from them. To fail to help them do this productively is to deny them opportunities for growth in many areas. Learning to relate to an increasing variety of environments is, in itself, growth. That kind of growth leads to a pyramiding array of possibilities for more learning.

THE INTELLIGENCE OF GROWTH

Our nature as learners contains an interesting contradiction: important growth requires change. We have to give up our comfortable ways of thinking and survive the buffeting involved in taking on unfamiliar ideas, skills, and values. The need to grow is built into the fiber of our being. We are impelled upward in a developmental sense. Paradoxically, however, we have an ingrained tendency to conserve our beings as they are or were. Nostalgia is, in fact, a yearning not to have grown or changed. We would like to go on and see things the way we could when we were young and untutored. Curiously, the answer is to produce disequilibrium—to create environments that impel us to change, not discarding what we were at any given stage, but learning to build on it productively. Thelen's advice to us is correct: the learner needs to confront problems and diverse opinions in order to reach beyond the present stage and develop the constructs that will sustain growth at another level.

When we are infants, the process of change is built into us. We do not intend to learn language, but we do, and in so doing we change. We do not expect to walk, but walking leads us where we could not go before. Not very many years later we learn our culture and begin to function at a level so satisfying that we can stay there forever. The purpose of education is to generate the conditions that will enable us to acknowledge the disequilibrium of change as a prerequisite to growth, so that we can reach beyond ourselves toward richer understanding and accept the wisdom that lies within ourselves—that discomfort is our lot if we are not to be arrested along our road to develop ourselves.

Emily Calhoun and I have developed a curriculum for "overage beginning readers," students from grades 4 to 12 who are struggling readers. About half of them are diagnosed as having learning disabilities. We have called this curriculum "A Second Chance to Learn to Read"; other school districts have called it "Read to Succeed," a term invented by the Northern Lights School District in Alberta (see Joyce, Hrycauk, Calhoun, & Hrycauk, 2006). Second Chance is a multiple-dimensioned approach that teaches students to develop sight vocabulary, inquire into the structure of words, read extensively, and write to learn to read. Prior to engagement with Second Chance, the students' average Grade Level Equivalent (GLE) gain in their history is about 0.5. After a year, the average gains for "regular" struggling readers and those with learning disabilities is about 2.0 GLE in both categories. These preadolescent and adolescent failing students are being brought into a new and optimistic world of achievement. Again, our curriculum has to give these students experiences that they will, in the beginning, find uncomfortable. But they have to overcome that discomfort or they will continue to use dysfunctional learning strategies.

If we ourselves are to grow we must learn that if we continuously use the same designs, our findings will not grow.

We are drawn to the perspective of Abraham Kaplan (1964) whose studies of the methodology of the behavioral sciences cover all the related disciplines and subdisciplines. As he introduces his inquiry, he comments:

> This book will contain no definition of "scientific method," whether for the study of man or for any other science . . . because I believe there is no one thing to be defined. . . . One could as well speak of "the method" for baseball. There are ways of pitching, hitting, and running bases; ways of fielding; managerial strategies for pinch hitters and relief pitchers; ways of signaling, coaching, and maintaining team spirit. All of these, and more besides, enter into playing the game well, and each of them has an indefinite number of variants. We could say, of course, that there is only one way to play: to score runs if you are batting, and to prevent them if you are not. And this statement would be about as helpful as any general and abstract definition of "scientific method." . . . If we are to do justice to complexity, I think it is hard to improve on P. W. Bridgman's remark that "the scientist has no other method than doing his damnedest." (Kaplan, 1964 p. 27)

Appendix

Peer Coaching Guides

The following pages contain peer coaching guides for use by pairs of teachers and by individual teachers as they inquire into models of teaching. These forms facilitate planning and communication between members of peer coaching groups who observe one another and try to profit from the observational experience. (For information about the peer coaching process and purpose, please consult Joyce and Calhoun, 2010.) The forms can also be used to facilitate sharing of ideas by study group members, regardless of whether observation of one another's teaching occurs.

Thus, they are addressed to both parties in the peer coaching process: the teacher who is planning and directing the teaching episode and the partner who is studying the model and helping both partners understand student responses. Both parties are involved in a continuing experiment on teaching. Each has the same purpose, which is to increase his or her ability to analyze the transactions between teacher and student and the ability to teach students how to learn information and concepts.

The guide is used to generate a productive interchange between peer coaching teams (usually two persons) over a specific teaching episode (about an hour) with one planning and leading the teaching and the other observing and studying the students' responses to the phases of the model. We refer to one member of the team as the teacher and the other as the observer.

The guide is used both to assist the planning of the teaching episode and to focus the observation on student response to the key features of the model. The teacher prepares the observer by filling out the entries in the guide that are intended to make the planning clear. The observer fills in the observation checklist and discusses the result with the teacher. Both parties will profit most by making a partnership that studies the student responses and plans how to help the students learn more effectively. The observer is present NOT to advise the one who is teaching on how to teach better (both are novices with the model they are learning), but rather to learn by observing and to help their partner by providing information about the students' responses.

When planning a session or lesson, skip through the guide to the entries marked "Tasks for the Teacher" and fill them in as needed. They will guide you through the model. Observers can use the guide to familiarize themselves with the plans of the teacher and to make notes about what is observed. Please remember, observers, that your primary function is not to give expert advice to your colleague, but to observe the students as requested by the teacher and to observe the whole process so that you can gain ideas for your own teaching. The teacher is the coach in the sense that he or she is demonstrating a teaching episode for you. When you teach and are observed, you become the coach.

Peer Coaching Guide:
Advance Organizer

Before beginning a lesson, the teacher discusses what the observer might concentrate on. These are prompts for the observation, which leads to a discussion. Both parties are watching the students respond, which will be the focus of the discussion.

The Teaching Process

Most teaching episodes have both content and process objectives. The content objectives include the information, concepts, theories, ways of thinking, values, and other substance that the students can be expected to learn from the experience. The process objectives are the ways of learning—the conduct of the social and intellectual tasks that increase the power to learn. In the case of a model of teaching, the process objectives are those that enable the students to engage effectively in the tasks presented when the model is being used.

Tasks for the Teacher

Do you want to suggest a focus for the observer?

Content Objectives

Please tell the observer the concepts and information that are the primary objectives of this teaching episode. What kind of information will be presented to the student? What concepts will be presented to organize the information? Are the concepts or information new to the students?

_____

_____

_____

_____

_____

Process Objectives

Please let the observer know any process objectives that are of concern during this episode. For example, are you trying to help the students learn how to comprehend and use organizers, how to relate material to the conceptual structure, how to tie new material to the organizers, or how to apply what is learned to new information and skills?

_____

_____

_____

_____

_____

Phase One: Presentation of the Organizer

The key aspect of this model is the use of organizing ideas to induce students to operate conceptually on the material they are trying to master. The teacher organizes the material with an intellectual scaffolding of concepts and presents those concepts to the students so that they can relate the new information to it—or reorganize familiar information within a more powerful conceptual framework. Although even the careful organization of information under a series of topics facilitates learning, we attempt to formulate organizing concepts that are at a higher conceptual level, so that students can process the information beyond associating it with a topic and think about the material at a more complex level than they would spontaneously.

Please describe the organizer (or system of organizers) and discuss how it will help the student conceptualize the material. How will you present the organizer(s)?

_____

_____

_____

_____

_____

Phase Two: Presenting Information

The purpose of the model, of course, is to facilitate the learning of material at any level of abstraction: data, concepts, theories, systems of thought—all the possibilities are there. The device is to place the student in the role of active receiver, getting information by reading, watching, or scrabbling around for information from formal resources or the environment. The information can be presented through readings, lectures, films or tapes, or any other mediated form or combination of forms.

Please describe the content that will be presented and how it will be presented. Emphasize the content you most want to be retained and how you want it to be applied in the future.

_____

_____

_____

_____

_____

Phase Three: Connecting the Organizer to the Presentation

The conceptual structure defined by organizers needs to be integrated with the information that has been presented and also reconciled with the students' personal intellectual structures. Though the students, with practice, will accomplish most of these tasks by themselves, it is wise to provide activities that make the relationship between concepts and material explicit and that provide the students with an opportunity to reflect on the organizing structure. For example, we can illustrate the connection between one of the organizers and some aspect of the information and induce the students to suggest further associations and relationships, or we can ask the students to reformulate the organizers in their own terms and indicate relationships between them and aspects of the material.

How will you make a presentation or provide a task to increase the possibility of integrating the organizing structure with the students' conceptual structure as well as connecting the organizer and the material that has been presented?

Phase Four: Application

Sometimes information is presented to students as a precursor to learning a skill (we may teach musical notation to facilitate learning to sing) and sometimes to assist in solving problems (knowledge of mechanics may be applied to problems requiring leverage). We also apply what is learned in subsequent learning tasks (the general concept of equation is useful in mastering many mathematical topics).

Do you wish to provide an explicit application task at this point? If so, please describe it briefly.

_____

_____

_____

_____

_____

Finally, do you want to suggest a focus for the observer? If so, what is it?

_____

_____

_____

_____

_____

Now, after the observation, let's think about the observer's analysis of the episode.

Tasks for the Observer

Phase One: Presentation of the Organizer

First, please make a general comment about the students' response to the organizer(s). Did they appear to absorb it? Did they appear to understand how organizers are to function and that their task is to learn new material and relate it to the organizer(s)?

_____

_____

_____

_____

_____

Phase Two: Presenting Information

Please comment on the student responses. Are the students clear about what they are to learn? Is it clear to you (thinking from the point of view of the students) how the organizer(s) may function in relation to the material?

_____

_____

_____

_____

_____

Phase Three: Connecting the Organizer to the Presentation

Please comment on this phase. Do the students appear to be clear about the organizing structure and its relation to the material to be learned?

_____

_____

_____

_____

_____

Phase Four: Application

If an application task is presented, please comment on the students' ability to make the transfer to the new material.

_____

_____

_____

_____

_____

Post-Observation Discussion

In most partnerships, leadership is shared. Sometimes the teacher has important issues to explore and those dominate the discussion. Sometimes some aspect of the students' responses catch the attention of the observer. Sometimes the discussion ends with the beginning of planning for the next episode. However, the discussion should not be endless. Twenty minutes is usually sufficient for an adequate debriefing.

Peer Coaching Guide:
Cooperative Learning Organization

Unlike the other guides in this series, this form to assist in the planning and observation of teaching is not built around a specific model of teaching. Thus, it does not deal with the specific cooperative learning strategies developed by Robert Slavin (1983) or David Johnson and Roger Johnson (2009), although the philosophy of the approach is similar, nor does it deal with group investigation (Sharan & Hertz-Lazarowitz, 1980b; Thelen, 1960), the major democratic-process strategy that is covered in another guide. But it is true to their spirit.

The focus is on setting up a cooperative organization within which the specific models can be used. The substance is the organization of students into study groups and partnerships. Those groups can study a substantive area using, for example, an inductive learning model (as in Chapter 3). Thus, the cooperative learning organization in the classroom or other instructional venue provides a setting for cooperative study that can be employed in combination with many approaches to teaching.

The guide describes some options and asks the teacher to select from them or to generate others. The observer analyzes the students' productivity and attempts to identify ways of helping the students engage in more productive behavior. The examples provided below are in reference to the inductive model of teaching. Using the two guides simultaneously may be useful.

When other models are used, analogous use can be made of cooperative learning.

Organizing Partners and Teams

Essentially, we want to organize the students so that everyone in the class has a partner with whom he or she can work on instructional tasks. For example, pairs of students can operate throughout the inductive model, collecting information, developing categories, and making inferences about causal relationships. The partnerships (which need not be long-term, although they can be) are collected into teams. For example, if there are 28 students in the class, there can be seven teams of four. We do not recommend teams larger than four. These teams can also operate using the inductive model, collecting and organizing data and making inferences. The partnerships provide an easy organization through which teams can divide labor. For example, each partnership can collect information from certain sources and then the information can be accumulated into a data set for the team. Similarly, team sets can be accumulated into a class set of data. Teams can then operate on these data sets and compare and contrast the results with those of other teams.

Team membership and partnerships can be organized in a number of ways, ranging from student selection, random selection, or teacher-guided choices to maximize heterogeneity and potential synergy.

Instruction of teams can range from explicit procedures to guide them through the learning activities to general procedures that leave much of the organization to the students. As in the other guides, the teacher gives the observer information about plans.

Tasks for the Teacher

Do you want to suggest a focus for the observer?

How will you organize the class for this teaching episode? How many groups of what sizes will be selected?

_____
_____
_____
_____
_____

How will memberships be determined?

_____
_____
_____
_____
_____

What approach to teaching/learning will be used? If you are not using a specific model of teaching, what will be your instructional strategy?

_____
_____
_____
_____
_____

How will cooperative groups be used throughout the teaching episode? What cooperative tasks will be given to pairs, study groups, or the whole class? For example, if this were an inductive lesson, partnerships might collect data, classify it, and make inferences. Or, partners might collect data, but it might be assembled by the entire class prior to the classification activity. Partners might study words, poems, maps, number facts and operations, or other material. What is your plan?

_____
_____
_____
_____
_____

And, before the observation, do you want to suggest a focus for the observer? If so, what is it?

_____

_____

_____

_____

_____

Tasks for the Observer

After you have familiarized yourself with the plan, situate yourself in the room so that you can observe several students closely. Throughout the teaching episode, concentrate on the behavior of those students, whether they are working in partnerships, study groups, or any other organization. Then comment on their performance.

_____

_____

_____

_____

_____

Did they appear to be clear about the tasks they were to accomplish? If not, can you identify what they were not clear about?

_____

_____

_____

_____

Did they appear to know how to cooperate to accomplish the tasks assigned to them? Is there anything they need to know in order to be more productive?

_____

_____

_____

_____

Do they regulate their own behavior, keeping on task, dividing labor, and taking turns? Could they profit from having any aspect of group management modeled for them?

_____

_____

_____

_____

What sort of leadership patterns did they employ? Did they acknowledge one or more leaders? Did they discuss process? Were they respectful to one another?

_____

_____

_____

_____

_____

Post-Observation Discussion

Following the episode, discuss the operation of the cooperative groups that the observer was close to. Is their productivity satisfactory? Their relationships? If not, see whether you can develop a plan for helping the students become more productive. Remember that:

1. Providing practice is the simplest and most powerful way to help students learn to work productively. This is especially true if they have not had much experience working in cooperative groups.
2. The smaller the group, the more easily students can regulate their own behavior. Reducing the size of study groups often allows students to solve their own problems. (This is also true for adults—peer coaching groups of two are more productive than larger groups; groups larger than seven usually can't get anything done.)
3. Demonstration gets more mileage than exhortation. A teacher can join a group and show the students how to work together. In fact, the observer can be a participant in a study group in future sessions.
4. Simpler tasks are easier for students to manage. Breaking complex tasks into several smaller ones often allows students to build their skills through practice.
5. Praising appropriate behavior gets results. If two groups are performing at different levels, it often helps to praise the productive group and then quietly join the less productive one and provide leadership.

Peer Coaching Guide:
Synectics

This guide begins with tasks for the teacher, who is orienting the observer about the lesson. The next section is a guide for the observer of the teaching/learning episode. After the episode, the partners meet to discuss the lesson, particularly the responses of the students to the phases of the model.

The Teaching Process

Most teaching episodes have both content and process objectives. Content objectives include the substance (information, concepts, generalizations, relationships, skills) to be mastered by students. Process objectives include skills or procedures the students need in order to learn productively from the cognitive and social tasks of the model.

Tasks for the Teacher

Do you want to suggest a focus for the observer?

Content Objectives

Please state the content objectives of the episode. What kind of learning will come from the activity? What is the nature of the area to be explored?

_____

_____

_____

_____

_____

Process Objectives

Are the students familiar with the model? Is there some aspect of its process where they need practice or instruction, and will you be concentrating on it in this lesson?

_____

_____

_____

_____

_____

Phase One: The Original Product

Commonly, synectics is used to generate fresh perspectives on a topic or problem, either for clarification or to permit alternative conceptions or solutions to be explored. Thus it generally begins by soliciting from students a product representing their current thinking. They can formulate the problem, speak or write about the topic, enact a problem, draw a representation of a relationship—there are many alternatives. The function of this phase is to enable them to capture their current thoughts about the subject at hand. Please describe how you will elicit the students' conceptions of the area to be explored. What will you say or do to orient them?

_____

_____

_____

_____

_____

Phase Two: Direct and Personal Analogies

The core of the model requires the development of distance from the original product through exercises inducing the students to make comparisons between sets of stimuli that are presented to them (direct analogy exercises) and to place themselves, symbolically, in the position of various persons, places, and things (personal analogy exercises). The analogy material generated in these exercises will be used later in the creation of further analogies called *compressed conflicts.*

What stimuli will you use to induce the students to make the direct and personal analogies? Please describe the material and the order in which you will proceed to stretch the students toward more unusual and surprising comparisons.

_____

_____

_____

_____

_____

Phase Three: Compressed Conflicts and Oxymoronic Analogies

The next task is to induce the students to operate on the material generated in phase two and create compressed conflicts. You need to be prepared to define compressed conflict, even if the students have familiarity with the model, and to continue eliciting material until a number of examples clearly contain the logical tension that characterizes a high-quality oxymoron.

Please describe how you will initiate phase three and how you will explain compressed conflict if you need to.

_____

_____

_____

_____

_____

Now we ask the students to select some compressed conflict pairs that manifest great tension and to generate some analogies that represent the tension. For example, we might ask them to provide some examples of "exquisite torture."

Please describe briefly how you will present these tasks to the students.

_____
_____
_____
_____
_____

Phase Four: Generating New Products

The compressed conflicts and the analogies to them provide material from which to revisit the original problem or topic. Sometimes we select or have the students select just one analogy with which to revisit the original material. At other times multiple perspectives are useful. What course to take depends on a combination of the complexity of the original problem or concept and the students' ability to handle new perspectives. For example, if a secondary social studies class has been trying to formulate potential solutions to a problem in international relations, we are dealing with a very complex problem for which multiple analogies are probably both appropriate and necessary. The task of helping the students share and assess a variety of analogies that can be used to redefine the problem and generate alternative solutions is complex, indeed.

Please describe how you will present the task of revisiting the original product. What will you ask the students to do?

_____
_____
_____
_____
_____

Now the new product needs to be examined. If the students worked as individuals or subgroups, the separate products need to be shared. If a problem is to be solved, new definitions and solutions need to be arranged. If written expression emerged, possibly it needs further editing. Unless the teaching episode is the conclusion of a topic of study, it generally leads to further study.

Please describe how products of the synectics exercises are to be shared and used. Will they lead to further reading and writing, data collection, or experimentation?

_____
_____
_____
_____
_____

Finally, do you want to suggest a focus for the observer? If so, what is it?

_____

_____

_____

_____

_____

_____

Tasks for the Observer

Phase One: The Original Product

Please comment on the students' response to the originating task. What is the nature of their conceptions?

_____

_____

_____

_____

_____

Phase Two: Direct and Personal Analogies

Please comment on the stimuli and the student responses. Did the students get "up in the air" metaphorically and generate less literal and more analogistic comparisons?

_____

_____

_____

_____

_____

Phase Three: Compressed Conflicts and Oxymoronic Analogies

Please discuss the students' understanding of the concept of *compressed conflict* and their ability to select the higher-quality examples. Also, comment on the product of their attempt to generate oxymoronic analogies.

_____

_____

_____

_____

Phase Four: Generating New Products

Please comment on the students' products. What do you think has been the effect of the metaphoric exercises?

_____

_____

_____

_____

_____

Next, comment on the use of the new products. Are the students able to see the effects of the metaphoric activity? If they are asked to participate in further activities or to generate them, are they bringing to those tasks a "set" toward the development of alternative perspectives or avenues?

_____

_____

_____

_____

_____

Comments on Student Training Needs

It is the student who does the learning, and the greater the skill of the student in responding to the cognitive and social tasks of the model, the greater the learning is likely to be. Practice alone will build skill, and we want to provide plenty of it. After students are thoroughly familiar with the structure of the model, we can begin to develop specific training to improve their ability to perform.

Please comment on the skills with which the students engaged in the activities and suggest any areas where you believe training might be useful. Think especially of their ability to make comparisons, their ability to take the roles required to make personal analogies, and their understanding of the structure of compressed conflicts and how to use them. Thinking back on the entire experience, is there any area where specific process training should be considered?

_____

_____

_____

_____

_____

Post-Observation Discussion

Have a good discussion—and discuss where both of you will go next with this model and the unit you are currently teaching.

Good luck!

Peer Coaching Guide:
Concept Attainment

The guide is designed to assist peer coaching partners as they work to master the concept attainment model.

The Teaching Process

Most lessons have both content and process objectives. Content objectives identify subject matter (facts, concepts, generalizations, relationships) to be mastered by students, whereas process objectives specify skills and procedures students need in order to achieve content objectives or auxiliary social objectives (e.g., cooperation in a learning task).

Tasks for the Teacher

Do you want to suggest a focus for the observer?

Content Objectives

Please let the observer know the concept that is the objective of the lesson. What are its defining attributes? What kind of data will be presented to the students? Is the information or concept new to the students?

_____

_____

_____

_____

_____

Process Objectives

Are the students familiar with the model? Do they need special assistance or training with respect to any aspect of the process?

_____

_____

_____

_____

Phase One: Focus

The focus defines the field of search for the students. It may eliminate irrelevant lines of inquiry. Often it is pitched at a level of abstraction just above the exemplars (e.g., "a literary device" might serve as a focus for the concept of metaphor). Formulating the focus is not easy. You do not want to state the concept or a name for it. But the students need some help as they focus on the exemplars. Please write the focus statement here.

_____

_____

_____

_____

Phase Two: Presenting the Data Set

The data set should be planned in pairs of positive and negative exemplars, ordered to enable the students—by comparing the positive exemplars and contrasting them with the negative ones—to distinguish the defining attributes of the concept.

Please describe the nature of the exemplars. (Are they words, phrases, documents, etc.? For example: "These are reproductions of 19th-century paintings. Half of them are from the Impressionists [Renoir, Monet, Degas] and the other half are realistic, romantic, or abstract paintings.")

_____

_____

_____

_____

As the students work through the data set, they are to examine each exemplar and develop hypotheses about the concept. They need to ask themselves what attributes the positive exemplars have in common. It is those attributes that define the concept. Please provide an example of what you will say as you present an examplar and label it.

_____

_____

_____

_____

Sometimes students are asked to record the progression of their thinking. Do you want to do this?

_____

_____

As the lesson progresses, we need to get information about whether the students are formulating and testing ideas. You need to ask them how they are doing without having them share their actual hypotheses. Please give an example of something you will say.

_____

_____

Phase Three: Sharing Thinking and Hypotheses

When it appears that the students have developed hypotheses that they are fairly sure of, they are asked to describe the progression of their thinking and the concept they have arrived at.

When to do this is a matter of judgment. How will you decide, and what will you say?

_____

_____

_____

_____

Phase Four: Naming and Applying the Concept

Once concepts have been agreed on (or different ones justified), they need names. After students have generated names, the teacher may need to supply the technical or common term (e.g., "We call this style *Impressionism*"). Application requires that students determine whether further exemplars fit the concept and, perhaps, find examples of their own.

An assignment to follow the lesson often involves the application of the concept to fresh material. For example, if the concept of metaphor had been introduced, the students might be asked to read a literary passage and identify the uses of metaphor in it.

Are you planning such an assignment? If so, please describe it briefly.

_____

_____

_____

_____

Tasks for the Observer

Phase One: Focus

Did the teacher deliver the focus statement?

Yes [ ]   No [ ]

In your opinion, was it clear to the students and did it function to help them focus on the central content of the lesson?

Completely [ ]   Partially [ ]   No [ ]

Comments:

_____

_____

_____

_____

How did the students respond to Phase One? Did students pay close attention to the focus statement and apply it to the examination of the exemplars? If not, is it worthwhile to give specific instruction? What might that be?

_____

_____

_____

_____

Phase Two: Presenting the Data Set

Did students compare and contrast the exemplars? Did they make hypotheses with the expectation that they might have to change them? Were they using the negative exemplars to eliminate alternatives? Is it worthwhile to provide specific training, and what might that be?

_____

_____

_____

_____

Phase Three: Sharing Thinking and Hypotheses

Were students able to debrief their thinking? Were they able to see how different lines of thinking gave similar or different results? Were they able to generate labels that express the concept? Do they understand how to seek exemplars on their own and apply what they have learned? Is it worthwhile to provide specific training, and what might that be?

_____

_____

_____

_____

Phase Four: Naming and Applying the Concept

Please discuss how well the students were able to name the concept—taking into account its attributes and how effectively they could make suggestions for its use.

_____

_____

_____

_____

Post-Observation Discussion

Teacher: Do you want to suggest a focus for the analysis? If so, what is it?

_____

_____

_____

_____

_____

As the discussion proceeds, process needs by the students is often a topic. When it comes up, we need to consider that, in order to improve student performance, the first option we explore is whether it will improve with practice. That is, simple repetition of the model gives the students a chance to learn to respond more appropriately. Second, we directly teach the students the skills they need to manage the cognitive and social tasks of the model. Much of your discussion might be about training needs and how to manage them.

Peer Coaching Guide:
Inquiry Training

Remembering that the episode will be followed by a discussion, we have tasks for the teacher as the lesson is planned. Then, as it takes place, the observer has tasks relating chiefly to the responses of the students to the various phases of the model.

The Teaching Process

Most lessons have both content and process objectives. Content objectives identify subject matter (facts, concepts, generalizations, relationships) to be mastered by students, whereas process objectives specify skills and procedures students need in order to achieve content objectives or auxiliary social objectives (e.g., cooperation in a learning task).

The content objectives for inquiry training reside in the information, concepts, and theories embedded in the problem or puzzling situation that is presented to the students. They have to discover the information, form the concepts, and develop the theories. The skills to do those things are the process objectives, as are the social skills of cooperative problem solving.

Tasks for the Teacher

Do you want to suggest a focus for the observer?

Content Objectives

What do you want students to gain from this task? What information, concepts, and theories do you wish them to learn?

_____

_____

_____

_____

_____

Process Objectives

Are the students familiar with the model? Do they need special assistance or training with respect to any aspect of the process? (For example, do they know how to obtain information through questioning? Can they work cooperatively with partners on a problem-solving task?)

_____

_____

_____

_____

Phase One: Encounter with the Problem

The primary activity of phase one of the inquiry training model is the presentation of the problem.

Please describe the problem to be used in this lesson and how you will present it.

_____

_____

_____

_____

Phase Two: Data Gathering and Verification

In this phase the students ask questions to gather information about the problem. As they begin, how well do you think they can distinguish between getting the facts straight and generating possible causal relations?

_____

_____

_____

_____

Phase Three: Experimentation

If the students do not do so spontaneously, the teacher will introduce this phase by instructing them to begin to develop causal hypotheses. Please provide an example of something you might say at this point.

_____

_____

_____

_____

Phase Four: Formulation of Likely Explanations

Now the students weigh the hypotheses and assess what the most likely explanations of the phenomena are. The teacher initiates the phase if this does not happen spontaneously. How might you do this?

_____

_____

_____

_____

Please rehearse how you will initiate the phase.

_____

_____

_____

_____

If students were successful in making inferences and conclusions about their data, the teacher may wish to push them a step further and ask them to predict consequences from their data by asking "What would happen if . . ." kinds of questions.

Please write one or two examples of hypothetical questions you might ask students about these data.

_____

_____

_____

_____

_____

Phase Five: Analysis of the Inquiry Process

In phase five the students are led to analyze their inquiry process and contemplate how to improve it. This activity provides the teacher with the opportunity to coach the students, explaining and even modeling how they can work together to collect and verify data, build concepts, and develop hypotheses and test them.

Tasks for the Observer

Phase One: Encounter with the Problem

Did the students understand the problem and find it puzzling? Were they able to ask questions to clarify it, and could they summarize it when asked to?

_____

_____

_____

_____

_____

Phase Two: Data Gathering and Verification

In your opinion, did the students understand the procedures they were to employ during this phase? Did they ask fact-oriented questions, and were they able to respond when the teacher modeled how to ask them? Could they distinguish between fact- and theory-oriented questions? How well could they "caucus" and summarize what they had learned and plan sets of questions to ask? Did they listen to each other?

_____

_____

_____

_____

_____

Phase Three: Experimentation

Please comment on the students' ability to organize the information and build hypotheses. Describe their social behavior as well as their ability to respond to the cognitive tasks.

_____

_____

_____

_____

Phase Four: Formulation of Likely Explanations

Discuss the students' response to this task. Were they able to state hypotheses clearly, summarize the evidence, and, where appropriate, weigh competing explanations?

_____

_____

_____

_____

Were students able to make logical predictions based on the foregoing categorization and discussion?

_____

_____

_____

For the whole episode, how did the students respond? What did they do most comfortably? Were there areas where they seemed stuck?

_____

_____

_____

_____

Post-Observation Discussion

Teacher: Do you want to suggest a focus for the discussion? If so, what is it?

_____

_____

_____

Observer: Please comment on the skills with which the students engaged in the activities and suggest any areas where you believe training might be useful.

Frequently the conversation returns, appropriately, to the issue of the skills of the students. In order to improve student performance, the first option we explore is whether it will improve with practice. That is, simple repetition of the model gives the students a chance to learn to respond more appropriately. Second, we directly teach the students the skills they need to manage the cognitive and social tasks of the model.

As the discussion ends, planning for the next episode is on the minds of the partners.

Peer Coaching Guide:
Assists to Memory

During the last 30 years there has been renewed research and development on strategies for assisting students to master and retain information. The science of mnemonics, as it is called, has produced some dramatic results (Pressley, Levin, & Delaney, 1982).

Rote repetition (rehearsing something over and over until it is retained) has until recently been the primary method taught to students for memorizing information and the primary method used by teachers as they interact with students. In fact, rote methods have become so used that they have become identified in many people's minds with the act of memorization. To memorize, it is often thought, is to repeat by rote.

Memorization Strategies

However, although rehearsal of material continues to be one aspect of most mnemonic strategies, a number of other procedures are employed that greatly increase the probability that material will be learned and retained. These procedures are combined in various ways, depending on the material to be learned. Most of the procedures help build associations between the new material and familiar material. Some of the procedures are shown below.

Organizing Information to Be Learned

Essentially, the more information is organized, the easier it is to learn and retain. Information can be organized by categories. The concept attainment, inductive, and advanced organizer models assist memory by helping students associate the material in the categories. Consider the following list of words from a popular spelling series, in the order the spelling book presents them to the children:

soft	plus	cloth	frost	song
trust	luck	club	sock	pop
cost	lot	son	won	

Suppose we ask the students to classify them by beginnings, endings, and the presence of vowels. The act of classification requires the students to scrutinize the words and associate words containing similar elements. They can then name the categories in each classification (the "c" group and the "st" group), calling further attention to the common attributes of the group. They can also connect words that fit together ("pop song," "soft cloth," etc.). They can then proceed to rehearse the spellings of one category at a time. The same principle operates over other types of material—say, number facts. Whether categories are provided to students or they create them, the purpose is the same. Also, information can be selected with categories in mind. The previous list is, to outward appearances, almost random. A list that deliberately and systematically provides variations would be easier to organize (it would already have at least implicit categories within it).

Ordering Information to Be Learned

Information learned in series, especially if there is meaning to the series, is easier to assimilate and retain. For example, if we wish to learn the names of the states of Australia it is easier if we always start with the same one (say, the largest) and proceed in the same order. Historical events by chronology are more easily learned than events sorted randomly. Order is simply another way of organizing information. We could have the students alphabetize their list of spelling words.

Linking Information to Familiar Sounds

Suppose we are learning the names of the states. We can connect "Georgia" to "George," "Louisiana" to "Louis," "Maryland" to "Mary," and so on. Categorizing the names of the states or ordering them by size or within region provides more associations.

Linking Information to Visual Representations

Maryland can be linked to a picture of a marriage, Oregon to a picture of a gun, Maine to a burst water main, and so forth. Letters and numerals can be linked to something that evokes both familiar sounds and images. For example, "one" can be linked to "bun" and a picture of a boy eating a bun, "b" to "bee" and a picture of a bee. Those links can be used over and over again. "April is the cruelest month, breeding lilacs out of the dead land" is more easily remembered thinking of an ominous metal spring, coiled malevolently over the spring flowers.

Linking Information to Associated Information

A person's name, linked to information such as a well-known person having the same name, a sound-alike, and some personal information, is easier to remember than the name rehearsed by itself. Louis (Louis Armstrong) "looms" over Jacksonville (his place of birth). Learning the states of Australia while thinking of the points of the compass and the British origins of many of the names (New South Wales) is easier than learning them in order alone.

Making the Information Vivid

Devices that make the information vivid are also useful. Lorayne and Lucas favor "ridiculous association," where information is linked to absurd associations. ("The silly two carries his twin two on his back so they are really four" and such.) Others favor the use of dramatization and vivid illustrations (such as counting the basketball players on two teams to illustrate that five and five equal 10).

Rehearsing

Rehearsal (practice) is always useful, and students benefit from knowledge of results. Students who have not had past success with tasks requiring memorization will benefit by having relatively short assignments and clear, timely feedback as they have success.

Tasks for the Teacher

Do you want to suggest a focus for the observer?

Planning with Memorization in Mind

The task of the teacher is to think up activities that help the students benefit from these principles. A teaching/learning episode that can be organized at least partly by these principles contains information to be learned. Both teacher and students should be clear that a very high degree of mastery is desired. (The students need to be trying to learn all the information and to retain it permanently.)

Please identify the information to be learned by your students in some curriculum area within a specified period of time.

_____

_____

_____

_____

Which principles will you emphasize in order to facilitate memorization?

_____

_____

_____

_____

Will these principles be used as the information is presented to the students? If yes, how?

_____

_____

_____

_____

How will rehearsal and feedback be managed?

_____

_____

_____

_____

Tasks for the Observer

During the teaching/learning episode, situate yourself so that you can observe the behavior of a small number of children (about a half-dozen). Concentrate on their response to the tasks that are given.

Comment on their response to the tasks. Do they appear to be clear about the objectives?

_____

_____

_____

Do they engage in the cognitive tasks that have been provided to them?

_____

_____

_____

Can they undertake these tasks successfully?

_____

_____

_____

Do they appear to be aware of progress?

_____

_____

_____

Post-Observation Discussion

The discussion should focus on how the students responded and ways of helping them respond more effectively.

Practice frequently enables students to respond more productively without further instruction. Where instruction is needed, demonstration is useful. That is, the teacher may lead the students through the tasks over small amounts of material.

Tasks can be simplified in order to bring them within the reach of the students. We want the students to develop a repertoire of techniques that enables them to apply the mnemonic principles to learning tasks. Making the process conscious is a step toward independence, so we seek ways of helping the students understand the nature of the tasks and why these should work for them.

Peer Coaching Guide:
Role Playing

The Teaching Process

Most lessons have both content and process objectives. Content objectives identify subject matter (facts, concepts, generalizations, relationships) to be mastered by students, whereas process objectives specify skills and procedures students need in order to achieve content objectives or auxiliary social objectives (e.g., cooperation in a learning task).

Tasks for the Teacher

Do you want to suggest a focus for the observer?

Content Objectives

What problem will be presented to the students, or in what domain will they construct a problem? Is the problem or domain of values new to the students?

Process Objectives

Are the students familiar with the model? Do they need special assistance or training with respect to any aspect of the process?

_____

_____

_____

Phase One: Warming Up

Role playing begins with a social problem. Often the problem is one in students' own interactions or interactions with others in their immediate situation, or the problem may be a real or student-generated human relations situation. Possibly the problem is one in their lives that simply needs exploration.

How will you present the problem to the students or help them develop it?

_____

_____

_____

Phase Two: Selecting the Participants

Please describe how the participants for the enactment (both role players and observers) will be selected.

_____

_____

_____

Phase Three: Creating the Line of Action for the First Enactment

How are you going to do this? Do you wish the first enactment to highlight certain aspects of values?

_____

_____

_____

Phase Four: Preparing the Observers

Once the characters have been identified and the story line generated, the observers are prepared.

What will you ask the observers to focus on?

_____

_____

_____

Phase Five: The Enactment

Now the students enact the problem for the first time.

Phase Six: Discussion

If necessary you may have to say something to get the ball rolling. What might you say?

_____

_____

_____

Phases Seven and Eight: Repeating the Enactment

From this point, phases five and six are repeated through several enactments. The teacher guides the students to ensure that the value questions are brought out.

Phase Nine: Analysis and Generalizations

When the teacher judges that sufficient material has been generated, a discussion is held (a cooperative learning format can be used for this phase to maximize participation, if desired) to ensure that the value positions are brought out and to put forth positions about what can be done to deal with the particular type of problem from a valuing basis rather than one of argumentation and conflict.

Please prepare the instructions you will give the students to inaugurate phase nine.

_____

_____

_____

_____

Tasks for the Observer

Phase One: Warming Up

In your opinion, was the problem clear to the students? Were they able to understand the nature of the problem and the type of human relations problem it represents? Could they identify the players in the situation and how they act? Can they see the several sides of the problem?

_____

_____

_____

_____

Phase Two: Selecting the Participants

How did the students respond to being selected? Did they seem ready and willing?

_____

_____

_____

_____

Phase Three: Creating a Line of Action for the First Enactment

Were the students able to generate a plausible and meaningful story line? Please note any difficulties they had.

_____

_____

_____

_____

Phase Four: Preparing the Observers

Did the observers appear to understand what they were to do? Did they seem to be prepared to focus on the enactment?

_____

_____

_____

_____

Phase Five: The Enactment

How well did the students enact the roles? Did they appear to empathize with the positions they were to take? Were the observers attentive and serious? Comment on any problems either role players or observers had.

_____

_____

_____

_____

Phase Six: Discussion

Were the students able to analyze the nature of the conflict and the values that were involved? Did they reveal their own value positions? Did they have any confusion about tactics of argumentation, skill, and values?

Phases Seven and Eight: Repeating the Enactment

Please comment on the student performance in the ensuing cycles of enactments and discussions. Did the students become increasingly able to distinguish value positions?

Phase Nine: Analysis and Generalizations

Please comment on the students' ability to handle the analysis of values that are central in phase nine.

Post-Observation Discussion

Following the teaching episode, the coaching partners might discuss ways of helping the students respond more effectively to the model. Remember that the early trials are bound to be awkward and that practice often does the trick. Also, problems can be adjusted to simplify the issues that have to be dealt with at any one time. Demonstrating the phases of the model to the students is also useful. The coaching partners can play the role of observer or even role player to give the students a model, or the two teachers can demonstrate together.

Please summarize the results of the discussion—the one or two chief conclusions you have reached to guide what you will next do as you use the model.

Peer Coaching Guide:
Inductive Thinking

The Teaching Process

Most lessons have both content and process objectives. Content objectives identify subject matter (facts, concepts, generalizations, relationships) to be mastered by students, whereas process objectives specify skills and procedures students need in order to achieve content objectives or auxiliary social objectives (e.g., cooperation in a learning task).

The content objectives for inductive thinking reside in the information and concepts embedded in a data set. Students categorize items in the data set by attributes held in common by subsets of items. For example, if the data set consisted of a collection of plants, students might classify plants by types of leaves (size, texture, patterns of veins, shape, connection of leaves to stems, etc.). Content objectives for this data set might include both information about specific plants and the building of a typology. Process objectives might include learning the scientific skills of the discipline (observation and classification) as well as the social skills of cooperative problem solving.

Tasks for the Teacher

Do you want to suggest a focus for the observer?

Content Objectives

What do you want students to gain from this classification task? What, in your opinion, are the critical attributes of the data set? What categories do you bring to the set?

Process Objectives

Are the students familiar with the model? Do they need special assistance or training in any aspect of the process? (For example, do students understand how to group items by common attributes? Can they work cooperatively with partners on a classification task?)

Phase One: Data Collection/Presentation

The primary activity of phase one of the inductive thinking model involves collection or presentation of a data set. The teacher may provide a data set or instruct students to collect the data that will be categorized. The data that will be scrutinized by the students are extremely important, because they represent much of the information the students will learn from the episode. The choice between data collection or presentation is also important—if students collect leaves, a different set of data will result than if they had been presented with them. Once a data set has been collected by or presented to students, the teacher may want to set parameters for the classification activity by orienting students to relevant attributes. For example, if the data are plants, the teacher may wish to narrow the field of observation by having students classify by types of leaves. On the other hand, the teacher may wish to leave the parameters open and simply instruct students to classify by common attributes. Generally speaking, the more open-ended the instructions, the better the results.

Items from a data set may be included in only one category or in multiple categories. You may want to experiment with different instructions regarding the classification of data and observe differences in the categories that result. Generally speaking, leaving open the possibility of multiple categories of membership for items from the data set provides the most energy.

Please describe the data set to be used in this lesson. Will you provide the data set or have students collect data? If the latter, what sources of information will they use?

Phase Two: Concept Formation

Once a data set is assembled and enumerated and students have been instructed on procedures for grouping the data, the teacher will need to attend to the mechanics of the grouping activity. Students may work alone, in pairs, in small groups, or as one large group. Working alone requires the least social skill, and working in small groups the greatest social skill. If one objective is to develop students' abilities to work cooperatively, assertively defending their categories but compromising when appropriate for group consensus, then students will need instruction and practice to develop these skills. If the teacher chooses to work with the entire class as a single group for the categorizing activity, he or she will need to exercise caution so that categories are not inadvertently provided for the students. Structuring students into pairs for the categorizing activity is the simplest way to have all students actively engaged in the task, although the teacher must again use considerable skill in keeping everyone involved while recording and synthesizing reports from the pairs. Teachers will probably want to experiment with different ways of structuring this activity. Pros and cons of each process can be discussed and problem solved with peer coaches.

Please describe how you will organize the students for the categorizing activity.

Also, please describe how you will instruct the students to classify the data that you have provided or that they have collected.

The names or labels students attach to groups of items within a data set will often accurately describe the group but not coincide with a technical or scientific name. For example, students may label a group of leaves "jagged edges," though the technical term would be "serrated edges." The teacher may choose to provide technical or scientific terms when appropriate, but not before students have attempted to provide their own labels.

For some lessons, the content objectives will be accomplished at the conclusion of phase two. When the teacher wishes to have students learn information by organizing it into categories and labeling it in order to gain conceptual control of the material, he or she may choose to stop here. When the objective is to learn what students see within a data set and what attributes they are unaware of, the grouping activity will suffice. However, when the objective is the interpretation and application of concepts that have been formed in phase two, the remainder of the inductive thinking model is appropriate. The final phases of the model result in further processing of the information and concepts embedded in the data set and should usually be completed.

Phase Three: Interpretation of Data

The purpose of phase three is to help students develop understanding of possible relationships between and among categories that they have formed in phase two. The class will need a common set of categories in order to work productively in this kind of discussion. Working off the descriptions of individual groups students have generated in phase two, the teacher asks questions that focus students' thinking on similarities and differences between the groups. By asking "why" questions, the teacher attempts to develop cause–effect relationships between the groups. The success of this phase depends on a thorough categorizing activity in phase two; the length of this phase is comparatively short.

Although you will not know during your planning what groups the students will form, make a guess about possible categories they might construct, and then write two sample questions that would explore cause–effect relationships between those groups.

_____

_____

_____

_____

If students were successful in making inferences and conclusions about their data, the teacher may wish to push them a step further and ask them to predict consequences from their data by asking "What would happen if . . ." kinds of questions.

Please write one or two examples of hypothetical questions you might ask students about this data set.

_____

_____

_____

_____

Tasks for the Observer

Phase One: Data Collection/Presentation

Data are easier to group if enumerated. For example, the teacher might place a numbered card under each plant so that students may discuss plants 1, 4, 7, and 14 as sharing a common attribute rather than by plant names (which students may not yet know).

Did the teacher/students enumerate the data before attempting to categorize it?

_____

_____

_____

Phase Two: Concept Formation

In your opinion, did the students understand the criteria and procedures they were to employ during the categorizing activity? Did the teacher inadvertently give clues about what the "right" groups would be?

_____

_____

_____

Did the students work productively on the categorizing activity?

_____

_____

_____

If the teacher had the students work in pairs or small groups, did the students listen as other groups shared their categories?

_____

_____

_____

Were students able to explain the attributes on which they grouped items within categories?

_____

_____

_____

Were students able to provide names for their categories that reflected the attributes on which the groups were formed?

_____

_____

_____

Phase Three: Interpretation of Data

Were the students able to discuss possible cause–effect relationships among the groups?

Did the teacher ask the students to go beyond the data and make inferences and conclusions regarding their data?

If yes, were the students able to do so?

If students were unable to make inferences or conclusions, can you think of any ideas to share with your partner that might help them do so?

Post-Observation Discussion

Teacher: Do you want to suggest a focus for the analysis? If so, what is it?

In order to improve student performance, the first option we explore is whether it will improve with practice. That is, simple repetition of the model gives the students a chance to learn to respond more appropriately. Second, we directly teach the students the skills they need to manage the cognitive and social tasks of the model.

At this point both teacher and observer might comment on the skills with which the students engaged in the activities and suggest any areas where training might be useful. Think especially of their ability to group by attributes and provide labels that accurately described the groups or synthesized characteristic attributes, their understanding of possible cause–effect relationships among groups, and their ability to make inferences or conclusions regarding their categories.

Peer Coaching Guide:
Picture Word Inductive Model

Peer coaches who are studying the PWIM model concentrate on the cycles, and these usually take three weeks or more.

Beginning Date of PWIM Cycle: _____

Description of Class (grade level, number of students, special needs):

_____

Tasks for the Teacher

Do you want to suggest a focus for the observer?

A. Describe your picture—actually, share it!

_____
_____
_____
_____
_____

B. List of words shaken out of the picture:

_____
_____
_____
_____
_____

Words added to the picture word chart and word sets after the first round:

_____
_____
_____
_____
_____

C. Examples of categories of words or phrases generated by students:

_____
_____
_____
_____
_____

D. Examples of categories or concepts selected by you for instructional emphasis:

Phonetic analysis categories or concepts:

_____

Structural analysis categories or concepts:

_____

Content categories or concepts:

_____

Other:

_____

E. Examples of titles generated by students from the picture:

_____

_____

_____

F. Examples of sentences generated by students:

_____

_____

_____

_____

_____

G. One of the informative paragraphs composed by you from student ideas:

_____

_____

_____

_____

_____

Be sure to do a think aloud with your students about how you put the ideas together to convey your message.

H. Sample(s) of student work: Be sure to take samples of student work, when they are available, to your sessions with your peer coaching partner and to designated sessions with the team as a learning community. You may take work from your whole class or group; however, we suggest you take, for collective study, the work of six students whose responses you are monitoring more formally and maybe more analytically than those of the whole class.

I. If you used tradebooks with the PWIM cycle, list the title, author, and strategy used (if applicable).

_____

_____

_____

_____

Number of lessons in PWIM cycle:

_____

Ending date of PWIM cycle:

_____

Number of times you planned with your peer coach in this PWIM cycle:

_____

Number of times you or your partner demonstrated for each other with your peer coach in this PWIM cycle:

_____

PWIM: Studying Student Performance

Emphasis: Vocabulary Development
Description of six students whose learning is being analyzed formally as part of studying the picture word inductive model:

1. Name _____ Birthdate _____ Gender: F/M

Other information that would be useful to understanding the student, such as learning history, etc.:

_____

_____

_____

2. Name _____ Birthdate _____ Gender: F/M

Other information that would be useful to understanding the student, such as learning history, etc.:

_____

_____

_____

3. Name _____ Birthdate _____ Gender: F/M

Other information that would be useful to understanding the student, such as learning history, etc.:

_____

_____

_____

4. Name _____ Birthdate _____ Gender: F/M

Other information that would be useful to understanding the student, such as learning history, etc.:

_____

_____

_____

5. Name _____ Birthdate _____ Gender: F/M

Other information that would be useful to understanding the student, such as learning history, etc.:

_____

_____

_____

6. Name _____ Birthdate _____ Gender: F/M

Other information that would be useful to understanding the student, such as learning history, etc.:

_____

_____

_____

Gender of Student	Total Number of Words	Date Asst.	Number of Words Read	Total Number of Words	Date Asst.	Number of Words Read	Gain
1.							
2.							
3.							
4.							
5.							
6.							

References and Related Sources

Achieve, Inc. (2013). *Next generation science standards.* Washington, DC: Author. Retrieved from www.achieve.org/next-generation-science-standards.

Adey, P., with Hewitt, G., Hewitt, J., & Landau, N. (2004). *The professional development of teachers: Practice and theory.* London, UK, and Boston, MA: Kluwer.

Adey, P., & Shayer, M. (1990). Accelerating the development of formal thinking in middle and high school students. *Journal of Research in Science Teaching, 27*(3), 267–285.

Adkins, D. C., Payne, F. D., & O'Malley, J. M. (1974). Moral development. In F. N. Kerlinger & J. B. Carroll (Eds.), *Review of research in education.* Itasca, IL: Peacock.

Akiki. (1989). *My five senses.* New York: HarperCollins.

Alexander, P., & Judy, J. (1988). The interaction of domain-specific and strategic knowledge in academic performance. *Review of Educational Research, 58*(4), pp. 375–404.

Alfasi, M. (1998). Reading for meaning: The efficacy of reciprocal teaching in fostering reading comprehension in high school students in remedial reading classes. *American Educational Research Journal, 35*(2), 309–332.

Allington, R. (2002). *Big brother and the National Reading Curriculum.* Portsmouth, NH: Heinemann.

Almy, M. (1970). *Logical thinking in second grade.* New York, NY: Teachers College Press.

Anderson, H., & Brewer, H. (1939). Domination and social integration in the behavior of kindergarten children and teachers. *Genetic Psychology Monograph, 21,* 287–385.

Anderson, L. M., Evertson, C. M., & Brophy, J. E. (1979). An experimental study of effective teaching in first grade reading groups. *Elementary School Journal, 79*(4), 191–223.

Anderson, L. W., Scott, C., & Hutlock, N. (1976). *The effect of a mastery learning program on selected cognitive, affective, and ecological variables in grades 1 through 6.* Paper presented at the annual meeting of the American Educational Research Association, San Francisco, CA.

Anderson, R. (1983). A consolidation and appraisal of science meta-analyses. *Journal of Research in Science Teaching, 20*(5), 497–509.

Anderson, R., Kahl, S., Glass, G., Smith M., & Malone, M. (1982). *Science meta-analysis project.* Boulder, CO: University of Colorado Laboratory for Research in Science and Mathematics Education.

Antil, L., Jenkins, J., Wayne, S., & Vadasy, P. (1998). Cooperative learning: Prevalence, conceptualizations, and the relation between research and practice. *American Educational Research Journal, 35*(3), 419–454.

Applebee, A., Langer, J., Jenkins, L., Mullis, I., & Foertsch, M. (1990). *Learning to write in our nation's schools.* Washington, DC: U.S. Department of Education.

Aristotle. (1912). *The works of Aristotle* (J. A. Smith & W. D. Ross, Eds.). Oxford, UK: Clarendon Press.

Arlin, M. (1984). Time variability in mastery learning. *American Educational Research Journal, 21*(4), 103–120.

Arlin, M., & Webster, J. (1983). Time costs of mastery learning. *Journal of Educational Psychology, 75*(3), 187–196.

Aronson, E., Blaney, N., Stephan, C., Sikes, J., & Snapp, M. (1978). *The jigsaw classroom.* Beverly Hills: Sage.

Aspy, D. N., & Roebuck, F. (1973). An investigation of the relationship between student levels of cognitive functioning and the teacher's classroom behavior. *Journal of Educational Research, 65*(6), 365–368.

Aspy, D. N., Roebuck, F., Willson, M., & Adams, O. (1974). *Interpersonal skills training for teachers.* (Interim Report No. 2 for NIMH Grant No. 5PO 1MH 19871.) Monroe, LA: Northeast Louisiana University.

Atkinson, R. C. (1975). Memnotechnics in second language learning. *American Psychologist, 30,* 821–828.

Augustine. (1931). *The city of God.* (J. Healy, Trans.). London, UK: J. M. Dent.

Ausubel, D. P. (1960). The use of advance organizers in the learning and retention of meaningful verbal material. *Journal of Educational Psychology, 51,* 267–272.

Ausubel, D. P. (1963). *The psychology of meaningful verbal learning.* New York, NY: Grune & Stratton.

Ausubel, D. P. (1968). *Educational psychology: A cognitive view.* New York: Grune and Stratton.

Ausubel, D. P. (1980). Schemata, cognitive structure, and advance organizers: A reply to Anderson, Spiro, and Anderson. *American Educational Research Journal, 17*(3), 400–404.

Ausubel, D. P., & Fitzgerald, J. (1962). Organizer, general background, and antecedent learning variables in sequential verbal learning. *Journal of Educational Psychology, 53,* 243–249.

Baer, J. (1993). *Creativity and divergent thinking.* Hillsdale, NJ: Erlbaum.

Baker, R. G. (1983). *The contribution of coaching to transfer of training: An extension study.* Doctoral dissertation, University of Oregon.

Baker, R. G., & Showers, B. (1984). *The effects of a coaching strategy on teachers' transfer of training to classroom practice: A six-month followup study.* Paper presented at the annual meeting of the American Educational Research Association, New Orleans, LA.

Bandura, A. (1969). *Principles of behavior modification.* New York, NY: Holt, Rinehart & Winston.

Bandura, A. (1971). *Social learning theory.* New York, NY: General Learning.

Bandura, A., & Walters, R. (1963). *Social learning and personality.* New York, NY: Holt, Rinehart & Winston.

Barnes, B. R., & Clausen, E. U. (1973). The effects of organizers on the learning of structured anthropology materials in the elementary grades. *Journal of Experimental Education, 42,* 11–15.

Barnes, B. R., & Clausen, E. U. (1975). Do advance organizers facilitate learning? Recommendations for further research based on an analysis of 32 studies. *Review of Educational Research, 45*(4), 637–659.

Barnett, W. S. (2001). Preschool education for economically disadvantaged children: Effects on reading achievement and related outcomes. In S. B. Neuman & D. K. Dickinson (Eds.), *Handbook of early literacy research* (pp. 421–443). New York, NY: Guilford.

Barron, F. (1963). *Creativity and psychological health: Origins of personal vitality and creative freedom.* Princeton, NJ: Van Nostrand.

Barron, R. R. (1971). *The effects of advance organizers upon the reception, learning, and retention of general science concepts.* (DHEW Project No. IB-030.)

Bascones, J., & Novak, J. (1985). Alternative instructional systems and the development of problem-solving in physics. *European Journal of Science Education, 7*(3), 253–261.

Baumert, J., Kunter, M., Blum, W., Brunner, M., Voss, T., Jordan, W., et al. (2010). Teachers' mathematical knowledge, cognitive activation in the classroom, and student progress. *American Educational Research Journal, 47*(1), 97–132.

Baveja, B. (1988). *An exploratory study of the use of information-processing models of teaching in secondary school biology classes.* Ph.D. thesis, Delhi University.

Baveja, B., Showers, B., & Joyce, B. (1985). *An experiment in conceptually-based teaching strategies.* Saint Simons Island, GA: Booksend Laboratories.

Beatty, A., Reese, C., Persky, H., & Carr, P. (1996). *NAEP 1994 U.S. history report card.* Washington, DC: U.S. Department of Education.

Becker, W. (1977). Teaching reading and language to the disadvantaged—What we have learned from field research. *Harvard Educational Review, 47,* 518–543.

Becker, W., & Carnine, D. (1980). Direct instruction: An effective approach for educational intervention with the disadvantaged and low performers. In B. Lahey & A. Kazdin (Eds.), *Advances in child clinical psychology* (pp. 429–473). New York, NY: Plenum.

Becker, W., & Gersten, R. (1982). A followup of follow through: The later effects of the direct instruction model on children in the fifth and sixth grades. *American Educational Research Journal, 19*(1), 75–92.

Becker, W., Engelmann, S., Carnine, D., & Rhine, W. (1981). In W. R. Rhine (Ed.), *Making schools more effective.* New York, NY: Academic Press.

Bellack, A. (1962). *The language of the classroom.* New York, NY: Teachers College Press.

Bencke, W. N., & Harris, M. B. (1972). Teaching self-control of study behavior. *Behavior Research and Therapy, 10,* 35–41.

Bennett, B. (1987). *The effectiveness of staff development training practices: A meta-analysis.* Ph.D. thesis, University of Oregon.

Bennett, L., & Berson, M. (Eds.). (2007). *Digital age: Technology-based K-12 lesson plans for social studies. NCSS Bulletin 105.* Silver Spring, MD: National Council for the Social Studies.

Bennis, W. G., & Shepard, H. A. (1964). Theory of group development. In W. G. Bennis, K. D. Benne, & R. Chin (Eds.), *The planning of change: Readings in the applied behavioral sciences.* New York, NY: Holt, Rinehart & Winston.

Bereiter, C. (1984a). Constructivism, socioculturalism, and Popper's World. *Educational Researcher, 23*(7), 21–23.

Bereiter, C. (1984b). How to keep thinking skills from going the way of all frills. *Educational Leadership, 42,* 1.

Bereiter, C. (1997). Situated cognition and how to overcome it. In D. Kirshner & W. Whitson (Eds.), *Situated cognition: Social, semiotic, and psychological perspectives* (pp. 281–300). Hillsdale, NJ: Erlbaum.

Bereiter, C., & Bird, M. (1985). Use of thinking aloud in identification and teaching of reading comprehension strategies. *Cognition and Instruction, 2*(2), 131–156.

Bereiter, C., & Englemann, S. (1966). *Teaching the culturally disadvantaged child in the preschool.* Englewood Cliffs, NJ: Prentice-Hall.

Bereiter, C., & Kurland, M. (1981–82). Were some follow-through models more effective than others? *Interchange, 12,* 1–22.

Berger, P., & Luckmann, T. (1966). *The social construction of reality.* Garden City, NY: Doubleday.

Berman, P., & McLaughlin, M. (1975). *Federal programs supporting educational change: Vol. 4. The findings in review.* Santa Monica, CA: Rand Corporation.

Biemiller, A. (2000, Fall). Teaching vocabulary early, direct, and sequential. *International Dyslexia Quarterly Newsletter, Perspectives, 26*(4), 206–228.

Bird, M. (1980). *Reading comprehension strategies: A direct teaching approach.* Doctoral dissertation, The Ontario Institute for Studies in Education.

Bishop, M. (2000). *Tunnels of time.* Regina, Saskatchewan: Coteau Books.

Block, J. W. (1971). *Mastery learning: Theory and practice.* New York, NY: Holt, Rinehart & Winston.

Block, J. W. (1980). Success rate. In C. Denham & A. Lieberman (Eds.), *Time to learn.* Washington, DC: Program on Teaching and Learning, National Institute of Education.

Bloom, B. S., ed. (1956). *Taxonomy of educational objectives. Handbook I: Cognitive domain.* New York, NY: McKay.

Bloom, B. S. (1971). Mastery learning. In J. H. Block (Ed.), *Mastery learning: Theory and practice.* New York, NY: Holt, Rinehart & Winston.

Bode, B. (1927). *Modern educational theories.* New York, NY: Macmillan.

Bonsangue, M. (1993). Long term effects of the Calculus Workshop Model. *Cooperative Learning, 13*(3), 19–20.

Boocock, S. S., & Schild, E. (1968). *Simulation games in learning.* Beverly Hills, CA: Sage.

Borg, W. R., Kelley, M. L., Langer, P., & Gall, M. (1970). *The minicourse.* Beverly Hills, CA: Collier-Macmillan.

Borman, G. D., Slavin, R. E., Cheung, A., Chamberlain, A., Madden, N., & Chambers, B. (2005). Success for all: First year results from the national randomized field trial. *Educational Evaluation and Policy Analysis, 27*(1), 1–22.

Bradford, L. P., Gibb, J. R., & Benne, K. D. (Eds.). (1964). *T-Group theory and laboratory method.* New York, NY: Wiley.

Bredderman, T. (1983). Effects of activity-based elementary science on student outcomes: A quantitative synthesis. *Review of Educational Research, 53*(4), 499–518.

Brookover, W., Schwitzer, J. H., Schneider, J. M., Beady, C. H., Flood, P. K., & Wisenbaker, J. M. (1978). Elementary school social climate and school achievement. *American Educational Research Journal, 15*(2), 301–318.

Brooks, J. G., & Brooks, M. G. (1993). *The case for constructivist classrooms.* Alexandria, VA: Association for Supervision and Curriculum Development.

Brophy, J. E. (1981). Teacher praise: A functional analysis. *Review of Educational Research, 51,* 5–32.

Brown, A. (1985). Reciprocal teaching of comprehension strategies (Technical Report No. 334). Urbana-Champaign, IL: University of Illinois Center for the Study of Reading.

Brown, A. L. (1995). Guided discovery in a community of learners. In K. McGilly (Ed.), *Knowing, Learning, and Instruction* (pp. 393–451). Hillsdale, NJ: Erlbaum.

Brown, A., & Palincsar, A. (1989). Guided, cooperative learning individual knowledge acquisition. In L. Resnick (Ed.), *Knowing, learning, and instruction* (pp. 234–278). Hillsdale, NJ: Erlbaum.

Brown, C. (1967). *A multivariate study of the teaching styles of student teachers.* Ph.D. dissertation, Teachers College, Columbia University.

Brown, C. (1981). The relationship between teaching styles, personality, and setting. In B. Joyce, L. Peck, & C. Brown (Eds.), *Flexibility in teaching* (pp. 94–100). New York, NY: Longman.

Bruce, W. C., & Bruce, J. K. (1992). *Learning social studies through discrepant event inquiry.* Annapolis, MD: Alpha Press.

Bruner, J. (1961). *The process of education.* Cambridge, MA: Harvard University Press.

Bruner, J., Goodnow, J. J., & Austin, G. A. (1967). *A study of thinking.* New York, NY: Science Edition.

Burkham, D., Lee, V., & Smerdon, B. (1997). Gender and science learning early in high school: Subject matter and laboratory experiences. *American Educational Research Journal, 34*(2), 297–331.

Burns, S., Griffin, P., & Snow, C. (1998). *Starting out right.* Washington, DC: National Academy Press.

Calderon, M., Hertz-Lazarowitz, R., & Tinajero, J. (1991). Adapting CIRC to multi-ethnic and bilingual classrooms. *Cooperative Learning, 12,* 17–20.

Calhoun, E. (1997). *Literacy for all.* Saint Simons Island, GA: The Phoenix Alliance.

Calhoun, E. (1998). *Literacy for the primary grades: What works, for whom, and to what degree.* Saint Simons Island, GA: The Phoenix Alliance.

Calhoun, E. F. (1994). *How to use action research in the self-renewing school.* Alexandria, VA: Association for Supervision and Curriculum Development.

Calhoun, E. F. (1999). *Teaching beginning reading and writing with the picture word inductive model.* Alexandria, VA: Association for Supervision and Curriculum Development.

Calhoun, E. (2004). *Using Data to Assess Your Reading Program.* Alexandria, Virginia: Association for Supervision and Curriculum Development.

Calkins, L. (2000). *The art of teaching reading.* Boston: Pearson.

Calkins, L. & Harwayne, S. (1987). *The writing workshop: A world of difference.* New York, NY: Heinemann.

Cambourne, B. (2002). Holistic, integrated approaches to reading and language arts instruction: The constructivist framework of an instructional theory. In A. Farstrup & J. Samuels (Eds.), *What research has to say about reading instruction.* Newark, DE: International Reading Instruction.

Cameron, J., & Pierce, W. (1994). Reinforcement, reward, and intrinsic motivation: A meta-analysis. *Review of Educational Research, 64*(2), 363–423.

Carr, N. (2010). *The Shallows.* New York, NY: Norton.

Carroll, J. B. (1963). A model of school learning. *Teachers College Record, 64,* 722–733.

Carroll, J. B. (1964). *Language and thought.* Englewood Cliffs, NJ: Prentice-Hall.

Carroll, J. B. (1971). Problems of measurement related to the concept of learning for mastery. In J. H. Block (Ed.), *Mastery learning: Theory and practice.* New York, NY: Holt, Rinehart & Winston.

Carroll, J. B. (1977). A revisionist model of school learning. *Review of Educational Research, 3,* 155–167.

Chall, J. S. (1983). *Stages of reading development.* New York, NY: McGraw-Hill.

Chamberlin, C., & Chamberlin, E. (1943). *Did they succeed in college?* New York, NY: Harper & Row.

Chesler, M., & Fox, R. (1966). *Role-playing methods in the classroom.* Chicago, IL: Science Research Associates.

Chin, R., & Benne, K. (1969). General strategies for effecting change in human systems. In W. Bennis, K. Benne, & R. Chin (Eds.), *The planning of change* (pp. 32–59). New York, NY: Holt, Rinehart & Winston.

Clark, C., & Peterson, P. (1986). Teachers' thought processes. In M. Wittrock (Ed.), *Handbook of research on teaching* (pp. 225–296). New York, NY: Macmillan.

Clark, C., & Yinger, R. (1979). *Three studies of teacher planning.* (Research Series No. 55.) East Lansing, MI: Michigan State University.

Clark, H. H., & Clark, E. V. (1977). *Psychology and language: An introduction to psycholinguistics.* New York, NY: Harcourt, Brace, Jovanovich.

Clauson, E. V., & Barnes, B. R. (1973). The effects of organizers on the learning of structured anthropology materials in the elementary grades. *Journal of Experimental Education, 42,* 11–15.

Clauson, E. V., & Rice, M. G. (1972). *The changing world today.* (Anthropology Curriculum Project Publication No. 72-1.) Athens, GA: University of Georgia.

Coiro, J. (2011). Talking about reading: Modelling the hidden complexities of online reading comprehension. *Theory into Practice 50*(2), 107–115.

Coleman, J. S., Campbell, E. Q., Hobson, C. J., McPortland, J., Mood, A. M., Weinfield, E. D., et al. (1966). *Equality of educational opportunity*. Washington, DC: U.S. Government Printing Office.

Collins, K. (1969). The importance of strong confrontation in an inquiry model of teaching. *School Science and Mathematics, 69*(7), 615–617.

Comenius, J. (1967). *The great didactic*. Brasted, Kent, UK: Russell and Russell Publishing.

Cook, L., & Cook, E. (1954). *Intergroup education*. New York, NY: McGraw-Hill.

Cook, L., & Cook, E. (1957). *School problems in human relations*. New York, NY: McGraw-Hill.

Cooper, L., Johnson, D. W., Johnson, R., & Wilderson, F. (1980). The effects of cooperative, competitive, and individualistic experiences on interpersonal attraction among heterogeneous peers. *Journal of Social Psychology, 111*, 243–252.

Cornelius-White, J. (2007). Learner-centered teacher-student relationships are effective: A meta-analysis. *Review of Educational Research, 77*(1), 113–173.

Counts, G. (1932). *Dare the school build a new social order?* New York, NY: John Day.

Courmier, S., & Hagman, J. (Eds.). (1987). *Transfer of learning*. San Diego, CA: Academic Press.

Crosby, M. (1965). *An adventure in human relations*. Chicago, IL: Follet Corporation.

Cunningham, J. (2002). The national reading panel report. In R. Allington (Ed.), *Big Brother and the national reading curriculum*. Portsmouth, NH: Heinemann.

Cunningham, J., & Stanovich, K. (1998). What reading does for the mind. *American Educator*, Spring/Summer, 1–8.

Cunningham, P. M. (1990). The names test: A quick assessment of decoding ability. *The Reading Teacher, 44*, 124–129.

Cunningham, P. M. (2005). *Phonics they use: Words for reading and writing* (4th Ed.). Boston: Pearson/Allyn & Bacon.

Daane, M., Campbell, J., Grigg, W., Goodman, M., & Oranje, A. (2005). *The Nation's Report Card*. Washington, DC: National Center for Educational Statistics.

Dale, P. (2007). *Ten in the bed*. Cambridge, MA: Candlewick.

Dalton, M. (1986). *The thought processes of teachers when practicing two models of teaching*. Doctoral dissertation, University of Oregon.

Dalton, M., & Dodd, J. (1986). *Teacher thinking: The development of skill in using two models of teaching and model-relevant thinking*. Paper presented at the annual meeting of the American Educational Research Association, San Francisco, CA.

de Jong, T., and van Joolingen, W. (1998). Scientific discovery learning with computer simulations of conceptual domains. *Review of Educational Research, 68*(2), 179–201.

Deal, T. E., & Kennedy, A. A. (1984). *Corporate cultures: The rites and rituals of corporate life*. Boston, MA: Addison-Wesley.

Deshler, D., & Schumaker, J. (2006). *Teaching adolescents with disabilities*. Thousand Oaks, CA: Corwin.

Dewey, J. (1910). *How we think*. Boston, MA: Heath.

Dewey, J. (1916). *Democracy and education*. New York, NY: Macmillan.

Dewey, J. (1920). *Reconstruction in philosophy*. New York, NY: Holt.

Dewey, J. (1937). *Experience and education*. New York, NY: Macmillan.

Dewey, J. (1956). *The school and society*. Chicago, IL: University of Chicago Press.

Dewey, J. (1960). *The child and the curriculum*. Chicago, IL: University of Chicago Press.

Dickinson, D. K., McCabe, A., & Essex, M. J. (2006). A window of opportunity we must open to all: The case for preschool with high-quality support for language and literacy.

In D. K. Dickinson & S. B. Neuman (Eds.), *Handbook of early literacy research: Vol. 2* (pp. 11–28). New York, NY: Guilford.

Downey, L. (1967). *The secondary phase of education.* Boston, MA: Ginn and Co.

Duffelmeyer, F. A., Kruse, A. E., Merkley, D. J., & Fyfe, S. A. (1994). Further validation and enhancement of the Names Test. *The Reading Teacher, 48*(2), 118–128.

Duffy, G. (2002). The case for direct explanation of strategies. In C. Block & M. Pressley (Eds.), *Comprehension instruction* (pp. 28–41). New York, NY: Guilford.

Duffy, G. (2009). *Explaining reading: A resource for teaching concepts, skills, and strategies* (2nd Ed.). New York, NY: Guilford.

Duffy, G., Roehler, E., Sivan, E., Racklife, G., Book, C., Meloth, M., et al. (1987). The effects of explaining the reasoning associated with using reading strategies. *Reading Research Quarterly, 22,* 347–367.

Duffy, G., Roehler, L., & Herrmann, B. (1988). Modeling mental processes helps poor readers become strategic readers. *The Reading Teacher, 41,* 762–767.

Duke, N., & Pearson, P. D. (undated). *Effective practices for developing reading comprehension.* East Lansing, MI: College of Education, Michigan State University.

Duke, N., Pearson, P. D., Strachan, S., & Billman, A. (2011). Essential elements of fostering and teaching reading comprehension. In A. E. Farstrup & S. J. Samuels (Eds.), *What research has to say about reading instruction* (pp. 48–93). Newark, DE: International Reading Association.

Dunn, R., & Dunn, K. (1975). *Educators' self-teaching guide to individualizing instructional programs.* West Nyack, NY: Parker.

Durkin, D. (1966). *Children who read early.* New York, NY: Teachers College Press.

Durkin, D. (1978/1979). What classroom observations reveal about reading comprehension instruction. *Reading Research Quarterly, 14*(4), 481–533.

Eastman, P. D. (1961). *Go, Dog, Go.* New York, NY: Random House.

Edmonds, R. (1979). Some schools work and more can. *Social Policy, 9*(5), 28–32.

Ehri, L., Nunes, S., Stahl, S., & Willows, D. (2001). Systematic phonics instruction helps students learn to read. *Review of Educational Research, 71*(3), 393–447.

Ehri, L. C. (1999). *Phases of acquisition in learning to read words and instructional implications.* Paper presented at the annual meeting of the American Educational Research Association. Montreal, Canada.

Ehri, L. C. (2005). Learning to read words: Theory, findings, and issues. *Scientific Studies of Reading, 9*(2), 167–188.

Elefant, E. (1980). Deaf children in an inquiry training program. *Volta Review, 82,* 271–279.

Elementary Science Study (ESS). (1971). *Batteries and bulbs: An electrical suggestion book.* New York, NY: Webster-McGraw-Hill.

Elkind, D. (1987). *Miseducation: Preschoolers at risk.* New York, NY: Knopf.

Ellis, A., & Harper, R. (1975). *A new guide to rational living.* Englewood Cliffs, NJ: Prentice-Hall.

El-Nemr, M. A. (1979). *Meta-analysis of the outcomes of teaching biology as inquiry.* Boulder, CO: University of Colorado.

Emmer, E., & Evertson, C. (1980). *Effective classroom management at the beginning of the year in junior high school classrooms.* (Report No. 6107.) Austin, TX: Research and Development Center for Teacher Education, University of Texas.

Emmer, E., Evertson, C., & Anderson, L. (1980). Effective classroom management at the beginning of the school year. *Elementary School Journal, 80,* 219–231.

Englert, C., Raphael, T., Anderson, L., Anthony, H., and Stevens, D. (1991). Making Strategies and Self-Talk Visible: Writing Instruction in Regular and Special Education Classrooms. (1991). *American Educational Research Journal, 28*(2), 337–372.

Englemann, S., & Osborn, J. (1972). *DISTAR language program.* Chicago, IL: Science Research Associates.

Erikson, E. (1950). *Childhood and society.* New York, NY: Norton.

Estes, W. E. (Ed.). (1976). *Handbook of learning and cognitive processes: Volume 4: Attention and memory.* Hillsdale, NJ: Erlbaum.

Farstrup, A. E., & Samuels, S. J. (Eds.). *What research has to say about reading instruction.* Newark, DE: International Reading Association.

Fisher, C. W., Berliner, D. C., Filby, N. N., Marliave, R., Ghen, L. S., & Dishaw, M. (1980). Teaching behaviors, academic learning time, and student achievement: An over view. In C. Denham & A. Lieberman (Eds.), *Time to learn.* Washington, DC: National Institute of Education.

Flanders, N. (1970). *Analyzing teaching behavior.* Reading, MA: Addison-Wesley.

Flavell, J. H. (1963). *The developmental psychology of Jean Piaget.* Princeton, NJ: Van Nostrand Reinhold.

Flesch, R. (1955). *Why Johnny can't read.* New York, NY: Harper Brothers.

Flint, S. (1965). *The relationship between the classroom verbal behavior of student teachers and the classroom verbal behavior of their cooperating teachers.* Doctoral dissertation. New York, NY: Teachers College Press.

Fromm, E. (1941). *Escape from freedom.* New York, NY: Farrar & Rinehart.

Fromm, E. (1955). *The sane society.* New York, NY: Rinehart.

Fromm, E. (1956). *The art of loving.* New York, NY: Harper.

Fuchs, D., Fuchs, L., Mathes, P., & Simmons, D. (1997). Peer-assisted learning strategies. *American Educational Research Journal, 34*(1), 174–206.

Fuchs, L., Fuchs, D., Hamlett, C., & Karns, K. (1998). High-achieving students' interactions and performance on complex mathematical tasks as a function of homogeneous and heterogeneous pairings. *American Educational Research Journal, 35*(2), 227–267.

Fullan, M. (1982). *The meaning of educational change.* New York, NY: Teachers College Press.

Fullan, M. G., Bennett, B., & Bennett, C. R. (1990). Linking classroom and school improvement. *Educational Leadership, 47*(8), 13–19.

Fullan, M., & Park, P. (1981). *Curriculum implementation: A resource booklet.* Toronto, ON: Ontario Ministry of Education.

Fullan, M., & Pomfret, A. (1977). Research on curriculum and instruction implementation. *Review of Educational Research, 47*(2), 335–397.

Gage, N. L. (1979). *The scientific basis for the art of teaching.* New York, NY: Teachers College Press.

Gage, N. L., & Berliner, D. (1983). *Educational psychology.* Boston: Houghton Mifflin.

Gagné, R. (1965). *The conditions of learning.* New York, NY: Holt, Rinehart & Winston.

Gagné, R., & White, R. (1978). Memory structures and learning outcomes. *Review of Educational Research, 48*(2), 137–222.

Garan, E. (2002). Beyond the smoke and mirrors: A critique of the National Reading Panel report on phonics. In R. Allington (Ed.), *Big brother and the National Reading Curriculum* (pp. 90–111). Portsmouth, NH: Heinemann.

Garan, E. (2005). Murder your darlings: A scientific response to the voice of evidence in reading research. *Phi Delta Kappan, 86*(6), 438–443.

Gardner, H. (1983). *Frames of mind: The theory of multiple intelligences.* New York, NY: Basic Books.

Garner, R. (1987). *Metacognition and reading comprehension.* Norwood, NJ: Ablex.

Gaskins, I., & Elliot, T. (1991). *Implementing cognitive strategy instruction across the school.* Cambridge, MA: Brookline Books.

Gentile, J. R. (1988). *Instructional improvement: Summary and analysis of Madeline Hunter's essential elements of instruction and supervision.* Oxford, OH: National Staff Development Council.

Gersten, R., Fuchs, L., Williams, J., & Baker, S. (2001). Teaching reading comprehension strategies to children with learning disabilities: A review of research. *Review of Educational Research, 71*(2), 279–320.

Giese, J. R. (1989). *The progressive era: The limits of reform.* Boulder, CO: Social Science Education Consortium.

Gilham, N. (2011). *Genes, Chromosomes, and Disease.* FT Press.

Glade, M. E., & Giese, J. R. (1989). *Immigration, pluralism, and national identity.* Boulder, CO: Social Science Education Consortium.

Glaser, R. (Ed.). (1962). *Training research and education.* Pittsburgh, PA: University of Pittsburgh Press.

Glass, G. V. (1975). Primary, secondary, and meta-analysis of research. *Educational Researcher, 7*(3), 33–50.

Glynn, S. M. (1994). *Teaching science with analogies.* Athens, GA: National Reading Research Center, University of Georgia.

Goffman, I. (1986). *Gender advertisements.* New York, NY: Harper.

Good, T., Grouws, D., & Ebmeier, H. (1983). *Active mathematics teaching.* New York, NY: Longman.

Goodlad, J. (1984). *A place called school.* New York, NY: McGraw-Hill.

Goodlad, J., & Klein, F. (1970). *Looking behind the classroom door.* Worthington, OH: Charles A. Jones.

Gordon, W. J. J. (1955, December). *Some environmental aspects of creativity.* Paper delivered to the Department of Defense, Fort Belvoir, VA.

Gordon, W. J. J. (1956). *Creativity as a process.* Paper delivered at the First Arden House Conference on Creative Process.

Gordon, W. J. J. (1961). *Synectics.* New York, NY: Harper & Row.

Graves, M. (2006). *The Vocabulary Book: Learning & Instruction.* New York, NY: Teachers College Press.

Graves, M. F., Juel, C., & Graves, B. B. (2001). *Teaching reading in the 21st century* (2nd Ed.). Boston: Allyn & Bacon.

Graves, M. F., Watts, S. M., & Graves, B. B. (1994). *Essentials of classroom teaching: Elementary reading methods.* Boston: Allyn & Bacon.

Greenberg, J. (2006) *Biological Sciences Curriculum Study: Blue Version—A Molecular Approach.* Glencoe, IL: McGraw-Hill.

Gunning, T. (1998). *Best books for beginning readers.* Boston, MA: Allyn & Bacon.

Halberstam, D. (1998). *The children.* New York, NY: Random House.

Halberstam, D. (2002). *Firehouse.* New York, NY: Hyperion.

Hall, G. (1986). *Skills derived from studies of the implementation of innovations in education.* Paper presented at the annual meeting of the American Educational Research Association, San Francisco, CA.

Hall, G., & Loucks, S. (1977). A developmental model for determining whether the treatment is actually implemented. *American Educational Research Journal, 14*(3), 263–276.

Hall, G., & Loucks, S. (1978). Teacher concerns as a basis for facilitating and personalizing staff development. *Teachers College Record, 80*(1), 36–53.

Hanson, R., & Farrell, D. (1995). The long-term effects on high school seniors of learning to read in kindergarten. *Reading Research Quarterly, 30*(4), 908–933.

Hart, B., & Risley, T. R. (1995). *Meaningful differences in the everyday experience of young American children.* Baltimore, MD: Paul H. Brookes.

Harvey, O. J., Hunt, D., & Schroeder, H. (1961). *Conceptual systems and personality organization.* New York, NY: Wiley.

Hawkes, E. (1971). *The effects of an instruction strategy on approaches to problem-solving.* Unpublished doctoral dissertation, Teachers College, Columbia University.

Hertz-Lazarowitz, R. (1993). Using group investigation to enhance Arab-Jewish relationships. *Cooperative Learning, 11*(2), 13–14.

Hill, H., Rowan, B., & Ball, D. (2005). Effects of teachers' mathematical knowledge for teaching on student achievement. *American Educational Research Journal, 42*(2), 371–406.

Hillocks, G. (1987). Synthesis of research on teaching writing. *Educational Leadership, 44*(8), 71–82.

Hoetker, J., & Ahlbrand, W. (1969). The persistence of the recitation. *American Educational Research Journal, 6*, 145–167.

Holloway, S. D. (1988). Concepts of ability and effort in Japan and the United States. *Review of Educational Research, 58*(3), 327–345.

Hopkins, D. (1987). *Improving the quality of schooling.* London, UK: Falmer Press.

Hopkins, D. (1990). Integrating staff development and school improvement: A study of teacher personality and school climate. In B. Joyce (Ed.), *Changing school culture through staff development. 1990 Yearbook of the Association for Supervision and Curriculum Development.* Alexandria, VA: ASCD.

Hrycauk, M. (2002). A safety net for second grade students. *Journal of Staff Development, 23*(1), 55–58.

Huberman, M., & Miles, M. (1984). *Innovation up close.* New York, NY: Plenum.

Huhtala, J. (1994). *Group investigation structuring an inquiry-based curriculum.* Paper presented at the annual meeting of the American Educational Research Association, New Orleans, LA.

Hullfish, H. G., & Smith, P. G. (1961). *Reflective thinking: The method of education.* New York, NY: Dodd, Mead.

Hunt, D. E. (1970). A conceptual level matching model for coordinating learner characteristics with educational approaches. *Interchange: A Journal of Educational Studies, 1*(2), 1–31.

Hunt, D. E. (1971). *Matching models in education.* Toronto, ON: Ontario Institute for Studies in Education.

Hunt, D. E. (1975). The B-P-E paradigm in theory, research, and practice. *Canadian Psychological Review, 16*, 185–197.

Hunt, D. E., Butler, L. F., Noy, J. E., & Rosser, M. E. (1978). *Assessing conceptual level by the paragraph completion method.* Toronto, ON: Ontario Institute for Studies in Education.

Hunt, D. E., & Joyce, B. (1967). Teacher trainee personality and initial teaching style. *American Educational Research Journal, 4*, 253–259.

Hunt, D. E., & Sullivan, E. V. (1974). *Between psychology and education.* Hinsdale, IL: Dryden.

Hunter, I. (1964). *Memory.* Hammondsworth, Middlesex: Penguin Books.

International Reading Association. (1998). *Position statement on phonemic awareness and the teaching of reading.* Newark, DE: Author.

International Reading Association & The National Association for the Education of Young Children. (1998). *Position statement on learning to read and write: Developmentally appropriate practices for young children.* Newark, DE: International Reading Association.

Ivany, G. (1969). The assessment of verbal inquiry in elementary school science. *Science Education, 53*(4), 287–293.

Johnson, D., Johnson, R., & Holubec, E. (1994). *Circles of Learning*. Alexandria, VA: Association for Supervision and Curriculum Development.

Johnson, D. W., & Johnson, R. T. (1974). Instructional goal structure: Cooperative, competitive, or individualistic. *Review of Educational Research, 44,* 213–240.

Johnson, D. W., & Johnson, R. T. (2009). An educational psychology success story: Social interdependence theory and cooperative learning. *Educational Research, 38*(5), 365–379.

Joyce, B., Bush, R., & McKibbin, M. (1982). *The California Staff Development Study: The January report*. Sacramento: The California Department of Education.

Joyce, B., & Calhoun, E. (1996). *Learning experiences in school renewal: An exploration of five successful programs*. University of Oregon, Eugene, OR: ERIC Clearinghouse on Educational Management.

Joyce, B., & Calhoun, E. (2010). *Models of professional development*. Thousand Oaks, CA: Corwin Press.

Joyce, B., Calhoun, E., & Hrycauk, M. (2003). Learning to read in kindergarten. *Phi Delta Kappan, 85*(2), 126–132.

Joyce, B., Calhoun, E., Jutras, J., & Newlove, K. (2006). Scaling up: The results of a literacy curriculum implemented across an entire 53-school education authority. Paper presented at the Asian Pacific Educational Research Association, Hong Kong.

Joyce, B., Hrycauk, M., Calhoun, E., & Hrycauk, W. (2006). The tending of diversity through a robust core literacy curriculum: Gender, socioeconomic status, learning disabilities, and ethnicity. Paper presented at the Asian Pacific Educational Research Association, Hong Kong.

Joyce, B., & Showers, B. (2004). *Student achievement through staff development*. Alexandria, VA: Association for Supervision and Curriculum Development.

Joyce, B., Weil, M., Calhoun, E. (2009). *Models of Teaching*. Boston, MA: Pearson Education.

Juel, C. (1988). Learning to read and write. *Journal of Educational Psychology, 80*(4), 437–447.

Juel, C. (1992). Longitudinal research on learning to read and write with at-risk students. In M. Dreher & W. Slater (Eds.), *Elementary school literacy: Critical issues* (pp. 73–99). Norwood, MA: Christopher-Gordon.

Kagan, S. (1990). *Cooperative learning resources for teachers*. San Juan Capistrano, CA: Resources for Teachers.

Kahle, J. (1985). *Women in science: A report from the field*. Philadelphia, PA: Falmer Press.

Kahle, J., & Meece, R. (1994). Research on gender issues in the classroom. In D. L. Gabel (Ed.), *Handbook of research on science teaching and learning* (pp. 542–557). New York, NY: MacMillan.

Kamii, C., & DeVries, R. (1974). Piaget-based curricula for early childhood education. In R. Parker (Ed.), *The preschool in action*. Boston, MA: Allyn & Bacon.

Kaplan, A. (1964). *The conduct of inquiry*. San Francisco, CA: Chandler.

Karplus, R. (1964). *Theoretical background of the science curriculum improvement study*. Berkeley, CA: University of California Press.

Kay, K. (2010). 21st Century Skills: Why they matter, what they are, and how we get there. In Bellanca, J., & Brandt, R. (Eds.), *21st Century skills: Rethinking how students learn* (pp. xiii–xxi). Bloomington, IN: Solution Tree Press.

Keyes, D. K. (2006). Metaphorical voices: Secondary students' exploration into multidimensional perspectives in literature and creative writing using the synectics model. Unpublished doctoral dissertation, University of Houston.

Kilpatrick, W. H. (1919). *The project method*. New York, NY: Teachers College Press.

Klauer, K., & Phye, G. (2008). Inductive reasoning: A training approach. *Review of Educational Research, 78*(1), 85–123.

Klein, S. (1985). *Handbook for achieving sex equity through education.* Baltimore, MA: Johns Hopkins University Press.

Klinzing, G., & Klinzing-Eurich, G. (1985). Higher cognitive behaviors in classroom discourse: Congruencies between teachers' questions and pupils' responses. *Australian Journal of Education, 29*(1), 63–74.

Knapp, P. (1995). *Teaching for meaning in high-poverty classrooms.* New York, NY: Teachers College Press.

Knowles, M. (1978). *The adult learner: A neglected species.* Houston, TX: Gulf.

Kohlberg, L. (1966). Moral education and the schools. *School Review, 74,* 1–30.

Kohlberg, L. (1976). The cognitive developmental approach to moral education. In D. Purpel & K. Ryan (Eds.), *Moral education . . . It comes with the territory.* Berkeley, CA: McCutchan.

Kohlberg, L. (Ed.). (1977). *Recent research in moral development.* New York, NY: Holt, Rinehart & Winston.

Kramarski, B., & Maravech, Z. (2003). Enhancing mathematical reasoning in the classroom: The effects of cooperative learning and metacognitive training. *American Educational Research Journal, 40*(1), 281–310.

Kucan, L., & Beck, I. (1997). Thinking aloud and thinking comprehension research: Inquiry, instruction, and social interaction. *Review of Educational Research, 6*(3), 271–299.

Kuhn, D., Amsel, E., & O'Loughlin, M. (1988). *The development of scientific thinking skills.* New York, NY: Academic Press.

Kulik, C. C., Kulik, J. A., & Bangert-Drowns, R. L. (1990). Effectiveness of mastery learning programs: A meta-analysis. *Review of Educational Research, 60,* 265–299.

Lavatelle, C. (1970). *Piaget's theory applied to an early childhood education curriculum.* Boston, MA: American Science and Engineering.

Lawton, J. T. (1977a). Effects of advance organizer lessons on children's use and understanding of the causal and logical "because." *Journal of Experimental Education, 46*(1), 41–46.

Lawton, J. T. (1977b). The use of advance organizers in the learning and retention of logical operations in social studies concepts. *American Educational Research Journal, 14*(1), 24–43.

Lawton, J. T., & Wanska, S. K. (1977a). Advance organizers as a teaching strategy: A reply to Barnes and Clawson. *Review of Educational Research, 47*(1), 233–244.

Lawton, J. T., & Wanska, S. K. (1977b, Summer). The effects of different types of advance organizers on classification learning. *American Educational Research Journal, 16*(3), 223–239.

Levin, J. R., McCormick, C., Miller, H., & Berry, J. (1982). Mnemonic versus nonmnemonic strategies for children. *American Educational Research Journal, 19*(1), 121–136.

Levin, J. R., Shriberg, L., & Berry, J. (1983). A concrete strategy for remembering abstract prose. *American Educational Research Journal, 20*(2), 277–290.

Levin, M. E., & Levin, J. R. (1990). Scientific mnemonics: Methods for maximizing more than memory. *American Educational Research Journal, 27,* 301–321.

Levy, D. V., & Stark, J. (1982). *Implementation of the Chicago mastery learning reading program at inner-city elementary schools.* Paper presented at the annual meeting of the American Educational Research Association, New York, NY.

Lewin, T. (1998, December 6). U.S. colleges begin to ask, Where have the men gone? *The New York Times,* pp. 1, 28.

Lindvall, C. M., & Bolvin, J. O. (1966). *The project for individually prescribed instruction.* Oakleaf Project. Unpublished manuscript, Learning Research and Development Center, University of Pittsburgh.

Linn, M., & Hyde, J. (1989). Gender, mathematics, and science. *Educational Researcher, 18*(8), 17–19, 22–27.

Lippitt, R., Fox, R., & Schaible, L. (1969a). *Cause and effect: Social science resource book.* Chicago, IL: Science Research Associates.

Lippitt, R., Fox, R., & Schaible, L. (1969b). *Social science laboratory units.* Chicago, IL: Science Research Associates.

Locke, J. (1927). *Some thoughts concerning education* (R. H. Quick, Ed.). Cambridge, UK: Cambridge University Press.

Lorayne, H., & Lucas, J. (1974). *The memory book.* Briercliff Manor, NY: Lucas Educational Systems.

Lortie, D. (1975). *Schoolteacher.* Chicago, UK: University of Chicago Press.

Loucks, S. F., Newlove, B. W., & Hall, G. E. (1975). *Measuring levels of use of the innovation: A manual for trainers, interviewers, and raters.* Austin, TX: Research and Development Center for Teacher Education, University of Texas.

Loucks-Horsley, S. (2003). *Designing professional development for teachers of science and mathematics.* Thousand Oaks, CA: Corwin Press.

Lucas, J. (2001). *Learning how to learn.* Frisco, TX: Lucas Educational Systems.

Lucas, S. B. (1972). *The effects of utilizing three types of advance organizers for learning a biological concept in seventh grade science.* Doctoral dissertation, Pennsylvania State University.

Luiten, J., Ames, W., & Ackerson, G. A. (1980). A meta-analysis of the effects of advance organizers on learning and retention. *American Educational Research Journal, 17,* 211–218.

Lunis, N., & White, N. (1999). *Being a scientist.* New York, NY: Newbridge Educational Publishing.

Maccoby, E., & Jacklin, C. (1974). *The psychology of sex differences.* Stanford, CA: Stanford University Press.

Madaus, G. F., Airasian, P. W., & Kellaghan, T. (1980). *School effectiveness: A review of the evidence.* New York: McGraw-Hill.

Madden, N. A., & Slavin, R. E. (1983). Cooperative learning and social acceptance of mainstreamed academically handicapped students. *Journal of Special Education, 17,* 171–182.

Mahoney, M., & Thoresen, C. (1972). Behavioral self-control: Power to the person. *Educational Researcher, 1,* 5–7.

Maloney, D. (1994). Research on problem-solving: Physics. In D. L. Gabel (Ed.), *Handbook of research on science teaching and learning* (pp. 327–354). New York: MacMillan.

Martin, M. O., Mullis, I. V. S., Foy, P., in collaboration with Olson, J. F., Erberber, E., Preuschoff, C., & Galia, J. (2008). *TIMSS 2007 international science report: Findings from IEA's Trends in International Mathematics and Science Study at the fourth and eighth grades.* Chestnut Hill, MA: TIMSS & PIRLS International Study Center, Boston College. Available from *http://timss.bc.edu/timss2007/intl_reports.html.*

Maslow, A. (1962). *Toward a psychology of being.* New York, NY: Van Nostrand.

Mastropieri, M. A., & Scruggs, T. E. (1991). *Teaching students ways to remember.* Cambridge, MA: Brookline Books.

Mastropieri, M. A., & Scruggs, T. E. (1994). *A practical guide for teaching science to students with special needs in inclusive settings.* Austin, TX: Pro-Ed.

Mayer, R. F. (1979). Can advance organizers influence meaningful learning? *Review of Educational Research, 49*(2), 371–383.

McCarthy, B. (1981). *The 4mat system: Teaching to learning styles with right/left mode techniques.* Barrington, IL: Excel.

McDonald, F. J., & Elias, P. (1976a). *Beginning teacher evaluation study: Phase II, 1973–74. Executive summary report.* Princeton, NJ: Educational Testing Service.

McDonald, F. J., & Elias, P. (1976b). *Executive summary report: Beginning teacher evaluation study, phase II.* Princeton, NJ: Educational Testing Service.

McGill-Franzen, A., Allington, R., Yokoi, I., & Brooks, G. (1999). Putting books in the room seems necessary but not sufficient. *Journal of Educational Research, 93,* 67–74.

McGill-Franzen, A. (2001). In S. Neuman & D. Dickinson (Eds.), *Handbook of early literacy research* (pp. 471–483). New York, NY: Guilford Press.

McGill-Franzen, A., & Allington, R. (1991). The gridlock of low achievement. *Remedial and Special Education, 12,* 20–30.

McGill-Franzen, A., & Allington, R. (2003). Bridging the summer reading gap. *Instructor, 112*(8), 17–19.

McGill-Franzen, A., & Goatley, V. (2001). Title I and special education: Support for children who struggle to learn to read. In S. Neuman & D. Dickinson (Eds.), *Handbook of early literacy research* (pp. 471–484). New York, NY: Guilford.

McGill-Franzen, A., Lanford, C., & Killian, J. (undated). *Case studies of literature-based textbook use in kindergarten.* Albany, NY: State University of New York.

McKibbin, M., & Joyce, B. (1980). Psychological states and staff development. *Theory into Practice, 19*(4), 248–255.

McKinney, C., Warren, A., Larkins, G., Ford, M. J., & Davis, J. C. III. (1983). The effectiveness of three methods of teaching social studies concepts to fourth-grade students: An aptitude-treatment interaction study. *American Educational Research Journal, 20,* 663–670.

McNair, K. (1978/1979). Capturing in-flight decisions. *Educational Research Quarterly, 3*(4), 26–42.

Medley, D. M. (1977). *Teacher competence and teacher effectiveness.* Washington, DC: American Association of Colleges of Teacher Education.

Medley, D. M. (1982). Teacher effectiveness. In H. Mitzel (Ed.), *Encyclopedia of educational research* (pp. 1894–1903). New York, NY: Macmillan.

Medley, D. M., Coker, H., Coker, J. G., Lorentz, J. L., Soar, R. S., & Spaulding, R. L. (1981). Assessing teacher performance from observed competency indicators defined by classroom teachers. *Journal of Educational Research, 74,* 197–216.

Medley, D., Soar, R., & Coker, H. (1984). *Measurement-based evaluation of teacher performance.* New York, NY: Longman.

Merrill, M. D., & Tennyson, R. D. (1977). *Concept teaching: An instructional design guide.* Englewood Cliffs, NJ: Educational Technology.

Metz, K. E. (1995). Reassessment of developmental constraints on children's science instruction. *Review of Educational Research, 65*(2), 93–127.

Miles, M., & Huberman, M. (1984). *Innovation up close.* New York, NY: Praeger.

Millar, G. (1956). The magical number seven, plus or minus two: Some limits on our capacity to process information. *Psychological Review, 63,* 81–87.

Minner, D., Levy, A., & Century, J. (2009). Inquiry-based science instruction—What is it and does it matter? Results from a research synthesis years 1984–2002. *Journal of Research in Science Teaching 47*(4), 474–496.

Mitchell, L. S. (1950). *Our children and our schools.* New York, NY: Simon & Schuster.

More, T. (1965). *Utopia.* New York, NY: Dutton.

Morris, R. (1997, September). How new research on brain development will influence educational policy. Paper presented at Policy Makers Institute, Georgia Center for Advanced Telecommunications Technology. Atlanta, GA.

Nagy, W., & Anderson, P. (1987). Breadth and depth in vocabulary knowledge. *Reading Research Quarterly, 19,* 304–330.

Nagy, W., & Anderson, R. (1984). How many words are there in printed English? *Reading Research Quarterly, 19,* 304–330.

Nagy, W., Herman, P., & Anderson, R. (1985). Learning words from context. *Reading Research Quarterly, 20,* 233–253.

Natale, J. (2001). Early learners: Are full-day kindergartens too much for young children? *American School Board Journal, 188*(3), 22–25.

National Center for Education Statistics. (2011). *The Nation's Report Card: Reading 2011* (NCES 2012-457). Washington, DC: U.S. Department of Education, Institute of Education Sciences. Available from *http://nces.ed.gov/nationsreportcard.pdf/main2011/2012457.pdf.*

National Council for the Social Studies. (2010). *National curriculum standards for social studies: A framework for teaching, learning, and assessment.* Silver Spring, MD: Author. (See also *www.socialstudies.org/standards/introduction.*)

National Governors Association Center for Best Practices & Council of Chief State School Officers. (2010a). *Common core state standards for English language arts & literacy in history/social studies, science, and technical subjects.* Washington, DC: Authors. Retrieved August 24, 2012, from *www.corestandards.org/assets/CCSSI_ELA%20St.*

National Governors Association Center for Best Practices & Council of Chief State School Officers. (2010b). *Common Core State Standards for English language arts and literacy in history/social studies, science, and technical subjects: Appendix A: Research supporting key elements of the standards and glossary of key terms.* Washington, DC: Authors. Retrieved from *www.corestandards.org/assets/Appendix_A.pdf.*

National Governors Association Center for Best Practices & Council of Chief State School Officers. (2010c). *Common Core State Standards for English language arts and literacy in history/social studies, science, and technical subjects: Appendix B: Text exemplars and sample performance tasks.* Washington, DC: Authors. Retrieved from *www.corestandards.org/assets/Appendix_B.pdf.*

National Governors Association Center for Best Practices & Council of Chief State School Officers. (2010d). *Common Core State Standards for English language arts and literacy in history/social studies, science, and technical subjects: Appendix C: Samples of student writing.* Washington, DC: Authors. Retrieved from *www.corestandards.org/assets/Appendix_C.pdf.*

National Governors Association Center for Best Practices & Council of Chief State School Officers. (2010e). *Common Core State Standards for mathematics.* Washington, DC: Authors. Retrieved from *www.corestandards.org/assets/CCSSI_Math%Standards.pdf.*

National Research Council. (2012). *A framework for K–12 science education: practices, crosscutting ideas, and core ideas.* Washington, DC: The National Academies Press.

Neill, A. S. (1960). *Summerhill.* New York, NY: Holt, Rinehart & Winston.

Neuman, S., & Dickinson, D. (Eds.). (2001). *Handbook of early literacy research.* New York, NY: Guilford Press.

New Standards Primary Literacy Committee. (1999). *Reading and writing: Grade by grade.* Pittsburgh, PA: National Center on Education and the Economy and the University of Pittsburgh.

Newby, T. J., & Ertner, P. A. (1994). *Instructional analogies and the learning of concepts.* Paper presented at the annual meeting of the American Educational Research Association, New Orleans, LA.

NGSS Lead States. (2013). *Next generation science standards: For states, by states.* Washington, DC: The National Academies Press.

Nicholson, A. M., & Joyce, B. (with D. Parker & F. Waterman). (1976). *The literature on inservice teacher education.* (ISTE Report No 3.) Syracuse, NY: National Dissemination Center, Syracuse University.

Nucci, L. P. (Ed.). (1989). *Moral development and character education.* Berkeley, CA: McCutchan.

Oakes, J. (1986). *Keeping track: How schools structure inequality.* New Haven, CT: Yale University Press.

Oczkus, L. (2010). *Reciprocal teaching at work.* Newark, DE: International Reading Association.

OECD. (2007). Science competencies for tomorrow's world. *OECD briefing note for the United States.* Retrieved from *www.oecd.org/dataoecd/16/28/39722597.pdf.*

OECD. (2009). *OECD programme for international student assessment (PISA) 2009 results.* Retrieved from *www.oecd.org/edu/pisa/2009.*

Oliver, D. W., & Shaver, J. P. (1971). *Cases and controversy: A guide to teaching the public issues series.* Middletown, CT: American Education Publishers.

Oliver, D., & Shaver, J. P. (1966/1974). *Teaching public issues in the high school.* Boston, MA: Houghton Mifflin.

Olson, D. R. (1970). *Cognitive development: The child's acquisition of diagonality.* New York, NY: Academic Press.

Parker, L., & Offer, J. (1987). School science achievement: Conditions for equality. *International Journal for Science Education, 8*(2), 173–183.

Pavlov, I. (1927). *Conditioned reflexes: An investigation of physiological activity of the cerebral cortex* (G. V. Anrep, Trans.). London, UK: Oxford University Press.

PBS Teacherline. (2005). An introduction to underlying principles and research for effective literacy instruction. PBS Electronic Catalog. Washington, DC: Author.

Pearson, P. D., & Dole, J. A. (1987). Explicit comprehension instruction: A review of research and a new conceptualization of instruction. *The Elementary School Journal, 88*(2), 151–165.

Pearson, P. D., & Gallagher, M. C. (1983). University of Illinois at Urbana-Champaign. Center for the Study of Reading.

Perkins, D. N. (1984). Creativity by design. *Educational Leadership, 42*(1), 18–25.

Perls, F. (1968). *Gestalt therapy verbatim.* Lafayette, CA: Real People Press.

Peterson, P., & Clark, C. (1978). Teachers' reports of their cognitive processes while teaching. *American Educational Research Journal, 15*(4), 555–565.

Peterson, P., Marx, R., & Clark, C. (1978). Teacher planning, teacher behavior, and student achievement. *American Educational Research Journal, 15*(4), 417–432.

Phenix, P. (1961). *Education and the common good.* New York, NY: Harper.

Piaget, J. (1952). *The origins of intelligence in children.* New York, NY: International University Press.

Piaget, J. (1960). *The child's conception of the world.* Atlantic Highlands, NJ: Humanities Press.

Piksulski, J., with Taylor, B. (1999). *Emergent literacy survey/K–2.* Boston, MA: Houghton Mifflin.

Pinnell, G. S. (1989). Helping at-risk children learn to read. *Elementary School Journal, 90*(2), 161–184.

Pinnell, G. S., Lyone, C. A., Deford, D., Bryk, A., & Seltzer, M. (1994). Comparing instructional models for the literacy education of high-risk first graders. *Reading Research Quarterly, 29*(1), 9–38.

PISA 2006: Science competencies for tomorrow's world. (2007). *OECD briefing note for the United States.* Retrieved from *www.oecd.org/dataoecd/16/28/39722597.pdf.*

Plato. (1945). *The Republic* (F. M. Cornford, Trans.). New York, NY: Oxford University Press.

Pollack, G. (1975). *Leadership in discussion groups.* New York, NY: Spectrum.

Pressley, M. (1977). Children's use of the keyword method to learn simple Spanish words. *Journal of Educational Psychology, 69*(5), 465–472.

Pressley, M. (1995). *Cognitive strategy instruction that really improves student performance.* Cambridge, MA: Brookline.

Pressley, M. (2002). Metacognition and self-regulated comprehension. In A. Farstrup & J. Samuels (Eds.), *What research has to say about reading instruction* (pp. 291–310). Newark, DE: International Reading Association.

Pressley, M. (2006). *What the future of reading research could be.* Paper presented at the International Reading Association's Reading Research, Chicago, IL.

Pressley, M., & Brainerd, C. (Eds). (1985). *Cognitive learning and memory in children.* New York, NY: Springer-Verlag.

Pressley, M., & Dennis-Rounds, J. (1980). Transfer of a mnemonic keyword strategy at two age levels. *Journal of Educational Psychology, 72*(4), 575–607.

Pressley, M., & Levin, J. R. (1978). Developmental constraints associated with children's use of the keyword method of foreign language learning. *Journal of Experimental Child Psychology, 26*(1), 359–372.

Pressley, M., Levin, J. R., & Delaney, H. D. (1982). The mnemonic keyword method. *Review of Educational Research, 52*(1), 61–91.

Pressley, M., Levin, J. R., & McCormick, C. (1980). Young children's learning of foreign language vocabulary: A sentence variation of the keyword method. *Contemporary Educational Psychology, 5*(1), 22–29.

Pressley, M., Levin, J., & Ghatala, E. (1984). Memory-strategy monitoring in adults and children. *Journal of Verbal Learning and Verbal Behavior, 23*(2), 270–288.

Pressley, M., Levin, J., & Miller, G. (1981a). How does the keyword method affect vocabulary, comprehension, and usage? *Reading Research Quarterly, 16,* 213–226.

Pressley, M., Levin, J., & Miller, G. (1981b). The keyword method and children's learning of foreign vocabulary with abstract meanings. *Canadian Psychology, 35*(3), 283–287.

Pressley, M., Samuel, J., Hershey, M., Bishop, S., & Dickinson, D. (1981). Use of a mnemonic technique to teach young children foreign-language vocabulary. *Contemporary Educational Psychology, 6,* 110–116.

Purkey, S., & Smith, M. (1983). Effective schools: A review. *Elementary School Journal, 83*(4), 427–452.

Purpel, D., & Ryan, K. (Eds.). (1976). *Moral education: It comes with the territory.* Berkeley, CA: McCutchan.

Qin, Z., Johnson, D. W., & Johnson, R. T. (1995). Cooperative versus competitive efforts and problem solving. *Review of Educational Research, 65*(2), 82–102.

Resnick, L. B. (1987). *Education and learning to think.* Washington, DC: Academic Press.

Resta, P., Flowers, B., & Tothero, K. (2007). The presidential timeline of the 20th century. *Social Education, 71*(3), 115–119.

Rhine, W. R. (Ed.). (1981). *Making schools more effective: New directions from follow through.* New York, NY: Academic Press.

Richardson, V. (1990). Significant and worthwhile change in teaching practice. *Educational Researcher, 19*(7), 10–18.

Rimm, D. C., & Masters, J. C. (1974). *Behavior therapy: Techniques and empirical findings.* New York: Academic Press.

Ripple, R., & Drinkwater, D. (1981). Transfer of learning. In H. E. Mitzel (Ed.), *Encyclopedia of educational research* (Vol. 4, pp. 1947–1953). New York, NY: Free Press, MacMillan.

Roberts, J. (1969). *Human relations training and its effect on the teaching-learning process in social studies.* (Final Report.) Albany, NY: Division of Research, New York State Education Department.

Roebuck, F., Buhler, J., & Aspy, D. (1976). *A comparison of high and low levels of humane teaching/learning conditions on the subsequent achievement of students identified as having learning difficulties.* (Final Report: Order No. PLD6816-76 re the National Institute of Mental Health.) Denton, TX: Texas Woman's University Press.

Rogers, C. (1961). *On becoming a person.* Boston, MA: Houghton Mifflin.

Rogers, C. (1969). *Freedom to learn.* Columbus, OH: Merrill.

Rogers, C. (1971). *Client centered therapy.* Boston, MA: Houghton Mifflin.

Rogers, C. (1981). *A way of being.* Boston, MA: Houghton Mifflin.

Rogers, C. (1982). *Freedom to learn in the eighties.* Columbus, OH: Merrill.

Rolheiser-Bennett, C. (1986). *Four models of teaching: A meta-analysis of student outcomes.* Ph.D. thesis, University of Oregon.

Romberg, T. A., & Wilson, J. (1970). *The effect of an advance organizer, cognitive set, and postorganizer on the learning and retention of written materials.* Paper presented at the annual meeting of the American Educational Research Association, Minneapolis, MN.

Rosenholtz, S. J. (1989). *Teachers' workplace: The social organization of schools.* White Plains, NY: Longman.

Rosenshine, B. (1985). Direct instruction. In T. Husen & T. N. Postlethwaite (Eds.), *International Encyclopedia of Education* (Vol. 3, pp. 1395–1400). Oxford, UK: Pergamon Press.

Rosenshine, B., & Meister, C. (1994). Reciprocal teaching: A review of the research. *Review of Educational Research, 64*(4), 479–530.

Rousseau, J. J. (1983). *Emile.* New York, NY: Dutton. (Original work published 1762.)

Rowe, M. B. (1969). Science, soul, and sanctions. *Science and Children, 6*(6), 11–13.

Rowe, M. B. (1974). Wait-time and rewards as instructional variables: Their influence on language, logic, and fate control. *Journal of Research in Science Teaching, 11,* 81–94.

Rutter, M., Maughan, R., Mortimer, P., Oustin, J., & Smith, A. (1979). *Fifteen thousand hours: Secondary schools and their effects on children.* Cambridge, MA: Harvard University Press.

Sadker, M., & Sadker, D. (1994). *Failing at fairness.* New York, NY: Touchstone (Simon & Schuster).

Sanders, D. A., & Sanders, J. A. (1984). *Teaching creativity through metaphor.* New York, NY: Longman.

Sanders, W., & Rivers, J. (1996). *Cumulative and residual effects of teachers on future student academic achievement: Research progress report.* Knoxville, TN: University of Tennessee Value-Added Research and Assessment Center.

Sarason, S. (1982). *The culture of the school and the problem of change* (2nd ed.). Boston, MA: Allyn & Bacon.

Scanlon, R., & Brown, M. (1969). *In-service education for individualized instruction.* Unpublished manuscript. Philadelphia, PA: Research for Better Schools.

Scardamalia, M., & Bereiter, C. (1984). Development of strategies in text processing. In H. Mandl, N. Stein, & T. Trabasso (Eds.), *Learning and comprehension of text* (pp. 370–406). Hillsdale, NJ: Erlbaum.

Schaefer, R. (1967). *The school as a center of inquiry.* New York, NY: Harper & Row.

Schaubel, L., Klopfer, L. E., & Raghavan, K. (1991). Students' transition from an engineering model to a science model of experimentation. *Journal of Research on Science Teaching, 28*(9), 859–882.

Schlenker, R. (1976). Learning about fossil formation by classroom simulation. *Science Activities, 28*(3), 17–20.

Schmuck, R. A., & Runkel, P. J. (1985). *The handbook of organizational development in schools* (3rd ed.). Palo Alto, CA: Mayfield Press.

Schmuck, R. A., Runkel, P. J., Arends, R., & Arends, J. (1977). *The second handbook of organizational development in schools.* Palo Alto, CA: Mayfield Press.

Schön, D. (1982). *The reflective practitioner.* New York, NY: Basic Books.

Schrenker, G. (1976). *The effects of an inquiry-development program on elementary schoolchildren's science learning.* Ph.D. thesis, New York University.

Schroeder, H. M., Driver, M. J., & Streufert, S. (1967). *Human information processing: Individuals and groups functioning in complex social situations.* New York, NY: Holt, Rinehart & Winston.

Schroeder, H. M., Karlins, M., & Phares, J. (1973). *Education for freedom.* New York, NY: Wiley.

Schutz, W. (1967). *Joy: Expanding human awareness.* New York, NY: Grove Press.

Schutz, W. (1982). *Firo.* New York, NY: Holt, Rinehart & Winston.

Schutz, W., & Turner, E. (1983). *Body fantasy.* Irvington, IL: Irvington Press.

Schwab, J. (1965). *Biological sciences curriculum study: Biology teachers' handbook.* New York, NY: Wiley.

Schwab, J. (1982). *Science, curriculum, and liberal education: Selected essays.* Chicago, IL: University of Chicago Press.

Schwab, J., & Brandwein, P. (1962). *The teaching of science.* Cambridge, MA: Harvard University Press.

Shaftel, F., & Shaftel, G. (1967). *Role playing of social values: Decision making in the social studies.* Englewood Cliffs, NJ: Prentice-Hall.

Shaftel, F., & Shaftel, G. (1982). *Role playing in the curriculum.* Englewood Cliffs, NJ: Prentice-Hall.

Sharan, S. (1980). Cooperative learning in small groups: Recent methods and effects on achievement, attitudes, and ethnic relations. *Review of Educational Research, 50*(2), 241–271.

Sharan, S. (1990). *Cooperative learning: Theory and research.* New York, NY: Praeger.

Sharan, S., & Hertz-Lazarowitz, R. (1980a). Academic achievement of elementary school children in small-group versus whole-class instruction. *Journal of Experimental Education, 48*(2), 120–129.

Sharan, S., & Hertz-Lazarowitz, R. (1980b). A group investigation method of cooperative learning in the classroom. In S. Sharan, P. Hare, C. Webb, & R. Hertz-Lazarowitz (Eds.), *Cooperation in education* (pp. 14–46). Provo, UT: Brigham Young University Press.

Sharan, S., & Hertz-Lazarowitz, R. (1982). Effects of an instructional change program on teachers' behavior, attitudes, and perceptions. *Journal of Applied Behavioral Science, 18*(2), 185–201.

Sharan, S., & Shaulov, A. (1990). Cooperative learning, motivation to learn, and academic achievement. In S. Sharan (Ed.), *Cooperative learning: Theory and research* (pp. 173–202). New York: Praeger.

Sharan, S., Slavin, R., & Davidson, N. (1990). The IASCE: An agenda for the 90's. *Cooperative Learning, 10,* 2–4.

Sharon, S., & Shachar, H. (1988). *Language and learning in the cooperative classroom.* New York, NY: Springer-Verlag.

Shaver, J. P. (1995). Social studies. In G. Cawelti (Ed.), *Handbook of research on improving student achievement* (pp. 272–300). Arlington, VA: Educational Research Service.

Showers, B. (1980). *Self-efficacy as a predictor of teacher participation in school decision-making.* Ph.D. thesis, Stanford University.

Showers, B. (1982a). *A study of coaching in teacher training.* Eugene, OR: Center for Educational Policy and Management, University of Oregon.

Showers, B. (1982b). *Transfer of training: The contribution of coaching.* Eugene, OR: Center for Educational Policy and Management, University of Oregon.

Showers, B. (1984). *Peer coaching and its effect on transfer of training.* Paper presented at the annual meeting of the American Educational Research Association, New Orleans, LA.

Showers, B. (1985). Teachers coaching teachers. *Educational Leadership, 42*(7), 43–49.

Showers, B. (1989, March). *Implementation: Research-based training and teaching strategies and their effects on the workplace and instruction.* Paper presented at the annual meeting of the American Educational Research Association, San Francisco, CA.

Showers, B., Joyce, B., & Bennett, B. (1987). Synthesis of research on staff development: A framework for future study and a state-of-the-art analysis. *Educational Leadership, 45*(3), 77–87.

Showers, B., Joyce, B., Scanlon, M., & Schnaubelt, C. (1998). A second chance to learn to read. *Educational Leadership, 55*(6), 27–31.

Shymansky, J., Kyle, W., & Alport, J. (1983). The effects of new science curricula on student performance. *Journal of Research in Science Teaching, 20*(5), 387–404.

Sigel, I. E. (1969). The Piagetian system and the world of education. In J. Hunt (Ed.), *Intelligence and experience.* New York, NY: Ronald.

Sigel, I. E., & Hooper, F. H. (1968). *Logical thinking in children.* New York: Holt, Rinehart & Winston.

Sill, C. (2013). *About birds.* Atlanta, GA: Peachtree.

Simon, A., & Boyer, E. G. (1967). *Mirrors for behavior: An anthology of classroom observation instruments.* Philadelphia, PA: Research for Better Schools, Inc.

Sitotnik, K. (1983). What you see is what you get: Consistency, persistence, and mediocrity in classrooms. *Harvard Educational Review, 53*(1), 16–31.

Sizer, T. R. (1985). *Horace's compromise: The dilemma of the American high school.* Boston, MA: Houghton Mifflin.

Skinner, B. F. (1953). *Science and human behavior.* New York, NY: Macmillan.

Skinner, B. F. (1957). *Verbal behavior.* New York, NY: Appleton-Century-Crofts.

Skinner, B. F. (1968). *The technology of teaching.* Englewood Cliffs, NJ: Prentice-Hall.

Skinner, B. F. (1971). *Beyond freedom and dignity.* New York, NY: Knopf.

Skinner, B. F. (1978). *Reflections on behaviorism and society.* Englewood Cliffs, NJ: Prentice-Hall.

Slavin, R. E. (1977a). How student learning teams can integrate the desegregated classroom. *Integrated Education, 15*(6), 56–58.

Slavin, R. E. (1977b). *Student learning team techniques: Narrowing the achievement gap between the races.* (Report No. 228.) Baltimore, MD: Center for Social Organization of Schools, Johns Hopkins University.

Slavin, R. E. (1977c). A student team approach to teaching adolescents with special emotional and behavioral needs. *Psychology in the Schools, 14*(1), 77–84.

Slavin, R. E. (1983). *Cooperative learning.* New York, NY: Longman.

Slavin, R. E. (1991). Are cooperative learning and "untracking" harmful to the gifted? *Educational Leadership, 48*(6), 68–70.

Slavin, R. E., & Madden, N. (2001). *One million children: Success for all.* Thousand Oaks, CA: Corwin Press.

Slavin, R., Madden, N., Dolan, L., & Wasik, B. (1996). *Every child, every school: Success for all.* Thousand Oaks, CA: Corwin.

Slavin, R. E., Madden, N. A., Karweit, N., Livermon, B. J., & Dolan, L. (1990). Success for all: First-year outcomes of a comprehensive plan for reforming urban education. *American Educational Research Journal, 27,* 255–278.

Smith, D. (2012). *State of the world atlas.* New York, NY: Penguin.

Smith, L., & Keith, P. (1971). *Anatomy of an innovation.* New York, NY: Wiley.

Smith, M. L. (1980). *Effects of aesthetics educations on basic skills learning.* Boulder, CO: Laboratory of Educational Research, University of Colorado.

Snow, C., Burns, M., & Griffin, P. (Eds.). (1998). *Preventing reading difficulties in young children.* Washington, DC: National Academy Press.

Soar, R. S. (1973). *Follow through classroom process measurement and pupil growth (1970–71).* (Final Report.) Gainesville, FL: College of Education, University of Florida.

Soar, R. S., Soar, R. M., & Ragosta, M. (1971). *Florida climate and control system: Observer's manual.* Gainesville, FL: Institute for Development of Human Resources, University of Florida.

Social Science Consortium. (1971, 1972, 1973). *Data handbook.* Boulder, CO: Author.

Spaulding, R. L. (1970). *E. I. P.* Durham, NC: Duke University Press.

Stallings, J. (1980). Allocating academic learning time revisited: Beyond time on task. *Educational Researcher, 9,* 11–16.

Stallings, J. (1985). A study of implementation of Madeline Hunter's model and its effects on students. *Journal of Educational Research, 78,* 325–337.

Stauffer, R. (1969). *Directing reading maturity as a cognitive-learning process.* New York, NY: Harper and Row.

Stauffer, R. (1970). *The language-experience approach to the teaching of reading.* New York, NY: Harper and Row.

Staver, J. (1989). A summary of research in science education. *Science Education, 70*(3), 245–341.

Steinbeck, J. (1952). *East of Eden.* New York: Viking.

Stenhouse, L. (1975). *An introduction to curriculum research and development.* London, UK: Heinemann.

Stenhouse, L. (1980). *Curriculum research and development in action.* London, UK: Heinemann.

Sternberg, R. (1986). Synthesis of research on the effectiveness of intellectual skills programs. *Educational Leadership, 44,* 60–67.

Stevens, R. J., & Slavin, R. E. (1995). The cooperative elementary school: Effects on students' achievement, attitudes, and social relations. *American Educational Research Journal, 32*(2), 321–351.

Stevenson, H. W., Lee, S., & Stigler, J. W. (1986). Mathematics achievement of Chinese, Japanese, and American children. *Science, 231,* 693–699.

Stevenson, H. W., & Stigler, J. (1992). *The learning gap.* New York, NY: Summit Books.

Stone, C. L. (1983). A meta-analysis of advance organizer studies. *Journal of Experimental Education, 51*(4), 194–199.

Suchman, R. (1981). *Idea book for geological inquiry.* Chicago, IL: Trillium Press.

Sullivan, E. (1967). *Piaget and the school curriculum: A critical appraisal.* (Bulletin No. 2.) Toronto, ON: Ontario Institute for Studies in Education.

Sullivan, E. V. (1984). *A critical psychology: Interpretations of the personal world.* New York, NY: Plenum.

Swartz, S., & Klein, A. (1997). *Research in reading recovery.* Portsmouth, NH: Heinemann.

Taba, H. (1966). *Teaching strategies and cognitive functioning in elementary school children.* (Cooperative Research Project 2404.) San Francisco, CA: San Francisco State College.

Taba, H. (1967). *Teacher's handbook for elementary school social studies.* Reading, MA: Addison-Wesley.

Taub, E. (2010). The web way to learn a language. *New York Times,* October 27. Technology, p. 1.

Taylor, C. (Ed.). (1964). *Creativity: Progress and potential.* New York, NY: McGraw-Hill.

Tennyson, R. D., & Cocchiarella, M. (1986). An empirically based instructional design theory for teaching concepts. *Review of Educational Research, 56,* 40–71.

Tennyson, R., & Park, O. (1980). The teaching of concepts: A review of instructional design research literature. *Review of Educational Research, 50*(1), p. 55–70.

Thelen, H. (1954). *Dynamics of groups at work.* Chicago, IL: University of Chicago Press.

Thelen, H. (1960). *Education and the human quest.* New York, NY: Harper & Row.

Thelen, H. (1981). *The classroom society: The construction of education.* New York, NY: Halsted Press.

Thompson, C. (2013). *Smarter than you think.* New York, NY: The Penguin Group.

Thoreson, C. (Ed.). (1973). *Behavior modification in education.* Chicago, IL: University of Chicago Press.

Thorndike, E. L. (1911). Animal intelligence: An experimental study of the associative process in animals. In *Psychological Review, 8*(Suppl. 2). New York, NY: Macmillan.

Thorndike, E. L. (1913). *The psychology of learning: Volume II: Educational psychology.* New York, NY: Teachers College.

Tobias, S. (1993). *Overcoming math anxiety.* New York, NY: Norton.

Tobin, K. (1986). Effects of teacher wait time on discourse characteristics in mathematics and language arts classes. *American Educational Research Journal, 23*(2), 191–200.

Torrance, E. P. (1962). *Guiding creative talent.* Englewood Cliffs, NJ: Prentice-Hall.

Torrance, E. P. (1965). *Gifted children in the classroom.* New York, NY: Macmillan.

Urdan, T., Midgley, C., & Anderman, E. (1998). The role of classroom goal structure in students' use of self-handicapping strategies. *American Educational Research Journal, 35*(1), 101–102.

Vance, V. S., & Schlechty, P. C. (1982). The distribution of academic ability in the teaching force: Policy implications. *Phi Delta Kappan, 64*(1), 22–27.

Vellutino, F., & Scanlon, D. (2001). Emergent literacy skills, early instruction, and individual differences as determinants of difficulties in learning to read: The case for early intervention. In S. Neuman & D. Dickinsons (Eds.), *Handbook of early literacy research* (pp. 295–321). New York, NY: Guilford.

Vellutino, F., Scanlon, D., Spay, E., Small, S., Chen, R., Pratt, A., et al. (1966). Cognitive profiles of difficult-to-remediate and readily-remediated poor readers. *Journal of Educational Psychology, 88,* 601–638.

Voss, B. A. (1982). *Summary of research in science education.* Columbus, OH: ERIC Clearinghouse for Science, Mathematics, and Environmental Education.

Vygotsky, L., (1986). *Thought and Language.* Cambridge: MA: MIT Press

Wade, N. (2002, June 18). Scientist at work/Kari Stefansson: Hunting for disease genes in Iceland's genealogies. *The New York Times,* p. 4.

Wadsworth, B. (1978). *Piaget for the classroom teacher.* New York, NY: Longman.

Walberg, H. J. (1985). *Why Japanese educational productivity excels.* Paper presented at the annual meeting of the American Educational Research Association, Chicago, IL.

Walberg, H. J. (1986). What works in a nation still at risk. *Educational Leadership, 44*(1), 7–11.

Walberg, H. J. (1990). Productive teaching and instruction: Assessing the knowledge base. *Phi Delta Kappan, 71*(6), 70–78.

Wallace, K. (2000). *Born to be a butterfly.* New York: Dorling Kindersley.

Wallace, R. C., Lemahieu, P. G., & Bickel, W. E. (1990). The Pittsburgh experience: Achieving commitment to comprehensive staff development. In B. Joyce (Ed.), *Changing school culture through staff development.* Alexandria, VA: Association for Supervision and Curriculum Development.

Walston, J., & West, J. (2004). *Full-day and half-day kindergarten in the United States.* Washington, DC: U.S. Department of Education, National Center for Education Statistics.

Wasik, B. A., & Slavin, R. E. (1993). Preventing early reading failure with one-to-one tutoring: A review of five programs. *Reading Research Quarterly, 28*(2), 186–207.

Watson, J. B. (1916). The place of conditioned reflex in psychology. *Psychological Review, 23,* 89–116.

Watson, J. B., & Rayner, R. (1921). Conditioned emotional reactions. *Journal of Experimental Psychology, 3,* 1–14.

Weikart, D. (Ed.). (1971). *The cognitively oriented curriculum: A framework for preschool teachers.* Washington, DC: National Association for Education of Young Children.

Weil, M., Marshalek, B., Mittman, A., Murphy, J., Hallinger, P., & Pruyn, J. (1984). *Effective and typical schools: How different are they?* Paper presented at the annual meeting of the American Educational Research Association, New Orleans, LA.

Weinstein, G., & Fantini, M. (Eds.). (1970). *Toward humanistic education: A curriculum of affect.* New York, NY: Praeger.

Wentzel, K. (1991). Social competence at school: Relation between social responsibility and academic achievement. *Review of Educational Research, 61*(1), 1–24.

Wertheimer, M. (1945). *Productive thinking.* New York, NY: Harper.

White, B. Y. (1993). ThinkerTools: Causal models, conceptual change, and science education. *Cognition and Instruction, 10*(1), 1–100.

White, S. (2002). *Developmental Psychology as a Human Enterprise.* Worcester, Massachusetts: Clark University Press.

Whitehead, A. (1929). *The aims of education.* New York, NY: Macmillan.

Wiederholt, J. L., & Bryant, B. (2001). *Gray oral reading tests.* Austin, Texas: Pro-Ed.

Wilford, J. (2013). Scull fossil suggests simpler human linkage. *The New York Times.* October 17, 2013, Science, p. 1.

Wilson, C. D., Taylor, J. A., Kowalski, S. M., & Carlson, J. (2010). The relative effects and equity of inquiry-based and commonplace science teaching on students' knowledge, reasoning, and argumentation. *Journal of Research in Science Teaching, 47*(3), 276–301.

Wing, R. (1965). *Two computer-based economic games for sixth graders.* Yorktown Heights, NY: Board of Cooperative Educational Services, Center for Educational Services and Research.

Wolfe, P., & Brandt, R. (1998). What do we know from brain research? *Educational Leadership, 56*(3), 8–13.

Wolpe, J. (1969). *The practice of behavior therapy.* Oxford, UK: Pergamon Press.

Wood, K., & Tinajero, J. (2002, May). Using pictures to teach content to second language learners. *Middle School Journal,* 47–51.

Worthen, B. (1968). A study of discovery and expository presentation: Implications for teaching. *Journal of Teacher Education, 19,* 223–242.

Xue, Y., & Meisels, S. (2004). Early literacy instruction and learning in kindergarten. *American Educational Research Journal, 41*(1), 191–229.

Young, D. (1971). Team learning: An experiment in instructional method as related to achievement. *Journal of Research in Science Teaching, 8,* 99–103.

Zhao, Y., Lei, J., Yan, B., Lai, C., & Tan, H. (2005). What makes the difference: A practical analysis of research on the effectiveness of distance education. *Teachers College Record, 107*(8), 1836–1884.

Ziegler, S. (1981). The effectiveness of cooperative learning teams for increasing cross-ethnic friendship: Additional evidence. *Human Organization, 40,* 264–268.

Relevant NAEP and Other U.S. Government Reports

Campbell, F., & Ramey, C. (1995). Cognitive and school outcomes for high-risk African-American students at middle adolescence: Positive effects of early intervention. *American Educational Research Journal, 32*(4), 743–772.

Campbell, J., Donahue, P., Reese, C., & Phillips, G. (1996). *NAEP 1994 reading report card for the nation and the states.* Washington, DC: U.S. Department of Education.

Campbell, J., Voelki, K., & Donohue, P. (1997). *Report in brief: NAEP 1996 trends in reading progress.* Washington, DC: National Center for Educational Statistics.

Donahue, P. (1999). 1998 NAEP Reading Report Card for the Nation and the States. Washington, DC: U.S. Department of Education.

Donahue, P., Flanagan, R., Lutkus, A., Allen, N., & Campbell, J. (1999). *1998 NAEP reading report card for the nation and the states.* Washington, DC: U.S. Department of Education.

Donahue, P., Flanagan, R., Lutkus, A., Allen, N., & Campbell, J. (2001). *The national report card: Fourth grade reading 2000.* Washington, DC: U.S. Department of Education, Office of Educational Research and Improvement, National Center for Educational Statistics.

National Assessment of Educational Progress. (2004). *Reading Highlights, 2003.* Washington, DC: National Center for Educational Statistics.

National Assessment of Educational Progress (NAEP). (1992). *The reading report card.* Washington, DC: National Center for Educational Statistics, U.S. Department of Education.

National Center for Education Statistics. (2000). *The condition of education.* Washington, DC: U.S. Department of Education.

National Institutes of Education. (1975). *National conference on studies in teaching (Vols. 1–10)*. Washington, DC: U.S. Department of Health, Education and Welfare.

National Reading Panel (2000). *Teaching children to read: An evidence-based assessment of the scientific research literature on reading and its implications for reading instruction*. Rockville, MD: National Institute of Child Health and Human Development.

National Center for Educational Statistics (1998). Long term trends in reading performance. NAEP Facts. Washington, DC: Office of Educational Research and Improvement, U.S. Department of Education.

National Reading Panel. (1998). *Teaching children to read*. Washington, DC: U.S. Department of Education.

O'Sullivan, C., Reese, C., & Mazzeo, J. (1997). *NAEP 1996 Science report card for the nation and the states*. Washington, DC: U.S. Department of Education.

Reese, C., Miller, K., Mazzeo, J., and Dossey, J. (1997). *NAEP 1996 mathematics report card for the nation and the states*. Washington, DC: U.S. Department of Education.

U.S. Department of Education. (1998). *NAEP Facts, 3*(1), 1.

Weiss, I. R. (1978). *Report of the 1977 national survey of science, social science, and mathematics education. National Science Foundation*. Washington, DC: U.S. Government Printing Office.

Selected Authors' Publications

Calhoun, E. (1997). *Literacy for all*. Saint Simons Island, GA: The Phoenix Alliance.

Calhoun, E. (1998). *Literacy for the primary grades: What works, for whom, and to what degree*. Saint Simons Island, GA: The Phoenix Alliance.

Calhoun, E. F. (1999). *Teaching beginning reading and writing with the picture word model*. Alexandria, VA: Association for Supervision and Curriculum Development.

Joyce, B. (1999). Reading about reading. *The Reading Teacher*, May, 1999.

Joyce, B., & Calhoun, E. (2010). *Models of professional development*. Thousand Oaks, CA: Corwin Press.

Joyce, B., & Calhoun, E. (2012). *Realizing the promise of 21st century education*. Thousand Oaks, CA: Corwin Press.

Joyce, B., Calhoun, E., Carran, N., Simser, J., Rust, D., & Halliburton, C. (1996). University town. In B. Joyce & E. Calhoun (Eds.), *Learning experiences in school renewal*. Eugene, Ore.: ERIC Clearinghouse for Educational Management.

Joyce, B., Calhoun, E., & Hopkins, D. (1998). *Models of learning: Tools for teaching*. Buckingham, UK: Open University Press.

Joyce, B., Calhoun, E., & Hopkins, D. (1999). *The new structure of school improvement*. Buckingham, UK: Open University Press.

Joyce, B., Calhoun, E., & Hopkins, D. (2000). *The new structure of school improvement*. Philadelphia, PA: The Open University Press.

Joyce, B., Calhoun, E., & Hrycauk, M. (2001). A second chance for struggling readers. *Educational Leadership, 58*(6), 42–47.

Joyce, B., Calhoun, E., Jutras, J., & Newlove, K. (2006). Scaling up: The results of a literacy curriculum implemented across an entire 53-school education authority. A paper delivered to the Asian Pacific Educational Research Association. Hong Kong.

Joyce, B., & Clift, R. (1984). The Phoenix agenda: Essential reform in teacher education. *Educational Researcher, 13*(4), 5–18.

Joyce, B., & Harootunian, B. (1967). *The structure of teaching.* Chicago: Science Research Associates.

Joyce, B., Hersh, R., & McKibbin, M. (1983). *The structure of school improvement.* New York, NY: Longman.

Joyce, B., Hrycauk, M., Calhoun, E., & Hrycauk, W. (2006). The tending of diversity through a robust core literacy curriculum: gender, socioeconomic status, learning disabilities, and ethnicity. A paper delivered to the Asian Pacific Educational Research Association. Hong Kong.

Joyce, B., Hrycauk, M., & Calhoun, E. (2001). A second chance for struggling readers. *Educational Leadership, 58*(6), 42–47.

Joyce, B., McKibbin, M., & Bush, R. (1983). *The seasons of professional life: The growth states of teachers.* Paper presented at the annual meeting of the American Educational Research Association, Montreal.

Joyce, B., Murphy, C., Showers, B., & Murphy, J. (1989). School renewal as cultural change. *Educational Leadership, 47*(3), 70–78.

Joyce, B., Peck, L., & Brown, C. (1981). *Flexibility in teaching.* New York, NY: Longman.

Joyce, B., & Showers, B. (1980). Improving inservice training: The message of research. *Educational Leadership, 37,* 163–172.

Joyce, B., & Showers, B. (1981a). *Teacher training research: Working hypothesis for program design and directions for further study.* Paper presented at the annual meeting of the American Educational Research Association, Los Angeles.

Joyce, B., & Showers, B. (1981b). Transfer of training: The contribution of coaching. *Journal of Education, 163,* 163–172.

Joyce, B., & Showers, B. (1982). The coaching of teaching. *Educational Leadership, 40*(1), 4–10.

Joyce, B., & Showers, B. (1983). *Power in staff development through research on training.* Washington, DC: Association for Supervision and Curriculum Development.

Joyce, B., & Showers, B. (2002). *Student achievement through staff development* (3rd ed.). Alexandria, VA: Association for Supervision and Curriculum Development.

Joyce, B., Showers, B., & Bennett, B. (1987). Synthesis of research on staff development: A framework for future study and a state-of-the-art analysis. *Educational Leadership, 45*(3), 77–87.

Joyce, B., Weil, M., & Wald, R. (1981). Can teachers learn repertoires of models of teaching? In B. Joyce, L. Peck, & C. Brown, *Flexibility in teaching.* New York, NY: Longman.

Joyce, B., & Wolf, J. (1996). Readersville: Building a culture of readers and writers. In B. Joyce and E. Calhoun (Eds.), *Learning experiences in school renewal.* Eugene, OR: The ERIC Clearinghouse in Educational Management.

Joyce, B., Wolf, J., & Calhoun, E. (1993). *The self-renewing school.* Alexandria, VA: Association for Supervision and Curriculum Development.

Index